William H. Kingston

My First Voyage to Southern Seas

A book for boys

William H. Kingston

My First Voyage to Southern Seas
A book for boys

ISBN/EAN: 9783337004125

Printed in Europe, USA, Canada, Australia, Japan

Cover: Foto ©Andreas Hilbeck / pixelio.de

More available books at **www.hansebooks.com**

ADEN.

Page 1046.

MY FIRST VOYAGE

TO

SOUTHERN SEAS.

A Book for Boys.

By

W. H. G. KINGSTON,

Author of "Old Jack," "A Voyage Round the World," &c.

LONDON:
T. NELSON AND SONS, PATERNOSTER ROW;
EDINBURGH; AND NEW YORK.

1876.

CHAPTER I.

My English Home and Family—My Brother goes to Sea—Hear of the Loss of his Ship—My Father's Death—We are Reduced to Poverty—Resolve to Visit my Grandfather, and to Search for Alfred—Kindness of my Schoolmaster and Companions—My dog Solon..................................... 9

CHAPTER II.

Our old Clerk—I find that he has a Heart—Look out for a Ship—The *Orion*—Her Officers and Crew—Last Day at Home—Part from Mr. Ward—The Passengers—Sail down the Thames—Change of Captain.................. 29

CHAPTER III.

At Sea—A Surly Mate—Solon's Astonishment at Seeing the Ocean—The Bay of Biscay—Madeira—Funchal—Visit on Shore—Story of the Discovery of Madeira—Trip to the Pico—Tommy Bigg—Roughness of Crew.......... 54

CHAPTER IV.

Natural Phenomena of the Ocean—Service at Sea—Mr. Vernon—A dead Calm—Fever breaks out—Dispute between Captain and First Mate—Its Consequences—Mortality among Passengers—Sight the Land—Teneriffe—Notice of History—Santa Cruz—Attack on it under Lord Nelson—An Excursion up the Peak... 76

CHAPTER V.

Sail again—The Trades—Cruelty of Master and Mate—Mutterings of Mutiny—A suspicious Sail—Boarded by Pirates—How they treated us.......... 104

CONTENTS.

CHAPTER VI.

Sight of Land not always pleasant—A suspicious Character on Board—A dangerous Predicament—How we made our Escape from it—The Cape of Good Hope—Land at Cape Town... 124

CHAPTER VII.

Cape Colony—Table Mountain and its Table-Cloth—A Storm—Sail for the Mauritius—Port Louis and Pieter Bot Mountain—Journey into the Interior—Paul and Virginia—Disappointment—An Estate in the Mauritius—Wild Animals—Sail for Ceylon....................................... 147

CHAPTER VIII.

Matters on Board as bad as ever—The Mate's Cruelty to poor Tom—I Interfere—An Island in Sight—An Expedition on Shore to Catch Turtle—Coco de Mer—A Night on Shore—Where is the Ship?—We are Deserted—A Ship on Fire—Mr. Henley puts off to her Assistance—Tom and I left on the Island.. 173

CHAPTER IX.

The Gale Increases—Fears for Mr. Henley's Safety—A Boat in Sight—Solon aids in Rescuing the Drowning Men—The Doctor Saved—His Illness—A Sail in Sight—Visit of a Slaver—Deserted by our Companions—Death of the Doctor—Tom and Solon on the Island—Our Comfort and Consolation 197

CHAPTER X.

A strange Sail—We Conceal Ourselves—More Visitors—Old Friends—Embark on Board a Man-of-War—Kindness of her Officers—Land at Point de Galle—A New Friend—Scenes in Ceylon—Sketch of the History of the Island—Colombo 217

CHAPTER XI.

My New Friends—Journey to the Capital—Kandy—Fine Roads—Magnificent Scenery—Coffee Plantation—Mountain Travelling—Neura-Ellia—Its refreshing Coolness—My First Buffalo Hunt—Unpleasant Consequences—Solon to the Rescue.. 236

CHAPTER XII.

Visit to great Elephant Corral—Mode of Capturing Elephants in Ceylon—Wonderful Sagacity of Tame Elephants—Mode of Taming Elephants—Their Habits when Tame—Habits when Wild................................. 253

CONTENTS. vii

CHAPTER XIII.

Singhalese Torches — Chewing Areca-Nut — The Veddahs — Devil-Dancers — Chena Cultivation — A Rogue Elephant — Rat Snake — My First Elephant Hunt — Horrible Situation — Nearly Killed by an Elephant — Providential Escape...... 273

CHAPTER XIV.

A Wounded Veddah — How a Christian can Die — Attacked by Black Ants — Abundance of Game — Catch a Crocodile Asleep — Fight with a Bear — Chase a Deer — Lose my Way — Climb up a Tree — What I saw when there. 303

CHAPTER XV.

Encounter with a Boa-Constrictor — Meet a Giant — Find myself among the Ruins of an Ancient City — Surrounded by Snakes — Take Shelter in a Ruin — Horrible Adventures in it — Attacked by Bears — How I passed the Night — Solon's Return — See a Leopard about to Spring on me — Solon Watches me while I Sleep...... 325

CHAPTER XVI.

Wonderful Statues — Dagobas — Temples and other Ruins — Consider how to find my way back to the Camp — Meet a Hermit — Attacked by a Buffalo — Kill it with one Shot — The Unexpected Meeting with an old English Gentleman — Accompany him to his Camp — Who he proves to be — Meet Lumsden, my Schoolfellow — Inquiries about Alfred — Anxiety as to Nowell's Fate — We set out in Search of him and Dango — Colony of Paroquets — The Anthelia — Find Dango — The Fate of an Elephant-hunter.... 347

CHAPTER XVII.

Grief of Mr. Fordyce — Mahintala — Catch a Crocodile — Singing Fish — Arrive at Trincomalee — Embark on Board the *Star* — Visit the Maldives — Aden — News of Alfred — Island of Perim — Magadona — Further News of Alfred — Find a Shipwrecked Seaman on a Rock — Who he proved to be........ 374

CHAPTER XVIII.

Old Bigg's Narrative — My Plan to Rescue Alfred — Fall in with an Arab Dow in a Sinking State — Catch Sight of the Pirate — She tries to Escape — The Chase — She blows up — The Fate of Sills...... 395

CHAPTER XIX.

Mozambique—Description of the Neighbouring Country—Slave-Trade—How carried on—Prepare for my Expedition into the Interior of Africa—Bigg and I land—Transformed into Blackamores—Fortunate Shot at an Elephant—Meet Natives—Feast off the Elephant—Search for Water—An Unwelcome Visitor—A Night in an African Desert.................. 414

CHAPTER XX.

Fresh Plan Adopted—Hunt for a Suit of Clothes—Kill a Lion—Turned into a Black Prince—Arrive at the Village—Cordial Reception—A Native Feast—How I established my Reputation—Find Alfred—Our Escape—Reach the *Star*—Sail for Cape Town—Conclusion............................... 434

MY FIRST VOYAGE

TO

SOUTHERN SEAS.

CHAPTER I.

My English Home and Family—My Brother goes to Sea—Hear of the Loss of his Ship—My Father's Death—We are reduced to Poverty—Resolve to visit my Grandfather, and to search for Alfred—Kindness of my Schoolmaster and Companions—My dog Solon.

OURS was a very united and a very happy family. We lived in the neighbourhood of London, near Blackheath, in Kent, on the elevated ground which overlooks Greenwich, its noble hospital, and the river Thames. I mention this because I think that the situation of the home of our boyhood has often much influence over our future career, as it has certainly in moulding our tastes and giving a direction to our pursuits in life.

Our father was a merchant, a thoroughly upright, industrious man, an honour to the profession to which he belonged. No man could be more attentive to business than he was, and yet no one enjoyed the country and the pursuits of the country more than he did. With what pleasure did we look forward,

MY ENGLISH HOME.

when we were children, to his return in the afternoon, and even now I think I hear his cheerful laugh, and see his bland smile, as he took us up one by one in his arms and kissed us, and then often, though he must frequently have been tired and harassed, had a game of boisterous romps with us, seeming entirely to have forgotten all his cares and troubles. Often, too, he brought down something for our amusement or instruction, not forgetting, also, that we were terrestrial beings, and would not object to wherewithal to please our palates. It was considered the privilege of little Kate, or one of the other young ones, to look slily into his pockets when, by a well-known significant gesture, he let us understand that they were not altogether empty. He had a little hand hamper or basket, such as many another paterfamilias possesses, which travelled with great regularity up and down nearly every day, and out of which all sorts of wonderful articles used to appear; and if a friend accompanied him unexpectedly down to dinner, our mother never had to complain that she was taken unawares and had nothing fit to offer him. The hamper, however, did not always contain eatables. Often our mother, or one of us, had been wishing very much for something which could not possibly have got into his pockets, and before many days were over, it was very nearly certain to make its appearance, when the top of the hamper was thrown back, imbedded in straw or paper. That dear old hamper always put us in mind of some magic chest in a fairy tale, only I doubt if any magic chest ever afforded so much pleasure, or produced so great a variety of articles as it did. I do not know if our kind father ever was out of humour; if he was, he left the appearance of it behind him in the city. Out of spirits he seldom or never was in my childhood's days.

The time was coming when a sad change was to occur. I mention these traits, trivial though they may seem, because I think that they speak well of my father's character. At the same time that he was a most affectionate father, he never forgot the necessity of correcting us for our faults; while he was deeply sensible of the importance of fitting us for the stations in life we might be destined to occupy, and of placing clearly before us the object of our existence on earth, and our duty to God and to our fellow-men. He watched over us with the most anxious solicitude during every moment he could spare; he took us out to walk with him, and had us constantly in his room, never wearying, apparently, of our society. This he did, I have no doubt, not only because he loved us, but that he might ascertain our different characters and dispositions, and at once eradicate, as far as he was able, each budding tendency to evil as it appeared.

Such was my father, a fine, intelligent, gentlemanly, handsome man; and though his hair was perfectly gray, his complexion was yet clear, nor had his eye lost the animation of youth. It is with great satisfaction that I can look back and picture him as I have now faithfully drawn his portrait.

Our dear mother, too, she was worthy to be his wife,—so amiable, and loving, and sensible, a pious Christian and a perfect gentlewoman, thoroughly educated, and capable of bringing up her daughters to fill the same station in life she occupied, which was all she desired for them. Indeed, we boys also received much of our early instruction from her, and I feel very certain that we retained far more of what she taught us than we acquired from any other source. To her we owed, especially, lessons of piety and instruction in the Holy Scriptures, never, I trust, to be forgotten, as well as much elementary secular knowledge, which probably we should otherwise have been very long in picking up. My mother had no relations of whom we, at all events, knew anything in England. She was the daughter of an Englishman, however, who had, when the Mauritius first came under the dominion of Great Britain, gone out there as a settler and planter, leaving her, his only child, to be educated in England.

Mr. Coventry, my grandfather, was, we understood, of a somewhat eccentric disposition, and had for some years wandered about in the Eastern seas and among the islands of the Pacific, although he had ultimately returned again to his estate. He had transmitted home ample funds for his daughter's education, but he kept up very little communication with her, and had never even expressed any intention of sending for her to join him. The lady under whose charge she had been left was a very excellent person, and had thoroughly done her duty by her in cultivating to the utmost all the good qualities and talents she possessed. That lady was a friend of my father's family, and thus my father became acquainted with her pupil, to whom he was before long married.

It was necessary for me to give this brief account of my family history, to explain the causes which produced some of my subsequent adventures.

We were a large family. I had several brothers and sisters. I was the third son, and I had two elder sisters. Alfred, my eldest brother, was a fine joyous-spirited fellow. Some said he was too spirited, and unwilling to submit to discipline. He was just cut out for a sailor,—so everybody said, and so he thought himself, and to sea he had resolved to go. Our father exerted all the interest he possessed to get him into the navy, and succeeded. We thought it a very fine thing for him when we heard that he really and truly was going to be a midshipman. It appeared to us as if there was but one step between that and being an admiral, or, at all events, a post-captain in command of a fine line-of-battle ship. Neither our mother nor sisters had at first at all wished that Alfred should go to sea; indeed, our father would, I believe, have much rather seen him enter into the business of a merchant; but as soon as the matter was settled, they all set to work with the utmost zeal and energy to get his kit ready for sea. Many a sigh I heard, and many a tear I saw dropped over the shirts, and stockings, and pocket-handkerchiefs, as they were being marked, when he was not near. Too often had they read of dreadful shipwrecks, of pestiferous climates, of malignant fevers carrying off the young as well as the old, the strong as well as the weak, not to feel anxious about Alfred, and to dread that he might be among those gallant spirits who go away outflowing with health, and hope, and confidence, and yet are destined never again to visit their native land, or to see the faces of those who love them so much. Alfred was full of life and animation, and very active in assisting in the preparations making for his departure. Well do I remember the evening when his uniform came down. With what hurried fingers we undid the parcel, and how eagerly I rushed up-stairs with him to help him to put it on! What a fine fellow I thought he looked; how proud I felt of him, as I walked round and round him, admiring the gold lace and the white patches worn by midshipmen in those days, and the dirk by his side, and the glossy belt, and the crown and anchor on his buttons and in his cap, and more than all, when I felt that he was really and truly an officer in the navy! Still more delighted was I when I accompanied him down-stairs, and heard the commendations of all the family on his appearance. Our father, with a hand on his shoulder, could not help exclaiming, "Well, Alfred, you are a jolly midshipman, my boy." And then all the servants had collected in the hall to have a look at him, and they were none of them chary of their expressions of admiration.

It was some days after this before all the multifarious contents of the chest were ready, and then came the parting day. That was a very sad one to our mother and elder sisters. I did not fully realize the fact that we were to be parted till he had actually gone, so my sorrow did not begin till I found his place empty, and had to go about by myself without his genial companionship. Our father took him down to Portsmouth, where he was to join his ship, the *Aurora* frigate, destined for the East India station, and our second brother Herbert accompanied him. Herbert was delicate, and required a change of scene and air. I longed to have gone too, but our father could not take both of us. My great desire was to see a large ship, a real man-of-war. I knew very well what a vessel was like, for I had seen numbers in the Thames, and one of Alfred's great pleasures was to take me with him to Greenwich Hospital, and to sit down on the benches and to watch the vessels sailing up and down the river, while we talked with the old pensioners, who were always ready to spin some of their longest yarns for our edification, though older people who went down there for the purpose found no little difficulty in getting anything out of them. This was not surprising. The old sailors found in us attentive and undoubting listeners. We never thought of even questioning them to let them suspect that we had not the most perfect reliance on what they said, which older people were apt to do, I observed, for the purpose of gaining more information from them. The old tars were either offended, from suspecting that their words were doubted, or fancied that their interrogators had some sinister motives in putting such questions, and, from an early habit of suspicion in all such instances, would shut up their mouths, and seem to have forgotten all about their early lives.

In the way I have mentioned, both Alfred and I gained a great deal of information about the sea and life in the navy, so that when he went afloat he was not nearly as ignorant as are many youngsters. In one respect, however, he had gained, unfortunately, no good from his intercourse with the old sailors. He had deeply imbibed many of the worst prejudices about the navy which even some old men-of-war's men retain to the present day, and he was taught to look upon all superior officers in the service as cruel and unjust tyrants, whom it was spirited to disobey when practicable, and ingenious to circumvent in every possible way. His feeling, in short, was very much that which schoolboys have for the ordinary run of masters whom they do not exactly detest for any unusual severity, but for whom they certainly do not entertain any undue affection. When he first received his appointment, he had forgotten all about this feeling; indeed, he had never expressed himself strongly on the matter; only I know that it existed. I mention it now as it accounted to me in some degree for his subsequent conduct.

When our father came back he gave a vivid description of the smart frigate in which dear Alfred was to sail, of the gentlemanly, pleasant captain, and of the nice lads in the midshipmen's berth who were to be his companions. The first lieutenant, he remarked, was a stern-looking, weather-beaten sailor of the old school, but he had the repute of being a first-rate officer, and the captain had told him that he was very glad to get him, as he was sure to make all the youngsters learn and do their duty, and to turn them into good seamen. Altogether, he was perfectly satisfied with all he had seen, and with Alfred's prospects.

Herbert's description of the midshipmen's berth made me regret more and more that I had not been allowed to accompany him, and I began to wish that I too might be able to go to sea. I did not talk about it; indeed, I tried to repress the feeling, because I knew that my father wished me to be brought up to his business. Herbert, it was seen, was not at all likely ever to become fitted for it. His health was delicate, and he was of a contemplative studious disposition, and of a simple trusting mind, which had a tendency to shut out from itself all thoughts or knowledge of the evil which exists in the world. This is, I believe, a very blessed and happy disposition, if rightly directed and educated, but, at the same time, those who possess it are not fitted for those pursuits in life which bring them into contact and competition with all classes and orders of men. They should not be thrown among the crowd struggling on to gain wealth, or name, or station, or they most assuredly will be trampled under foot. So our father said, and I think he judged rightly, when he advised Herbert to fix his thoughts on becoming a minister of the gospel. "If I am considered worthy, there is no vocation I would so gladly follow," was dear Herbert's answer. Those who knew him best would most assuredly have said that he was worthy, compared to the usual standard of frail human nature.

The time to which I have now been alluding was during our summer holidays. We all three went to a first-rate school near Blackheath, where I believe we were general favourites. I know that Alfred and Herbert were, and I had many friends among the boys, while the masters always expressed themselves kindly towards me. If not exactly what is called studiously disposed, I was, at all events, fond of learning and reading, and gaining information in every variety of way, and the commendations I received from my masters encouraged me to be diligent and attentive. My father also was pleased with my progress; and as I delighted in giving him pleasure, I had another strong motive to study hard, not only what I especially liked—for there is very little virtue in that—but what I was told would ultimately prove a benefit to me. I was especially fond of reading about foreign countries, and I thought to myself, if I am not allowed to enter the navy, I will, at all events, become a great traveller, and, perhaps, as a merchant, be able to visit all those wonderful lands, with the accounts of which I am now so much interested. I will not dwell upon my school life. It was a very happy one. We were boarders, but we came home frequently, and we did not thereby lose the love of home; for my part, I think we loved it the more for frequently going to it. We kept up our home interests, had our home amusements, and our home pets Our more particular friends among our school-fellows frequently came home with us, especially to spend their Easter and Michaelmas holidays, when they would otherwise have had to remain at school. We had also generally a good supply of eatables, and for these and the reasons of which I have before spoken, we were probably altogether the most popular boys at school. Alfred had been so, and so was Herbert, and I in time came in for my share of popularity, and, as I found, for what is far more valuable, of sincere, true friendship. We all at that time undoubtedly enjoyed the sunshine of prosperity.

We heard occasionally from Alfred; but he was not an apt penman, and did not prove himself so good a correspondent as we had hoped. We had a letter from him written at Rio de Janeiro, and a short one from the Cape of Good Hope. Then the ship went to India, and was there a couple of years, during which time he wrote occasionally. At last he sent us a few hurried lines from the Mauritius, saying that he was well, but that the frigate was about to return to India, and on her way to visit several interesting places.

Waiting for some time after the receipt of that letter, we began to be anxious about receiving another, but none came. Day after day, week after week, and month after month passed by, and we heard nothing. Our disappointment was great, but our anxiety did not increase in the same proportion, as we had no doubt that his letters had by some means miscarried. We never allowed ourselves to suppose for a moment that the ship had been lost, or that any other misfortune had occurred, still less that Alfred himself was ill or had died. None of us, it seemed, could have borne that thought. At last my father became really anxious and wrote to the captain. He waited for a long time for a reply, and at last he got one, not from the former captain, who had died from fever, but from the officer who had been first lieutenant when my brother sailed, saying that Mr. Marsden had thought fit to quit his ship without leave; he could not be considered as belonging to the navy, and that, therefore, he had no further charge over him. He did not say where Alfred had left the ship, or when, or why, allowing us to remain most cruelly in a dreadful state of suspense. My father instantly wrote again to make further inquiries, but during the time we were waiting for the reply to the second letter, we saw it stated in the papers that the gallant frigate had been lost, and that all hands on board had perished.

We grieved much at the idea that Alfred should have left his ship and brought disgrace upon himself by becoming a deserter. At the same time, we could not but with gratitude rejoice that he had escaped the dreadful fate which had overtaken his companions. This circumstance was one of the first griefs which had befallen our family. My father was much troubled by it. He wrote again and again to various correspondents in that part of the world, but received no satisfactory replies; none of them had heard of Alfred. The surprising thing was that he did not write himself. His silence was most unaccountable and painful. We could not believe that he was lost to us for ever, nor could we suppose for a moment that he whose memory was so fondly cherished, and who had loved us all so much, had so completely changed as not to think it worth while even to communicate with us, and to let us know that he was alive.

"Oh no, no! that is impossible," exclaimed our mother, with tears in her eyes, when one day our father remarked that lads scarcely were aware how quickly time flew by, and that they often put off writing home from day to day till they forgot all about the matter. "I am sure our dear Alfred would have written if he could. Perhaps he has written, and his letters have been lost. This is by far the most likely thing to have occurred. So affectionate, kind, and dutiful as he always was, he certainly has not forgotten us."

Mary, and Charlotte, and Herbert, all thought the same. So did I. I felt sure that he had not forgotten us, and that, had he possessed the means of writing and of sending us a letter, that he would have done so; but I could not help fancying that he must have been made prisoner by some savages, or carried into slavery by some Malays or Malagash or other eastern people, or perhaps that he had been wrecked on some desolate island from which he had no means of escaping. I reasoned thus: Fond as he was of the sea, after he had left his ship and virtually quitted the navy, he was not at all likely to live a shore life. It was much more probable that he would engage in some trading voyage or other, and the more romance and adventure it might appear to offer, the more likely he was to select it; and thus he would have gone away to the South Seas or to the East Indian Islands, where all the contingencies I have just spoken of were very likely to occur. It at last became a fixed idea in my mind that poor Alfred was groaning somewhere or other in slavery, but the where was the question to solve. I told my sister Mary my idea, but she entreated me on no account to mention it to our mother, or to anybody else, as she was certain that it would make them still more unhappy about him than they were already.

At length a strong desire grew up in my bosom to set out and try to discover Alfred. I had heard my father quote a Portuguese proverb, "He who does not want sends, he who wants goes." Now, I certainly wanted very much indeed to find out where poor Alfred was, and I was ready and eager to sail the world round to discover him; but I was still very young, and I knew that there would be a great deal of difficulty in getting my father to allow me to go, if indeed he would give me permission at all. When or how the idea came into my mind I could not tell. There it was, however, and once there it was not likely to die out, but would grow with my growth and strengthen with my strength, till at length I was able to act upon it.

About this time I observed a great change coming over my father. He was kind and affectionate as ever, but his spirits were lower than I had ever known them; and day after day he came down late from London, looking weary and fagged. My mother, too, looked anxious and sad. Whatever was the cause which affected him, she was fully aware of it. He had always from the first told her how his affairs were going on, and he was not the person to conceal any expected misfortune from his long-trusted wife.

The looked-for blow which was to lay him low, destroy his credit, and bring him to utter ruin, came even more quickly and suddenly than he had anticipated. He had some heavy liabilities, but at considerable loss had collected the necessary sums, which were placed in the hands of his bankers to meet them. The morning of the very day on which the money was to be paid, his bankers failed, and he was in consequence compelled to stop payment. Still, his creditors had so much confidence in him that they would have enabled him to continue business; but scarcely a week had passed before he received news that two of his principal foreign correspondents, with whom he had at the time very large transactions, had likewise failed. Thus the remittances he was expecting from them did not arrive, and he was utterly unable to meet other and still heavier liabilities which were daily falling due. He at once manfully called his creditors together, and explained clearly to them the state of the case, and handed all his available property over to them. He bore up well under the trying situation in which he was placed; he even, I heard, looked cheerful. He was doing what he felt to be his duty. He trusted still, by industry and energy, to be able to support his family; but there was something working away at his heart which those who saw him did not suspect, and of which he himself possibly was not aware. He went back to his counting-house after this last meeting of his creditors. He wrung the hand of his faithful head-clerk, Mr. Ward, who had himself suffered severely by the failure of the bank; and then, scarcely venturing to speak, set off to come home.

That home he never reached alive. Between the station and his house he was seen to fall, and being carried into the nearest shop, immediately breathed his last. Sad and almost overwhelming was the account which was brought us. I will not enter into the particulars, with which my readers generally cannot be interested.

Deep was our grief at our kind father's loss. We were left also almost penniless. He had insured his life, but by some unaccountable neglect of his trustees, we could not benefit by the insurance. Had Alfred been at home, we should, it appeared, have been placed above want, at all events. A considerable sum of money had been left him by his godfather, the interest of which was to be paid over to our father or mother for his use from the time he was sixteen. In case of his death, it was to go to another godson of the same old gentleman. Unless, therefore, the trustees in whose names the capital was invested were assured that he was alive, they, of course, could not venture to pay our mother the money.

After our first burst of grief was over, and we could talk with some calmness, I told my mother of the idea which had so long occupied my mind, and besought her to allow me to carry it into execution. Herbert, it was very clear, was not so well fitted for the undertaking as I was. Somebody, I argued, ought to go, and as I had long set my heart on the work, and thought, or fancied that I had thought, of all the difficulties I should have to encounter, I was better fitted for it than anybody else. I would also visit my grandfather in the Mauritius, and he certainly would give me important assistance in tracing out my brother. Steadily and strenuously I pressed the point, till at length my mother came entirely into my view of the case, and gave me her full permission to set off, and to make such arrangements as I thought necessary.

As soon as she had done this, though her fast falling tears told me how much the effort cost her, a load appeared to be taken off my heart. I felt as if I had at once grown into a man, and was about to begin the serious business of life. Scarcely a fortnight had elapsed after my father's funeral before it was arranged that I was to go. How to carry out my purpose was the next consideration. On one point I was resolved—not to deprive my mother and sisters of a farthing of the small sum which could be collected for their support. I had a fair stock of clothes, and Herbert insisted on my taking some of his, so that I was at no expense for my outfit. The first thing Herbert and I did was to set off for the London Docks, where I had been several times with my father, to try and find a ship bound for the Cape of Good Hope or the Mauritius, at one of which places I proposed commencing my search. I was ready to enter on board in any capacity in which I was not called upon to pay a premium; but as I had never been at sea, and knew nothing practical about the sea, it may be supposed that, although I had heard of several ships at the point of sailing to the very places I wished most to visit, I could not succeed in obtaining a berth on board any of them. We walked home again somewhat dispirited with our want of success; but, nevertheless, I was still as resolved as before to go by some means or other.

We had arranged the next day to visit our school, that I might take leave of our excellent master and school-fellows.

I could not bear to go away without seeing them, though I fancied that I should find it a painful ceremony. I shall never forget how warmly and kindly I was greeted by every one; and still more gratified was I when one boy after another brought me up some present, which he asked me to accept as a keepsake. Some were trifles, but everything was of a character likely to prove useful to me. One gave me a knife with a hole in the handle, through which I might pass a lanyard to wear it round my neck; another a small writing-case; a third, a drawing-case; others, such things as sketch-books, pencils, some useful tools; and one of my greater friends, who was well off, gave me a first-rate spy-glass; while my kind master called me into his study, and showed me a serviceable sextant.

"There, Ralph, I hope that, as you are going to sea, you will endeavour to acquire all the information in your power respecting nautical matters, even though you may not ultimately follow a sea life as your profession. Of course, you will fit yourself to become an officer by the study of navigation, which, you will find, is a distinct branch of a sailor's profession from seamanship. The possession of the sextant you will, I hope, find a considerable advantage to you, as it will enable you to gain experience in taking observations of the celestial bodies as you traverse the ocean. I offer you this gift on the condition that you accept another one. It consists of these two stout volumes of blank paper, and I shall expect you to do your best to fill them with the result of the observations you make during your voyages and travels. I want you to keep not merely an ordinary sea-log, remember, but a complete journal, as diffuse as you can. Never trust to your memory. Points which at the time you fancy you will never forget are often completely obliterated in a few months. I have frequently myself found this to be the case. So put down everything worth noting as soon after it has occurred, or you have seen it, as possible; and especially understand that no point connected with natural history, or science generally, is too trivial to be noted. Great and important truths are often discovered by what at first might have appeared a collection of trivialities."

I repeat these remarks of my master's, because I think that they may be of use to my readers, as I certainly found a very great advantage in following his advice. He gave me also a number of pocket-books with pencils, for producing indelible writing, which I also found very useful. Other friends gave me books to form a complete sea-library; indeed, I strongly suspected, from their character, that my master had assisted in their selection. I need not say that I was very grateful for all these numerous marks of kindness, and it made me very happy and proud to feel that I was so much esteemed by my companions; at the same time, I daresay I owed some of the kindness I received to the commiseration my friends felt for me in consequence of the misfortunes which had overtaken my family. Nearly everybody had given me something, except my friend, Henry Raymond. I knew that his means were not large; but still, I felt sure that he would wish to make me some trifling present or other. After all my treasures had been collected, I found him standing by my side.

"Come along, Ralph," he said, with the pleasant smile which constantly lighted up his countenance; "I want to give you something which you will like and value." He was leading me towards the courtyard at the back of the house. "I wish that I could go with you myself, that we might take care of each other; but as I cannot do that, I beg that you will take Solon with you. He will fight bravely in your cause, and will, I am sure, prove watchful and faithful; and it will be a great satisfaction to me to know that you have got so stout a friend by your side."

There stood Solon with a new chain and collar, with my

SOLON.

name engraved on it. He was wagging his tail, and looking up with a pleased expression in our faces, as if he was fully aware of what had been said, and was perfectly ready to undertake the charge committed to him. He was an old friend of mine, and would follow me as readily as he would Henry if I let him loose, so that he possibly did not consider that he was about to change masters. He was a very intelligent and powerful dog, a cross between a mastiff and a Newfoundland dog. He was born in the island of Portland, in Dorsetshire, his immediate ancestors having belonged to some of the free trading population of that district, and employed in the not very creditable occupation of carrying casks of spirits and small bales of silks and laces into the interior, past the revenue officers stationed there to prevent smuggling. So sagacious were those dogs that they knew the appearance of a coast-guardsman at a great distance, and employed every stratagem to avoid him, so that they were seldom captured or shot. Dogs trained in the same way are employed by the contrabandists to carry smuggled goods across the frontiers of both France and Portugal into Spain, in which country the high duties make smuggling a profitable business. We had called Henry's dog

Solon, from the sagacity he displayed in everything in which he was called on to take a part.

"The very thing, of all others, I am delighted to have," I exclaimed, wringing Henry's hand. "I would rather have had you; but next to you, I think Solon is likely to prove as true a friend as any one I shall meet with. Dear old Solon, you will stick by me, I know, and help me to find out Alfred, won't you? That I know you will, old fellow." Solon, as I spoke to him, wagged his tail and licked my hand, and looked up in my face, as if he thoroughly understood all I was saying.

Henry Raymond that day accompanied me and Herbert home, to assist, as he said, in carrying my presents. My mother was much affected by the kindness of my school-fellows, and more especially with the liberality and consideration of our master, when Herbert told her that he was to go back and attend school regularly as before.

"Your father was very kind, and procured me many pupils," he remarked. "You need not consider yourself under any special obligation to me, for I should indeed regret if you had not the opportunity of continuing your studies at the most important period of your life. I need scarcely say that the best way you can repay me is to study hard, and to obtain all the advantage you can from the instruction I am happily able to afford you."

The circumstances I have been describing shed a gleam of bright sunshine over our late sorrowing household, and, as our mother said, she was sure that the widow and the fatherless who place their trust in God's protecting care will not be forgotten by him. The exertions my mother and sisters were compelled to make to prepare my kit, allayed somewhat their grief, at the same time that it reminded them of poor Alfred's departure, and many a tear they dropped on account of both of us.

I had still to hunt about to get a ship, and as I was anxious to lose no time, I resolved not to relax my search till I had found one. Of course, I knew that if I had been able to go to one of the large shipowners with a premium in my hand, and requested to be taken as an apprentice, I should have had little difficulty about the matter; but as I could not do that, I was compelled to try and obtain a berth by some other means. One night I scarcely closed my eyes, being employed in turning over in my mind various plans by which I fancied I might succeed in my object. I bethought me at length that I would go to Mr. Ward, my father's old clerk. He had been very unwell ever since hearing of my father's death; but I knew his lodgings, and I was sure he would give me the best advice in his power, though he might not be able to help me in a more practical way. This resolution may not appear a very great result of a sleepless night's cogitations, yet I have found it often to be the case, that although during the night I have fancied that I have been thinking all sorts of important things, I have in the morning been unable to derive from them more than some very simple and insignificant results. I advise my readers, if they can help it, never to think at night. Let them go to sleep, get up early, and while they are taking a brisk walk in the bright, fresh air, let them think as much as they can—their thoughts then will be of ten times more value than all the produce of a sleepless night. A successful merchant once told me that he made a practice of rising with the sun, and walking round and round his grounds, while he laid plans for the day's work; and thus he got nearly all his thinking done while enjoying pure air and exercise, and while in the city had only to perform the less fatiguing duty of an overseer to watch that his plans were carried out. The result of my visit to Mr. Ward I will detail in the following chapter.

CHAPTER II.

Our old Clerk—I find that he has a Heart—Look out for a Ship—The *Orion*—Her Officers and Crew—Last Day at Home—Part from Mr. Ward—The Passengers—Sail down the Thames—Change of Captain.

OLD Mr. Ward rose from his chair by the fire when, accompanied by Solon, I went in; and he made me sit down beside him with a great deal of courtesy and kindness, while the dog crouched down at my feet. The old gentleman sighed very much, and blew his nose, and wiped his eyes, when I told him of the plan I had resolved to follow. I ought to have said that I had not had much communication with him, for he was of a somewhat eccentric character; and although my father had frequently invited him, he would never come down and dine with us, as it is the custom of many head-clerks to do with their principals.

"Ah, Mr. Ralph," he said, still sighing, "till our misfortunes came I always looked forward to your joining us in Crooked Lane when you were old enough; and now to have you go wandering about the world by yourself—so young as you are, too—I cannot bear the thoughts of it."

I did my best to persuade him of the importance of my object; and I argued that my youth was no disadvantage, and that I should enjoy the sort of life I proposed leading.

"Well, if that is the case, Mr. Ralph, I will see what I can do," he exclaimed, getting up with more activity than I expected, and preparing to put on his great-coat and hat, though, by-the-by, the day was warm and genial.

I begged him, however, not to venture out if he was still ill. He looked at me almost reproachfully.

"Ah, Mr. Ralph, for your honoured father's son it is a slight thing indeed that I am undertaking to do," he answered. "We will first go to Lloyds' and ascertain what vessels are on the berth for those places, and then I will go to the agents and see if I know any of the owners, or captains, or other officers of the ships, and endeavour to make some arrangement with them about you."

Mr. Ward, though usually very silent, showed that he was a man of prompt action, which is much better than being a talker.

"Leave your dog, Mr. Ralph, till we come back," he observed as we were about leaving the room; so patting Solon on the head, and making him lie down on the rug, I saw that he clearly understood that he was to stay where he was.

Mr. Ward said very little during our walk to the Exchange. He went up into Lloyds' room, leaving me waiting on the pavement at the foot of the stairs. He was not long absent.

"Come along, Mr. Ralph; it is possible we may be successful," was all he said, as he hurried me off to Billiter Street, and St. Helen's, and to one or two other places in the neighbourhood, where some of the large ship-brokers have their offices.

He made a great variety of inquiries at a considerable number of offices, where he seemed always to be kindly received; but as he invariably spoke in a low tone of voice, and was answered in the same, I did not exactly comprehend the tenor of the information he obtained. I only know that he exhibited a great deal of patience and perseverance in going about from office to office, in waiting till some one was at leisure to speak to him, and in asking questions. I made some remark to that effect.

"Yes, Mr. Ralph," he replied. "We have in the city to exercise patience as well as perseverance. We have often to hurry along as fast as our legs can carry us, for ten minutes, while perhaps we may at the end of it be kept waiting for an hour before we can speak to the person we have come to see; but you will understand that if we had not hurried along at first, we might have had to wait two hours, or have missed the interview altogether. Sailors are tried much in the same way, I fancy, as you will learn when making a voyage. Sometimes they get a fair breeze, and run before it for many days; and then they fall into a calm, and have to float about doing nothing, or they are driven back by contrary winds, and lose all the ground they have gained. Such is our voyage through life, Mr. Ralph; and it is better to know beforehand what we are likely to meet with, and be prepared for it. That is the reason why I wish to draw your attention to the subject, my dear young gentleman, and to urge you to be prepared. Because the sun shines sometimes, and we have a fair breeze, we must not suppose that the sun will always be shining, or that we shall at all times enjoy a favourable wind."

These remarks were made by the kind old man as we sat waiting in one of the offices to see the principal, to whom he was well known. One so often reads in stories of roguish, or hard-hearted, or narrow-minded head-clerks, that it is pleasant to be able to record from my own experience an example of a very different character. I believe that clerks are often made hard-hearted or selfish, if not rogues, by the unsympathizing or supercilious way in which they are treated by their employers. The successful general will always be found to have taken an interest in the welfare of the humblest private among his troops; and in the same way I am certain that the successful merchant has always shown that he can enter into the domestic affairs of his subordinates, and has treated them with kindness and consideration. At last Mr. Ward was summoned into the private office of the broker. When he came out he took me by the arm.

"Come along, Mr. Ralph," he said; "we will look in at my lodgings, and then hie off to the docks."

He hurried along the streets at a great rate without speaking. Not that he was really, I found, in a great hurry, but it was his habit to get over the ground as fast as possible when he could, so that he might not be inconvenienced by delays from impediments when they might occur. A very nice luncheon was spread out on the table, over which Solon was keeping a dutiful ward and watch. This, I knew, could not be according to the old gentleman's custom; but he had ordered the meal, I suspected, that I might not have the expense of paying for my own luncheon, and that he might not run the risk of hurting my feelings by paying for it himself at a chop-house.

"Perhaps you would like to take your dog with you, Mr. Ralph," said the old man, when the meal was over, looking down kindly on Solon, who wagged his tail on being thus noticed. He had come in for his share of the bones of the mutton-chops we had had for luncheon.

"Yes, indeed, I should, thank you," I answered. "I never wish to be parted from Solon. Do you know, Mr. Ward, I always fancy he knows that he has especially to look after me, and to keep me out of harm."

Mr. Ward smiled. "He looks very intelligent, and I have no doubt will do his best for you on all occasions," said he. "But, my dear young gentleman, I must not lose the opportunity of urging you ever to look to One, our great and merciful Maker, for protection and support. But then, you cannot look to him for protection unless you show your love to him by obeying him, and trying to please him in all things. Do that, pray to him always, and then boldly and fearlessly go through life. You will be equipped with a better tempered armour, a larger shield, a stronger helmet than any steel-clad knight of old. Next trust to yourself, to your own energies, courage, and perseverance. Don't fancy that other people are to do things for you. Others, however good their intentions, may fail you. Just be true to yourself, and don't fear. The lad who is always fancying that his friends are going to do something for him (as the foolish phrase goes), is very sure to be left behind in the race. You will be surprised, I daresay, how a London counting-house clerk came to get these ideas into his head. Look—there are my masters." He pointed to some shelves well filled with books, not remarkable for the elegance or uniformity of their binding. " I have read every one of these—not once, but over and over again. When I have wanted a new friend to dine with me, I have stopped at a book-stall, and have managed to pick him up at the cost of sixpence or a shilling; sometimes I have expended several shillings on him, but I have seldom paid so much for any work as some of the city gentlemen pay for one dish of fish to feed three or four friends who have given them very little entertainment in return, whereas my new friend has afforded me interest for days and weeks afterwards. But I must not go on babbling in this way. Call your good dog. Come along, Mr. Ralph."

Off we set, Solon keeping very close to my heels, as if he were afraid of losing me in the crowd, and whenever I put down my hand I felt him licking my fingers to show that he was near me. Mr. Ward was again taciturn as before. He felt that, as a city man, he was among people who knew him, and lest he should be overheard he was habitually silent. He now appeared to me quite a different person to what I had fancied him to be. I had thought him what the world calls a very worthy, faithful, but rather stupid old man. I found him to be kind, thoughtful, and intelligent, and I felt very sure that my dear brother and sisters would find him the same, and that he would, in some way or other, prove a valuable friend to them.

The London, as well as the East and West India and several other docks, are well worthy of a visit. There are immense warehouses both under and above ground, those below being called vaults, by-the-by; and there are broad quays with huge basins, or 1 might describe them as vast tanks, which are full of fine ships, each of many hundred tons. The names of the ships were painted in large letters on black boards and hung up on the rigging, so that we had no necessity to make inquiries for the ship Mr. Ward wished to find.

"We had not much to do with vessels," he observed. "We took freight, and shipped our cargoes, and received them in return without any communication with the master or his officers, so that I do not know many sea-going people. However, I have, fortunately, a cousin, who is second mate of a ship—the *Orion*—just sailing for the Cape of Good Hope and the Mauritius. My friends, Minnories, the brokers, have given me a letter to the master, and if we can arrange matters with him, you will, I hope, from what I hear, find him a pleasant man to sail with. At all events, I know that my cousin, William Henley, is a very fine young fellow, and will prove a good friend to you. If I am not too presumptuous, Mr. Ralph, I might say, also, a worthy companion, though his birth was not much less humble than was mine."

"My father would not have allowed such a consideration to weigh with us in the choice of our companions, I assure you, Mr. Ward," I answered, promptly; for well did I remember hearing him remark, that he would far rather his sons chose their friends from among right-principled, steady, industrious lads, than from among the most wealthy or high-born in the land.

"That was like him, Mr. Ralph—that was like him," said the old man, warmly. "Now, here we are at the *Orion*. She

THE ORION IN DOCK.

is a fine-looking ship for her size—some four or five hundred tons, I should guess. Ah, there is William Henley himself!"

As he spoke, a dark man with a large black beard and whiskers looked over the bulwarks, and seeing Mr. Ward, came along the plank which connected the ship with the quay towards us. He shook hands warmly with Mr. Ward, who took him aside, while I stood patting Solon's head and admiring the appearance of the ship—the neat way in which she was rigged and painted, and the massive masts and yards to which the white sails had just been bent. I seldom had had an opportunity of examining so large a ship ready for sea so near, and I thought her, as she truly was, a very handsome production of human art.

"And so you wish to go to sea with us," said the mate, when he and Mr. Ward rejoined me. I liked his tone of voice, and I saw that he was a much younger man than his dark appearance at first led me to suppose.

"Yes, indeed I do," I answered; "I always have wished to go to sea, and now I have a stronger motive than ever. Perhaps Mr. Ward has told you."

"Yes; I know all about it—very right," said Mr. Henley. "And you want to secure a berth for your four-footed companion there. He's a fine fellow. I'll try and arrange that for you. Captain Seaford is a very reasonable man, and you will like him, I know. We shall go out of dock to-morrow, or the next day at furthest. You may join us at Gravesend, if you like, but I would advise you to come on board here. It will save you expense and trouble, and you will find much to interest you in seeing the ship go out of dock."

All this seemed very easily and agreeably arranged. Mr. Henley was, I found, a connection of Captain Seaford's, and much trusted by him, so that he did not speak without authority in what he said. He then took us round the ship. She had her cargo on board, but she was taking in stores and provisions, and appeared to be in a state of great confusion. She was, I found, to carry a certain number of first and second class emigrants to the Cape. Mr. Ward insisted on accompanying me to London Bridge, declaring that the walking about in the service of my father's son did him more good than all the doctor's physic he could take. On our way there he told me that the first mate of the *Orion*, Mr. Paul Grimes, was a very different sort of person to William Henley, and that he was certainly a bad-tempered and not a well-disposed man, at all events.

"Never mind, though," said my old friend. "Keep on doing your duty. Do not retort. Return good for evil, and so you will in the end 'heap coals of fire on his head.' There are few men's hearts which cannot be softened in that way."

Mr. Ward kindly shook my hand when I parted from him, and begged that I would come to him early the next day with my chest before going on board the *Orion*.

I saw the tears trickling down my dear mother's cheeks as I gave her an account of what had occurred during the day.

"Surely He does not desert the fatherless and widows who cry unto him; and he employs his emissaries often in the shape of human beings to do his work," she exclaimed, as she put her head upon my shoulder while I stood by her side.

The next morning I was up by daybreak finishing all my preparations. I will not describe the parting at last. It was very grievous for us all to bear. I knew too well how much my poor mother felt it, for she could not help allowing the idea to enter that perhaps Alfred might be lost to her for ever, and that I, too, subject to the numberless vicissitudes of a sea-life, might never return. Herbert was to go with me to see the *Orion*, and Henry Raymond got leave to accompany us. We all four—that is to say, Solon, Herbert, Henry, and I—started away after an early breakfast, and in spite of the sad events which had occurred—such is the buoyancy of young spirits—a very merry party we soon became. Perhaps our spirits were rather forced at times. Mr. Ward was not ex-

THE PARTING.

pecting so large a party, but he was not displeased at seeing us. I found a tailor waiting to take my measure.

"You are to be received on board as a midshipman, Mr. Ralph," said the kind old man, in a sort of hesitating way. "There are two other youngsters, I find, and as they wear uniforms, it is right that you should be dressed like them. Mr. S—— will get you yours ready in a few hours, and I can settle all about it some day with your mother, you know."

"But I do not like to put my mother to the additional expense," said I, drawing back.

Mr. Ward almost gave me a hug, while a smile of satisfaction beamed brightly on his countenance. "Never mind, my dear lad," he exclaimed. "Mr. S—— is very liberal, and the whole matter will be arranged without the slightest difficulty, or having to trouble your mother in any way. You must have the uniform, and it would be a great disappointment to have to give up the expedition because you would not get it."

I saw that there was no use disputing the point further, so wringing Mr. Ward's hand to show that I understood him, I let the tailor take my measure. The cab, with my sea-chest on the top of it, and a portmanteau, hat-box, and several other articles inside, was waiting at the door.

"We will put your property on board, Mr. Ralph, and ascertain at what time the *Orion* goes out of dock," observed Mr. Ward. "You will have plenty of time to come on shore again, and purchase any trifles you may have forgotten. William Henley will tell us all about the matter."

We were somewhat of a cabful, as Henry Raymond observed, for though Mr. Ward said he would go outside, we would not let him, nor would he let Henry go on the box. At last the cab reached the docks, and disgorged its contents on the quay just before the *Orion*. While we watched over my property, Mr. Ward went on board. Soon a couple of seamen appeared, and made very little difficulty in hauling my mighty chest on board. Mr. Henley then came and showed me a place between decks, near his and the third mate's cabin, where I and the other first-class apprentices, or midshipmen, were to swing our hammocks. It was a gloomy, very unattractive spot, I thought; but I had made up my mind to be contented with whatever was provided for me, so I did not even think of grumbling. Herbert, however, whose tastes were very different from mine, shuddered when he found that this low, confined spot, was to be my future abode for so long a period.

"Horrible!" I heard him whisper to Henry Raymond. "Poor dear Ralph! it is sad indeed that he should have to live in so dark a hole."

Henry laughed. "If no worse fate befall him, I do not think that he should be unhappy," he answered.

We were all introduced to Captain Seaford, who had come on board to visit the ship only, and we found that he was going on shore again, and that she would after all not leave the docks for a couple of days. I liked Captain Seaford's appearance very much. He was a fine, gentlemanly-looking man, with a very kind expression of countenance; and Mr. Henley, who had before sailed with him, assured us that his character was in accordance with his features. He looked unwell, and complained of being ill when he left the ship. He told me as he went away that I might, if I wished, remain on shore for at least forty-eight hours longer, as there was nothing just then for me to do on board. I scarcely knew whether to be glad or sorry at this. I should again see my mother and sisters, but then there would be the parting to go through once more.

"As you are to remain, we must try and get Mr. Ward and Mr. Henley to come down and dine with us to-morrow," observed Herbert, who was always thoughtful. "It will be a very great comfort to our mother to know one of the officers of the ship you are to sail in, and it will be gratifying to her to be able to thank Mr. Ward for all his kindness to you."

We accordingly agreed that we would give the invitation, although I was afraid that Mr. Ward, at all events, would not accept it. What was my surprise, therefore, to find that he did so readily and cheerfully, and he added that he was certain that William Henley would come if he could. The reason

why he now came so readily was this. He had so much tact
and consideration, and he knew that his so doing would gratify
my mother, and that having to entertain him would assist to
keep up her spirits, and prevent her from thinking too much
of her forlorn condition. Mr. Ward would not let me go back
to Blackheath till my uniform was ready, when he made me
put it on, not a little to my inward satisfaction, and said that
he would send my other things on board the *Orion*. He made
during the day many minute inquiries about my kit, and the
various articles I possessed; and in a list he showed me in his
lodgings, he made me point out what I did not possess, and
insisted in supplying the deficiency. He also added all sorts
of odds and ends, and many little articles which he said William
Henley told him that I should find useful.

The next day both he and Mr. Henley came down to Blackheath to dine with us. How gentle and kind they both were!
That strong, weather-beaten, dark-whiskered young man, who,
from his appearance, I should have expected to have a loud
gruff voice, spoke on the contrary in the most quiet, pleasant
way; and in a very little time, after having at first eyed him
askance, the younger children collected round him, and were soon
listening eagerly to an account he was giving them of some of
his sea adventures, and which, when I overheard, I found he
was exactly adapting to their comprehensions. A very pleasant
afternoon was spent. My mother and sisters did their best to
amuse Mr. Ward, and to show him how much they appreciated
his kindness to me. They were also, as I knew they would
be, very much pleased with Mr. Henley; and I am sure that
the kind old gentleman must have been satisfied with the
result of his unusual excursion. He asked my mother's leave,
as he was wishing her good-bye, to be allowed to call in occasionally to see if he could be of use to her or to any of the
little ones, and just to hear also if she had received any news

of Mr. Ralph. From the diffident way in which he spoke, it might have been supposed that she was a lady of rank and wealth, and that he was a humble person asking some great favour. Yet there was certainly no false humility in anything he said. I am very sure that he felt as he spoke, and that my mother's loss of property made no difference in his sight, but rather, from the way she bore it, raised her still higher in his estimation.

The next morning Herbert accompanied me and Solon once more on board the *Orion*. She was just then getting ready to move out of dock, it being close upon high water. Captain Seaford was not on board. He was still ill, and it was understood that he would join us at Gravesend. Mr. Ward was on board, according to promise, to see me off.

"I wish, my dear Mr. Ralph, that you would make me your banker," he said, after shaking hands, and leading me aside. I was not aware that he had already paid a considerable sum towards the premium required by the owners, though in my case they liberally lowered it.

I told him that I hoped to get assistance from my grandfather in the Mauritius, and that I ought not to take further advantage of his kindness.

"It is you who do me the favour, Mr. Ralph," he answered warmly. "You may, indeed you are certain to want money at the Cape or elsewhere. You cannot carry out your object without it, depend on that, and so you see I have already directed William Henley to honour your drafts on me; and here, my dear Mr. Ralph, I know that you will pardon an old man who made all he possesses through your father's means, take this little bag, it contains only twenty sovereigns—a mere trifle. Sew it up carefully in a belt about you; very likely you may find them useful. Sovereigns go everywhere, remember. They are just bright from the bank, and full weight.

Oh no, no; don't thank me—there's a good boy—just take them, and stow them away at once. That matter is settled; not another word—not another word."

Thus he liberally and delicately made me a present which I could not help feeling might be of the greatest service to me. I shall have to mention several valuable and expensive presents which I afterwards found he had made me.

"But I thought that you suffered as did my father when the bank failed."

"Ah, well, I did lose something, certainly," he answered quickly; "but that would be but a bad excuse for not trying to do as much good as I can with the remainder which Providence has allowed me to retain. Ah, yes, I know people do make it an excuse, but it is a very bad one, and will not prove valid, I suspect, in the day of judgment. That is the time we should always be looking forward to, Mr. Ralph; and we should ask ourselves, whatever we are doing, How will this stand the test on that great day? They have begun, sir, to cast off the wharfs. Good-bye, dear Mr. Ralph. May you be preserved from all danger, and be successful in your search. Mr. Herbert will go with you to Gravesend, and I shall esteem it a favour if he will come and let me know how you were, and how you got on at the last."

Saying this, the kind, generous old man wrung my hand and hurried on shore. When I looked at the vast crowd of mighty ships as well as smaller craft of all sorts with which we were surrounded, it seemed impossible that the *Orion* could ever be got clear of them; yet by a proper application of hawsers, and by due pulling and hauling, she was, in a wonderfully short time, warped clear of all impediments, and then a steam-tug taking her in tow, away she went, aided by the ebb, down the stream, and past many of the scenes with which I was so familiar.

THE ORION LEAVING THE DOCKS.

Solon and I looked our last on the old *Dreadnought*, the hospital ship for seamen of all nations, which lies just above Greenwich. I had more than once visited her with my father, who was a warm supporter of the institution. What a noble employment for a green old age, like that, I believe, of many a gallant sailor who, having fought the battles of his country in his youth, now employs himself by going about among his humble fellow-creatures, and doing all the good he can to their bodies and their souls! I have heard of several such men, admirals and others of high rank, who have thus happily occupied their declining years, just as the old ship is employed in receiving all who come to be cured of sickness and disease

THE DREADNOUGHT.

Then I gazed at Greenwich Hospital—a building I could never look at without the greatest interest. I knew so many of the old inmates, and so many pleasant hours had been passed there. What a blessing it has proved to thousands of England's brave tars, who would otherwise in their decrepitude have been cast helpless on the cold world! Above the hospital is another magnificent institution connected with it, I believe, where the sons of naval officers, as well as seamen, receive a first-rate nautical education. I thought as I looked over the ship's side that I recognized some of my old acquaintances, and then there were some white handkerchiefs waved by some ladies in black. I felt certain that my mother and sisters had come to take a last glance at me. I waved and waved in return, and Solon stretched out his neck and barked in a low, significant way; for Henry Raymond was with them, I guessed, and the dog recognized him. The incident, however, very nearly unmanned me. Blackwall was next passed, and Woolwich, where several men-of-war were fitting out; but I will not further describe our voyage down the Thames.

Herbert and I continued our walk on the quarter-deck, with

THE ORION PASSING GREENWICH.

Solon pacing up and down between us. No one had told me to do any duty; and as Herbert was with me, I naturally did not ask what I was to do, as I should have thus been separated from him. Suddenly, however, I heard a gruff, harsh voice hailing me from the poop.

"Hillo, youngster, what are your dog and you come aboard here to do, I should like to know?" These words were spoken by Mr. Grimes, the first mate. "That dog of yours will be hove overboard if he misbehaves himself, and that gold lace cap and those black kid gloves will follow, unless you can find something to do with your hands, let me tell you."

I looked up and caught the very unpleasant glance of the

mate fixed on me. He was a tall, thin, light-haired man, with a freckled complexion—wiry and bony—his eyes were large and gray, but bleared, with a remarkably hard, sinister expression in them. I had read about people in whose eyes the light of pity never shone, and as I looked up at that man's, I could not help feeling that he belonged to that miserable class. I had been too well trained both at home and at school not to answer properly.

"I am ready to do anything I am ordered, sir," I replied promptly, taking off my gloves and putting them in my pocket, while I whispered to Herbert to take Solon out of the way.

The ill temper of the mate was disarmed for the moment. However, a minute afterwards, as I stood where he had at first addressed me, I heard him sing out,—

"What's your name, youngster?"

I told him.

"Well, then, Mr. Ralph Marsden, up aloft with you, and help to loose that fore-top-sail. We shall be wanting a little head sail on the ship presently."

I knew perfectly well which was the fore-top-sail, but how to loose it was a piece of practical seamanship of which I was as yet entirely ignorant. Up the rigging, however, I went as fast as I could—greatly, I fancy, to poor Herbert's horror, who trembled in every joint as he saw me, wondering how I could do such a thing, while Solon looked up and barked, and would, I am persuaded, have come up likewise, could he have managed it with his four legs, to help me. I knew that some of the seamen would be on the yard, and I hoped to get them to show me what was to be done. I never felt particularly giddy on a height, so I was not at all unhappy waiting in the top till some one came to join me. I found, however, that Mr. Grimes had only sent me up there, as he said, to give me something to do. He knew at the same time that he was without necessity separating me from my brother. Still, I gained an advantage even from his ill nature, as I was thus somewhat accustomed to go aloft before the ship was in the open sea, and exposed to rough weather. I stood, therefore, in the fore-top watching what was going on below me on deck.

Many of the first-class passengers were walking the poop. They were mostly going out as settlers to Cape Colony and Natal, while a few merchants, planters, and clerks were proceeding on to the Mauritius. The second-class passengers were nearly all emigrants to the first-mentioned places. They were mostly small shopkeepers, farmers, servants who had saved up a little money, and others who had belonged to a superior class, but were broken down, and all of whom had paid for their passages. They were a very independent set of people, apparently, and not at all inclined to submit to discipline. They were wonderfully varied in the style of their costume, and it struck me that all were aiming to be considered as belonging to a rank superior to what I suspect they had in general held. They were scattered about, sitting on the bulwarks or holding on by the main rigging, watching the vessels and the shores of the river, which few of them were destined ever to see again. There were fathers and mothers, with their young children, and single men, shopmen, and farmers, and artizans going out to seek their fortunes alone, and a few unmarried women, mostly connected with the married couples. There were even some old men, whom I should have supposed would have been content to spend their latter days at home; but, strange as it may seem, they were urged on by the same desire which animated many of their younger companions—to make money—to do what they had failed to do at home. As I watched the motley collection of people from my high perch, I observed that some were laughing and joking as if nothing important was taking place. Others were thoughtful, as if conscious that they were taking an important step in life, while others looked very sad, evidently feeling that they were quitting for ever the home of their birth. The little children were playing about, unconscious that they were going to sea, and running a great risk of tumbling down the hatchways, while several of the men were arguing and wrangling as if the welfare of the nation depended on the result of their discussions. I thought to myself, I am well out of all that. Belonging to the ship, I shall not have to associate with those people.

I had been some time in the top when the other two new midshipmen joined me. They had never been to sea before; and there we all stood looking very foolish, and staring at each other, wondering what we were to do. They also had been sent up by the first mate, as he told them to loose the top-sail. To them it signified very little; but as I wished to be with poor Herbert, I was very much vexed at being kept up there doing nothing. At length several seamen did come into the top in a lazy, half-asleep sort of way. I found that they had all been tipsy the previous night, and were even then scarcely sober. They cut their jokes at us, loud enough for us to hear them, and addressed us as the three Master Greenhands with much mock respect, begging to know if they really were expected to loose the top-sail, and to be informed how they were to do it. I was pretty well versed in nautical phraseology, though my practical experience of sea affairs was very limited; so, knowing that there was nothing like making a good impression at first, I turned round on them, and said quickly,—

"Come, bear a hand, my hearties! You are sent up here to loose that top-sail,—I was sent to see you do it. You do your duty; I'll do mine."

They looked at me with surprised glances, never suspecting my ignorance; and instantly laying out on the yard, they cast off the gaskets and let fall the top-sail; which done, as soon as it was sheeted home, I descended on deck. I determined to try and make myself acquainted with everything about the ship as soon as I could, and to maintain, if possible, the superiority I had gained over the seamen in the top.

Among Mr. Ward's many valuable gifts was one on practical seamanship, full of prints and diagrams, which made it very easy to understand. This also I resolved to study with all the attention I could give it, so that I might avoid the necessity of constantly asking questions of the seamen,—at the same time, I must say that it is very much wiser to ask questions about things than to remain ignorant of what one wants to know. When I got on deck I found Herbert and Solon waiting for me at the foot of the fore-mast, and we agreed to remain there, hoping by keeping out of the sight of Mr. Grimes to avoid more of his annoyance. As I watched the scenes which were taking place, and the look of the crew, and the way they went about their work, I began to be sorry that Herbert had accompanied me on board to witness them, as I knew the unfavourable impression they would create in his mind—which was of an especially refined order—and that either he would fear that I might become vitiated by them, or that I should be made very unhappy by the sort of people with whom I should have to associate. I tried, therefore, to relieve his mind on that point.

"You know, Herbert, that I shall have to associate chiefly with Mr. Henley and the third mate, Mr. Waller, who seems a quiet sort of young man, while there appears to be no harm in my two fellow-midshipmen, Sills and Broom, though they certainly do not look very bright geniuses. I like the look, too, of Dr. Cuff, the surgeon; so, depend on it, people will soon shake into their proper places, and everything will turn out right in the end."

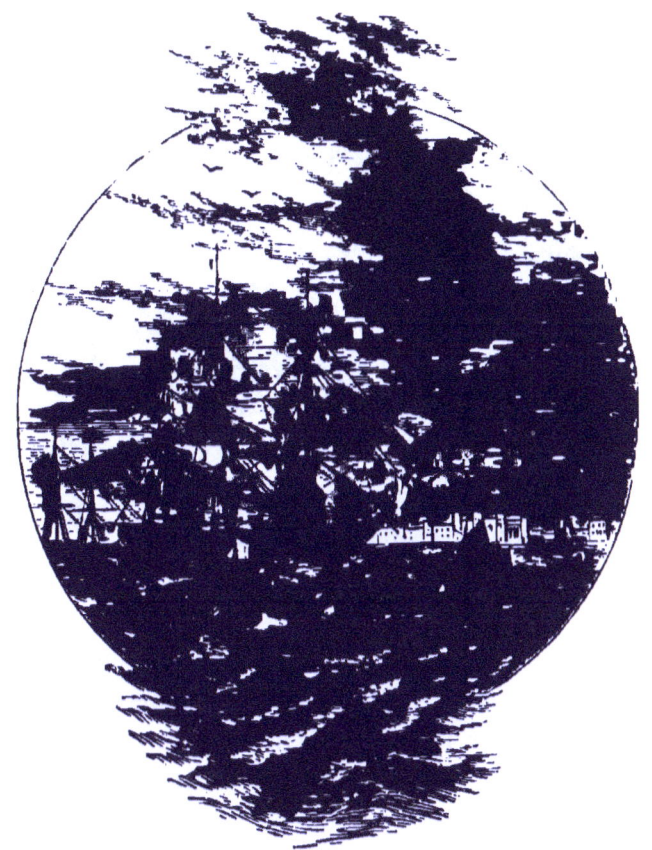

GRAVESEND.

We brought up at Gravesend, and had to remain there another twenty-four hours, that certain officers from the Government Emigration Board might visit the ship. That night Herbert would have had to go on shore, but Mr. Henley very kindly told him that he should have his cabin, and thus we were able to remain longer together.

The next morning the passengers were all employed in arranging their berths, and the crew were busy in stowing away casks and bales, and so no one attended to me—which was an advantage, as I was thus able to be much more with Herbert.

STOWING AWAY BOXES, ETC.

As the time for sailing approached, it was whispered about that Captain Seaford was very ill, and would be unable to take charge of the ship. Still, nothing certain was known. At length the hour arrived when it was necessary for Herbert to take his leave.

After Herbert had gone, it became known positively that Captain Seaford was unable to make the voyage; and after waiting a whole day longer, another master came on board with one of the owners, who formally put him in charge of the ship. I did not at all like his looks; nor did Solon, I suspect, for he snarled loudly at him, and in consequence, when getting in his way, received a severe kick in his ribs. It seemed as if there was at once an open declaration of war between the two. I was very sorry for it; for I was afraid that poor Solon, being the less powerful of the belligerents, would come off second best. Once more the anchor was hove up, and with a fair breeze we ran past the Nore, and stood down Channel under all sail. Captain

THE ORION PASSING THE NORE LIGHTSHIP.

Gunnell was the name by which our new master was known. I asked Mr. Henley what sort of a man he was.

"I sailed with him once, and I had hoped never to sail with him again," was his unsatisfactory reply.

CHAPTER III.

At Sea—A surly Mate—Solon's Astonishment at seeing the Ocean—The Bay of Biscay—Madeira—Funchal—Visit on Shore—Story of the Discovery of Madeira—Trip to the Pico—Tommy Bigg—Roughness of Crew.

AT length we were fairly on our voyage, far away out on the wide ocean without the most distant glimpse of land. Nothing but dark, heaving, white-crested waves around us. To me, as I looked over the bulwarks, the scene was inexpressibly strange, and grand, and awe-producing. I should have liked to have been for a short time perfectly alone, to have enjoyed it to the full, not another human being near me, with only Solon, my dumb companion, by my side. Far more I could have enjoyed it, I thought, than among the noisy, quarrelling crowd of passengers who formed the little coarsely composed world confined within those wooden walls, as the expression runs. Still, I did not think that I could have endured the solitude I wished for during any long period, but felt that I should soon have been glad to return to the midst of my noisy associates. Solon seemed as much surprised as I was when, looking out first at one port, then through the other, he found that there was no land to be seen. Several times he ran backwards and forwards, evidently trying to settle in his mind the state of the case. At last he was satisfied; then came up and licked my hand, as much as to say,—" I understand it all now, master. We are embarked in the same boat; and whatever befalls us, I intend to stick by you." Thanks to Mr. Henley's kindness, I had been allowed to arrange a berth for Solon just outside his cabin, between two chests, and within sight of my hammock. I made a mattress for him with some bits of old canvas stuffed with straw; for although a dog will do well enough even without a rug on the quiet ground, when a ship is pitching and rolling about he is very much the better for something soft to protect his ribs, as well as to keep him off the damp deck. He was also able in his snug corner to save himself from slipping about. Mr. Grimes, I suspect, never discovered where he slept, for the place was so dark that when he passed through that part of the ship he did not perceive him, and Solon, whose instinct told him that an enemy with whom he could not compete was near, always kept perfectly quiet and silent, with his bright eyes closed or hid away under his paws. His movements were regulated entirely by mine. When I went below, so did he, either to crouch at my feet at meals, or to go to his berth when I turned into my hammock; and the instant I was summoned by the hoarse voice of the boatswain, or of one of his mates, to keep my watch, he was on his feet ready to accompany me on deck. He was only unhappy when I had to go aloft, and then Sills and Broom told me that he kept running under wherever I was, looking up into the rigging, and watching me with intense earnestness —evidently showing that he was ready to run to my assistance if he could possibly get to me, and they declared that they saw him often examining the ratlines, and considering whether he could manage to get up them. He soon became a great favourite with most of my messmates, who appreciated his affection for me; but he was certainly not one with the first mate or the captain. He gave further evidence of his sagacity by managing, in the most active manner, to keep out of their way whenever they came on deck. The moment they appeared, although he might just before have been frolicking and frisking about in the merriest style possible, he slunk away with his tail between his legs, and hid himself forward, at some spot, if possible, whence he could see the quarter-deck, and watch for their retiring. Then he would run out from his hiding-place and look about on every side to be sure that they really were not on deck, and would again come bounding aft as joyous as before. I could not help fancying sometimes that he must have understood the threat Mr. Grimes uttered against him the first day he came on board. At all events, he evidently mistrusted the first mate's tone of voice, as he did the stern eye of the captain.

I must not enter very minutely into what may be called the nautical particulars of the voyage, interesting as they were to me. Our start was not satisfactory. No sooner did some heavy weather come on than the working of the ship opened the seams of her decks, and numerous other crevices through which wet could find its way—the bull's-eye lights, screw bolts, and skylights—the water poured down upon the unfortunate passengers, as it did, indeed, into all the standing bed-places both of officers and men, and soon made everybody in a most wretched condition. Neither the captain nor Mr. Grimes seemed to care about the matter. Mr. Henley and I, therefore, accompanied the surgeon round the between-decks to try and assist the suffering passengers. Never had I seen any set of people more thoroughly wretched. The deck was in some places an inch or more deep in water, the bedding was saturated, and the women's petticoats and shoes and stockings were wet through and through, while all sorts of articles were floating about amid a mass of dirt.

"We shall have fever break out among these poor people before long," observed Dr. Cuff to the second mate. "I must represent the state of the case to the captain, and advise him to put back to Plymouth."

"I am glad to hear you say so, as I have thought the same," said Mr. Henley. "The cargo, too, which I have to think about, will be damaged, if not destroyed; and the ship, from being overloaded, steers so badly, that it is a work to get her about, and if she was caught on a lee shore with a heavy sea, so that we could not tack, but had to wear, the chances are that we should run aground before we could do it. It would require two or three miles to wear this ship with any sea on in her present state."

This was unpleasant information. I had learned enough seamanship by this time fully to comprehend what Mr. Henley meant. Tacking and wearing are both manœuvres to get a ship's head round so as to have the wind on the side opposite to what it was at first. In tacking, the helm is put down, and the head comes up close to the wind, and then is forced round by it till it strikes the sails on the opposite side. Wearing, on the contrary, is performed by putting the helm up and keeping the ship's head away from the wind, gradually squaring the yards till she is directly before it. Then the helm is put down, and the yards are braced up till she is once more brought as close to the wind as she will lie. As she must be kept moving all this time, and as, in a gale, the ship moves very rapidly, it may be conceived that a great extent of ground must be run over before the whole manœuvre can be completed. I thought to myself, I hope that we shall not have to tack or wear ship on a lee shore in a dark night,—for although a shipwreck is a very interesting incident to read about, it is a thoroughly disagreeable one to suffer.

When Dr. Cuff made his report, the captain was highly indignant. "He would sooner see the ship go down, or all the people rot with fever, than put back,—that was not his way," was the answer he was reported to have made.

"Awful is the responsibility that man has taken on his shoulders!" observed Dr. Cuff to Mr. Henley.

I have scarcely spoken of Waller, our third mate. He was a rough, uneducated young man; not much, even, of a practical sailor; and Mr. Grimes soon made a complete, though not a willing tool of him. He was like Caliban under Prospero,— he grumbled, but could not help himself. After knocking about with heavy, contrary winds, somewhere in the latitude of Cape Ushant, and running a great risk of being driven up either the Irish Channel or on to the English coast, we at

THE BAY OF BISCAY.

length shaped a course across the Bay of Biscay. That bay, famed for turbulent seas, did not lose its character with us.

What a dark mass of troubled waters were around us! how gloomy the sky overhead! I could not help fancying that disasters were about to overtake us; and, indeed, the aspect of affairs on board was sufficiently discouraging. I never, indeed, had before felt so low-spirited. The second mate predicted shipwreck; the doctor, pestilence and death. What else was to happen I could not tell. Several sharp showers fell, then suddenly the sun burst forth from behind some dark clouds with resplendent beauty, spreading over, with a sheet of silver, a wide extent of the raging sea, along which flitted the sombre shadows from masses of clouds, casting an occasional gloom, but leaving the ocean once more to roll on in glorious brightness.

After all, I thought to myself, the evil anticipated may pass away like the clouds; I was wrong to have desponded.

"You admire this, my lad," said Dr. Cuff, in a kind way, as he came up to take a short turn on deck after attending to his laborious duties below. "The sea presents changeful scenes and extraordinary beauties, of which those who live always on shore have little conception. You will find yourself, I hope, amply repaid in the life you have chosen, by the numberless objects of interest you will meet with in your voyages. It is a grievous pity that lads are so often sent to sea with so small an amount of education that they cannot appreciate the advantages they enjoy, or make use of the opportunities which are presented to them of acquiring information. A sailor—an officer, I mean—unless he is content not to be superior to a waggoner who drives his team up and down between London and his native town, should have a fuller and more varied style of education than men of any other profession. He should know the history of every country he visits, the character of its people, and their institutions and language, its natural productions and natural history,—indeed, no knowledge will come amiss to him."

As may be seen, I was more fortunate in my associates than I might have expected. I had often read of waves running mountains high in books of poetry and other works, and I fully expected to see them as high as the mast-heads. I was surprised, therefore, to find our big ship tumbled about so much by those over which we sailed, and which seldom rose very much higher than the bulwarks. I told Mr. Henley what I had expected to see. He laughed very much, and said that it was fortunate they did not run to the height I had supposed. He then told me that those we were watching were generally not rising more than twenty feet, though, occasionally, some attained an elevation of from twenty-two to twenty-four feet. He calculated the height of the wave by first estimating the height of our eyes above the water, and then the height of the crest which intercepted the horizon.

A fortnight after leaving London the gale passed away, and the next morning we sighted a high land to the south, which was announced to be the island of Madeira. Latterly, we had made a good run of it. The captain was for giving it a wide berth, but Dr. Cuff made such strong representations as to the condition of the passengers, that, with a very bad grace, he stood towards it. Brightly the sun shone forth, and, with a light breeze, we soon found ourselves enjoying a summer climate. I was surprised to find that the captain consented to put into Funchal, but the doctor represented to him that if he kept at sea any longer, he could not answer for the lives of any of the passengers from day to day, so sickly had they become, and in such a wretched condition was the between-decks. Though he had refused to go back to an English port, he did not object to visit a foreign one.

I was much struck with the extraordinary beauty of Funchal and the surrounding country, as we brought up in the roads, which are on the south side of the island. Before us, piled one upon another, were numberless precipitous hills, separated by ravines, with houses, churches, and public buildings perched on every accessible point, and climbing up, as it were, from the sea-beach to a considerable height above the water. On our left, on the summit of some rocks, were two forts of some-

FUNCHAL.

what ancient appearance, the guardians of the town, while on the west was another fort of no very terrific aspect. But, perhaps, the chief attraction of the landscape next to the picturesque outline, was its exquisitely varied tinting and colouring, and the ever-changeful shadows which were cast over it by the passing clouds. White and bright are the houses in the town, with their red tiles; and green and shining are the quintas in the suburbs, with orange groves and coffee plantations, extending far and wide up the hills to the height of 1500 feet or more. One of the most conspicuous objects, standing high above the town, is the Church of Nossa Senhora do Monte—the Lady of the Mount—a well-known landmark to heretics as well as Catholics. The latter, however, offer up their vows while they look towards it as they start on their voyage, and pay their tribute to it, if they have escaped the perils to which they may have been exposed, on their return.

Dr. Cuff, who had been there frequently before, told me that some of the native residents had assured him that Nossa Senhora worked all sorts of miracles. On one occasion a famine threatened the island. A pilgrimage was accordingly made to the mount with great ceremony, to entreat the beneficent lady to supply them with food. The very next morning a vessel laden with corn arrived from Portugal. There could be no doubt that the saint had had a hand in the matter. So said the priests of the Church; and on examining her clothes, they were found to be perfectly wet with salt water. The sailors, too—so it was said—confirmed this statement by asserting that, while their vessel lay becalmed, a white figure had risen suddenly out of the ocean, and towed them into the roads. Of course, the truth of the miracle being thus satisfactorily established, the Church gained immensely by it; and no one thought of asking the sailors whether they really had seen the figure towing them into harbour or not.

"The way any new miracle is managed is this," continued the doctor: "The priests boldly assert that the saint has done some wonderful thing or other, and then they tell another story, without any foundation in truth, as a proof of the first.

The credulous people go about and say there can be no doubt as to such a miracle having been worked, because so and so happened, whereas so and so never did happen. That reminds me of the old story of the wicked baker having been seen by the crews of several merchantmen anchored off Stromboli, in the Mediterranean, being driven down the crater by a number of black imps. The proof adduced is, that an action was brought by the widow of the old baker, who had died at the time specified, against some of the maligners of her husband's character. The case was tried before Lord Eldon, or some other learned judge, who decided against the widow, in consequence of the exact agreement of the logs of all the vessels as to the incident narrated. The real state of the case is, that no trial took place, and that the whole story is a complete fiction; yet I have heard people argue on the subject with the greatest warmth, and bring forward the trial as a proof that such an occurrence had taken place."

However, I must not repeat the numberless yarns I heard, or I shall not have space for my own adventures. As soon as we had anchored, the health-boat came off to us. She was a large, gaily-painted boat, manned by a mahogany-coloured crew with red caps and sashes, and white shirts, all jabbering away in very unpleasant-sounding Portuguese. As no one had actually died on board, the passengers were allowed to go on shore; but the captain warned them that, should a southerly wind spring up, he would have instantly to put to sea, and that, should any of them not have returned on board, they would lose their passages. Very few, therefore, took advantage of the privilege. Meantime all the passengers' bedding and clothes were got up on deck, and their berths were well fumigated and dried with hanging stoves, and the whole space they occupied thoroughly cleansed.

The great difficulty was to get the ship into better trim by heaving overboard some of the ballast. Mr. Henley exerted himself greatly to get this done by shifting a little of the cargo at a time, so as to get down to the ballast; but after all, very little could be done to remedy the evil.

I was very anxious to get on shore, both for my own sake to see the place, and also to give Solon the means of stretching his legs. I was delighted, therefore, when Dr. Cuff told me that he had obtained leave for me to accompany him. We went in a shore boat. Dr. Cuff advised me always to make use of the boats belonging to a place, as more suited for the purpose. He said that he had seen so many accidents occur in consequence of officers despising this caution, and insisting on landing without necessity in their own boats. An unexpected roller has come in and turned them over and over, drowning all hands, while the odd-looking and despised native boat has landed her passengers in perfect safety.

Away bounded Solon the moment he saw me fairly landed, scampering along the sand, throwing it up and barking, and then hurrying back to me and licking my hand, and leaping up over and over again, and then, in the exuberance of his joy, away he went once more to repeat the same manœuvres.

Funchal struck me as a clean, well-paved town, built entirely of brick, and free from mud and dust; indeed, from the steepness of the streets and the constant supply of running water, it would be a disgrace if it were not clean. I fancy that the English residents have contributed much to effect this object. The streets are narrow, and thus shade is obtained, a great object in a hot climate. The largest houses are occupied by the merchants, whose stores of wine and other goods are on the ground floor, they living in the upper rooms. The dress of the peasants we met in the town on landing I thought very picturesque. The cap, worn both by men and women, is like an inverted funnel, made of blue cloth lined with red, and covers only the crown of the head. The men have as little clothing as is consistent with decency,—a pair of full linen drawers reaching to the knees, with a loose linen shirt, and sometimes a jacket thrown over the shoulder, completes the costume of most of them, stockings and shoes not being thought of. Some, however, we saw with trousers and long yellow boots, turned over at the tops. They were evidently the dandies of the population. The women appeared in coloured petticoats, with a well-fitting bodice and a red cape. Some wore handkerchiefs instead of the funnel cap, and others mantillas and black hoods, by which the whole face and figure can be concealed. In consequence of the steepness and hardness of the roads, wheeled vehicles cannot be used, and a sort of sledge, a cart on runners, is employed instead. In the town people who cannot walk are carried about in palanquins, slung on a long pole, and borne on the shoulders of two men. The passenger can sit upright in them; but as they are very heavy, people travelling to any distance into the country use hammocks, or as the natives call them *rêdes*, made of fine network, and also slung on a single pole and borne by two men. With cushions arranged in them I can fancy no more luxurious conveyance for an invalid, though for my part, as I think exertion gives zest to travelling, I should prefer being bumped on the back of a mule, or employing my own legs. As Dr Cuff was anxious to return on board to look after his charges, we had not seen much of the town.

Just before embarking we went into the counting-house of a merchant, to whom the doctor happened to speak about me. While I was waiting outside a gentleman came forward and invited me into an inner office, and told me that he knew my father, and begged that I would remain with him till the ship sailed. I could only say that I should like it very much, if the captain would allow me.

"Oh, we will settle all that," he answered promptly. "We are the agents of the owners here; he will not refuse us."

Still, I said that I must go back with the doctor, for I had determined not in the slightest degree to disobey orders, notwithstanding any excuse I might have to offer, and the captain had directed me to return with the doctor.

My new friend thereupon gave me a letter containing his request, and walked with us down to the beach. On the way, however, we met the captain, and I was much amused with the deferential, almost servile, manner in which he addressed the wealthy merchant, so different to the rough blustering way in which he treated all on board.

As William Henley observed when I told him of it, "That man is very different on blue water and on shore."

When Solon saw the captain he grew as sedate as a judge, and shrunk back behind my heels, scarcely venturing to lift his eyes from the ground. The captain instantly granted the merchant's request, with many polite expressions, warning me to keep an eye on the weather, and to return instantly at the slightest sign of a change of wind.

My adventures in Madeira were not very exciting; I shall, therefore, be brief. Mr. Marshall, my new friend, told me, however, much about the place during our walk to his quinta, where I went to dine with him. Madeira is situated between the thirty-second and thirty-third parallels of north latitude. Its extreme length is about 33 miles, and its greatest breadth 14, and it contains about 115,000 inhabitants. It was well known to the ancients, and re-discovered by the Portuguese captain, Zarco, sent out by the great Don Henry. Zarco was appointed governor of the southern and western portion of the island, and Captain Vaz of the northern and eastern. It afterwards, with the mother-country, fell under the dominion of Spain, who ruled it, as she has invariably done her foreign settlements, with cruelty and oppression; but at length, in 1640, under Don João IV., it was restored to Portugal, and the island recovered its prosperity. For a short time in 1801 and 1807, the English held it to protect it from the French. Mr. Marshall told me an interesting story about its early discovery. An Englishman, Robert Machin, in the reign of Edward III., fell in love with a lady, Anna D'Abret, whose father would not consent to his marriage with her. He at length, however, succeeded in running off with her, and embarked in a vessel, intending to proceed to France. He was, however, driven by a storm to the southward, and the first land he saw was that of Madeira. He having landed with the lady Anna and some of the ship's company, the vessel was driven out to sea. Those who remained on shore underwent great suffering, in consequence of which the lady died. Heartbroken Machin, refusing all food, died also, desiring to be buried in the same grave with her whose untimely end he had caused. The survivors escaping in a boat, landed on the coast of Barbary, where they were made prisoners by the Moors. Having related their adventures to a fellow-prisoner, the information at length reached the ears of Gonçalves Zarco, who certainly brought the first news of the discovery of the island to Europe. The tale, however, is doubted; but there is an air of probability about it, which makes me fancy that it has its foundation in truth, and I can no more speak of Madeira without thinking of the unfortunate, high-born, and lovely Anna D'Abret, and the bold plebeian, Robert Machin, than I can of the Mauritius, and forget Paul and Virginia, or of Juan Fernandez, without believing that Robinson Crusoe lived on it.

There was something particularly cool and pleasant in the appearance of Mr. Marshall's house. The rooms were large, the floors covered with matting instead of carpets, and the furniture consisted chiefly of cane-bottom sofas and chairs, while in front were shady verandahs with banana trees, their long fan-like leaves waving before them, and contributing, by their continual movement, to keep the air cool and fresh.

The next morning Mr. Marshall went on board, and ascertained that the ship would not sail that day, unless compelled to do so by a shift of wind, which was not likely to occur. He accordingly invited me to take a ride with him and two other gentlemen to the Pico Grande, above the Curral das Freiras, whence a superb view over a large portion of the island is obtained. We were mounted on small horses active as goats. Each horse was attended by a *burroquero*, literally a donkey driver. They were fine athletic fellows, armed with a *rabo*, a cow's tail at the end of a stick, to flick off the venomous flies which worry both animals and riders. They carried also cloaks and umbrellas, to shield their masters from cold and mist. We rode out of the town between walls covered in profusion with heliotropes, roses, geraniums, fuchsias, and other sweet-smelling flowers, often having trellises of vines completely closing over our heads for many yards together, while here and there were *mirantes*, or summer-houses, literally *Gaze-out-of-places*, very properly so called, for they were filled with ladies, and often gentlemen, who seemed to have nothing else to do than to watch the passers-by all day. The road for some way was not bad, being paved with stones set edgeways and tolerably even. Solon followed us with great gravity, looking up at the mongrel curs which ran along the tops of the quinta walls, barking and yelping in tones sufficiently loud to crack the drums of our ears. Never before had I seen views so varied and beautiful of mountains, and round hills, and precipitous cliffs, and rugged peaks, green plantations, vineyards, orangeries, white buildings, deep valleys and gorges, and the blue sea beyond, all forming the setting to the picture. The first place we stopped at was the little church of the Estreito, the padre of which, habited in a gay robe, invited us to take a view of the surrounding scenery from the top of his tower. When three thousand feet above the sea, we found ourselves surrounded by a grove of Spanish chestnuts, at the habitation of the late consul, Mr. Veitch, a lovely spot, the house in the Italian style. It is called the Jardin. In the grounds the chief varieties of tea cultivated in China are grown, as well as many other rare and curious plants. Mounting higher and higher, we reached at last the Curral das Freiras. Girls surrounded us begging, and men and boys offering us sticks to ascend to the Pico.

"Stay," said Mr. Marshall, after we got off our steeds, and leading us over the green sward, we stood at the edge of a precipice nearly 5000 feet above the blue ocean.

It was difficult at first to distinguish the numberless objects which appeared before us, far, far away below our feet. Gradually, however, sky and sea as it were separated, woods and fields, and hills and valleys, and convents and churches, and quintas and cottages, came out, and colours divided themselves, and the wonderful landscape, in all its beautiful variety, appeared before us. Still every object was diminished so much, that even the Church of Libramento, which is itself situated 2000 feet above the sea, appeared but a small speck at the bottom of a huge basin. After enjoying the scene for some time we were summoned to proceed, and higher still we went, round and round by winding paths, superb views bursting on our sight each instant, for an hour or more, till we reached the foot of the *Pico Grande*, higher than which our four-footed beasts could not go. However, one of my companions and I, with a guide, climbed to the very top of the Pico, and such a view as that of mountain, valley, and blue laughing ocean, I had never before beheld. On one side was the *Pico Ruivo*, the embattled *Torrinhas*, the rugged *Sidrao* and *Arnero* ; and on the other, the long unbroken ridge of Paul with the Terra d'Agoa, clothed in an evergreen mantle of forest far below it. Our burroqueros had brought on their shoulders some baskets of provisions, off which we made a capital luncheon. I could not help wishing all the time that Herbert and Henry Raymond could have been with me—they would have so enjoyed the scenery; for though Solon seemed to think it all very good fun, he evidently would have said that the luncheon was the best part of the expedition. We got back much faster than we went up, for our horses were far less inclined to stop to allow us to admire the views. Somehow or other, one is always influenced, even in that respect, by the animal one bestrides.

MADEIRA.

Madeira may be said to consist of a mass of mountains, the highest points of which rise in a central ridge. Cliffs varying in height from 100 to 2000 feet form the coast boundary of the island. On the north they are the highest and most abrupt, while on the south they are lower and more accessible. The central mountains branch down to the sea in ridges parted by deep ravines, in some places full of dark forests, adding to their gloomy grandeur. The towns are generally situated in the more open parts of these ravines. From the tops of the mountains the sea can be discovered on all sides; but this adds to the grandeur of the prospect, as a person cannot but experience a feeling of awe when he considers that he is thus perched aloft, as it were, on a mere point in the centre of the vast Atlantic. I have only described one of the many very interesting excursions which may be made in Madeira. I should think it must be a delightful place in which to spend a winter, and I wonder more people do not go there. My friend described the Portuguese inhabitants as the most polite and good-natured of all the people with whom he ever had any intercourse; and as provisions are plentiful and cheap, and the voyage can be performed in a week, I am surprised it is not more frequented.

I thought it prudent to go on board that night, and fortunately I did so, for at daybreak the next morning the captain ordered a gun to be fired, the anchor to be hove up, and sail to be made. There was but little wind, so a boat-load of passengers who had slept on shore had just time half-dressed to reach the ship before she stood out of the bay. Of course it was provoking to have to lose so much of a fair breeze, but the ship was, I found, very far from being in a proper condition to put to sea. We were to prove the proverb true, that "too much haste is bad speed."

The condition of the passengers was somewhat improved, but still there had not been time thoroughly to clean and dry their berths, or to wash their clothes, while the decks were in want of calking, and very little of the superabundant ballast had been removed. Mr. Henley had been working very hard with those under him, but Mr. Grimes declared that he did not consider that the matter was of any consequence, and would do nothing. Three or four days more spent in making the required alterations would have prevented much after-suffering.

It was some hours before we sunk the lofty eminences of Madeira below the horizon.

I have hitherto said very little about my shipmates. The men were mostly a rough set, now brought together for the first time, and without that confidence which long acquaintance gives either in their officers or in each other. Without being unduly familiar, I was on good terms with most of them. I had done my very utmost to gain a knowledge of everything about the ship, and had thus kept the respect which I at first had gained, before they found out that I was really a greenhorn. I now knew so much that I did not fear having to ask them questions, and I thus quickly became versed in all the mysteries of knotting and splicing, and numberless other details of a seaman's work. I found, however, that many of the older sailors had a very rough and imperfect way of doing those ordinary things, and that some of the younger ones, who had been brought up under a better system, did them in a superior style, and far more expeditiously.

My most willing instructor was an oldish man, John Spratt by name; Johnnie Spratt he was generally called. He was very short and very fat. It was a wonder how he could get aloft as rapidly as he did; but no man stepped more lightly along the decks. He also said the reason of that was that his heart was so light. In spite of the rubs he received, he was the merriest, and apparently the happiest fellow on board; nothing put him out. He was very independent in his manner, and had gained the ill-will of the captain and first mate, as well as of the boatswain and some of the men. "Though I get more kicks than halfpence, what are the odds?" he was wont to say. "My fat shields my bones, and I've got quite used to such compliments." In some ships Johnnie would have been valued and made much of, from his sterling qualities—on board the *Orion* he was despised and ill-treated. He and Solon took a great liking to each other, and I knew that if he was on deck my dog would be watched by him and protected.

I could not manage to make companions of my messmates Sills and Broom. Their education was very limited, and the few ideas they possessed were frequently erroneous. Sills was not ill-natured, though weak, and easily led by anybody who would take the trouble to lead him. Broom I found at times surly and quarrelsome, and inclined always to grumble. However, as I had been a good many years at school, and had often met similar characters, though my school-fellows were more refined, I knew pretty well how to deal with him.

There was a great deal of bullying and tyranny going on on board from the very first. The captain and mates, except Mr. Henley, bullied the men, and the men bullied the boys, and the boys bullied each other, and teased the dumb animals, the pigs, and the goats, and the fowls, and a monkey—the weakest, or the best natured, as usual, going to the wall. The worst treated was a little fellow—Tommy Bigg by name. His size was strongly in contrast to his cognomen—for his age he was one of the smallest fellows I ever saw. He was nearly fifteen years old, I fancy—he might even have been more, but he was a simple-minded, quiet-mannered lad, and from the expression of his countenance, independent of his size, he looked much younger. He had no friends, having been sent on board the ship from the workhouse when she was first fitted out. He had belonged to her ever since, having remained to assist the ship keeper in sweeping her out, and looking after her when he had to leave her. He had never, I believe, set foot on shore since the first moment he had been sent on board. He was as cheap to keep as a dog, and was as vigilant and more useful, and he got dog's fare, and received dog's thanks—more kicks than halfpence. He had no parents and no friends. His father, he told me, was a sailor; and as he had gone away some years ago, and never come back, it was supposed that he had been lost at sea. He had a fond recollection of his father as the only being who had ever cared for him, and he remembered how he used to carry him in his arms, and jump with him, and bring him all sorts of curious things to play with, and how he kissed him and wept when he had to go away again to sea. Tommy had been left in charge of a poor woman, who treated him very kindly, but she died, and no news coming of his father, he had been sent to the workhouse of the parish to which one of the owners of the *Orion* belonged. Through him Tommy was sent on board to fight his way onward in the world. Under Captain Seaford his life had been happy enough—now it was very much the contrary; and poor Tommy, when kicked and cuffed without mercy, often in his misery threatened that he would jump overboard and drown himself, and that his ghost would ever after haunt the ship. I heard him one day make the threat, and at once spoke to him on the subject, showing him that it was wicked even to threaten to do so, although he might not intend to commit the act; but much more horrible would it be actually to destroy his life, because he would have to appear in the presence of an offended God without having the possibility of repenting and seeking for forgiveness for one of the greatest crimes a man can commit—murder—self-murder being of equal magnitude with it. Tommy listened very attentively; a new light seemed to beam upon him—he had evidently not considered the subject in that way, and in very thoughtlessness might have thrown himself overboard. I had early in the voyage observed the poor lad, and taken an interest in him from his seeming youth and helplessness; and I resolved, as far as I had the power, to stand his friend, and to protect him from the cruelty of his messmates—with what result was to be seen.

When on deck, if I observed a seaman about to bestow the end of a rope or a kick on him, I sharply hailed either one or the other, and gave some order, which for the time prevented the punishment, but I fear Tommy seldom failed to receive it when my back was turned.

There are numberless objects to be observed at sea, if people do but know how to appreciate them. Dr. Cuff pointed out many to me; and one of the passengers, a clergyman, when he found that I took a deep interest in such matters, showed me many others. Just before entering the trade-wind region we observed several whales sporting round the ship. Directly afterwards we found ourselves in a shoal of medusæ or jellyfish. The least diameter the scientific men on board assigned to the shoal was from thirty to forty miles; and, supposing that there was only one jelly-fish in every ten square feet of surface, there must have been 225,000,000 of them, without calculating those below the surface. They moved by sucking in the water at one end of the lobe, and expelling it at the other. When I watched them I said they put me in mind of a white silk parasol opening and shutting. Dr. Cuff had a powerful microscope, through which he examined one of the stomachs of the medusæ. It was found to be full of diatoms, which are flinty-shelled microscopic animals of every variety of shape, such as stars, crosses, semicircles, and spirals—yet soft as are the jelly-fish, they can consume them. This one medusa had in its stomach no less than seven hundred thousand diatoms, so that it would be rather difficult to compute how many the whole shoal consumed for their dinner—they in their turn having to be eaten by the huge whales.

CHAPTER IV.

Natural Phenomena of the Ocean—Service at Sea—Mr. Vernon—A dead Calm—Fever breaks out—Dispute between Captain and First Mate—Its consequences—Mortality among Passengers—Sight the Land—Teneriffe—Notice of History—Santa Cruz—Attack on it under Lord Nelson—An Excursion up the Peak.

HAD during my voyages and travels ample proof of the truth of the remark, that different people see the same object in very different lights. Frequently I had heard persons declare that nothing is more dull and stupid than a long sea voyage—that there is nothing on the ocean to afford interest—nothing to look at, or think about—nothing to do. I have every reason to assert the contrary of this to be the case. Of course I had plenty to do in learning my profession; I did not forget to make ample use of my master's gift—my sextant; and in this Mr. Henley gave me all the assistance in his power. I never failed to make use of it on all occasions, so that in a short time I became a very good observer. I do not say this as a boast, but that others may understand what may be done by attention and perseverance. Sills and Broom used to say that it would be time enough by-and-by to begin learning navigation, and so weeks passed away, and they knew nothing whatever about it.

With regard to objects to be noted at sea, I will only touch on a few of them. The form of the waves varied much as we advanced southward. In the Bay of Biscay they had been exceedingly irregular, and now the crests formed almost straight lines, only one sea now and then rising above his fellows like some huge marine monster, and rolling on in potent majesty, till lost to sight in the distance. The clouds, too, were even for a time varying; one day especially I remember remarking some masses of clouds collecting in the east—Mr. Waller called them lightning clouds—their shadowy parts were of a peculiar steel blue, while the brighter portions glowed with a fleshy tint. At dusk, catching the reflection of the sun, they seemed to shine out of the dark sky like pale spectres of gigantic size, casting their supernatural lights over the waves. At midnight the expected lightning burst forth with an almost terror-inspiring grandeur; sometimes eight or ten flashes of forked lightning darted forth at once, lighting up the whole ocean, and showing the dark banks of clouds assembling in the distance. Even when the lightning ceased, so great was the phosphorescence of the ocean, that, as the ship surged onward through it, she seemed to be throwing off masses of sparkling gems from her bows; and as I was looking over the side, I observed a huge shark, or some other ocean monster, swim by amidst a blaze of light. The clouds, like the waves, grew more regular as we sailed south, and at length formed long parallel lines, radiating out of the north-east, and converging into the south-west points of the horizon—finally forming one unbroken sheet over the Canary Islands.

The great difficulty of making observations at sea, except with a sextant—and such, it must be remembered, are of a very rough nature compared with those made on shore—is want of steadiness. The sea is never quiet, and no machine has as yet been invented to counteract the movement of a ship, and obtain a perfect level.

Mr. Vernon, the clergyman passenger I spoke of, told me an anecdote of Galileo, showing that, great as he was as an astronomer, he might make a great mistake by forgetting to

ANECDOTE OF GALILEO.

PHOSPHORESCENCE OF THE OCEAN.

take all points into consideration. He fancied that he had discovered a method of determining longitudes at sea by observing the eclipses of Jupiter's satellites. He accordingly went to the King of Spain and offered to manufacture telescopes to enable his navigators to sail across the ocean without fear or hesitation. His telescopes were unexceptionable, and his method excellent, but it depended entirely on the perfect steadiness of the observer; and, as even the biggest ships of the mighty monarch of Spain could not be taught to keep quiet, the great astronomer's telescopes were perfectly useless.

I was much struck with the fine deep Prussian blue of the waters, which had changed from the cobalt blue of more northern latitudes, as also with its extraordinary power to froth and effervesce. The water, as it was dashed about the decks in the morning from the buckets, sparkled like champagne; but perhaps that was owing more to the nature of the atmosphere than to any peculiarity in the water.

I found that I had several erroneous notions of my own to correct. I always fancied that a porpoise was a great fat lumbering sleepy animal, simply because people are accustomed

THE PORPOISE.

to say "as fat as a porpoise." In reality he is a gracefully formed, remarkably fast, sociable, warm-hearted, or rather warm-blooded fellow, with a coat of fat like a paletot on his back, to keep out the chill of the icy seas. He is more like a hunter than a pig; and, as to "rolling and wallowing," those are expressions used by poets who never saw a porpoise dashing away at twenty or thirty knots an hour, or a whole shoal bearing down upon a ship like a troop of light horse, and escorting her for miles and miles, careering away, darting round and round her as if she were only going at the speed of some heavy baggage waggon; and humbling the pride of those who have been before hugging themselves with the pleasing idea that she has been moving along at a tremendous speed. The back fin is triangular and near the tail; and as the active fish plunges forward through the tumbling seas, the fin seen for an instant, and looking like his back, makes him appear as if he was rolling slowly on in the water—a very different movement from what he really makes, which is rapid in the extreme. While talking of cetaceous animals, to which order the porpoise belongs, I must remark on a very common error held by seaman as well as landsmen, that whales spout out water. The idea is, that the water is taken into the stomach while the whale is feeding, and ejected when he rises to the surface. This is in no sense the case. What the whale spouts forth is a steam-like air, dense with mucous vapour, of which he must empty his lungs before he can take in a fresh supply of atmospheric air to enable him to dive down again to the depths of the ocean.

We were now enjoying the north-east trade wind. The latitude in which these winds are to be met with varies by several degrees, according to the season of the year. An indication that we were entering them was shown by the barometer, which had previously been low, falling still more from 30° 3′ to 30° 2′, and even lower. But if I was to go on describing all the phenomena I observed, and all the information on natural history I obtained, I should have no space left for my own adventures, or an account of the countries I visited.

I spoke of Mr. Vernon, a clergyman. At first he had been ill, but when he recovered he made a great effort to have religious services held on board on each Sunday, as well as on other days of the week. The captain and first mate, as may be supposed, objected to the measure.

"People might go to church when they got on shore if they liked, but on board his ship he was not going to have anything of that sort," was the captain's reply.

"But our worship is to praise and to pray to that God who protects us equally at sea as on shore," was Mr. Vernon's mild reply. "It will be such that all denominations may join in it, and surely no one on board would wish to be without God's protection and help; yet, if we do not ask for it when we have the power, how can we expect to obtain it?"

The captain could make no reply to this question, and though he went away grumbling, and would afford no assistance to the arrangements, he did not prevent Mr. Henley from rigging an awning on deck, or oppose the assembling together of the passengers and some very few of the crew under it. The second mate, the doctor and I, and Spratt and Tommy Bigg, were the only ones of the ship's company who took the trouble to attend. Some kept away, they said, because the captain did not encourage the movement; and others had no better reason to offer than that as they never had had to attend services at sea, they did not know why they should now begin. Broom said that he didn't come to sea to have to go to church; and Sills remarked that, as the captain did not patronize the affair, he did not think it right for the officers to do so, and he wondered how we ventured to be so mutinous. Now, strange as it may seem, these are in no degree more absurd or more contemptible than the kind of excuses offered constantly by people on shore for not attending religious worship; in other words, for not offering up their meed of adoration, for not praying to that great and good Being from whom we all receive our existence and everything we enjoy in this world, and in whose presence and sight we can alone hope to enjoy happiness in the life to come. Mr. Vernon, however, persevered; and Sunday after Sunday fresh members, if not converts, were added to his little congregation, till even Sills and the rough Waller, and the still rougher boatswain, occasionally appeared among them.

We had, for the sake of obtaining the north-east trade-wind, kept closer to the coast of Africa than usual; and whether it was from keeping too much to the eastward, or that for some reason the wind did not reach that point, we found the breeze fail us, and the sails began to flap lazily against the masts. There we lay day after day with the hot sun beating down on our heads, making the pitch in the seams of the decks boil and bubble, and drawing up dense masses of steam from the damp and crowded berths below.

One day observing the doctor looking graver than usual, I inquired, as he was passing along the deck, "What is the matter, doctor?"

"Fever has broken out among these poor people, in consequence, it is pretty evident, of the measures I advised not having been taken at Madeira; and if something is not done to get the ship to rights, one-half of them may be carried off," he replied, with some bitterness in his tone.

"What ought to be done?" I asked.

"Put into port and land the passengers," he replied. "A bad commencement is certain to cause a great deal of trouble. Had we put back to Plymouth the ship might at once have been set to rights, and we should probably have reached the Cape in less time and with less suffering than it is likely will now be the case. If this were a Government emigrant ship, I should have the power of compelling the captain to put into port; but all I can do is to represent the state of the case and protest."

Day after day we lay on the glass like shining ocean, surrounded by the straw and empty hampers and bottles, and all sorts of things thrown overboard, showing that we had not in the slightest degree moved from the spot where the wind last left us. The people grew paler, and more wan and sickly. Many took to their beds; and now one death occurred, and now another. A strong, hardy young man was the first to succumb to the fever, and then a young woman, and then a little child; next a mother was carried off, leaving six or seven poor children to the care of the heart-broken father. Again death came and carried off an old man, one of those who had left home in the hope of making gold in the far-off land to which we were bound.

A funeral at sea is a very impressive ceremony. Had Mr. Vernon not been on board, the dead would have been committed to their floating grave with a scant allowance of it. He, however, came forward and read some portions of Scripture, and offered up some short and appropriate prayers—not for those who had departed; he had prayed with them and for them while they were yet in the flesh—but that strength and support might be afforded to the survivors, and that they might be induced to repent and rest their hope on One who is all-powerful to save, ere they too might be called away. Painful, indeed, were the scenes which took place—the cries and groans of some of the bereaved ones—the silent grief and trickling tears of others, while ever and anon the despairing shrieks or ejaculations of those who feared that they too might speedily be summoned from the world, were heard ascending from below. Notwithstanding this, the captain vowed that he would continue the voyage as soon as the wind returned, without again putting into port.

I had observed that though the captain carried it with a high hand over all the other officers and crew, he always treated Mr. Henley with considerable respect, and never swore at or abused him. They, however, very seldom exchanged any words with each other; and, indeed, never spoke except on duty. I had lately remarked Mr. Henley constantly watching the captain, who seemed to shrink away from him at times, and avoid his gaze; though when he saw that the second mate was not looking at him, he turned on him a glance of the most intense hatred. One day, after this sort of work had been going on for some time, I asked Mr. Henley why it was that he had said he would not, if he could have helped it, have sailed again with Captain Gunnell.

"Have you remarked anything strange about him lately, Marsden?" he asked in return.

I said that I thought he looked flushed and hurried in his manner, and that he often spoke thick, and said things without meaning.

"You have divined one of the many reasons I have for not liking him," he observed. "He has one of the worst vices which the master of a ship can possess, or any man who has the lives of hundreds committed to his charge. He is desperately addicted to liquor; yet, strange to say, he has sufficient command over himself to keep sober in harbour, or when he is approaching a port, so that the owners and consignees, and others who might have taken notice of it, have never discovered his failing, as it would be called, while an inferior officer like myself would feel that it would be perfectly useless to report him. I thought of doing so for the sake of my fellow-creatures who might have otherwise to sail with him, but I knew that there would be great difficulty in substantiating my charge, and that if I failed I should ruin my own prospects; so, right or wrong, I abandoned the idea."

"And so once more you have to sail with him," I could not help remarking.

"You are right, Marsden; I ought to have had more moral

courage," answered the second mate. "And now I fear that he will get us into greater trouble than he did those on board the ship in which I before sailed with him. The way the men are treated is very bad; and his refusal to put into harbour may be productive of very serious consequences, especially should we be caught by bad weather."

Scarcely had Mr. Henley said this than the captain made his appearance on deck with his sextant in his hand, as if to take a meridional observation. Though it was thus early in the day, I remarked the peculiarities about him of which I had been speaking. He looked around him angrily.

"Are none of the officers here?" he exclaimed, turning away, however, from the second mate. "Where is Mr. Grimes? what is the fellow about? send him here, some one. And you, sir—you think yourself a navigator—go and get your sextant and prove yourself one," he added, turning fiercely to me. "You young slips of gentility must be kept in order."

Of course I made no other reply than, "Ay, ay, sir," and went below to get my sextant. I kept it, I should have observed, in Mr. Henley's cabin. The door was locked, so I had to return to him for the key, and some little time had thus elapsed before I got back on deck. I found the first mate and captain in high dispute. The origin of the quarrel I could not comprehend. They had differed, I found, as to their readings on their instruments which is not surprising, for, horrible to relate, as I watched them attentively the conviction forced itself on my mind that they had both deprived themselves of the right use of their intellects—they were both drunk, verging towards the condition of brute beasts. Presently Mr. Grimes said something which still more offended the captain, who, lifting up his sextant—a valuable instrument belonging to Captain Seaford—threw it with all his force at the mate's head, and it was dashed to pieces on the deck.

The latter, whose ear had been struck, with the same thoughtless impulse, and furious at the insult, rushed towards the captain, and striking him with his sextant in return on the face, knocked him over, when, falling forward with the impetus, it also was rendered hopelessly useless. There they both lay, grovelling, kicking, and swearing, and abusing each other in a manner truly terrible; while the cabin passengers who were on the poop, witnesses of the scene, looked on with dismay, not knowing what might next happen.

"I have seen something like this occur before," said Mr. Henley to me. "Call Mr. Waller and the boatswain, we must carry them to their cabins."

I hurried to obey the order. Some of the men had observed the occurrence, and I feared that the officers would scarcely be able to maintain any authority over them after it. The master and first mate were carried to their cabins; but they both contrived to get more spirits brought to them, I afterwards found, by the steward, and for several days they remained almost in a state of insensibility. During this time three or four more of the second-class passengers had died; the first, or, as some of the people forward called them, the aristocrats, had hitherto escaped, as their cabins were better ventilated and dryer, and they had better food, and, more than all, generally knew better how to take care of themselves. But now they also began to sicken, and look pale, and anxious, and sad. Well they might indeed!

Mr. Vernon's character as a minister of the gospel now appeared to great advantage. Fearless himself, he went among the sick and dying, encouraging, consoling, and warning. Many of those who had before refused his ministrations now listened to him eagerly. Vain they felt was any hope in man. He offered foundation for hope, but it was from above. Fond of science as he was, all his scientific pursuits were now laid aside that he might devote himself to the duties of his far higher ministerial calling.

Mr. Grimes made his appearance on deck before the captain. He could scarcely be persuaded that some days had passed while he was below, and was much puzzled to account for it. He thought that he had had the fever, but never appeared to suspect the true cause of his illness, till, asking for his sextant, the fragments were brought him by the steward, who minutely explained how it had been broken. Then the truth burst on him, but it did not make him at all ashamed; he only became more savage and tyrannical. I felt very sure that, although I had hitherto enjoyed a tolerable immunity from ill-treatment, my time would come before long.

For some days, though the people continued sickly, death had not visited us, and the spirits of the crew and passengers rose accordingly. The great desire was to get a breeze. Sailors have a trick of whistling when they want wind—trick it is, because very few really believe that their whistling will bring a wind. It was amusing to see everybody whistling; the boys forward took it up—the passengers aft; the gruff old boatswain was whistling more furiously than anybody, but I saw him cock his eye knowingly at some clouds gathering to the northward. Just then, as I was looking aloft, I saw a bird pitch on the fore-top-gallant yard-arm.

"A booby! a booby!" was the cry.

Tommy Bigg was in the fore-top, sent up for something or other, and the desire to possess the bird seized him. Any incident, however light, creates a sensation in a calm. All eyes were directed towards Tommy and the bird. It was a great doubt whether the latter would not fly away, however, before Tommy got him.

"What is it you are looking at?" asked Sills, just then coming on deck.

"A booby, lad," answered the doctor, to whom he spoke, regarding him calmly; whereat Broom and Waller laughed, but Sills only said: "See now, what's that?" and looked up at the yard-arm whereon the bird sat perched.

"We've two of them aboard just now," observed Broom, who never lost an opportunity of having a fling at his chum.

TOMMY ON THE FORE-TOP.

Tommy had reached the cross-trees; now he had his feet on the top-gallant yard. He looked at the booby, and the booby looked at him, as much as to say, "What do you want with me?" but had not the sense to make use of his wings. A great ado and discussion arose among the passengers, as to whether boy or bird would prove the victor. Tommy worked his way along the foot-ropes, holding on tightly with one hand while he lifted up the other, and down it came on the neck of the bird. Tommy in triumph brought him on deck, and in spite of the grabs made at him by the seamen, succeeded in conveying him safely to me.

"There, sir, you'd like to have a look at that thing," said he, putting the poor bird, whose windpipe he had pressed so tightly that it had little power to struggle, into my hands.

The little fellow wanted to show his gratitude to me, so I thanked him, and examined the bird. It was larger and longer in the body than a common duck—a species of gannet—with a brown body, and under-part white, and a long beak; its expression of countenance indicating, I declared, the excessive stupidity it is said to possess. Several of the passengers crowded round to have a look at the stranger, and while thus engaged I was startled by hearing Mr. Waller, who had charge of the deck, sing out,—

"Hand top-gallant sails! brail up the main-sail! let fly mizzen-top-sail sheets! up with the helm!"

Mr. Henley, hearing the orders, hurried on deck, while Mr. Grimes, scarcely yet having recovered his senses, came out of his cabin and looked stupidly about him. The example he set, of course, had a bad effect on the crew, already badly enough disposed; so they slowly and lazily prepared to obey orders which should instantly have been executed. A heavy squall, which the third mate ought to have foreseen, struck the ship. Over she heeled to it, till she was borne down on her beam ends. Away flew royals, top-gallant sails, main and mizzen-top-sail-sheets, and the stout ship, before she righted and obeyed the helm, was deluged with water, and reduced almost to a wreck. At length she was got before the wind, and away she ran towards the south and east, surrounded by a cloud of mist and foam which circumscribed our view to a very narrow compass. The sea, too, got up with a rapidity truly astonishing. It seemed as if the giant waves had been rolling on towards us from some far-off part of the ocean. All that day and night we ran on. Scarcely had the first streaks of dawn appeared, when the look-out aloft shouted,—

"Land on the starboard bow!"

Startling, indeed, was the cry. Mr. Henley and I, and Mr. Waller, had been watching to take observations after the captain and mate had broken their sextants, but we had not been able to ascertain our position with the exactness we wished; and the second mate thought the ship might have been set by some current to the eastward of her course. The first mate now came on deck; he examined the land as we drew in with it, and then ordered the ship to be kept more to the southward, but still the land appeared more and more ahead. I asked Mr. Henley what he thought about the matter.

"I have some fears that it is the coast of Africa. It may be the north-east coast of Grand Canary," he answered; but even while we were speaking, we observed a line of dark rocks over which the sea was breaking furiously, heaving up on high, dense masses of foam.

Shipwreck, in one of its worst aspects, on a wild coast, without help at hand, stared us in the face. The passengers soon got notice of the condition of the ship, and came hurrying, pale and trembling, on deck. Never had I seen so many horror-stricken countenances collected together, as they gazed forth on the rock-bound desolate shore towards which the ship was hurrying. Mr. Henley had carefully been watching the land.

"I have hopes," he observed at last, "that the land we see is Point Arraga in Teneriffe, and if so, we shall soon see a long continued coast-line."

Anxiously we kept our eyes fixed on the shore. Just then an apparition appeared in the shape of the captain, his coat only half on, and his hair streaming in the wind. He looked about him, trying to comprehend what had occurred. Then suddenly he ordered the helm to be put to port, with the idea of hauling up to the westward, and trying to escape the danger in that direction. Before the order was obeyed Mr. Henley stepped boldly up to him.

"If we do that, sir, the ship will be cast away," he said firmly. "That is the island of Teneriffe aboard of us, and we shall soon be getting round its eastern point and into smooth water."

By this time all the cabin, as well as second-class passengers and the crew, were collected on deck, listening anxiously to what was going forward. The captain stamped about the deck once or twice, as if undecided what to do.

"You may be a very good navigator, Mr. Henley, and you may have taken very good care of the ship while I have been ill," he exclaimed at last; "but to tell me that the land we see there is the island of Teneriffe, is perfectly ridiculous. I'd just as soon believe that that is Teneriffe as I would what you and the parsons would tell us, that there's a heaven and all that."

Just as he was speaking, the dark clouds which had hitherto, as if they had been thick folds of drapery, completely shut out the sky and all surrounding objects, were suddenly widely rent asunder, and high above our heads appeared, like a mass of burnished gold lit up by the rays of the fast rising sun, the lofty peak of Teneriffe towering in majesty towards the blue sky, 12,000 feet above the ocean.

PEAK OF TENERIFFE.

"As surely as there exists before us that grand mountain, so surely is there a heaven," said the deep-toned voice of Mr. Vernon. "And, my friends, ere it be too late, seek the only path by which that glorious heaven can be gained, and eternal misery and self-reproach avoided."

Some listened and crowded round the clergyman, but the captain turned aside, observing with a half sneer, "That's Teneriffe, there's no doubt about that; and so I suppose we shall have to bring up at Santa Cruz to get some fresh vegetables and fish for some of you good people."

He was evidently wishing just then to ingratiate himself with the passengers, while, from the state of the ship, he knew that he would be compelled to put into the nearest port to repair damages.

As we sailed along, one headland after another came into view, and then we began to distinguish the varied and very bright colours of the land,—reds, browns, and yellows of every degree. While sheltered by the coast we no longer felt the force of the wind, but glided calmly on in comparative smooth water. Again, however, the glorious peak, by the intervening clouds which played wildly around it, was hid from sight, and only the slopes of the town hills, the green valleys, or mountain glens, coming down to the very water, could be seen. By degrees, however, the trees, and even the solitary Euphorbia bushes, could be distinguished, and then a long, low, white line appeared, which our telescopes divided into the houses, and churches, and towers of Santa Cruz, the capital of the island. Before long the *Orion* was rolling her sides in the glassy waters of the bay opposite the town. Once upon a time the island possessed a magnificent harbour—that of Garachico —but it was filled up by a stream of red-hot lava which flowed into it from an eruption of the mountain in 1705, and which committed much other damage. Glassy as was the surface, the rollers from the ever unquiet ocean came slowly in, causing the vessels at anchor to dip their sides alternately in the water up to their bulwarks, and, as we stood on the deck of the *Orion*, making it seem now and then as if the town, by a violent convulsion of nature, had been suddenly submerged before our very eyes. This was not a place to remain in longer than could be helped, and accordingly the captain directed Mr. Henley, as the only officer in whom he could confide, to go on shore and to bargain for the necessary assistance we required to fit new spars and masts, and in other respects to repair our damages. Mr. Henley, knowing how anxious I was to go on shore at every place we visited, got leave for me to accompany him. Away we glided on the summit of the glassy roller towards the mole, and as we passed by, active hands being ready to catch the boat, we stepped out, and away went the watery mass broken into sheets of foam along the sandy shore, making all the Spanish boats hauled up on it bump and thump and grind together as if it would knock them to pieces; but I suppose that they were accustomed to such treatment, for no one interfered to place them in safer positions.

I was particularly struck on landing with the brilliant colours and varied hues, not only of the sky and water, the earth and the buildings, but of the dresses and very skins of the peasantry. Every cake out of my paint-box would have been required, I was sure, to give effect to the scene. Even the barefooted porters wore red scarfs round their waists, while shawls and handkerchiefs of every tint adorned the heads and shoulders of the women—hats, however, being worn generally by the older dames. Then there was the fine tawny colour of the persevering oxen who dragged after them little sledges laden with casks and bales. Camels also we saw introduced from the not far off coast of Africa, patient as ever, bearing heavy weights balanced on their hump backs. Madeira was hot, but we were much hotter now, as the basalt-paved streets and the white glittering buildings sent back the burning rays of the almost vertical sun. Thus fired and scorched, we could not help gazing with a somewhat envious glance into some of the Moorish-looking houses, not unlike the model of the Alhambra or the Pompeian house at the Crystal Palace, only not quite so fine as the former, with bananas growing in the centre of their court-yards, and fountains throwing up cool jets of water, and shady corridors and alcoves, the wide-spreading leaves of the banana throwing a refreshing coolness around. Having heard that Santa Cruz was a very poor place, we were astonished to find it really a fine city with handsome houses, spreading backwards a considerable distance from the sea, with gardens and villas beyond, and outside all cactus plantations and cultivated terraces rising up the slopes of the mountains. I was proceeding with Mr. Henley in search of the consul, who was to arrange matters about the ship, when I felt a hand placed on my shoulder, and I heard a voice say,—

"Halloa, old fellow!—Marsden! what wind has brought you here in that rig?"

"A pretty stiff gale," I answered, looking up and recognizing an old school-fellow, Tom Lumsden, who, though older than Alfred, was a great friend of his.

"Come along, then, and tell me all about it," said he. "I have an uncle settled here, and I have been sent out to learn business with him. Come and stay with us while your ship remains here. He'll get you leave from the captain. You can spare him us?" he added, addressing Mr. Henley, who laughed, and said that he hoped I should always find friends wherever I went.

Lumsden at once got his uncle to send off a note to the captain, who replied in the most courteous way that I was welcome to remain as long as the ship was there.

"Capital!" exclaimed Lumsden. "We were on the point of starting up the peak just for a pic-nic of three or four days. The ship won't sail before that time. You shall go with us."

Of course I was delighted. We were to start after an early dinner, and in the interval Lumsden took me round the place to show me its lions. I can only venture to give a rapid and brief summary of what I saw and heard. The Canaries were known to the ancients, and were called the fortunate or happy isles. Their present name is derived from *Canis*—dogs of a peculiar breed having been found in them. The inhabitants were a fine and brave race, of whom little is known except that they had the custom of embalming their dead. The Spaniards made several attempts to take possession of the islands, but did not succeed in overcoming their aboriginal inhabitants till about 1493, since which time the latter have become completely amalgamated with the conquerors.

The group consists of seven islands of volcanic origin. The principal islands are Teneriffe and Grand-Canaria. Teneriffe is sixty miles long and thirty broad. The peak, called also the Peak of Teyde, is about the centre of a dormant volcano nearly 12,000 feet high. Connected with it are numerous mountain-ridges, out of which sulphuric vapours constantly ascend, and another crater called Chahorra, close upon 10,000 feet high, and to the west of it are several cones which were in a state of eruption in 1798. Surrounding the peak is a plain bordered by mountain-ridges and covered with pumice stones, the only vegetable which grows on it being the *retama*. Indeed, only one-seventh of the whole island is fit for cultivation, the rest being composed of lava and ashes, or rocky heights and precipitous cliffs. Still, many of the portions which can be cultivated are of extraordinary fertility; and the contrast is very great between the richly-cultivated plains and valleys, and the leafy forests, with the barren, scorched, and burnt sides of the peak and its surrounding heights. I ought to have said that the houses of Santa Cruz are of several stories, with the verandahs one above another, looking into the interior courts, in which grow not only bananas, but all sorts of tropical shrubs, and fruit, and flower-bearing plants, in the most luxurious manner.

In speaking of Santa Cruz, I must not forget that it was here one of the greatest of England's admirals, Nelson, lost his arm; and here alone he failed of success among the numerous expeditions in which he was engaged. He commanded a squadron under Lord St. Vincent, who despatched him to take Santa Cruz, and to cut out a valuable Spanish ship, *El Princesse d'Asturias*, from Manilla, bound to Cadiz, which it was reported had put in there. The first attempt to effect a landing having failed, Nelson took command of the expedition. The directions were that all the boats should land at the mole, but the night was very dark, and the greater number having missed it, were driven on shore through the surf I have described, and stove, while the admiral, with only four or five boats, found the mole. This they stormed, though a terrific fire was opened upon them; and Nelson, who was about to draw his sword as he was stepping on shore, was struck by a musket-ball on the right arm. Had not his step-son, Lieutenant Nisbet, and one of his bargemen, John Lovel, bound up his arm, he would in all probability have bled to death. Captain Troubridge having, in the meantime, succeeded in collecting two or three hundred men on the beach, all who had escaped being shot or drowned, marched to the square, and took possession of the town. He, of course, had to abandon all hopes of taking the citadel; but, though eventually hemmed in by eight thousand Spaniards, he was able, by threatening to burn the town, to make terms, and to retire with his little band from the place. In this disastrous affair, the English lost, killed and wounded, two hundred and fifty men, and several captains and other officers. Blake, it may be remembered, in the time of the Commonwealth had cut out from this same bay some rich Spanish galleons, and it was hoped that Nelson would have been equally successful in a like attempt. The islanders do not bear us any ill will in consequence, and I found a good many Englishmen living in the place. Many of them are engaged in exporting Teneriffe wine, in days of yore well known as Canary wine.

Talking of wine, the disease which has destroyed the vines of Madeira has also committed great havoc here, but the people have been saved from ruin by the discovery of a new article of export. The cactus, that thick-leaved, spiny plant used often in the south to form hedges, which look as if the ground was growing a crop of double-edged saws, flourishes in the most arid soil in Teneriffe. The cactus had some time before been introduced from Honduras with the cochineal insect, which feeds on it, by a native gentleman; but his fellow-islanders turned up their noses at the nasty little creature, and said that they would rather produce wine as had been done for the last three hundred years or more. When, however, their vines sickened and died, too glad were they, one and all, to have such for their support, and everybody, nigh and low, took to planting cactus and breeding the cochineal. The female insect is in form like a bug, but white; the male turns into something like a gnat, and soon dies. The insects are shut up in boxes to lay their eggs on bits of linen, which are pinned to the cactus plants by one of their own thorns. In six months after planting the cactus, the harvest begins. The insect, which has secreted a purple fluid, is swept off the plant on to a board, and then baked to death in an oven. This constitutes the cochineal as imported. A single acre of land planted with cactus will produce from three hundred pounds to five hundred pounds of cochineal, worth £75 to the grower.

Teneriffe produces the dragon-tree—*Dracena draco*—which gives forth in the form of gum a splendid scarlet, known of old as dragon's blood; but as they take a century or more to grow into trees, and several centuries before they attain any size, he would be a daring man who would attempt their cultivation for the sake of profit.

In strong contrast to the luxurious habitations of the upper classes were the abodes of many of the poorer orders. When the now silent peak sent forth streams of lava, it flowed down towards the sea, covering the sandy shore, where, cooled by the water, it stopped short. In many places, in process of time, the sand has been washed away, leaving rows of caverns, with flat lava roofs. Numbers of poor people have taken up their abode in these nature-formed recesses; and if they have no windows, they have plenty of sea air, and pay no taxes.

I had an opportunity of seeing something of the fish of these regions. A net, as we passed near the beach, was being drawn on to it. There was a shout, and a rush towards it. A huge monster of a ray, with the sharpest of stings, was seen floundering amid a number of other creatures, the most numerous being hammer-headed dog-fish, which were quickly knocked on the head to be turned into oil, while the ray (*Pteroplatea Canariensis*) was set on by a host of enemies, and speedily despatched.

Now, dinner being over, mounted on horses, Lumsden and I, with his uncle and three other friends, trotted off along a not bad road, lately constructed by the Government, for Orotava, a town standing high above the sea, not far from the base of the peak. The cross is the great symbol, not only in Santa Cruz, but throughout the island; and in front of nearly every house and on every height it is seen conspicuous. We slept that night at that very sedate town of Orotava. We started at a very early hour, having exchanged our horses for sure-footed, active mules. As we ascended, the botanical changes were remarkable. The gardens on either side of us were for some way filled with orange, lemon, fig, and peach trees; 2000 feet higher, pear trees alone were to be seen; and 2000 feet more, the lovely wild plants of the hypericum in full bloom, with their pink leaves and rich yellow flowers, covered the ground, and then a few heaths appeared, followed by English grasses. We were then high above the clouds, the whole country below our feet being entirely shut out by them. The region of the retama was at last gained, 7000 feet above the sea. It is a peculiar broom found nowhere else but in Teneriffe. We stopped before this in a shady spot, where, among heaths and ferns, a few laurels waved around, imparting coolness to the air. A flock of goats were driven past us, from which we abstracted an ample supply of milk. The only milk to be obtained in the island is from goats, as the inhabitants never milk their cows. Goats in great numbers are kept, and are often eaten, while their skins supply their owners with clothing or with roofs for their huts. The two gentlemen who accompanied us had some astronomical instruments with them; and when the simple-minded people saw them looking in the evening at the moon, they could not believe but that they were trying to discover if there were any goats there to make it a fit abode for man. Without goats they could not conceive that any place could be habitable. At length we reached a spot where even goats could find no pasture. Vegetation there was none: the surface of the ground was composed of ashes of pumice, with cascades of black stones, while far below us floated a vast level plain of mist. The heat was much greater than I expected to have found it in so elevated a region.

"We shall soon arrive at a spot where we may be cool enough," observed Lumsden, pointing to a little cross, which rose out of the lava.

We scrambled towards it, and on getting to the spot, found a hole about four feet square. A rope-ladder and ropes had been brought. By their means we descended about twenty feet, when we found ourselves in a large cavern, with a pool of pure water at the bottom, and surrounded by masses of snow—a curious and unexpected scene in that arid region of lava and pumice stone. Of course, the scientific gentlemen eagerly discussed the reason why the water was there retained. All agreed that the snow—of which great quantities fall on the peak in winter—beat into it at that time, and was thus preserved from the effect of the sun's rays. I think they con-

A SNOW CAVERN. 101

cluded that the floor of the cavern may have been formed by a sheet of lava, and that thus a natural basin was created. At the bottom of the water, however, we found a thick mass of ice. Even in this cool spot we discovered a jet of smoke or vapour coming out from amidst a heap of stones not far from

TOP OF THE CRATER.

the entrance hole. As we proceeded on our ascent, 11,600 feet above the sea, we came upon a jet of steam, at a temperature of 100 degrees, coming out of crevices in the rocks three inches in diameter, and known as the Narix of the Peak. As it was condensed on the surrounding stones, it gave nourishment to a small quantity of moss growing among them. At last we reached the base of the cone, and had to climb up about 470 feet; at first over loose pumice, but soon coming to some red lava crags, the ascent was easy enough. Often we found the ground hot beneath our feet, while jets of sulphurous vapour greeted our olfactory nerves in an unpleasant way. Still on we climbed till we found ourselves on the very basin of the culminating crater, but were almost driven back by the jets of steam and sulphurous vapours which surrounded us.

"A mighty tall chimney to a huge fire burning down below somewhere," observed Lumsden. "I have no wish to go down and try and sweep it, to cure it of smoking, however."

The interior of the crater was judged to be about 300 feet in diameter and 70 deep. A remarkable feature was its extraordinary whiteness when not covered with sulphur. The surrounding wall was so narrow at the top that there was scarcely standing room for two persons. In many places, however, it has given way, and crumbled down into the interior floor. We walked about over the whole of the floor, searching for specimens of sulphur, without the slightest fear of falling through the crust, and slipping down the chimney, as Lumsden called it. Again we were on our descent. I remember stopping to lunch in a grassy ravine, under the shade of a superb laurel, by the side of a clear stream, amid a profusion of green leaves and lovely wild-flowers, on some delicious bananas, and other fruits, cold tea, and biscuits.

Never did I more enjoy an excursion; and then I had many a long talk with Lumsden about old times, and especially about Alfred. He entered—as I knew he would—warmly into my projects and when we got back to Santa Cruz, procured me several valuable letters both to the Cape, the Mauritius, Ceylon, and many other places.

"I wish that I could go with you to assist in finding Alfred," he exclaimed, as I was wishing him good-bye. "I'll see what my uncle will say. Perhaps he may cut out some work for me in that direction; and if so, depend upon me joining you sooner or later."

I have not mentioned Solon. By Lumsden's advice I had left him in his house, lest he might suffer from the heat to which we were exposed. I had a narrow escape from being left behind. Scarcely had Solon and I got on board by a shore boat, than a breeze coming off the land, the *Orion's* anchor was hove up, and we stood out of the bay of Santa Cruz.

CHAPTER V.

Sail again—The Trades—Cruelty of Master and Mate—Mutterings of Mutiny—A suspicious Sail—Boarded by Pirates—How they treated us.

WE had now got the steady north-east trade-wind, and away went the *Orion*, at the rate of nine knots, through the water. Fresh meat and vegetables, with dry clothing and free ventilation, had contributed to arrest the progress of the fever, and people were recovering their usual spirits, forgetting, apparently, the trials they had gone through. The captain was at first very quiet, and scarcely spoke to any one; then he grew sulky, and muttered threats and curses against any one who opposed him; and very soon he broke into open violence, and, in conjunction with Mr. Grimes—with whom he had made up his quarrel, it seemed—began to ill-treat the crew as before. If any man did not do exactly what he wanted, the captain would tear off his cap, seize his hair, and then, kicking his legs, bring him down on the deck. One day he knocked a poor fellow down with a hand-spike, and thrashed him with a boat-stretcher; and soon afterwards threw a marlin-spike at the head of another, and wounded him severely in the ear. It surprised me that the men did not turn upon these tyrants.

"They know full well that if they did they would come off the worst," observed Mr. Henley. "It is not fear, but wisdom, keeps them obedient. However, they may be over-tried, and then, as in numberless cases, they will not fail to exact a bitter retribution."

He then told me of several instances on board merchantmen, and some few on board men-of-war, where the crews, driven to desperation, had risen against their officers, and either put them to death or turned them adrift, and run off with the ship. He, however, did not seem to dream of any such thing taking place in our case. I at the same time was much struck with his remarks, and could not help keeping my ears and eyes open to watch the proceedings of the crew. From what I had seen of the men, I considered that they were very likely some day to turn suddenly on their persecutors. Still, ill as the captain was behaving, I felt that at all hazards he must be supported against the men. Indeed, no instance occurs to my memory in which a crew who have mutinied have made even a sensible use of their success, and mostly they have come to untimely and miserable ends.

We were standing to the southward, with the north-east trade well on our port-quarter, the captain intending to keep close to the African coast, instead of standing across to Rio de Janeiro, as is often done, and keeping to the southward of the south-east trade-winds. We sighted the Cape de Verde Islands, which, eight in number, extend between 14° and 17° of north latitude. Ribeira Grande, on the island of Santiago, is the capital, but Porto Praya, on the south coast, is the chief harbour. They belong to the Portuguese; but the greater number of the inhabitants are either blacks or mulattoes. The islands are all of volcanic origin; and Fogo, one of them, contains a still active volcano. They produce all sorts of tropical fruits, as well as asses, goats, and poultry. I did not regret being unable to touch at the Cape de Verdes.

Now, for the first time, I saw what is called the zodiacal light. It commenced below the horizon with a considerable breadth, and as luminous as a moderate aurora, and extended upward in the direction of the star Aldebaron, thus forming a triangle. Mr. Vernon explained to me the supposed cause of this phenomena. It is that the sun is surrounded by a mass of nebulous matter, of which this light is but a manifestation. Some philosophers have an idea that the matter has solid particles in it, which, when they pass through the earth's atmosphere, produce shooting stars, or are drawn towards it in the shape of meteoric stones. It is seen always, it must be remembered, nearly in the elliptic, or sun's path. Now, too, my eyes gazed for the first time on the magnificent constellation of the Southern Cross, which rose night after night higher in the heavens. Greater, also, grew the heat, till it was impossible to sit, walk, or stand—indeed, to exist—without being in rather an uncomfortable state of moisture. I had expected to see more living beings—birds and fish—than we had hitherto met with. When the ocean was rough, only the larger sorts—whales and dolphins, porpoises and sharks—were likely to be distinguishable; and now in the calmer and hotter latitudes the inhabitants of the deep seemed to eschew the surface, and to keep to the cooler regions below. Now and then, however, as some of the sportsmen on board declared, we flushed a covey of flying-fish, or rather, they rose out of the water to avoid their enemy the boneto. A hundred yards is said to be the utmost extent of their flight; and that is a good flight, considering the weight of their bodies and the size of their gauze-like wings. They can also turn at an angle; but they seldom rise more than a dozen or twenty feet above the surface. They thus frequently fall on the decks of vessels of no great burden. When getting up a bucket of water from alongside, I was often interested in examining the variety of minute creatures which it contained. Among others, I found some beautiful specimens of swimming crabs, with paddles instead of the usual sharp-pointed legs, by which they propel themselves rapidly along.

Day after day, as we approached the line, our shadows grew less and less, till at length those of gentlemen or ladies wearing wide-brimmed hats were represented by circular discs on the deck, as the sun became perfectly vertical. The alarm and anxiety of the passengers seemed now to have ceased. The cabin passengers had their chairs up on the poop deck, and sat talking, and working, and singing long after sunset, enjoying the cool air and the magnificent display of stars which spangled the dark sky. The whole expanse below the Southern Cross down to the horizon was covered with the glorious luminosity of the Milky Way, their thousand times ten thousand worlds then glowing before us; while in the direction of Orion was another rich assemblage of stars, presenting one of the most glorious of spectacles, speaking loudly of the eternal power and might of the great Creator. As I gazed at that innumerable multitude of worlds beyond worlds, all circling in their proper orbits round one common centre, and thought that all might be peopled with beings with minds perhaps far superior to the inhabitants of our small globe, all engaged in praising and honouring Him who made them all, I felt my own utter insignificance; and yet, at the same time, my soul appeared to soar upward to a point far higher than it had ever before reached, and got, as it were, a glimpse of the mighty scheme of creation far more vivid and magnificent than I had ever before attained. In a future world, I thought to myself, man will be able to comprehend the wondrous mysteries of the universe, and the mists will be cleared away which prevent him, while in his present mortal state, from beholding all those unspeakable glories which he will fully comprehend surely in a more spiritual state of existence. The soul of man is made to soar. Its wings become helpless and weak, and without

God's grace it no longer has the desire to rise above the grovelling money-making affairs of life; but, depend on it, those who would enjoy the purest delights this world is capable of affording, must never lose an opportunity of raising their thoughts to contemplate the mighty works of the Lord of heaven. Sailors, of all men, have great advantages in that respect; but how few comparatively benefit as they might by them!

The night after this, during my watch on deck, I went forward, and stood some time gazing on the sky, lit up by the new constellations that were gradually rising. When tired from standing so long, I sat down on the break of the forecastle. After I had been there for some time, I heard two or three men speaking in low voices below me. As I was leaning forward, they could not perceive me. I hate the feeling of being an eaves-dropper; but I could not help listening to what they said, and soon felt that it was important to hear more. Solon was at my feet. I was afraid that their voices might arouse him. Only fragments of what they said reached my ears. I could not, however, be mistaken as to the meaning of their words.

"It might be done; and many's the like deed has been done ere now," observed one of the speakers, whom I suspected to be a fellow of the name of Cobb, the greatest ruffian in the ship.

"And the passengers who won't join—what's to be done with them?"

The immediate answer I did not hear. The first words which reached me were,—

"They'll do very well. Some ship will take them off by-and-by."

Then another remarked,—

"Drowning is too good for him. Turn him adrift with a cask of brandy; that's what he'd like best."

This last suggestion seemed to please all the speakers, for they laughed heartily, but in a low tone, as if they knew that some were near in whom they could not confide. I had heard quite enough to convince me that a plot was hatching among some of the men to run off with the ship; but it was also important to ascertain when the precious scheme was to be put into execution. That point, though I listened eagerly, I could not ascertain. I was anxious that the men should not suspect that I overheard them, which, if I moved, I was afraid they might do; so I sat quiet, pretending to be asleep. I considered what course I ought to pursue. Had Captain Gunnel been a different sort of man to what he was, I should, of course, have at once informed him; but as his ill-conduct had made the men think of the scheme I had heard them discuss, I felt that it would be better to try and counteract it, without letting him know anything about the matter. I resolved, therefore, only to tell Mr. Henley and Mr. Vernon, on whose discretion I knew that I could rely, and let them consider what course to pursue. The mutineers went on talking; and from further words I occasionally caught, I discovered that the conspiracy had existed for some time, and had spread much further than I at first supposed. At last, losing patience at having to sit so long, I rose and went forward, as if about to look over the bows. I had stood there a minute, when I felt two hands grasping my shoulders.

"You've heard what we've been talking about," whispered Cobb—I was certain it was him—in a deep, fierce tone.

"And if I have, what is that?" I asked with an unfaltering voice.

"That dead men don't tell tales," answered the seaman in the same tone of concentrated fierceness.

"It is folly for you to talk to me in that way," I answered. "Though I am young, I am not a child to be frightened by you. You will get no good by doing what you are talking of, let me tell you that at all events, and advise you to give up your notable scheme."

"Then you did overhear us," said the ruffian Cobb; "it won't do to trust him."

Before I had time to open my mouth I found myself gagged, so that I could not give the alarm, and I felt that the ruffians were about to lift me up and heave me overboard. At that moment an ally came to my aid, on whom the mutineers had not reckoned. The moment the fellows laid violent hands on me, Solon, who had been standing unobserved under the bowsprit, sprung on them, biting them right and left, and barking loudly. They sung out to each other to knock him on the head with a handspike, but he avoided their blows, now leaping on one side, now on the other, and with the greatest fury tearing at the legs of the men who had hold of me, though the others, it seemed to me, he let alone. The moment, however, that one of them touched me, Solon made his teeth meet in the calves of his legs. I struggled as hard as I could to free myself, but what could I do, a mere boy, in the hands of powerful and desperate men. Knowing that I must be aware of their plot, they seemed bent on my destruction. Already they had got me off my legs, close to the bulwarks, and were about to heave me overboard; the gag slipped from my mouth, and I shouted out hastily for help. The mutineers, alarmed by my cry, let me go, and aided by Solon, who had not ceased his furious onslaught at their legs, I made a desperate leap off the top-gallant forecastle, and rushing aft, followed by my faithful ally, I gained the poop. Looking forward, I saw that several of the men were coming aft. It was the third mate's watch on deck. He had been asleep, I suspect, or at all events pretended not to have heard my cry. Happily, however, it had reached the ears of Mr. Henley, even in his berth, and so it had of Johnnie Spratt, forward, and of Mr. Vernon, and several of the gentlemen passengers, whom the heat of the weather prevented sleeping. Mr. Henley and several of the others had pistols in their hands. Their appearance awed the mutineers, who stopped a little abaft the main-mast, while Solon stood on the break of the poop, barking furiously at them.

"What is the matter? who cried out, Marsden?" asked Mr. Henley, recognizing me.

"I did, sir," I answered. "To the best of my belief some of those men there were about to throw me overboard, and would have done so if my dog had not helped me to get away from them."

"Throw you overboard! nonsense," exclaimed Mr. Waller; "what should they want to do that for?"

"Because I overheard them proposing to turn the captain and some of the officers adrift, land the passengers on a desolate coast, and then to run off with the ship," I replied in a loud tone, so that the men might hear me.

"A likely story enough. It is perfectly ridiculous and improbable," exclaimed the third mate, vehemently; "you were dreaming, Marsden. The men finding you forward, I daresay as a joke, lifted you up to frighten you, though probably they did not like your dog biting their legs."

The mutineers had come sufficiently aft to hear what was said. Cobb, who was the instigator—so it seemed to me—of the rest, sung out,—

"Yes, sir, you're right. It was only a joke. Mr. Marsden was frightened, do ye see, and so we carried it on till his confounded dog bit our legs, so that we were obliged to let him go."

This explanation appeared to relieve the minds of all on deck. It seemed so natural, and the seaman spoke in so calm a way, corroborating so completely the suggestions of the third mate, that I felt I had then but little chance of having my statement credited.

"All right, my men," said Mr. Waller; "go forward, the youngster's cock and bull story is not likely to be believed."

I said nothing, but I felt that it would be most important to persuade Mr. Henley that I had had all my senses about me, and that we ought to be on our guard against any treachery, as it was not likely that the men would abandon their plans, if they thought that they were not suspected. During all this time neither the captain nor first mate had come on deck. Once more the passengers retired to their cabins, and Mr. Henley went back to his. I felt that it would be more prudent to pretend to yield to the general opinion that my fancy had deceived me, and so I resolved to walk the deck with Solon by my side till my watch was out. I had a suspicion, however, of Mr. Waller, from what he had said; and also, though the men had not mentioned his name, they spoke of some one on whom they could rely to navigate the ship for them. Neither Sills, nor Broom, nor the boatswain could do so, and except that there might be some seaman who had concealed his calling among the passengers, I could think of no one else to whom they could allude. Solon was no more pleased with this state of things than I was, and as he walked up and down with me he kept a bright look out on every side, frequently peering forward into the darkness and giving a low dissatisfied growl.

At length eight bells struck; the first mate, who had the middle watch, was called, and as soon as he made his appearance, I went below. Mr. Waller did not at once go to his cabin, so I forthwith went to Mr. Henley's. I found him sitting up reading. I told him briefly all that had occurred, and assured him that I could not have been deceived.

"I believe you completely," he answered. "We must be

cautious. We may easily put the ruffians down, but I would avoid bloodshed. Their plans are not yet matured, so we have time to reflect on the matter. Our difficulty will be to warn the captain and first mate. I doubt, indeed, whether they will believe your statement. However, we must take our own measures according to circumstances."

Mr. Henley said that he would not turn in, but would go on deck, and get Spratt and some few of the other men in whom he had confidence, as well as some of the passengers, to appear with him, and thus to make the conspirators fancy that their plans were well known. His measures had a good effect, for Spratt told him that all the men had taken off their clothes, and gone quietly to their berths, showing that they had no thoughts of putting their scheme into execution that night.

"Forewarned, forearmed," observed Mr. Henley; "it will be our own fault if they overpower us."

Thus we continued on our course, no longer benefiting by the trade-winds, but having frequently to encounter the light and baffling breezes to be met with off the African coast, and now and then to contend with the heavy black squalls of those regions, which more than once carried away some of our spars and blew our lighter sails out of the bolt ropes. By keeping in with the African coast, we had a strong current in our favour, which helped us along materially, at the same time that we were exposed to the risk of a westerly gale, which might send us helplessly on shore. With careful navigation there would have been little danger of this, but unhappily, with the exception of Mr. Henley, not one of the officers could be depended on. Some of my readers may be astonished at hearing of a ship sailing from the port of London, towards the middle of the nineteenth century, being in the condition in which I describe the *Orion*, but if they will look at the newspapers they will see not once, but frequently, accounts of circumstances occurring on board ships both from London and Liverpool, and other parts, fully as bad as those of which I was a witness.

It surprised me often to see how calm and collected Mr. Henley could keep, knowing as he did the dangers with which we were surrounded. He was constantly observing the compass, and several times he got the chart of the African coast, and examined it in his own cabin. He told me also one morning to tend the chronometer for him, while he made a set of observations with the sextant to ascertain our exact longitude. When he had worked them out, his countenance assumed a graver aspect than I had ever before seen it wear.

"We are far more to the eastward than we ought to be," he remarked. "There are hereabouts strong currents setting on shore, and with the light winds we may expect we are too likely to find ourselves hard and fast on the African coast some night. How it has happened, I don't know, but depend on it there is some vile treachery concocting on board. Those villains have not abandoned their designs, as I hoped they might have done."

This appeared very evident, and we agreed to make every preparation in our power for any emergency which might occur, and to try and induce Dr. Cuff, Mr. Vernon, and two or three other gentlemen among the passengers, to see the state of affairs in the light we did. I have been unwilling to sicken my readers with a repetition of the accounts of the captain and chief mate's barbarity to the crew. Not a day passed but what they ill-treated one or more of them, and my surprise was, not that the men should be plotting revenge, but that they had so long endured these sufferings.

Mr. Henley undertook first to speak to Dr. Cuff. The doctor, however, made very light of his suspicions.

"Very careless steering, I have no doubt, and we have got

closer to the coast of Africa than may be altogether pleasant. No wonder at that. Then the lad dreamed he heard the sailors plotting mutiny—that is not surprising; they are not attractive looking fellows. Then it is not unusual for a set of old salts to attempt to play off a trick on a young midshipman who holds himself somewhat a cut above the common run. No fear. All will come right at last; just do you keep the ship to the westward for the present, and then get into Table Bay as fast as you can. We shall have to put our noble skipper into the sick-lists there, or I am very much mistaken."

Such was the reply the doctor made to all Mr. Henley told him. His opinion had great weight with all the other gentlemen, though Mr. Vernon did not altogether discredit my account. The result, however, of the affair was, that no especial steps were taken to counteract the schemes of the mutineers, if such schemes were still entertained by them. All Mr. Henley and I could do, therefore, was to keep a watchful eye on the movements of the suspected men.

Two days after this we lay becalmed on the smooth shining ocean with all our sails flapping against the masts, when just after daybreak a vessel was made out to the eastward, and with a fair though light breeze standing towards us. As she drew near, carrying the wind along with her, we made her out to be a large black brig, probably, from her appearance, it was supposed, a man-of-war. She was still at some distance when the passengers came on deck to take their usual walk before breakfast. Of course she excited no small amount of interest, and many opinions were passed as to her character, and to what nation she belonged. Whatever she was, it was pretty evident that she intended to come and speak us. I asked Spratt if he thought she was an English man-of-war.

"Not she," was his answer. "That spread of white canvas cloth is of Brazilian cotton stuff. To my mind she has a wicked, unsatisfactory look I don't like. There's no good about her, depend on that, Mr. Marsden."

I found, on going aft, that the captain and mates entertained the same opinion of the stranger which Spratt had expressed.

"What can he want with us?" was the question asked by several.

"Perhaps only to know his longitude," observed the captain. "By the cut of his sails he looks like a slaver, and, from his size, he is not likely to be one to knock under to any man-of-war's boats he might fall in with."

"But suppose he should be a pirate," observed some one.

"A pirate! Oh, there are no pirates now-a-days who would dare to attack a big ship like this," answered the captain, laughing. "In the Indian seas or the China coast there are fellows who would come on board and cut our throats if they could catch us all asleep; but such a thing never happens about here now."

"I am not quite so sure of that, sir," remarked Mr. Henley. "I was not long ago on this coast, and I heard of severa' piratical vessels which did not always let even English merchantmen go free, though the British blockading squadron has made their game rather a hazardous one."

On came the stranger. We now could make out that she had at least four ports on each side, with some heavy guns looking out at them; but she showed no colours from which we might ascertain her nation. We expected that, as she brought up the breeze, we should feel it also; but as she approached us it seemed to die away, till she lay becalmed about half a mile from us. That she had hostile intentions regarding us was soon evident. Three boats were lowered from her sides, and we saw numbers of men crowding into them.

"They intend to attack us!" exclaimed the captain, now

almost too late beginning to wonder what steps he should take for the defence of his ship.

We had only two guns—six-pounders—intended more for firing signals than for defence; but there was an arm-chest, with a couple of dozen muskets and some pistols and cutlasses, and a small amount of ammunition.

The captain, having opened the chest, was about to distribute the arms generally among the crew. "Stay, sir," exclaimed Mr. Henley; "there are some of the men cannot be trusted with arms. Let them be given to the cabin passengers and officers, and to three or four of the men I will call aft. Let them serve the guns, but don't trust them with other firearms. They may be pointing them aft, depend on that, sir."

"What are you talking about, Mr. Henley?—the crew not to be trusted? We'll soon see what they dare to do when we've settled with these slaving fellows."

"It's a fancy, sir, Mr. Henley has taken into his head in consequence of a cock and bull story of young Marsden's," put in Mr. Waller. "If we are not sharp about it, the boats will be alongside before the arms are served out."

Without waiting for the captain's answer, and before Mr. Henley could interfere, he handed both muskets and pistols to Cobb and Clink, another of the men who had tried to heave me overboard. Mr. Henley, seeing this, as quickly as he could, aided by me, served out the arms to the passengers and to those of the crew he fancied he could trust. The captain, however, had the sense to follow his advice, and to give only three rounds of ammunition to each man. When this was done, I had time to look towards the approaching boats. They were filled full of fellows armed to the teeth, and dressed in every variety of costume. Some of them were whites, but many were mulattoes and blacks. There could not be a shadow of doubt as to their intentions being hostile, though it was doubtful how far they might venture to proceed, when they saw us in a way prepared to receive them. Some of the passengers were very full of fight; others I saw skulking below, either not liking the look of things, or going to secure about their persons any articles of value they might possess. Some of the seamen handled their muskets as if they were prepared to use them; but others, especially two or three who had been lately ill-used by the captain and first mate, threw their weapons down on the deck, and, folding their arms, declared that they would see the ship sink before they would use them. The captain swore at and abused them most vehemently; but they listened to him with perfect unconcern, while Cobb, and Clink, and their companions, backed them up in their mutinous conduct. Our imperfect preparations, such as they were, had hardly been completed, when the pirate's boats dashed alongside.

"Don't fire till I give the order!" shouted the captain; but he did not speak in time, and several of the passengers and crew discharged their muskets at the boats. No one was hit that I could see, and the pirates shouted and shrieked in return as they began to scramble up the sides. They were bravely opposed aft, and pistols were fired in their faces, and pikes plunged at them, so that numbers were hurled back into their boats; but, to my dismay, I saw a band of them beginning to clamber up about the forechains, where Cobb and his associates had posted themselves. I shouted to the seamen to drive them back, but instead of doing so, they only laughed, and, putting out their hands, welcomed the strangers on board. Mr. Henley had been so busily engaged in defending the after-part of the ship, that he did not see what was occurring. I shouted to him to call his attention to the circumstance. He instantly, collecting around him all the men who were disengaged, made a rush at the pirates; but so many had gained a footing, that the rest had no difficulty in clambering up, and, notwithstanding his desperate onslaught, he could make no impression on them, but was compelled to retire with a wound in his sword arm, several of the rest being also much hurt. I was by his side, using a cutlass to some effect. I had learned the broadsword exercise at school, and was considered a first-rate hand at single-stick. It gave me a wonderful confidence in the *mêlée*, which I should not otherwise have felt. A shot, however grazed my arm. At that instant a big mulatto made towards me. The pain I felt caused me to drop my arm for an instant, and my antagonist would certainly have cut me down, had not my faithful Solon, who had been keeping at my heels, rushed in, and, with his usual tactics, bit the mulatto's legs so severely, that he had to try and drive off his new opponent. I sprang back, and Solon, seeing that I was safe, beat his retreat before the fellow had time to strike him. Tyrannical and cruel as the captain and first mate were, they proved themselves very far from being brave in the hour of danger. The pirates, having made good their footing on board, took entire possession of the forecastle; and when the captain saw this, he declared that there was no further use in resisting I felt that even then, had we made a bold rush forward, they might have been driven overboard; but, instead, taking out a white flag from the locker, he waved it above his head, and shouted out to the pirates, to ask them if they would come to terms.

"You are a sensible man, Senhor Capitan," answered one of them in return, in very fair English. "If you had not made any resistance at all, you would have saved a great deal of trouble and some hard knocks. We see that you are a passenger ship, and not laden with Manchester or Birmingham goods, as we hoped. We don't want to harm you, but we must be paid for our hot pull and the fighting you have given us. Here, Antonio, let the captain have a list of the stores we require, and the provisions and some water. You see your cruisers have driven us off the coast, and we are rather in want of such things. And then, let me see—we have been put to a good deal of expense—we shall require some eight or ten dollars a-head from the passengers and crew. That will not be much. We should have asked ten times the sum had you been going home; but we wish to be moderate in our demands."

Thus the pirate captain ran on. Whether he was an Englishman or an American I could not make out; but he was either one or the other. Captain Gunnell stood astounded. He began to consider whether it was still too late to resist; but on glancing towards the brig, he saw that she had her sweeps out, and was gradually creeping up towards us, to strengthen with her broadside the arguments which might be employed to induce us to comply with the requests just made to us. When he saw this, our captain stamped with rage.

"You have got the better of us," he exclaimed. "But look out. Some of the men-of-war in these seas may catch hold of you, and they are not likely to let you go without punishment for this day's work."

"Not the first time I have got the better of you, Captain Gunnell," answered the stranger, laughing. "And as for your men-of-war, my brig can show a faster pair of heels than any of them. However, we are only indulging in child's play talking thus. We'll proceed to business, if you please."

The two guns I spoke of were forward. Hauling them inboard, the pirates turned them aft; and while one party had charge of them, another was stationed on the top-gallant forecastle, and the rest, headed by their captain, advanced aft, compelling, as he did so, all the seamen and passengers he met to give up their arms. The best way I can express our sensations is to say that we all felt very small; at least I did, I know. The pirates set about the business in such a quiet, matter-of-fact sort of way, that I cannot say I was in any way alarmed as to the result of the affair. Having disarmed everybody fore and aft, the pirates proceeded to get what they wanted. The mate—at least, so I supposed the man called Antonio to be—pulled out a huge pocket-book, and in the most systematic way wrote down what was wanted, —so many casks of biscuit, so many of flour, so many of beef, and so on. He even insisted on having tea and sugar. Then he came to paint and oil, and so many fathoms of rope, and so much canvas; indeed, it was very clear that they would not be content without a complete new outfit for their brig. More than once Captain Gunnell showed signs of becoming restive, and vowed that he would give no more, when with the blandest smile the captain pointed to the guns of his black-looking craft, and intimated that in that case he should be compelled to call her alongside, when, perhaps, some of his comrades might not be so leniently disposed as he was. As soon as the boats were loaded they shoved off, and very quickly returned for a fresh cargo. At last all Antonio's demands were satisfied.

"I will give you an acknowledgment for all the supplies with which you have been good enough to furnish me," said the captain, turning to Captain Gunnell; "nay, you must not refuse me—we always do that. My owners will repay you when you call on them; and now, by-the-by—the dollars—we must not forget them."

The bystanders looked very blue; they fancied that the polite captain would not press that point. In spite of his politeness, however, there was a grim, determined look about him which showed that he was a man not accustomed to be trifled with where his interests were concerned. He pulled out a gold watch set with jewels from his waistcoat,—

"Come, gentlemen, I can but give you ten minutes," he observed, quietly. "The dollars must be forthcoming or their equivalent—two sovereigns a-piece for every man, woman, and child on board. The rich must pay for the poor; but I know well there are very few on board who cannot afford to pay that trifle. I am letting you off cheap—you ought to be grateful. Antonio, rouse up everybody from below, and make them come round and pay their mite into our coffers; be smart about it, lad: the time is up, and we ought to be parting company with these good people."

Saying this, the pirate captain stationed himself just below the poop, and he insisted on everybody on board passing in review before him, and as they did so, dropping into his hat either eight dollars or a couple of sovereigns. When anybody appeared without the required coins he sent them back, and would allow no one else to pass till the money was forthcoming. At first, when any one appeared without the money he took it very quietly, but the second time he spoke very angrily, and the third time stamped and swore with rage, threatening to throw overboard any who had not the required sum. This made their friends very quickly find it, and, consequently, after this there was very little delay. At length came Cobb and Clink, and the rest of the men who had joined them in their conspiracy. I saw Cobb wink to the captain.

"You'll not make us pay, at all events," he said, in a low voice, which he thought would not be heard. "We helped you aboard, and if you've berths for us, we shouldn't mind joining you, do ye see."

"You scoundrels," answered the pirate captain, "pay that you shall, and double too. You betrayed your own shipmates, and do you think that I would trust you and such as you? No; my fellows would cut a man's throat without ceremony, but they are faithful to each other."

He spoke loud enough for all to hear him.

"We have to supply our necessities now and then, but we don't go and harm our fellow-creatures, if we can help it. But quick, quick, you fellows, hand out your four sovereigns or your sixteen dollars."

The mutineers at first thought that he was joking with them, but he very quickly showed that he was in earnest, and suddenly clapping a pistol to Cobb's head, he told him that if he did not instantly pay the sum he would be a dead man. Cobb's countenance fell; but fumbling in his pocket, he produced the four sovereigns which had been demanded, while the pirate captain allowed the other men to pass by paying the usual sum. As the money was collected he turned it into bags, which he handed to Antonio and two or three other men, who formed a sort of body-guard behind him.

"Now, gentlemen and ladies, I wish you a good morning and a prosperous voyage," he said, making a polite bow to all around, and going down the side—his retreat being covered by a body of armed men—he stepped with the treasure he had collected into one of his boats and pulled on board his brig.

She once more got out her sweeps, and slowly glided away towards the African coast. We watched her with no very friendly feelings till night at length hid her from our sight.

CHAPTER VI.

Sight of Land not always pleasant—A suspicious Character on Board—A dangerous Predicament—How we made our Escape from it—The Cape of Good Hope—Land at Cape Town.

THE blue outline of the distant land, speaking of home and all its endearments and comforts, is welcomed joyfully by the weary seaman after a long voyage; but with a very different feeling does he view it when it appears where he does not expect to see it, and when he would rather be many miles away from it. It was in the latter way that we received the cry of "Land ho!" on board the *Orion*, when one morning it was shouted by the look-out from the mast-head.

"Where away?" asked Mr. Henley, who was the mate of the watch.

"Right a-head, and a little on the starboard bow, sir," was the answer.

"I have thought so before," he whispered to me; "our compasses have been tampered with. There exists some vile conspiracy on board to cast the ship away—of that there can be no doubt. We must keep our counsel, however, this time, Marsden, and try and counteract it by ourselves."

I assured him that I would gladly support him in any plan he might have to suggest. Things had been going on much as usual since our encounter with the pirate. The captain at first talked of going in search of a man-of-war; but he abandoned that idea, and we continued our voyage, he drinking as hard as usual, and often continuing in his cabin for three or four days together, the passengers being informed that he had a bad headache or a bilious attack. The first mate was almost as bad; and if he was not so often tipsy, the reason was that he had a stronger head and could take more liquor with impunity. The attack of the pirate on us had been the subject of conversation for many a day. Those who knew the coast of Africa best, said that there were many such vessels fitted out as slavers under the Brazilian, Spanish, Portuguese, and sometimes United States flags. If a favourable opportunity offered, they would take a cargo of slaves in on the coast, and make the best of their way to Cuba or the Brazils. If not, they would attack a slaver, take out all her slaves, and paying her with manufactured goods, would send her back to take in a fresh supply, and, of course, to run the chance of being captured. As, however, manufactured goods were not always to be procured, such fellows would not scruple to attack an outward-bound merchantman, and having taken out of her what they required, let her go free, pretty certain that she would not have the means of lodging a complaint against them on board a man-of-war till they were far beyond reach. Such was, undoubtedly, the character of our polite friend. It occurred to me that possibly Cobb and his friends might have secretly communicated with the pirate, and that the indignation of the latter was only pretended, while they had between them arranged where to cast the ship away.

"No, no," answered Mr. Henley; "they are both villains, but of a different stamp. The low, brutal Englishman and the keen, cunning Yankee have few feelings in common. The latter looks upon all the world as his prey; the former commits an atrocity for the sake of some especial revenge, or to attain some particular object of sensual gratification. We have only traitors on board to guard against, of that I am certain."

"What do you propose to do, then?" I asked.

"Put the ship's head off shore, and try and get a good offing," he answered. "But go aloft, and see what you can make out of the land."

I gladly obeyed, and went to the fore-top-gallant mast-head. There I saw clearly to the east and south-east of us a long blue irregular line, which I took to be highland with a mountainous range beyond. Having arranged in my mind in what words I should make my report, so as best to make Mr. Henley understand what I had seen, I descended on deck. I have always found it very useful to settle on the spot exactly the terms I would use to describe an object, so as to give those to whom I have had to report the clearest view of it.

"I suspect that there is some extent of lowland between us and the mountains you have seen," observed Mr. Henley. "Report the facts to the captain, and say that I am about to haul the ship up to the south-west."

I heard Mr. Henley issue the order to brace up the yards as I was about to enter the captain's cabin. I could scarcely make him comprehend what had occurred.

"Make it so. Tell the second mate to do what he thinks best," he answered, and then turned round and went off into a deep slumber again.

I told Mr. Henley. "That is well; I will take him at his word," he observed. "We will now have a look at the compass."

Fortunately Johnny Spratt was at the helm. He took off the top of the binnacle, and examined it carefully in every direction.

"I thought so," he exclaimed at last, unscrewing a piece of steel which had been secured to the west of the northern points, giving it a strong westerly variation.

Thus, when the man at the helm, unconscious of the trick, fancied that he was steering to the south, he was in reality steering east or south-east. The second mate having removed the steel, charged Spratt to say nothing about the matter. When breakfast was over, I saw Cobb come on deck and look up at the sails. Then he strolled carelessly aft to the compass, and in another minute he, with the same assumed look of indifference, ascended the fore-rigging. He was some time aloft, and when he came down he again went below to his companions. Our difficulties were much increased by our not being able to trust Waller, or indeed Sills and Broom. Sills, I believe, wished to be honest, but he had no discretion. Broom, I feared, was an ill-disposed fellow, without even a knowledge of what was right and wrong. I have met many such persons possessed of a perfect moral blindness, who do all sorts of wicked things, without in the slightest degree making their consciences uncomfortable, or fancying that they are doing any harm. Mr. Henley again spoke to Dr. Cuff, and was this time more successful in persuading him that there was something wrong going forward on board. The plotters, however, knowing that we suspected them, were on their guard, and committed no acts to betray themselves.

Soon after our discovery that the compass had been tampered with, it fell a dead calm. It continued all night and the following day. Mr. Henley and I never left the deck together all the time. One or the other of us was always on the watch. At length, after sunset on the second day, he told me to turn in. I did so, for I was nearly tired out. I had been asleep some time, when I felt some one touch my hammock.

"Hist, sir," whispered a voice close to my ear; "don't speak, please—'tis only me, Tommy Bigg. They are going to do it this very night—I've heard all about it, and I thought I'd come and tell you first. There's some use in being little, for I was stowed away in a corner where they didn't think a human being could have got."

"What is it, Tommy?" I asked, in a low voice.

I thought all the time he had been speaking that I had been dreaming, and could not believe that the reality of what I had so long apprehended had arrived.

"They intend just at eight bells, in the middle watch, to seize the captain and all the officers, and those of the crew who won't join them, and to turn them adrift in the long boat. Then they propose to run into the coast, which they say is close aboard of us, land all the passengers, and then make sail for America, or round Cape Horn for the Pacific. At first there was a doubt about their having provisions enough, from the pirates having taken so much from us; but then they agreed that as they had been robbed, they might rob others in the same way—they needn't be afraid about that matter."

I had so long expected an announcement of this sort in one form or other, that I was not surprised at what little Tommy told me. His lucid and brief statement showed me that he was a sharp, clever lad, and might be relied on. I told him to go back quietly to his berth, and if he could gain any further information, to try and let Mr. Henley or me know. I immediately dressed, and, followed by Solon, who jumped up as soon as he saw me afoot, went on deck. I found Mr. Henley standing near the binnacle. It was a star-lit night. He was noting the bearing of the stars by the compass.

"Ah, is that you, Marsden?" he said carelessly. "You cannot sleep with this hot weather, nor can I—that is not surprising. What is strange, however, is that our compasses are still in error—a wonderful variation."

Taking another observation, he stepped forward with me to the break of the poop, whence we had a clear view of the deck below us, and could be certain that no one overheard what we said. I then informed him briefly of what Tommy Bigg had told me, and asked what was to be done.

"I must consider," he answered. "We must take care, in the first place, that the mutineers do not observe our movements. Do you wait a few minutes, and then quietly slip below, and let the doctor and Mr. Vernon know, and tell them to be prepared." He mentioned also four or five of the cabin passengers. "I will wait till just before the time to call the first mate. He would only bluster now, and betray all our plans. As to Waller, I doubt the fellow. If we could show him that he was running his head into a halter, he would side with us. If you can get hold of Tommy Bigg again, let him tell Spratt that I want him, quietly. The doctor will do best to rouse all the second-class passengers who can be trusted. There are four or five among them who would do anything rather than work for an honest livelihood; but we shall not have much difficulty in keeping them down, unless, as I suspect, there is some seaman, a desperate character, among them, who is the real instigator of this long meditated plot."

I asked him who he thought the man could be, for I had watched narrowly since he had before suggested the idea to me, and could fix on no one as at all likely to be the man. He, to my surprise, mentioned a quiet, middle-aged looking man, dressed in a brown coat and wide-awake hat, who wore large green spectacles, and announced himself to be a shoemaker—Barwell he called himself.

"He is a seaman, of that I am very certain," observed Mr. Henley. "And I am almost equally so that he never made a pair of shoes in his life. Why he conceals his calling, I do not know. Perhaps he has committed some crime afloat or ashore, and is escaping from justice. I have observed him more than once in close conversation with Cobb, and for some time he seldom lost an opportunity of speaking to Waller whenever he went forward, though he himself has never ventured aft. He evidently has had a good education, and is a plausible, long-tongued fellow, well able to influence men of inferior station."

From what Mr. Henley said, I saw the man Barwell in a new light, and quickly recalled to my mind several circumstances connected with him which I had before forgotten. As it was still some time to midnight, we were in no hurry to arouse our friends, but at length having arranged our plans, I went below to perform the part I had undertaken. As I was leaving the deck I patted Solon on the head, and made him understand that he was to keep watch on the poop till my return. I was very certain that I should hear his bark if anything unusual took place.

Mr. Vernon was not much surprised nor alarmed with the information I gave him. "I cannot fancy that such a scheme as these wretched men have concocted has a chance of success," he observed calmly. "Forewarned, as we providentially have been, we can easily counteract their plans."

The other gentlemen I summoned did not take things quite so coolly. They all dressed immediately, and examined their pistols, which they put in their pockets. They then declared themselves ready to obey the second mate's orders. I therefore went to report this to him. I found that he had collected a quantity of small rope, as also some of the arms which the captain had so injudiciously distributed to the crew. I asked him for what purpose he had got the rope.

"To steal a march on the mutineers, to seize their ringleaders, and to lash them down in their berths," he answered. His plan was generally approved of. We had now altogether twelve or fourteen persons prepared for the expected emergency. It was important to communicate with Spratt, to collect the men forward who could be trusted. I volunteered immediately to do this. I knew that there was considerable risk, for I had already had an example of the way Cobb and his associates would treat me if they suspected my object. Calling Solon, however, I went forward. The watch were standing, with their hands in their pockets, on the top-gallant forecastle.

"Keep a bright look out, my lads," said I. "We are not far off the land, and it won't do to run the ship ashore."

I wanted to ascertain who the men were, but none of them spoke. I felt pretty sure that one of them was Cobb. Presently I saw Mr. Barwell come up the fore-hatchway. I knew him by his dress and figure.

"A fine night, Mr. Barwell," said I, as he stepped up on the top-gallant forecastle. "It's a sort of night you landsmen don't often meet with, I suspect."

"Not often, youngster," he answered. "But one might suppose, from the way you talk, that you had been all your life afloat."

"No, it's my first voyage, like yours, Mr. Barwell; only, as you see, I have taken kindly to the life; now, you probably would never become a better seaman than you are now," I could not help replying. "However, if you have a fancy to learn, I will teach you to knot and splice, and show you all I know myself."

"Thank you, but I am contented to know how to make shoes," he drawled out, in quite a different tone to that in which he had before spoken. I was convinced that Mr. Henley was right.

"Mend shoes! I wouldn't wish for a better man at the weather earing when reefing top-sails in a gale of wind—that is to say, if you were but a seaman," I observed, laughing, as I turned to go aft.

He started, and my remarks evidently puzzled him not a little, as I intended they should. As I was just abaft the main-mast, I heard my name called, and looking under the booms, I discovered Tommy Bigg.

"Just step this way, sir, in case I should be seen," he whispered. "I have heard more of their plans. They are going to shut up Spratt and the rest who won't side with them in the fore-peak, and then hurry aft and seize the arms, lock the cabin-doors, and lash the officers down in their berths. They have divided themselves into three parties, and they think that the whole work can be done in a couple of minutes or so. If any resist on deck, they vow that they'll knock them overboard. They'll not commit murder if they can help it, they say, but they'll not stand on ceremony about the matter."

"Very well done, Tommy," I replied. "Get forward as quietly as you can, and tell Spratt I want him and any true men he can bring; and, if possible, not to let Cobb and the rest know that they have come aft. If they slip out one by one, they can manage it. Do you then, Tommy, join us, unless you find that you can stow yourself away safely forward."

"If you'll let me, sir, I'll do what seems best," answered Tommy. "Maybe by stopping I may help you more than by being with you."

I told Tommy to do as he judged best, and returning to the poop, resumed my usual walk. The night was very dark. The conspirators reckoned on this to assist them, but it was of more use to us, as it enabled us to move about and arrange our counter-plot without their discovering us.

Six bells struck. In the merchant service the bell is generally struck only every hour. All our plans were arranged. As the time approached I joined Mr. Henley. We were all well armed. I found Spratt and some other men had managed to come abaft, unperceived by the mutineers. Just under the break of the poop there was an empty cabin. Some of our party were concealed in it with lanterns. Others the doctor had stowed away in his dispensary, close to which the mutineers must pass on their way aft. I, with a third party, under Mr. Henley's command, were concealed in a cabin close to the arm-chest. We expected here to have the most desperate resistance. All was ready.

Eight bells struck. I had a loop-hole to look out forward. I could just distinguish the dark forms of the men, as, without their shoes, they hurried aft. Their plans were well arranged. At the same moment that one party rushed past the doctor's dispensary to secure the mates, and another to overpower the cabin passengers, and the third to break open the arm-chest, we all sprang out upon them. Cobb and Clink struggled desperately, but Mr. Henley and those with us soon had them under. Mr. Vernon showed that he could fight as well as preach, and not one of the men about to enter the cabin escaped, while the doctor secured most of those below. Two or three, however, in the scuffle with us managed to escape forward before we had time to get our lanterns lighted, and so furiously did the others resist, that we were unable to spare any of our hands to follow them; we had not also discovered who they were. We had ropes ready, and so we lashed all the fellows' arms and legs, and made them fast to the ring bolts in the deck, where they lay without power to move. Never was success so complete; no one was hurt; not a pistol had been fired. The captain was not in a condition to understand what had occurred, but Mr. Grimes, hearing the scuffle, rushed out of his cabin; he, however, stood irresolute, not knowing whether friends or foes had the upper hand; and very much astonished was he when he was told what had occurred. He did not receive the information very graciously, and grumbled at not having been aroused before. Mr. Henley and I, with a strong party, meantime, holding lanterns in our hands, commenced a search round the between-decks and forward, to try and discover the people who had escaped from us. The second-class passengers were all in their berths, and many of them asleep. Mr. Barwell was in his, and snoring loudly—so loudly, that I could not help fancying it was feigned. Mr. Henley threw the light of the lantern in his face, and shook him by the shoulder. I expected to find that he was dressed, but if he had been among the mutineers, he had had time to take off his clothes.

"What's the matter? who wants me?" he exclaimed, in a husky voice.

"Up, up, sir," answered Mr. Henley. "There's mutiny on board, and we want you to help us."

"Mutiny! who's going to mutiny?" he said, rubbing his eyes. "I'll be up soon and help you, of course."

I could not tell what Mr. Henley thought about this reply. We met three or four people coming aft, who seemed very much astonished at hearing what had occurred, while all the suspected men whom we had not secured were in their berths. Our difficulty was to secure those we had captured, to guard against their being liberated. We had a dozen pair of irons on board, which we clapped on those most likely to prove refractory, and so there was little chance of their escaping. The third mate came out of his cabin soon after eight bells, as he was to have had the morning watch, but by that time all the mutineers were secured. The remainder of the night passed slowly away. It was a time of great anxiety. When the morning broke we looked eagerly towards the east. There was the land not eight miles off—a rocky shore with a sandy beach—trees in the foreground, and then ridges of hills rising into mountains in the distance. There was not a breath of wind. The sea on every side was like a polished mirror; but every now and then it seemed to heave up as if a pulse beat beneath, and away towards the shore progressed at a slow pace—not like a roller, but one swell rising at an interval after the first had fallen, and I could well fancy with what a roar it must be dashing on the rocky coast. The first mate, as he looked towards the shore, ordered the lead to be hove, but no bottom was found.

"I doubt if there is any holding-ground till close in-shore," observed Mr. Henley. "I pray that we may find a breeze to carry us away from it before we get much nearer."

"More likely to have one to drive us on to it," answered the first mate, in a gloomy tone. "How we managed to get here, I can't tell."

"We have now to consider how we may best secure an offing," remarked Mr. Henley. "We could do little at towing, even if we had all hands at work; but with more than half the crew in irons— No, Mr. Grimes; we must trust in Providence, for vain is the help of man."

The first mate uttered some sneering expression; but still he could not help acknowledging that the latter part of the remark was true. As I looked over the side, I could see the circling eddies of a current which was evidently setting in at a rapid rate towards the shore. Nearer and nearer we got. There were reefs laid down in the chart as running a long way off the coast, and we could not tell at what moment we might be driven on them. As I watched I found that we were being swept, not directly towards the shore, but to the southward and eastward, so that, though the current was strong, our progress towards destruction was slow, though not the less sure. Our position was already painful and dangerous enough, with a drunken, half-mad master, a mutinous crew, many of the passengers ready for any mischief, several of the officers worse than useless, and on a dangerous, little known coast.

The cabin passengers and the most trustworthy of the second-class ones formed themselves into a guard, and kept regular watch over the prisoners, so as to prevent any attempt which might be made to rescue them. Hour after hour passed away, leaving us still in a state of great suspense and anxiety. Evening approached—the calm continued. Darkness at length descended once more over the waters, and, though it concealed, much increased our danger. We could feel, too, by the increased motion of the ship, that although the calm continued, the form of the undulations had changed, and that heavy rollers were now moving under us towards the shore. Still the water was far too deep to allow us to anchor with the slightest hope of our anchors holding. I asked Mr. Henley what he thought of the state of things.

"Why, Marsden, that I have never been in so dangerous a position in all my life," he answered; "and to this condition we have been brought by the folly and wickedness of one man. Had he done his duty, nothing of this sort would have occurred. However, it is too late now to complain. Let us, at all events, try to do ours. Oh, that we had but a breath of wind, to get steerage way on the ship!"

As helpless as a mere log floated on our gallant ship, her head slowly pointing round to all the points of the compass. How anxiously did every one look out for the sign of a coming breeze! As to turning in, no one who had the sense to comprehend the condition of the ship thought of doing so. Sills and Broom came up, and inquiring what I thought of the state of affairs, bitterly regretted their folly in coming to sea, and asked me if I was not very sorry at having left home.

"No, far from it," I answered. "I had an important object to gain, and I knew that it could not be obtained without encountering many dangers and difficulties. This is one of them; but I do not despair of escaping, though at present I do not see the way we shall do so."

"Ah, I am glad to hear you say that, Marsden," said Sills. "It's a comfort, isn't it, Broom, to find that anybody thinks we shall escape?"

"If his opinion was worth much, it would be," growled out Broom. "For my part, I have no great faith in what anybody says."

I answered that I would not quarrel with him on account of his polite remarks, but that I only hoped my opinion would prove correct in this instance, at all events.

About midnight, in spite of the darkness, we could see the land about a mile and a half, or even less, from us, while the roar of the surf as it broke on the shore could be heard with distinctness. Suddenly, as I was standing on the deck, I felt one side of my cheek grow colder than the other. I wetted my finger and held up my hand. There was a sensible difference in the temperature. In another minute I had no doubt about it. A breeze was springing up. The sails gave two or three loud flaps against the masts. I looked at the compass; the breeze was from the westward. Still, any wind was better than none at all, provided there was not too much of it. Mr. Henley felt it as soon as I did. I heard his clear, manly voice issue the order to brace the yards sharp up; and the ship, at length feeling her helm, was brought close to the wind. Had the breeze been off the shore, our difficulties would have been over; as it was, they were only mitigated. The land lay broad on our port beam; and when I looked over the port bow I could not help believing that I saw a cape or headland which it seemed scarcely possible that we should weather. I pointed it out to Mr. Henley. He had seen it, and told me I was right. To go about was useless.

"Unless the wind shifts some four or five points, we shall have gained but little," he observed.

Higher and more distinct drew the headland. Then it seemed to stand out in the dark ocean like some monster of the deep about to overwhelm us. It was a remarkable headland—once seen not likely to be forgotten. As we all stood gazing at it with dread and anxiety, I observed a person coming up on the poop deck. He advanced rapidly towards where the mates were standing. I thought I recognized the figure and appearance of Mr. Barwell, who had never before come, that I was aware of, to that part of the deck.

"There appears no small chance of the ship being cast away, and of our losing our lives," he observed abruptly. "The ship will never weather that point, let me assure you."

"Who are you?—what do you know about the matter?" exclaimed Mr. Grimes, turning sharply round on him.

"Who I am is of little consequence, provided I do know something of the matter," answered the pretended shoemaker. "This is not the first time by many that I have been off here, and if you will trust to my pilotage I will take you into a bay where you may lie as securely as in Plymouth Harbour. If you stand on as you are now doing, the ship will inevitably be cast away."

This painful fact was too evident; still, I could not be surprised that the mates should hesitate, even in this extremity, to trust a man who was more than suspected of being one of the chief movers in the late mutiny.

"You must decide quickly, gentlemen," he continued. "For my own sake, I hope that you will accept my offer. I cannot compel you to trust me; but I do tell you, that if the ship once strikes yonder headland, not a plank of her will hold together, and not one human being on board will ever reach the shore alive."

"I'll shoot him through the head if he plays us false," I heard Mr. Grimes say to the second mate.

"You'll do as you please," observed the stranger, with a low laugh. "I don't fear your threats, but I must make a bargain with you. If I take the ship into a safe anchorage, you must promise to grant me any request I may make, provided it is not extravagant or injurious to you."

After a short consultation with Mr. Vernon and other gentlemen, the mates agreed to the stranger's terms, and the ship was put under his charge.

"Starboard the helm! Square away the yards! Be smart, my lads!" he shouted, and the ship was headed in towards the land.

The tone of voice and mode of speaking showed that the pretended Mr. Barwell was not only a seaman, but well accustomed to command. No longer slouching about as he had been accustomed to do, he was quick and active in all his movements. He took his post in the main rigging to con the ship, and his full and clear voice was heard ever and anon issuing his orders. As we stood on, high cliffs appeared right ahead of us, and I fancied that I could distinguish one long, unbroken line of surf directly across our course. It required great faith in the stranger's assurances to believe that we were not rushing to destruction. Every moment the breeze freshened, and shortened the interval which must elapse before the point was settled. I heard Mr. Grimes cock his pistol. The dark outline of the land seemed to rise above our mast-heads. Still on we went. I held my breath; so, I doubt not, did every one on deck. I could not help expecting every moment to hear the terrific crash of the ship striking on the rocks. Suddenly, as I looked, I fancied that I could distinguish an opening in the surf. It grew wider and wider. The ship entered it, while on either side the white foam danced up frantically, as if trying to leap on board of us. The next instant we were between high cliffs. Still on we glided.

"Starboard!" sung out her pilot; and the ship standing to the northward, in a few minutes we were in a perfectly sheltered position. The sails were furled, and the ship was brought to an anchor. Rocks and cliffs appeared around us on every side, with here and there a palm-tree standing up against the clear sky; and so completely land-locked were we, that I could not discover the passage by which we had entered the bay.

"There!" exclaimed Mr. Barwell; "I have performed my share of the agreement. Now I will ask you to perform yours."

Most of the passengers and the officers of the ship were assembled on the poop.

"What is your demand?" asked the first mate, who had not uttered a word of thanks to the stranger who had certainly saved all our lives.

"My demand is that you land any of the unfortunate men you have in your power who may desire to be liberated," answered the stranger firmly. "I intend to leave the ship here; I have had enough of her. Of course, if they do not wish to go, I can say nothing further; but ask them, and fulfil your contract."

"I will see what the captain has to say to the matter," began the first mate.

The stranger stamped on the deck with anger. "The captain has had nothing to do with the affair!" he exclaimed. "I appeal to all on board whether you did not make the promise, and whether, had I not performed what I undertook to do, you would not ere this have been dashed helplessly amid the breakers on the cliffs we saw ahead of the ship."

I heard Mr. Henley asking Mr. Vernon's opinion.

"There is one simple rule to go by," he answered. "If

you make a promise, fulfil it. Of course, I know that certain inconveniences may arise in consequence. The authorities at the Cape will probably find fault with you, and various complaints may be made; but still, Mr. Barwell has a perfect right to demand the fulfilment of the promise you made him, and you cannot in justice refuse to do so."

I was sure that Mr. Vernon was right, and I knew that Mr. Henley thought the same, so I was very glad when it was settled that all the prisoners who might wish it were to be landed with Mr. Barwell. Whatever opinion might have been formed of him, one thing was certain—he had been the means of preserving the ship and the lives of all on board. I talked over the matter with Mr. Henley as we walked the deck during the remainder of the night. We might fancy the man a slave-dealer or pirate, or an outlaw of some sort; but we had no proof of this, and if so, he would be able to commit as much mischief at the Cape as here. Our chief fear was that he might lead the prisoners we were about to liberate into crime. Then again came in the promise made to him, and we felt that they had been driven to mutiny by the greatest cruelty, and that if carried on to the Cape they would be severely punished. Thus I must leave it to others to decide whether we were right or wrong in liberating the prisoners. The offer was made to them by the doctor, who explained the nature of the country, and the hardships they would have to go through, and the dangers to which they would be exposed; but notwithstanding this, they all at once preferred being landed to undergoing a trial for the crime they had committed.

When daylight came we found ourselves in a strangely wild place. Near us were rocks, and cliffs, and sandbanks, and further inland palm-trees and other tropical productions, with a wide extent of grassy, undulating plains, or rather uplands, between the shore and the hills; but not a sign was there of human habitations or human beings. Mr. Barwell was busy in making preparations for his departure. Certain trunks and packages were got up, and he begged to purchase some sail-cloth for a tent, and some provisions, which of course were not refused. We had altogether fifteen prisoners. When Barwell, dressed in his brown suit, and looking perfectly the unassuming artisan he had pretended to be, had taken his seat, six of them were told off into the boat and carried on shore. The boat then returned for the remainder, and for the stores and provisions which Mr. Barwell—for so I will still call him —had purchased. The mates added several more things, so that altogether the party were not ill supplied; and in that climate, with an abundant supply of food to be found in its wild state, they might very well be able to support existence till they could find means to quit it. Barwell had, it appeared, a rifle and a supply of ammunition, and he had purchased a fowling-piece from one of the passengers, and five or six muskets for his companions, so that they might be able to defend themselves against any attack from the natives they might fall in with. Mr. Henley told me, however, he believed that in that southern part of the African coast the natives were scattered widely apart, and that in many extensive districts none were to be found.

Climbing to the mast-head, I had a look round with my telescope, and I felt certain that I saw several herds of animals feeding on the plains in the interior. Some were antelopes and deer of various sorts; and then, as I watched, to my great delight I saw a number of large animals come out of a wood. They were elephants—not two or three, such as might be seen in the Zoological Gardens—but a whole drove, fifty or sixty at least, magnificent, big fellows. They were on their way, apparently, to a river to drink. I longed to be on shore to hunt them, and I almost envied Barwell and his companions the sport I fancied they would enjoy. I was called on deck by the order to make sail. The wind had come round to the north-east, and was fair for running out of the harbour. As the anchor was hove up the people we had left behind waved to us, and, it appeared, were cheering; but whether they did so to wish us farewell, or in derision, we could not tell. With our sadly-diminished crew we stood away to the southward. Just as we left the harbour the captain once more came on deck. The mates could scarcely convince him of what had occurred.

"I knew that we were not far off land," he remarked. "The smell of the shore brought me to myself."

Strange to say, this was perfectly true; and from that time till they were again in harbour neither he nor Mr. Grimes touched spirits, and appeared to be as sober as any man could be.

Such were some of my early experiences in the merchant service. It must not be supposed that all ships are like what the *Orion* then was, or that there are many of her size commanded by such a man as Captain Gunnell, with such a first mate as Mr. Grimes; but still there are some, and I might almost venture to say many, which are in no better condition, and I have met with numerous instances where a state of things equally bad had existed on board. This has arisen from the absence of religious principle, from the want of education, and from the intemperate habits of the officers. I am far from wishing to dissuade any of those who read my travels from entering the merchant service. It is an honourable and useful career; but I would urge them to endeavour, by every means in their power, to improve their minds, and especially to be on their guard against the vice of drunkenness, which has proved the destruction of so many gallant seamen. Far more would I urge them to make it their highest aim to become true Christians, not only in name, but in word and in deed.

Once more the sound of "Land ahead!" greeted our ears. It was a clear, bright morning; and as the sun rose we had before us a fine mountainous line of coast, running down from Table Bay to the extremity of that lofty headland known as the Cape of Good Hope. Everywhere the coast appeared bold and high. The mountains seemed to rise abruptly from the sea in a succession of ledges, steep, rugged, and bare, with rough and craggy crests. As we stood in close to the shore, the sun shining on the crags and projections made them stand out in bold relief, throwing the deep furrows of their steep sides into dark shades, while the long line of white surf dancing wildly at their bases formed a fitting framework to the picture. Table Mountain appeared to be the highest point of the whole range, though it was not till we got closer in that it assumed its well-known form of a table. As we opened Table Bay we caught sight of the picturesque mountains of Stellenbosch and Hottentots Holland in the background, with a line of sand hills in front. It was not till the evening that we at length dropped our anchor.

Cape Town stands on nearly flat ground. Immediately behind it rises abruptly the Table Mountain, most appropriately, from its shape and appearance, so called. On our left, joining the Table Mountain, was the bold and rugged peak called the Devil's Mountain, and on the right the rocky height known as the Lion's Head, while a long, round-backed hill, running north from the Lion's Head, is known as his Rump, the two hills together having somewhat the appearance of a lion couchant. Cape Town has not lost the character given to it by its Dutch founders. Down the principal street runs a canal, and several are shaded by rows of trees. The houses are flat-roofed, with glass windows composed of a number of small panes. They are either white-washed or gaily painted, and in front of each of them are brick terraces called *stoeps*, where, in the summer, the inhabitants sit and talk to their acquaintances who may be passing. The houses are rather low, there are no regular foot-pavements, the roads are very dusty, and the streets cross each other at right angles. Though the place has a

CAPE TOWN.

decidedly foreign look, and people of all nations are to be seen there—especially Dutch, Hottentots, Malays, and Negroes—still the greater number are English, and one fully feels that he is in an English town, and living under English laws. The most remarkable feature of the picture, to be seen in every direction, is the Cape waggon—long and low when laden with heavy goods, drawn by twelve or more oxen, and driven by a Hottentot with a long bamboo whip. Lighter articles are conveyed in lighter waggons, and drawn at a quick pace by horses. The town is defended by a castle of considerable strength, and several lesser forts. The dust, which sprinkles everybody and everything with red, and the strong winds, which blow ships on shore, and commit other species of damage, are the things most objected to in Cape Town.

Having introduced them, I hope that I may be considered to have given a fair picture of the place as it appeared to me when, the day after our arrival, I went on shore in the afternoon with Mr. Henley. All the passengers who were to remain at the Cape had disembarked, and the rest, who were going on to Natal and the Mauritius, had gone on shore to live till the ship again sailed.

I at once delivered the letters I received from my old schoolfellow Lumsden at Teneriffe, and met with the kindest reception from all his father's friends to whom they were addressed. My story excited a great deal of interest among them, and they all expressed an anxiety to help me in finding out my brother Alfred. This, from their connections with all the ports in that part of the world, they were well able to do, and my hopes of success increased as I talked the matter over with them; and they suggested various places to which he might have gone, and the different occupations in which he was likely to have engaged. On one point I felt very certain—and may all those similarly placed feel the same. I had passed through many and great dangers, and had been mercifully preserved by Providence; and I had the assurance that the same kind Providence would continue to watch over and preserve me in all the perils and difficulties I might have to undergo.

CHAPTER VII.

Cape Colony—Table Mountain and its Table-Cloth—A Storm—Sail for the Mauritius—Port Louis and Pieter Bot Mountain—Journey into the Interior—Paul and Virginia—Disappointment—An Estate in the Mauritius—Wild Animals—Sail for Ceylon.

MY ship, I found, was to remain but a short time at Table Bay before proceeding on to the Mauritius. I had been in great hopes of going to Natal, but the passengers all left here rather than attempt to land at the port of that province from so large a ship. I thought that I might there possibly hear of my brother, but as I had as yet received no information to lead me to suppose that he was there, I felt that it would be far better to get as soon as possible to the Mauritius, which was the place where we had last heard of his being. It must be understood that of this, the main object of my voyage, I never for a moment lost sight, though in the account I am giving of my voyages and travels I may not on all occasions bring it prominently forward.

A great deal might be said about Cape Colony, and I will not leave it without giving a very short description of it. The country in the neighbourhood of Cape Town is fertile and picturesque, and the south-western districts produce wine and corn in abundance; but the larger portion is sterile and uninviting, with a sad absence of shade, verdure, and water. At the same time there are numerous, but unnavigable rivers. It improves, however, in the direction of Natal; but in the north, towards the Orange River, it is said to be again barren. To the north and north-east are the districts inhabited by the Amakosa Caffres, the Tambookies, and the Amaponda; while along the coast round and beyond Port Natal is the country of

HOTTENTOTS.

the fierce Zooloos. Bartholomew Diaz discovered the Cape of Good Hope in 1493; and it was doubled four years afterwards by Vasco de Gama. The inhabitants found there were called Hottentots. They attacked the Portuguese who first attempted

THE CAPE CONQUERED BY THE ENGLISH. 149

to settle at the Cape, and it was not till 1650 that the Dutch East India Company formed a thriving establishment there. A large addition was made to the colonists by many French Protestants, who had escaped into Holland from the tyranny

CAFFRES.

of Louis XIV. after the revocation of the Edict of Nantes. The Dutch remained in possession of the country until the year 1795, when Holland, having become subject to France, the English sent out an expedition which conquered it. It was restored to the Dutch at the Treaty of Amiens; but in 1806, they and the English having again become enemies, it was taken from them by an army under Sir David Baird. In 1814 it was confirmed to the British. The Hottentots were a mild, inoffensive race, but were cruelly treated by the Dutch, who, however, as they advanced inland found a very different race to contend with in the Caffres, with whom a constant feud was maintained. The English also found them a fierce, warlike, and treacherous people, and have constantly been at war with them, or engaged in forming treaties which were as often broken. Happily, by the judicious management of Sir George Grey, the enlightened governor of Cape Colony, the disputes with the Caffres were terminated; the Boers—as the Dutch farmers are called — were satisfied; while the contented Hottentots, long kept in slavery, were freed at the passing of the Slave Emancipation Bill, when the glorious announcement was made throughout the world that no human being could be longer held in slavery on British soil.

I forgot before to mention that as soon as we reached Table Bay a full statement had been lodged with the proper authorities of the attack which had been made on us by the pirates, and of the mode in which we had been robbed. Full particulars were accordingly sent to all the vessels on the west coast, and directions given to them to look out for the pirate; but we learned that there was very little chance of our having any redress, as of course he would take care to keep out of the way of all men-of-war for some time to come, at all events. I cannot say that I felt very much interested in the matter, and my chief fear was that, should the pirate be captured before the *Orion* sailed, we might be detained to give evidence against the crew. All my thoughts were occupied with devising means by which I might discover Alfred.

We were not to leave the Cape without a gale. I had been

walking the deck with Mr. Henley, expecting to receive our orders for getting under way, when he pointed to Table Mountain.

"See, the table-cloth is spread right over the table," he observed. "We shall not get to sea without a storm."

Then, as I looked up, I saw a dense white cloud which seemed to be ever pouring over the edge of the table, but never to get lower; indeed, most appropriately, from its appearance, is it called the table-cloth.

TABLE BAY.

Mr. Henley explained how this happened. "Table Mountain terminates in a ridge of high land, which covers the larger portion of the promontory of the Cape of Good Hope. The side immediately above the town is 4000 feet high. During the day, when the air is warmer than the water," he observed, "there is a considerable evaporation which saturates the warm air overhanging the basin. The warm air thus laden with moisture rising to the edge of Table Mountain meets with the prevalent cold south-east wind, which immediately condenses it into a cloud. Then it hangs suspended above the mountain, and is then called the table-cloth. Sometimes it is precipitated on the ridge in the shape of dew or rain, and thus forms a stream of cool water for the inhabitants of Cape Town."

The table-cloth growing thicker and thicker, Mr. Henley gave the necessary orders to prepare for the coming gale. Everything was made snug on board the *Orion;* the topmasts were struck, and fresh cables were laid out.

The people on board several vessels did not take the precautions we did in time, and were consequently exposed to great risk of driving from their anchors. Had they done so they would not only have been lost themselves, but would have damaged, if not destroyed, any other craft against which they might have run. The boatmen in Table Bay have, however, fine boats, and are gallant fellows, and in spite of the heavy sea which came rolling in, brought out additional cables and anchors to the assistance of those who required them. I will not describe the gale further than to say that it blew terrifically, and that I was very thankful that our cables held; for had they parted, I felt sure the stout ship would immediately have been dashed to pieces on the rocks, and not one of us would have escaped.

As soon as the gale was over the captain came on board. He appeared quite a different man to what he had been during the voyage. He was quiet, and kind, and gentlemanly in his manner. Several merchants accompanied him from the shore, and he seemed to be on excellent terms with them.

I told Mr. Henley that I hoped things would improve on board.

He shook his head. "All is not gold that glitters. He was much the same when he first took command. Wait till we are out of sight of land before we begin to congratulate ourselves."

Mr. Henley had doubted whether, should Mr. Grimes return, he would remain in the ship. The first mate had pretended to be ill as soon as we arrived, and had gone into hospital. However, directly after Captain Gunnell appeared so did he. He too seemed changed, and was very polite to all the officers, and quite mild in his manner. Though the second mate had little confidence in him, he still made up his mind, greatly to my satisfaction, to remain in the ship. His prognostications proved too true. By the time we had been three days at sea, the captain began to resume his bad habits, and of course the mate followed his example. The voyage was comparatively short, so they took care not to lose their senses altogether, and were tolerably sober when we came in sight of the Mauritius.

I had never seen anything more beautiful than the scenery of Port Louis harbour. High above the town rises La Pouce, or the thumb mountain, clothed with trees to its very top. It forms one of an amphitheatre of queer-shaped mountains, at the foot of which nestles comfortably the capital of the island. To the left, seen over a range of hills, rises "Pieter Bot," a mountain so called from a Dutchman who, in a spirit of adventure or pot valour, attempted to ascend its summit, and was dashed to pieces. The compliment paid him was of a doubtful character, as "Bot" means silly, a *sobriquet* he obtained probably in consequence of his failure. Some English officers, cleverer than silly Pieter, by means of a line thrown over the summit, by which a ladder was drawn up, managed to reach it, and moreover, to the great disgust of the French inhabitants, to place the Union Jack there. The difficulty of the feat exists in consequence of the upper portion overhanging that immediately below it, as a man's head does his neck. I had been reading the account of the ascent in a book I had with me, and therefore looked at silly Pieter with considerable interest, and thought how much I should like also to get to the top of his pate. The harbour is small, and the entrance is defended by heavy batteries. As we sailed in, with the pretty little town before us, and the finger-like mountains rising in a semicircle behind it, we had on our right the mountain of Morne Fortunée, where is the signal station at which the famous ship-seer, who could see ships nearly a hundred miles off, was stationed. He saw them, it was supposed, reflected in the clouds. When the island belonged to the French, he used to give notice in the war time of the whereabouts of the English cruisers.

As I stood on the deck watching the shore, my heart beat with anxiety to get there, that I might visit my grandfather, and commence my inquiries for Alfred. I had little expectation of being able to accomplish my wish. I went, however, to the captain, expecting to be told that the duties of the ship required my attendance on board. What was my surprise, therefore, to find him bland and courteous in the extreme.

"You wish to pay a visit to your grandfather, Mr. Coventry, you say?" answered the captain; "certainly, Mr. Marsden— certainly. Give my compliments to him. I have the pleasure of his acquaintance, and I conclude that he has not forgotten me. And hark you, Mr. Marsden, you will not allow anything which has occurred on board here to transpire: we shall be very good friends if we keep council, but if not, the consequences will be disagreeable."

I scarcely knew what answer to make to this observation. I felt how low a man must have fallen to find it necessary to speak thus. I considered a moment, and then answered boldly,—

"Unless I am specially questioned, I will say nothing about the matter. If, however, I am asked the particulars of what has occurred, I will not refuse to reply; for, should I do so, I

PORT LOUIS.

should probably myself be looked on as having taken part in the mutiny."

"No fear of that. I must trust to you," he answered. "But mark me, Mr. Marsden; you will find that I am a firm friend, but I can be a bitter enemy."

"I hope I shall not lose your friendship, sir," I answered, hurrying away, and shocked that a man who professed to be a Christian could give expression to so dreadful a sentiment.

I was glad to find that Dr. Cuff was going on shore; so he and I and Solon set off together. We landed on the beach in front of the town, amid swarms of black men entirely naked, with the exception of a blue cotton handkerchief tightly fastened round their thighs. However, their colour in a degree answers the purpose of dress. As we walked through the town we thought it a very pretty place. None of the houses are crowded together, while most of them stand in a small garden, amid a profusion of trees and flowers; and even in the streets we observed growing luxuriantly the banana, the bread fruit, the palm, and other tropical trees and shrubs. The most conspicuous building is Government House, with a broad verandah running round it; but it has no pretensions to architectural beauty. Behind the city is the Champ de Mars, a small level space, above which, on three sides, rise the rugged, curious shaped hills we had seen from the harbour. The Champ de Mars is the race-course and the general resort of the inhabitants, and was, we were told, in days of yore the usual duelling-place. From all I saw and heard of the Mauritius, I believe it is one of the richest and most fertile of the British insular possessions. Yet, to garrison it and defend it from our enemies, not an entire regiment is to be found in the whole island, while the French have in the island of Réunion, formerly called Bourbon, a force of not less than six thousand men, ready to take advantage of any dispute which may occur between the two countries, and to pounce down upon the Mauritius once more, to make it what the French still call it —an isle of France. The blacks from Mozambique, we were told, do all the rough and dirty work in the city, such as dragging the sugar casks down to the quays, and loading the vessels. They seemed a merry set; and Dr. Cuff and I could not help stopping to watch some of them, as they met each other, indulging in their hearty laughs, one with a cocked hat and feather on his head, and another with a round hat which even an Irish carman might decline to wear. What their jokes were about it was impossible to tell. One would say something, and then the other would answer him, and both would burst into the most absurdly noisy roar, turning back to back to support each other, then clinging together, rising, and falling, and twisting, and turning, and finally rolling over on the ground, as if completely overcome. It seemed a matter of constant occurrence, for no one stopped even to take notice of these strange performances. I know that I felt inclined to burst into laughter too, either for very sympathy, or on account of the ridiculousness of the scene.

My grandfather's estate was, I found, about fifteen miles from Port Louis. The people at the hotel said they knew him, but that they had not seen him for months. However, that was not extraordinary, as he often went a whole year without coming into the city. I asked the doctor to accompany me, which, as he was anxious to see the island, he consented to do. We hired two horses, and a black man who was to act as our guide, take care of our steeds, and carry our luggage. This consisted chiefly of a change of linen and trousers, which the doctor put into a tin case, to preserve the things from the attacks of the numerous insects in the island, who would quickly eat them up. Solon followed us on foot. Our guide carried in his hand a piece of sugar-cane about six feet long, which served him as a walking-stick, while at the same time he amused himself and kept away hunger by chewing the upper end. Shorter and shorter grew the stick, until he had eaten it down till it was scarcely three feet in length.

"I suppose we have got through more than half our journey, for see, blackie has eaten up the best part of his cane," said the doctor; but he was mistaken, for our sable guide knew that he could get another at any estate we passed, and soon sucked up his first walking-stick.

We found that we were passing the village of Pamplemousses, close to which is an estate where, we heard, are to be seen the tombs of Paul and Virginia, whose history, written by St. Pierre, I had read. Not a moment had I ever doubted the truth of their history; still, not being sentimentally disposed, I had no great wish to visit their graves, especially as I was in a hurry to hear of Alfred. Our guide, however, had no notion of our passing a spot which everybody visited, without paying it our respects; so, before we were aware of it, we found ourselves standing before two pretty urns in a garden of roses.

"And so here sleep at rest poor Paul and his devoted Virginia," said I, with a sigh; for I was beginning to feel sentimental.

"Fiddlestick!" answered the doctor, laughing. "The *St. Geran* was, I believe, wrecked hereabouts, and some of her passengers were drowned; but whether there was a Paul or a Virginia on board, I cannot say. Certainly the French author had no other foundation for his tale than the mere wreck of a ship of that name; and as the language is good, and the moral is less exceptionable than that of most French tales, it is put into the hands of most young people beginning to learn French, and has thus become universally known."

I felt almost vexed to find that two such people as Paul and

PAUL AND VIRGINIA'S TOMBS.

Virginia never really did exist, till the doctor laughed me back into my usual state of mind.

"Fictitious sentiment I cannot abide," he observed. "There is quite enough of real sorrow and suffering in the world to excite our sympathies; and if we employ them on fiction, we are very apt to exhaust them before they can be employed to some useful end."

The scenery at the foot of Pieter Bot is very fine, as, indeed, was all we passed through. It was only towards the evening that we reached my grandfather's estate of Eau Douce, or Sweet Water, as he called it. How my heart beat as our guide pointed out the house, a single-storied building with a wide verandah round it, standing in a garden filled with trees and shrubs of the most luxuriant growth, and of every variety of shape and colour.

"Can Alfred himself be here?" I thought, as I eagerly jumped off my horse, and letting our negro guide take the reins, ran up the steps to the front door. The doctor followed slowly. Though the door was open, I did not like to go in. I waited and waited, and rang two or three times, and no one came. At last I heard a shuffling in the passage, and an old black man, dressed in a white shirt and trousers and yellow slippers, made his appearance. In broken English, with a French accent, he asked me what I wanted. I told him.

"Oh, Master Coventry! He gone away—no come back for one year, two years, or more," he replied, with a grin.

I asked him if he knew where Mr. Coventry was gone. His notions of geography were limited; he could not tell. I felt very dispirited.

"But I am his grandson. Is there no one here who can tell me about him?" I exclaimed.

The negro looked at me hard. "Oh yes, there is Mr. Ricama, the steward; he will tell you all about the master," he answered. "Come in, gentlemen, come in."

The doctor said, however, that he would prefer waiting under the shade of the balcony till invited to enter by the officer in command. I accordingly followed the old black, who showed me into a cool sitting-room, the floors covered with matting, and furnished with cane-bottomed sofas and marble tables, the windows opening to the ground looking out on the sea, whence a delicious breeze came blowing freshly in. In a short time a tall, dark-skinned man, in a light calico dress, and with straw hat in hand, came into the room. He bowed as he entered, and advanced towards me.

"I am the overseer here left in charge by Mr. Coventry, whose grandson I understand you are," he said in very good

English. "I shall be glad to do everything you may wish which is in my power."

"Thank you," I answered. "First, then, tell me where Mr. Coventry is; I am most anxious to see him."

"That is a very difficult question to answer," he replied. "I can tell you where he was when I last heard from him; but where he now is I cannot say, and where he may be in another month no man can tell."

"Where was he then?" I asked eagerly.

"In Ceylon. He purposed remaining some time there, but many months have passed since I last heard of him," was the answer I received.

Here again was a bitter disappointment. If my grandfather was away, still less likely was I to hear of Alfred. The next question I put to the overseer was about him.

"Yes, a young midshipman had been to visit Mr. Coventry, belonging to a ship in Port Louis harbour. He had come once again without his uniform, when he seemed very sad and unhappy. Mr. Coventry had spoken kindly to him, and had given him assistance." What had become of him afterwards, the overseer could not say positively. He had an idea, however, that he had been sent to Ceylon, where Mr. Coventry had an estate. That he was not aware if Mr. Coventry had again heard of him; but he seemed little troubled by this, as he, Mr. Coventry, was himself so eccentric in his movements, and so seldom wrote letters, that he could not be surprised at others altering their plans, or at not writing to him.

This was the sum total of the information I obtained from the overseer. It was altogether far from satisfactory. I felt sure that Alfred, after having been kindly treated by our grandfather, would not have failed, had he possessed the power, to communicate with him. Still it was possible, as Dr. Cuff reminded me, that he might have done so without the overseer knowing anything about the matter. The moment the overseer heard that Dr. Cuff was with me, he went out and brought him in, insisting on our making ourselves perfectly at home.

"Pray, do not thank me," he observed; "I feel that I am but doing my simple duty in treating you with all the attention in my power."

There was something particularly pleasing and attractive about the overseer. From his colour, he was evidently a native of the East, but he spoke English well, though with a foreign accent. He was, as the doctor called him, one of nature's gentlemen. In the course of conversation we learned that his name was Ricama—that he was a native of Madagascar, and had at an early age been converted, as were many of his countrymen, to Christianity. He had come over with his father to the Mauritius in charge of cattle, dressed, as he said, in a long piece of yellow grass matting with green stripes wound round his body, with the end thrown over his left shoulder and hanging down at his back. His hair was long, and fastened up in large bunches about his head. Persecution against the Christians in Madagascar having arisen, he had remained in the island, but his father had returned, and with many other Christians had been put to death. Ricama had before that time entered the service of Mr. Coventry, who, appreciating his high principles and honesty, raised him to the highest office of trust he had to bestow. From all I saw and heard, the overseer was well worthy of the confidence placed in him. A very tempting repast was soon prepared for us, to which we were well inclined to do ample justice. At first Ricama would not sit at table with us, but we entreated him to do so, nor could the most polished Englishman have behaved in a more appropriate manner. He was perfectly free and unembarrassed in his conversation, and gave us a great deal of information about the island.

MR. COVENTRY'S GARDEN.

Before it grew dark we took a turn in the garden, where he showed us the Indian rubber tree, the tea plant, and many other trees and plants which Mr. Coventry had wished to cultivate. With regard to the Indian rubber tree, the doctor said that it was only one of many trees producing caoutchouc —the *Ficus elastica*, I believe. To produce it the tree is, during the rainy season, pierced, when a yellowish-white coloured and thickish juice runs out into the vessels prepared to receive it. If kept in a corked air-tight bottle, it will remain liquid and retain its light colour for some time. Heat coagulates it, and separates the juice from the Indian rubber. If exposed to the air in thin films, it soon dries. In this way it is prepared for exportation :—lumps of clay, generally in the shape of bottles, are spread over with successive coats, and to hasten the process dried over fires, the smoke from which gives the black colour which it generally possesses at home. The marks we see on the Indian rubber bottles we buy are produced by the end of a stick before they are quite dry.

"How wonderful are the ways with which Nature supplies our wants!" observed the doctor. "Not only do trees give us fruit in every variety of shape, consistency, and flavour, but even their juices minister to our gratification. How many valuable gums do they exude! The maple-tree of North America gives excellent sugar, and certainly the discovery of caoutchouc has added very much to our comfort and convenience. Just think of the number of elastic articles, the waterproof dresses, the piping, and even the boats which are made with it."

Ricama assisted us to pick some leaves from the tea plants, with which, in their raw state, we afterwards made an infusion, and we found it differ little from ordinary tea, except that it possessed a richer aromatic flavour and scent.

Ricama told us that great numbers of his countrymen came over to the Mauritius, and among others the son of the famous King Radama had been sent to learn various useful trades. As his majesty had considered that the first step towards civilizing his subjects was to have them dressed, he had requested that his son might learn the trade of a tailor. The young prince, however, was said not to have taken very kindly to the goose, and had soon returned.

Among other trees were guavas, bananas, mangoes, breadfruit palms, and two or three fern-trees. The leaves of the latter are in shape like those of the English fern, but of gigantic proportions, and grow on the top of a stem thirty feet in height.

SUGAR CANES.

The sugar-cane is the chief cultivated production of the island on all the more level parts. The fields are surrounded with pine-apple plants; the fruit is, therefore, so abundant that the pines are sold for a penny a-piece. A small insect had, however, lately attacked the sugar-canes, eating their way into them and destroying them utterly. Though fresh canes had been introduced, they had suffered in the same way. The proprietors, like those of Madeira, had therefore lately taken to cultivating the mulberry tree to feed silk-worms. The overseer entreated that we would remain at the estate as long as we could. I had got leave to be away from the ship for a week, and the doctor said that he need not return for some days. Could I have forgotten my disappointment in not meeting with Alfred and our grandfather, I should have considered those some of the most delightful days in my existence. Yet we did little but converse with Ricama and go about the estate, with short trips into some of the wilder regions of the island, and examine and hear about the trees, and shrubs, and fruits, and flowers, and animals, and insects, and reptiles of the country.

On desiring to be shown our bed-rooms, on the first night of our arrival, the overseer, to our surprise, conducted us out into the garden. Here we had observed a dozen or more little pavilions, with windows opening nearly all the way round, so that from whatever direction the wind came, it could find a passage through them. Some light gauze curtains, an iron bed-stead, a table and chair, with a tin box, constituted the furniture of these temples dedicated to Morpheus. The tin box was, I found, to hold my clothes; for though the ants and other insects might not carry them off bodily during the night, they were likely to inflict much mischief on them in a short space of time.

The white ants of the Mauritius generally build their nests in trees, where one of them looks like a huge excrescence of the stem. Numerous covered ways approach it along the branches and up the trunk. Not a single insect is seen, though thousands may be employed in bringing to this castle the produce of the tree or the booty they have collected from the neighbouring country. They have a pale, long-buried look, caused probably from living so entirely in the dark. When attacking a house, they run a tunnel with wonderful expedition through the floor and up a wall, always taking care to have a case of some sort to work in. If anything particularly tempting to their appetites is discovered, they immediately branch off to it, and if it is inside a wooden box, or chest of drawers, or bureau, they take up their abode in the interior till they have completely gutted it. They think nothing of eating up a library of books, or cutting out the whole interior of the legs of tables and chairs, so that, should a stout gentleman sit down on one of them, he would be instantly floored.

I saw the negro servant who attended me to my bower hunting about in every direction. I asked him what he was looking for.

" Scorpions, master," was his answer.

Presently he produced from a corner, holding it by the head, what looked like a spider with a very long tail, which latter adornment was curled up over his back like that of a squirrel. He put it down close to the table, when down came its tail with considerable force. He showed me a sort of claw in the tail, through which the poison, which lies in a bag at the bottom of it, is projected. I called to the doctor, whose house was within hail of mine, to come and look at it. He told me that it belonged to the class *Arachnida*. It had two claws and eight legs, or stigmata, with a very long tail. He laughed at the common notion that the scorpion will sting itself to death when surrounded by fire, and showed how that would be impossible, as he has no muscular power to drive his sting through his breast-plate, nor could he do much more, when curling it up, than tickle his back with it. He cannot even twist his tail to strike, so that the only dangerous point on which to assail him is his rear.

Cockroaches, of course, abound. They are frequently destroyed by a peculiar sort of large fly, the female of which lays her eggs in them while they are alive, the larvæ afterwards eating them up.

The prettiest little creatures I saw were lizards, which ran quite tame about the house in search of flies, their usual food. Their feet are furnished with a pneumatic apparatus like those of the house fly, by which means they are able to run along the ceiling, or even any surface as smooth as a mirror. They are of a whity-brown colour. I watched one of them shuffling along with an awkward gait, consequent on the peculiar formation of his feet. When about two inches from a fly, out he darted his tongue, and it had disappeared.

The most curious insect I saw was the leaf-fly, the wings of which so exactly resemble the leaf on which it feeds that it is impossible to distinguish them from it. It is said that if a number are put into a box without food, they will eat up each other's wings.

I heard of deer and wild boars, and saw plenty of monkeys. They are of a small size. They are here rapacious and cunning as usual. It is said that a large number will concert to rob a plantation, and forming a line, will pass the fruit from hand to hand till it is deposited safe in their mountain fastnesses. I doubt, however, whether there is honour among such thieves, and I suspect that those at the home end of the line would in most instances get the lion's portion.

I did not see many birds; indeed the island does not boast of any large number, though the dodo once inhabited it, and perhaps still exists among some of the thick jungles in the interior, into which no human being has as yet penetrated. The only songster is called a martin. He is somewhat larger than a blackbird, and pied like a magpie. He is a lively, chattering fellow, very good-looking into the bargain, and, from his sociable qualities, a great favourite with everybody. There are several species of amadavides, or love birds, of the finch tribe, with red beaks, which, as they live on seeds, are easily kept. Had I been going home, I should have liked to

MONKEYS ROBBING A PLANTATION.

have taken some with me. The most conspicuous bird is the cardinal, though scarcely larger than a bullfinch, as his bright scarlet plumage is seen flitting about amid the dark green jungle. But I might fill my pages with descriptions of the various wonderful things I saw and heard about, and have no space left to give an account of my own adventures.

I awoke cool and refreshed the morning after our hot ride,

and had a delicious bath in a stream which ran close to the garden. Solon sat by the pool watching my proceedings, and evidently ready to lay hold of any noxious creature which might come to interfere with me. He seemed very glad when I was out again, and bounded back with me to my bower, where I went to finish my toilet. The overseer was ready to receive us at breakfast. It consisted of bread in various forms, rice, and every variety of fruit, with tea, and coffee, and cocoa.

"Some English gentlemen take all sorts of hot and exciting dishes, as well as strong beverages," observed Ricama, "but Mr. Coventry never takes them himself, and never gives them to his guests. I have followed his custom, and let me assure you that, especially in a hot climate, it is a very wise one. Depend upon it, Europeans would not suffer nearly so much from hot climates if they would but alter their mode of living to suit them. Adhere to this plan while you are here, and you will at once perceive its advantage by the sound and refreshing sleep you will enjoy."

The doctor agreed with Ricama, and I ever afterwards, notwithstanding many temptations to act in a contrary way, strictly followed his advice, and most certainly benefited greatly by it. One day was spent very much like another, in going about the estate, seeing the labourers at work, and taking rides about the neighbourhood. We were obliged to keep on the beaten paths, for so dense a barrier did the masses of creepers form amid the boughs of all the trees, that a company of pioneers could alone have penetrated into the woods.

At the end of a week we took our departure to return to Port Louis. We were both much pleased with Ricama, and I felt a sincere friendship for him. He furnished me with letters to two friends of my grandfather's at the capital, as he thought they would be glad to be of assistance to me. They could tell me nothing about my brother, but they both thought it most probable that he had been sent to Ceylon. I was now only anxious once more to continue my voyage. I forgot the misconduct of the captain and first mate, and all the dangers to which, in consequence, all on board had been exposed, and was quite ready once more to trust myself at sea with them.

CHAPTER VIII.

Matters on board as bad as ever—The Mate's Cruelty to poor Tom—I Interfere—An Island in Sight—An Expedition on Shore to Catch Turtle—Coco de Mer—A Night on Shore—Where is the Ship?—We are Deserted—A Ship on Fire—Mr. Henley puts off to her Assistance—Tom and I left on the Island.

ONCE more we were upon the ocean, the tall finger-like peaks of the beautiful Mauritius fading from our sight. Captain Gunnel was as pleasant and kind in his manner as could be desired, the first mate as glum and surly as usual. It was curious to observe the sagacious manner in which Solon avoided him, as if perfectly well aware that if he got in his way a kick or a rope's end would be his inevitable portion.

For three or four days things went on somewhat quietly; we had fair winds and fine weather, and there was nothing to put any one out. Before long, however, some trifle caused the first mate to lose his temper, and he began ill-treating the men as before. He seemed inclined especially to vent his rage against Johnny Spratt.

The fat old fellow used to rub his sides, and, as usual, as he limped away from his tyrant, say, "Well, it's fortunate the bones are so thickly cased, or they'd have been broken every one on 'em before now."

He never made a reply to all the abuse showered on him; but this silence, instead of appeasing the mate's anger, only seemed to increase it. Poor Tommy Bigg, too, got more knocked about than ever. My blood used to boil as I saw the poor friendless little fellow kicked, and cuffed, and rope's-ended without mercy, day after day, and more than once I felt inclined to rush to his rescue, and to tell his tyrants what cruel brutes they were. In vain Mr. Henley expostulated with Mr. Grimes. He got only abused in return.

"Wait till you are kicked yourself and then cry out," was the answer.

Mr. Henley could make no reply to this remark, but walked quietly away. He took good care, however, that while he was on deck none of his inferiors should bully anybody; and I, to the best of my power, assisted him. I soon found that I had made mortal enemies of Sills and Broom, who had never liked me. Several times I reported them to Mr. Henley for striking the men and using foul language towards them. They called me a sneak and a tell-tale, and said that I was fitter for a nursery or a girls' boarding school than to come to sea. I said that I saw nothing sneaking in preventing men from being ill-treated, and reminded them of a proverb I had met with, "That curses, like pigeons, are sure to come home to roost at night."

"Hang your proverbs — what do you mean?" exclaimed Broom.

"That curses are sure to recoil on the heads of those who utter them," I answered. "I earnestly hope that the dreadful ones to which you have been giving expression may not overtake you; but remember, that though he may delay, God's arm is not shortened that he cannot strike."

"Now you have taken to quoting Scripture, you canting hypocrite," cried Sills. "Do you think we are afraid of any such thing happening to us? Our curses may come back for what we care."

"Oh, it's all humbug! Nothing you can say will make me hold my tongue," added Broom, with a hoarse laugh.

"In mercy to yourself do not say such things," I exclaimed, as I turned away from my two messmates.

Mr. Henley had warned me, when some days before I had observed that I hoped the captain had improved, that before long he would break out as bad as ever. Such in a few days I unhappily found to be the case. Not only did he become as bad, but worse than ever, and I heard Dr. Cuff tell Mr. Henley that he did not think that he could possibly survive such continued hard drinking. The first mate overheard the remark, which was made probably in kindness as a warning to him. It had in one respect the effect intended. He kept himself perfectly sober, and attended carefully to the navigation of the ship; but I could not help strongly suspecting that he was seized with the ambition of becoming captain, and of having to take the ship home. Mr. Henley and the doctor thought so likewise, for he at once assumed the airs of a master, and became more dictatorial and overbearing than ever.

There lay the wretched captain, unconscious, in his berth, and of course this man was virtually in command of the ship. One day, after we had been rather more than a week at sea, I had called Tommy Bigg aft, and was speaking to him, directing him to do something or other, when Mr. Grimes came up close to us.

"What do you do here?—go forward to your kennel, you young ——," he exclaimed, with an oath.

Tommy heard him, but his impulse was to wait till I had finished my sentence. This momentary delay so enraged the first mate, that he flew at the poor little fellow, knocked him down with his fist, and then began to kick him along the deck as if he had been a foot-ball.

"Coward! brute!" I exclaimed, gasping for breath; and losing all command of myself, I rushed in before Tommy. "Let alone the child—you'll kill him if you continue to treat him thus; if you do I will brand you as a murderer. Help! help! he is killing the boy."

My cries were heard throughout the ship. The first mate, as was to be expected, turned his fury upon me.

"Mutiny! mutiny!" he exclaimed, lifting up his fist to strike me.

He would have felled me to the deck, and I should have received the same treatment from which I had attempted to save Tommy Bigg, when his arm was seized by Mr. Henley, who had at that instant sprung on deck.

"What are you about, Grimes?" he exclaimed; this behaviour is unworthy of an officer. He is no mutineer. Anybody with feeling would have attempted to save that poor boy from your cruelty."

"I didn't doubt that you would have shoved in your officious interference at every opportunity," growled out the first mate, turning fiercely on Mr. Henley; "you'll find, however, before long, that you have interfered once too often, and that you have caught a Tartar."

"I am doing my duty as much towards you as towards others," said Mr. Henley calmly. "I entreat you, for your own sake as well as theirs, do not again strike the boys. You cannot tell what the consequences may be. We have had an example already on board this ship what men may be driven to do."

Mr. Grimes turned pale on hearing these words, partly from suppressed rage and partly from fear, I suspect, and giving a threatening look at me and Mr. Henley, walked aft. I felt sure that I had made the first mate my most bitter enemy, but I could not regret what I had done. Probably, had not Mr. Henley interfered at the moment he did, he would have declared me a mutineer, and had me put into irons.

We had unusually light winds, though fair, and nothing could be more pleasant than the weather; but there was every appearance of the passage being a long one.

Dr. Cuff, meantime, was doing his best to restore the captain to a state of consciousness, and after a time he once more made his appearance on deck. His temper was not improved; but the doctor had so far alarmed him by putting clearly before him the inevitable result of his intemperance, that he appeared more inclined than usual to remain sober.

"Our captain is the most miserable man on board the ship," observed Mr. Henley, as we saw him walking up and down on the poop, muttering to himself, and wildly waving his arms about. "He is suffering all the horrors of the drunkard deprived of the stimulants to which he has accustomed himself. Indescribable horrors—dreadful recollections of the past—fears of the present—anticipations of coming evil, not the less fearful because indefinite and uncertain! O Marsden, as you value your peace and happiness here and hereafter; avoid every temptation which may lead you to drink, and do your utmost to warn your friends and all you meet of the dangers of intemperance."

A day or two after this, when the sun arose, we found ourselves becalmed little more than a couple of miles from a small island, apparently about three or four miles in length, with trees and rocks, and a high conical hill rising up in the centre. There appeared some islets about it but a few hundred yards across, scarcely elevated above the level of the sea. When the captain and first mate came on deck they examined them narrowly with their telescopes, and were seen to talk together earnestly for some time. Breakfast was just over when the captain observed to Mr. Henley,—

"There are fine turtle to be got on these islands. Fresh meat would be a good thing for the people, who are getting sickly for want of it, and not a bad thing for us. What say you to taking a boat and trying to catch a few? There is Johnny Spratt and one or two other men well accustomed to the work. Take them with you. You'll have plenty of time; these calms often last many days."

The second mate said that he would be very happy to go, and instantly set about getting a boat ready.

"You'll like to go, Marsden," said the captain to me, in a good-natured tone of voice.

Of course it was just the thing I wished to do. I bethought me of taking my sketch-book with me; but I could not find it, and so I carried off the book in which I wrote my journal, as it would serve my purpose. As I went on deck I saw the first mate send Johnny Spratt and Tommy Bigg into the boat, but his doing so did not at the moment excite my suspicions.

"Come, shove off, lads," he sung out, looking over the side.

"Stay," said Mr. Henley, ascending on deck again, "I never go away in a boat without a compass, and provisions, and water. A fog may come on, or we may be benighted, or a breeze might spring up, and we might have some difficulty in getting on board again."

Mr. Grimes made no answer to this remark, but turned away whistling. Mr. Henley had, I found, put together a number of things, which were handed into the boat. I slung my spy-glass over my shoulder, and, thinking that I might get a good shot at some birds, filled my powder-flask and shot-belt, and rifle in hand, followed by Solon, stepped into the boat. I took one oar and Spratt another, and we had two black men whom the chief mate had observed were first-rate hands at turning turtles. Mr. Henley had brought the boat's masts and sails, because, as he observed, a breeze might spring up, and we might find them useful. As we pulled away from the *Orion* I could not help admiring her size and build, and regretting that she was not better commanded.

"There are many like her, and there will be, till young men intended for the sea are educated and brought up as gentlemen and Christians," observed Mr. Henley, divining my thoughts. "All I can hope is that before we leave Colombo Captain Seaforth will come out and take command. I wrote home from the Cape entreating him to do so."

This was good news, and the bare hope of having a change for the better on board put me in good spirits. I had never encountered any heat equal to what we were now enduring. The sea was as smooth as glass, and glittered like a sheet of polished silver; there was not a breath of air, and the sun was almost perpendicular. Oh, how hot it was!—the perspiration was running from every pore. The sight of some trees, however, on the islands we were approaching encouraged us to persevere, and we contemplated the satisfaction of enjoying their cool shade, and then a plunge in some quiet pool before we returned on board. But as we drew near we began to fear that our anticipations would be disappointed, for on every side appeared a line of surf beating against what Mr. Henley at once pronounced to be a coral bank.

"Still, there may be an opening which may lead to the island," he remarked. "We'll not give up till we have tried in every direction."

Accordingly, keeping at a little distance from the thin white line of surf, we continued pulling slowly round to the eastward of the island. The island had, I observed, a peak rising in the centre to a considerable elevation, and Mr. Henley remarked that it looked like the cone of a volcano. After pulling on for another half hour a space appeared where the water was as smooth and glassy as that on which we floated. We instantly pulled in towards it, and, passing between the end of the lines of surf, found ourselves in a small bay lined with pure white sand, and here and there dark rocks rising up among it, while cocoa nut and other palm-trees came almost close down to the water's edge. I had never seen a prettier or more romantic spot. Here and there along the shore we caught glimpses of other similar bays. Scarcely a ripple broke on the beach, so we ran the boat up on the sand, and jumped on shore. Not a sign of human beings or of inhabitants of any sort had we yet seen. Having hauled up the boat, we therefore proceeded without hesitation towards the summit of the peak, that we might enjoy a more extensive view of the surrounding scenery. There are two sorts of turtle found on the shores of the islands of these seas—the hawk-billed and the green turtle—Mr. Henley told me. From the former the tortoise-shell, so valuable for making combs and other articles, is taken; but the flesh is considered poisonous. The shell of the green turtle is of comparatively little value, but then the flesh is excellent, and it was this turtle we wished to catch. It, however, comes on shore to lay its eggs chiefly at night, while the hawk-bill lands in the day-time for that purpose. Had we known this we should have waited till the evening to pay our visit to the island. It was only when we asked the blacks why we saw no turtle that we ascertained the fact. Still, as there appeared every chance of the continuance of the calm, we agreed to wait till the evening that we might capture some of the green species. Both lay many hundred eggs, and deposit them in large holes which they make with their flappers in the sand. Having with the same implements covered up the eggs, they leave them to be hatched by the rays of the sun, which strike down with great force on the white sand; indeed, the heat I should have thought would have been enough to bake them. Probably the moisture coming through the sand prevents this, and keeps up a regular temperature. As we advanced we came to an open space, in which grew a clump of tall trees, which Mr. Henley looked at with much interest.

"I have seen such before at the Seychelles," he remarked. "We are about the latitude of those islands. These trees are some of the rare and celebrated coco de mer. See, they must be nearly a hundred feet high, and little more than twelve or thirteen inches in diameter. There is scarcely any difference in their size to the very top, where observe that curious crown of leaves, which has the fruit—the double cocoa-nut—inside it. If there was a breeze we should see the trees bending about like whips, of so flexible a nature is the stem."

We calculated that each leaf was upwards of twenty feet long, including the petioles or stalks. These are of strength sufficient to bear a person's weight. One of the blacks coming up made preparations to climb to the summit of one of the trees. First, he fastened a band round the stem, sufficiently large at the same time to admit his body; then, pressing his back against the band, he worked his way up to the top. Securing the band, he disappeared among the leaves. Presently he returned with a bundle tied round his neck, and quietly descended the stem as he had ascended, by means of the band. On reaching the ground he presented us with what looked like three young cocoa-nuts growing together. Sometimes I found that the fruit not only grows double, but triple, and even quadruple. We broke the shell, and found the fruit far superior to that of any cocoa-nut I had ever tasted, though resembling it in flavour: in appearance and consistency it was more like the ice in a pastry-cook's shop. We found it particularly refreshing, and there was enough to supply all our party. The black had brought also the germ of another fruit, and the crown of the trunk, which, like that of the true cabbage-tree, makes an excellent dish like asparagus. It bears flowers and fruit of all ages at the same time. The black showed us the rings on the stem, which were about four inches apart.

They are left by the leaves falling off as the palm grows; and as two leaves fall off every year, I conclude that they grow about eight inches in that time. The coco de mer is as useful as the more common cocoa-nut. With the leaves houses are thatched; the trunk serves for troughs and piping; with the leaves and fibres of the petiole baskets and brooms are made; from the fibrous bark rope called coir is manufactured—so are hats and baskets; a beverage is extracted from the sap; beautiful cups are made from the shell; oil is pressed from the fruit; and mattresses are stuffed with the fibre which surrounds the shell; even the farinacious matter contained in the stem is used as food, and is not a bad substitute for sago. Indeed, there is no end to the useful ways in which it may be employed.

We were not long in reaching the highest point in the island. This, Mr. Henley said, he had no doubt was the crater of a volcano which had long ceased to emit fire; for though here and there we discovered lava and ashes, the ground was almost entirely covered with a luxuriant vegetation. We had a view of the unbroken horizon on every side, with a number of little green gems of islands scattered over the blue shining ocean around us. Mr. Henley said he suspected that it was one of the islands which the French frequented during the wars of the first Napoleon, and where their privateers used to conceal themselves when they had to refit or refresh their crews to be again ready to go in search of our merchantmen. In the distance lay our ship with her sails hanging idly against her masts. There was not a sign of a breeze, so Mr. Henley determined to wait till the night in the hopes of catching some green turtle. We now returned to the beach where we lighted a fire and cooked some provisions, not forgetting our tree-cabbage, and most delicious we found it. After our dinner we wandered along the shore, admiring the beauty of the spot and the thin reefs of coral which surrounded it.

"To think that all that work has been produced by small insects, and, so to speak, out of nothing, is indeed wonderful," observed Mr. Henley as we strolled along together. "Do you know, Marsden, I have often thought that it is intended that we should learn from these coral reefs what great results are produced in the moral world by apparently small means, at the will of our almighty Creator. Sometimes, I daresay, the agents are conscious that they are working for a great end; sometimes—still oftener—perhaps not. It should encourage us to persevere when we are working in a good cause, though our progress may not be quicker than that of the coral insects. Yet see the result of their labours! In time these rocky islets may increase to a size sufficient to support a large population."

I understood what he meant, and fully agreed with him. We found a number of beautiful shells on the beach of every shape and size, most of them empty, so that any hermit crabs wandering about in search of a new home could easily suit themselves with a habitation.

We enjoyed also a bath in a pool surrounded by rocks, where the water was so clear that we could see to the bottom. I had proposed bathing in the open bay, but Mr. Henley said he would on no account venture to do so, as we could not tell what sharks there might be in the neighbourhood. He told me that he knew of so many instances where people had lost their lives from incautiously venturing in where sharks had seized on them, that he was always very careful where he bathed. I remembered his advice and followed it. Had I not done so, I believe that I should very soon have shared the fate of the unfortunate people he spoke of.

The time passed quickly away, and hunger at last made us turn our steps towards the spot where we had left the boat. We found that Johnny Spratt had got some water boiling to make tea, and Tommy Bigg had collected some shells, while the blacks had brought in some cocoa-nuts and several other tropical fruits and roots whose names I do not remember.

"Wait till turtle come, then plenty supper," they observed.

After supper, while the men smoked their pipes, Mr. Henley and I, followed by Solon, walked on to a rock from which we could watch the proceedings in the next bay, which more directly faced the opening in the reefs. We had not long to wait before we observed some black objects slowly emerging from the water and crawling up the beach. We at once guessed that they were turtle, and not knowing how long they might be occupied on shore we hurried back to call the blacks to our assistance. Solon was for dashing in at them at once, and I had some little difficulty in restraining his impatience.

"Very good—no hurry—sure more come," was the answer of the blacks when I told them what we had seen.

However they got up, and all the party set off towards the rock where Mr. Henley and I had been watching. By the time we got there the entire line of beach from one side of the bay to the other was swarming with turtle. It was now growing so dark that they could only just be distinguished. Away we all ran armed with handspikes towards the shore. Our appearance did not seem to create any commotion among them. We watched the proceedings of the blacks. One of them seized a flapper, while the other insinuated his handspike under the animal, and by a sudden jerk turned her over. Mr. Henley and I, and Spratt and Bigg did the same, but we found that the blacks had turned three or four while we could scarcely get over some of the smaller ones. We had another companion who showed that he had no wish to be idle. As soon as we began the onslaught on the creatures Solon commenced an attack on them also. As he had no handspike to turn them over, all he could do was to lay hold of their flappers, and to try to hold them till we came up; many a severe knock on the nose, though, he got in the attempt as he flew

CATCHING TURTLE.

from one to another barking furiously. After some time I did not hear him, and on looking about I found that at last he had resolved to attempt to capture one entirely by himself. He had seized a good large turtle by the flapper, and was trying to haul it away from the water, which it was doing its best to reach. Now, as the turtle weighed nearly one hundred and fifty pounds, Solon would have had very little chance of victory if he had trusted only to his strength; so sometimes he would let go and leap round to the other side of the turtle, and would bite away at its flapper. This made it retreat once more up the beach. Solon, discovering the good effect of his tactics, would continue them till the turtle refused to go further, and then he would seize the former flapper and begin pulling away again. Though he stopped the turtle's way, still she made progress towards the ocean, and I doubt whether he would have let go till she had pulled him in. He was highly delighted when at last we went to his assistance and turned the turtle on her back. He still, however, seemed to consider it as his own especial property, and sat sentry over it, barking whenever it moved its flappers, as if he thought that it was going to get up and escape him. At length we had turned as many turtles as we would possibly require on board, or carry off; so we looked out for the ship, purposing at once to return to her. It had, however, now become very dark, and she was nowhere to be seen.

"Never mind, lads," observed Mr. Henley; "we will light a fire and make ourselves comfortable. They will see the light on board, and know that we are all right."

We did not want the fire to keep ourselves warm or to scare off wild beasts, as there were not likely to be any in that small island, but the smoke kept off the insects, and we hoped that our shipmates would understand, by seeing the fire continually blazing, that we were waiting till the morning to return on board. We sat round our fire talking and spinning yarns. Mr. Henley encouraged the men to speak of themselves, and to tell their adventures. Nothing so much induces the men to place confidence in their officers as to show them that an interest is taken in their welfare. The blacks told us how they had been kidnapped in their youth from the interior of Africa, carried down to the coast, confined in barracoons for some weeks till they were shipped on board a Spanish schooner. They pictured vividly the horrors of the middle passage, shut up in a hold three feet only between decks, where, with nearly four hundred of their fellow-creatures, they sat crouched up together as closely as they could be stowed for many weeks; how sickness got in among them and carried off great numbers, who were dragged out and thrown overboard as if they had been rotten sheep; how at last the schooner had been chased by a British cruiser and captured, and they had been carried to Sierra Leone and restored to liberty. There they had served in various vessels, both merchantmen and men-of-war, and had made several whaling voyages. The two had never been separated. Though not brothers by birth, they had become more than brothers— where one went there went the other. It was a strong proof that the gentler and purer affections are not excluded from the bosoms of the sons of Africa. Indeed, I suspect it is their very simplicity of mind and gentleness which make them so much more readily yield to the yoke of slavery than the white races. One went by the name of Jack, and the other Gill. When I asked them if these were their real names, they laughed and said no, but that they were as good as any others; they were not particular about names.

Though there was little chance of anything happening during the night, we agreed that one at a time should sit up and watch to give notice of danger. The atmosphere was far fresher than it had been, for a light breeze had sprung up, but as it was directly contrary to the course of the ship, it did not seem necessary to set off in the attempt to find her, especially as we could not possibly carry all the turtles we had caught in one trip. I took my watch in the first part of the time. The early part of the night, it must be remembered, we were employed in turning the turtles, so that it was past midnight before we lay down. I was kept awake by having continually to throw dry leaves on the fire to keep up a smoke; but even had it been otherwise, the beauty and strangeness of the scene would have kept me awake. Still, the moment I was relieved and put my head on the ground, I fell asleep with my faithful Solon by my side. I knew that he would keep a careful watch over me.

I awoke by hearing Johnny Spratt exclaim—

"Where can she be?"

It was broad daylight. I jumped up and looked about me. All the party were gazing seaward in the direction where the ship should have been. Not a glimpse of her was to be seen!

"They cannot have deserted us," said Mr. Henley to himself, as he led the way towards the peak to which we all instinctively directed our steps.

We hurriedly climbed to the top of it, then cast our eyes round in every direction. There was a speck in the horizon to the southward, but only a speck. There was no doubt that it was a sail. It might have been the *Orion*, considering the direction of the breeze which had been blowing all night; it was the point she would most likely have attained had she made sail the instant darkness set in. It became too evident that we had been intentionally deserted, for there was not the slightest necessity for her quitting the neighbourhood of the island. Strange and almost overwhelming were the feelings we experienced.

"What is to be done, sir?" I asked of Mr. Henley. "Shall we try to overtake her in the boat?"

"That would be utterly hopeless," he answered. "That was the reason Grimes pressed me to take the pinnace. Her planks are rotten, and she was scarcely fit even to pull the short distance we came in her, much less is she capable of carrying us safely away from this."

This was very evident, for we had had constantly to bale her out on coming from the ship to the island. The feelings of all the party can better be imagined than described when we were convinced that we had been thus purposely and cruelly deserted, and that until some vessel should come off the island, or we could contrive to build one capable of navigating the Indian seas, we should have to remain where we were. Months or even years might pass before we could get away. Our chief hope was that Dr. Cuff would give information at Colombo of our having been left on the island, and that a vessel might be sent for us, though, of course, Captain Gunnel and the first mate would try to persuade him that the boat was lost, or that we had deserted. None of the party, however, were inclined to despair. As soon as Mr. Henley had got over his first sensations of indignation, he did his best to keep up our spirits. Having breakfasted, the first thing we did was to haul up the boat to examine her thoroughly.

"It will never do to venture to sea in her," said Mr. Henley, and Johnny Spratt agreed with him. "She would answer, however, to form the centre of a raft, on which, if strongly put together, we might venture to sail for some port in India or Ceylon."

These and similar remarks cheered us more than anything. There is nothing like action or anticipation of active work for keeping up the spirits. We dragged the boat still further up the beach, and covered her completely over with branches of palm and other broad-leaved trees, so as to save her from being yet more destroyed by the heat of the sun. We then set to work and built ourselves two huts for sleeping in, and a shed which served us as a mess-room, open on every side. Mr. Henley and I intended to occupy one of the huts and the crew the other. We had found a pure, abundant stream of water, so that we were in no way badly off.

On the possibility of the ship having merely stood off for the night, and having been becalmed and unable to get back in the evening, we again ascended to the peak to look for her. Curiously enough, there was the same speck in the horizon which we had observed in the morning. There had been all day but a slight breeze on the island, and as the sea in the direction of the sail looked especially calm, it was very probable that she lay becalmed where we had first seen her. If so, we might, had we pulled off at once, very probably have got on board her. Still, we could scarcely blame ourselves for not sailing after her; for had the breeze again caught her, she would have gone away and left us in the lurch. Yet it must be owned that it was very tantalizing to see our ship still in sight; for we did not suppose that, had we got up to her, Captain Gunnel would have ventured to refuse to admit us on board. He would probably have tried to turn the tables on us, and have abused us for remaining so long away from the ship.

In a short time the whole party were assembled on the peak. There we all stood, forgetful of everything else, gazing at the far distant sail. The sun went down, and for a few minutes we could almost distinguish the outlines of her loftier sails as they rose above the water clearly defined against the bright sky. The darkness came rushing on with a rapidity unknown in northern climes, and shrouded her from our sight. Mr. Henley had before this been examining a pocket compass.

"Lads," he said suddenly, "I have taken the bearings of that sail. She may be the *Orion* or she may not—will you make the attempt to get on board her? I warn you that I believe there is great risk in doing so. Our only hope will be that the calm may continue, and that we may be able to get on board before a breeze spring up or before we are discovered."

The men unanimously declared that they were ready to do exactly what he wished.

"Well, then, we will make the attempt," he exclaimed. "But what is that? What can be that red glare over where we just saw the ship?"

SHIP ON FIRE.

"She is on fire, sir," answered Spratt, after attentively watching the point indicated. She's not the first ship I've seen burning at sea, and I know for certain that is one. She may be the *Orion*, or she may be some other unfortunate craft, that I can't say."

"Whatever may be the case, we must go to her assistance," exclaimed Mr. Henley. "We may be able to save some of the poor fellows clinging on to part of the wreck or to a raft, and we will bring them back to the island."

"Gladly," said I; "we have no time to lose."

"No, Marsden," he answered; "I have made up my mind what to do. It will not do to have more in the boat than is absolutely necessary, and I intend to leave you and Tommy Bigg and your dog behind. I would leave one of the black men, but they will not part from each other; and I wish to have Spratt with me. It is settled; say no more about it. Believe me, my dear Marsden, I am anxious to save you from unnecessary peril. If I survive I will come back, and if I am lost it will be better for you to have remained as I wish."

"I am sure that you desire what you believe to be the best for me," said I, warmly wringing his hand. "I'll do as you order me, though I wish that you had allowed me to go with you."

This conversation took place as we were hurriedly descending the mountain. We had some little difficulty, in our haste, in finding our way down to the beach. Putting some provisions and water into her, including some of the turtle we had cooked, we once more launched her, and then, with no small amount of sorrow and apprehension, I saw my companions pull out towards the passage through the reef, when they were soon lost to sight in the gloom of night. One of Mr. Henley's last charges to me had been to keep up a large fire all night, to enable him the better to steer his course, and also to find the island again. Indeed, that this might be done, he assured me, was another strong reason for his wishing me and Tommy to remain on the island.

As soon as we had lost sight of the boat, Tommy and Solon and I hurried back to the spot where it was agreed the fire should be lighted, and we soon had a magnificent one blazing away. It was on a rock free from dry grass, or bushes, or other combustible matter, or we should have run a great risk of setting the island on fire. The previous night our aim had been to collect leaves to create a smoke; now we wished to make as bright a flame as possible. We had no difficulty in collecting an abundance of dry sticks for this purpose. Solon looked on for some time at our proceedings, and then, apparently discovering our object, ran about till he found a good-sized branch, which, seizing hold of with his mouth, he dragged up to the fire; then, wagging his tail, he came up to me to show me what he had done. Great was his delight when I put it on the fire, and immediately off he set and brought up another. He seemed to consider light sticks, such as Tommy and I had been collecting, as beneath his notice. When he found that I did not put the next stick on the fire, he sat down to watch proceedings. When, however, I patted him on the head, and pointing to a distance, cried, " Go fetch more," away he went, and in a short time collected almost as much wood as Tommy and I had each of us done, so that he was really of great use.

" Solon is coming out," said I to Tommy; " I thought he would, but hitherto he has had few opportunities of exhibiting his sagacity and talents."

" Well, sir, I am certain as how Solon could speak if he had a better made tongue," observed Tommy. " Often and often I have sat by him, and I have talked to him, and he has opened his mouth and twisted and turned about his tongue and lips till he has all but spoke. More than once I have thought he was going to say something, but he never has yet."

I was very much inclined to be of Tommy's opinion, and often almost expected Solon to give expression to some wise sentiment worthy of his name. When our fire was well made up, I retired to a distance from it that I might look out for the burning ship. Though, from where I stood, her topgallant masts would not have been visible above the horizon in the day time, a bright glare, which lighted up the whole sky above where she was, showed me that she was burning still more fiercely than when we first discovered the fire. It made me fear that there was not a possibility of her escape. I was afraid, too, that Mr. Henley would have his long pull to no purpose. What would become then of the unfortunate people on board? Poor Dr. Cuff! I thought of him more than any one. He was a friend in whom I could place perfect confidence, and had so often been my companion that I thought more of his fate than of that of anybody else on board. While I stood watching the far-distant conflagration, I felt a stronger puff of wind on my cheek than had for some time been blowing. It rapidly increased, but it blew off the land. After I had waited some time till I thought I ought to go back to assist Tommy in keeping up the fire, the wind again fell. I had been longer away than I supposed, and I was obliged to set to work again to collect sticks—a more difficult task than it had first been, as we had to go to a greater distance beyond the light of the fire to find them. Solon now even surpassed us, for he was able to discover the dry sticks in the dark far better than we could. I could not help thinking at times of the risk we were running from venomous creatures, and more than once drew back my hand under the idea that I was about to catch hold of a snake. However, though I daresay we might have put many of them to flight, neither of us were bitten, and at length we were able once more to sit down before our fire and rest from our labours. We should have preferred a cooler situation, but it was more important to have the smoke to keep off the mosquitoes. I should have preferred a more intellectual companion than Tommy Bigg, but there was so much honest simplicity and good-nature about him, that I could not help feeling a regard for him. The night passed slowly by. I could not venture to go to sleep, though Tommy begged I would, promising to call me should our supply of sticks run short; but I felt the importance of keeping up the fire as long as it might serve as a beacon to our friends, and the further they were off the larger I was anxious to make it.

For some time I had been aware that the wind was again getting up. It continued to come in fitful gusts, but each of them grew stronger and stronger. I feared that a regular gale was coming on; and if it did, I knew that our boat must be exposed to very great danger. As morning approached I began anxiously to look out for the return of the boat. I got up over and over again, and walked to a distance to endeavour to see her through the gloom; and frequently I shouted in case Mr. Henley had landed at any other spot, to guide him to where we were. No one replied to my shouts; not a sign of the boat could I see.

The glow in the sky over the spot where we supposed the ship was burning had by this time much decreased in brilliancy. I stood earnestly watching it. Suddenly it burst out brighter than ever, extending far round on every part of the sky. While I was looking, wondering what next would happen, it as rapidly vanished, and not the faintest trace of the fire remained. I immediately surmised what had happened—the deck had been blown up, and the hull had sunk beneath the waves.

The gale now grew rapidly more and more furious, and the wind veered about till it blew directly on the shore. I went back once more to the fire.

"I am afraid, Tom, that Mr. Henley and the rest are in great danger," said I, as I sat down on a stone, and employed myself in throwing the sticks we had collected to feed the flames, and told him what I had seen. " I do not think that they could have reached the burning ship before the gale came; and as for those who might have escaped from her, I fear that there is not a chance of their escaping."

" I'm afraid not, sir, if they have only themselves to trust to," answered Tom, quietly looking up in my face. " But you know, sir, God can do everything."

" He can—he can," I answered warmly. " We will pray to him, Tom, and perhaps he may think fit to preserve our friends."

" Yes, sir; but we should pray for our enemies too," said Tom.

" You are right again, boy," I answered. " We will pray for them also."

And we two knelt down on the rock looking towards the wild, troubled sea, and offered up our humble though fervent prayers to the throne of Heaven, that He who could calm the waters of Gennesaret would preserve both our friends and those who had ill-treated us from the destruction which seemed to us inevitably to await them. I could not have prayed in the same way at home; and I little thought that the poor little insignificant ship-boy by my side could have prayed in the way he did. I firmly believe that earnest prayers are answered, though often in the world we do not discover how or when they are so. Still, we may depend on it, all that is right is done in God's own good time.

CHAPTER IX.

The Gale Increases—Fears for Mr. Henley's Safety—A Boat in Sight—Solon aids in Rescuing the Drowning Men—The Doctor Saved—His Illness—A Sail in Sight—Visit of a Slaver—Deserted by our Companions—Death of the Doctor—Tom and Solon on the Island—Our Comfort and Consolation.

THE morning came at last, wild and tempestuous as had been the night. As soon as the beacon-fire no longer required our attention, Tom and I, accompanied by Solon, set off to the peak to take a look round, that we might discover if Mr. Henley's boat was returning, or if any other boat or a raft might have escaped from the burning ship. In vain we cast our eyes on every side; a thick mist, caused by the driving spray, hung over the ocean, and had any floating thing been on it, would have completely hid it from our sight. Sad, indeed, we felt as we two stood on that high solitary peak rising up amid the Indian Ocean.

"I am afraid that they are all gone in," said Tommy after a long silence.

"I do not despair, Tom," I answered. "A raft would take a long time driving from where the ship was burned to the island. We will wait and see what happens. Perhaps we may get a better view from a lower point."

Accordingly we went down the hill, and walked along the high ground above the beach, looking out from every spot among the trees where we could get a clear sight of the sea. As the sun rose his rays penetrated through the mist, but still no boat could we see; there was nothing before us but dark, leaden waves, with white crests and sheets of foam blown like driving snow from off them. We returned, therefore, with sad hearts to the embers of the fire, where we cooked some turtle and drank some cocoa-nut milk for breakfast. Our hearts, I believe, were grateful that we had been preserved from the destruction which we believed had overtaken our companions. After recruiting our strength, we again climbed up to a high point in the neighbourhood, where we sat for a long time without speaking, watching the foaming ocean, with Solon crouching at our feet. Suddenly Solon sprung up, and looked seaward with his head and neck stretched out to the utmost. Tom and I gazed eagerly in the same direction. After looking for a little time I caught sight of a black spot amid the white crests of the waves. It seemed like a mere speck. I should have thought that it was merely a man's head or hat, or nothing larger than a cask. After searching about for some time I brought my glass to bear on it. It was a boat, and a large one; it seemed full of men. I could scarcely hope that it was Mr. Henley's. On she came. Some of the men appeared to be rowing, but there was a small sail set—a mere table-napkin it seemed. Still we had a prospect of having companions, and if the boat was as large as I fancied, we might be able to get away in her from the island. We hurried down to the beach. If Mr. Henley was in the boat he would make, we knew, for the opening in the reef; but if there were only strangers to the place we could not tell where they might steer for. We did our best, therefore, to make signs to them to keep for the opening, but our telegraphing was not, we feared, received or understood, for the boat ran on directly towards a part of the reef over which the sea was breaking with especial fury. We waved, we shouted, we made every sign we could possibly think of to warn the unhappy people of their danger. They could scarcely have seen us, much less could they have heard our voices amidst the wild turmoil of waters.

"O Tom, how dreadful!" I exclaimed. Now the boat was lifted up by the seas, now she was hid among the foaming

BOAT DASHED ON ROCKS.

surf. I scarcely think that those on board were aware of their danger.

In an instant more we saw that they would be on the reef. Down we rushed to the wreck. It was scarcely possible that the boat could wash over it. We reached the edge of the calmer water of the lagoon inside the reef, but even there the waves came rolling up with considerable force, sufficient, at all events, to carry us off our legs had we ventured within their power. We looked eagerly for the hapless boat. She might still be concealed by the masses of white surf which flew high up in the air. We looked in vain. At last we saw some dark objects tossed up and down among the breakers. Now one, now another was cast over the reef, but whether they were human beings or merely fragments of the wreck we could not at first tell. We watched—now we saw an arm lifted up, then a head emerged from the foam—there could be no longer any doubt about the matter. At last we could almost see the features of the unfortunate wretches. Had it even been smoother in the lagoon we had no means of going out to the assistance of our drowning fellow-creatures. Oh, how dreadful it was to see people thus perishing before our eyes and to be unable to assist them! Still we could not withdraw our gaze from the spot where we had last seen the boat. Presently a larger wave than any of the previous ones came rolling in. As it broke several pieces of the wreck seemed as it were to fall out of it. To one of them a human form was by some means secured, but whether it was that of a living or a dead person we could not tell. He appeared, at all events, to be making no effort to save himself. He was at first washed some way across the lagoon, and then carried swiftly back again. It became soon evident that if not already drowned he very soon would be, when Solon, who had been earnestly watching what was taking place, uttering a loud bark, plunged fearlessly into the waves, and swam boldly out towards him. The next wave again set him in. Solon with wonderful sagacity at that moment seized his arm, and directing his course towards the shore, brought him within our reach before the force of the wave had time to force him out again. Tom and I rushed in, and grasping his clothes, ran with him with all our might up the beach, and placed him beyond the power of the waves before the next rolled in on us.

"Why, it is Dr. Cuff!" exclaimed Tom.

So it was, indeed, but till that moment I had not observed the man's features. Now, as I looked at his pallid countenance, with a blue tinge over it, and saw that his eyes were closed and teeth clenched, I feared that he was indeed gone. We took off his neckcloth, and I bethought me of putting some of the hot white sand round his feet, and some on his stomach, which I rubbed gently, while Tom brought some grass and leaves, which we placed under his head. While we were thus employed Solon dashed again into the water, and we saw that he had seized another person who was clinging to an oar. We discovered a third also struggling in the waves. We waited till Solon had brought the person of whom he had now got hold within our reach, and then, leaving Dr. Cuff for a moment, we rushed down to his assistance. Solon, the moment he had given him into our charge, darted off to the relief of the other drowning men. We at once recognized the man he had now rescued as one of the crew of the *Orion*. We dragged him up out of the reach of the sea, and hurried back to resume our efforts to resuscitate Dr. Cuff, for the sailor, though unconscious, gave evident signs of life. While we were rubbing away at the doctor's body, every now and then looking to see if an eyelid moved, and feeling if his heart beat, we kept watching Solon's proceedings. Wearied by his previous exertions, he swam out to the struggling person, who was further off than the other two had been, and, waiting till he had ceased to fling his arms about, he seized him by the collar, and swam on towards the beach. The man seemed to float much lighter than had either of the other two, and the cause of this we discovered, when we got hold of him, to be owing to a life-buoy round his waist. He would, however, notwithstanding this, have been drowned, had not Solon gone to his assistance, and had we not been ready to drag him up the beach, for he was quite unconscious when we got hold of him, and unable to help himself. On looking at his face I discovered that he was my messmate Sills. Believing that he would soon recover without our help, we again returned to the doctor. We rubbed and rubbed away with the greatest energy, till Tom said he felt that there was some warmth coming back into the body. I felt the same, and this encouraged us to persevere, till at length, to our great joy, the doctor partly opened his eyes and looked up at us.

"He's alive! he's alive!" cried Tom, clapping his hands.

Then he set to work and rubbed away harder than ever. The doctor still remained unconscious, or, at all events, unable to speak, but yet we had great hopes that he was recovering. At last he sat up and looked about him, trying to recover his power of thinking, and to ascertain what had happened.

"Thank you, lads, thank you," were the first words he uttered; "I see what you have done for me. Now go and help those other two who have been saved. They will want your aid. I will come presently and assist you, when I am a little stronger. But, lads, where is Mr. Henley and the others who were left here with you?"

I did not like to agitate him by telling him that I feared they were lost, so I said that they were not on that part of the island.

We had some difficulty in recovering Sills and the seaman, but at length they came entirely to themselves. The seaman took all that had happened to him as a matter of course, but Sills seemed to be somewhat horrified when he found how narrowly he had himself escaped death, and that so many of his companions had lost their lives. When all the party were sufficiently recovered to walk, we set off for our huts, which were at no great distance. I felt very sad, for the doctor told me that they had seen nothing of Mr. Henley's boat, so that I feared she must have foundered without even reaching the *Orion*. He said that he fully believed the burning of the ship was a judgment on those who had deserted us. He had little doubt, from what afterwards transpired, that treachery was from the first intended us, though, ill as he thought of the captain and first mate, yet he could not, when he saw us leaving the ship, believe that they would be guilty of such an atrocity.

During the day they had abused us for not returning, though they did not propose to fire a gun, or to make any other signal to recall us; and when night came on the first mate observed that he concluded we should not attempt to come back till the morning, but that he would keep a bright look-out for us. This disarmed any suspicions which were rising in the doctor's mind, and he turned in, expecting to see us soon after daybreak. What, then, was his astonishment, on going on deck, to find the ship under all sail, standing away from the island, and to be told that we had not come back. The captain might have been a party to the act, but he was already perfectly tipsy, and could make no coherent remark; and when the first mate came on deck, he said that the ship had been driven off the island by a sudden squall, and that he had no doubt our boat had been swamped in attempting to come off. The doctor had in vain entreated him to beat back, and to send another boat on shore to ascertain our fate. He made all sorts of excuses, till at length when the island could no longer be seen the *Orion* was once more becalmed. The doctor said that he endeavoured to get a boat, and, in spite of the heat and the distance, offered to pull back to look for us; but the first mate refused, and at length grew perfectly furious on his persisting in making the offer. At dinner the first mate drank more wine and spirits even than usual, and towards the evening was in no better a condition than the captain.

At this juncture dense masses of smoke were seen to burst suddenly out of the captain's cabin. The crew, part of whom were below, and part lying about the decks nearly asleep, were hurriedly summoned to extinguish the flames, but they obeyed lazily. The third mate got completely bewildered, and gave nothing but contradictory orders, so that the fire had taken complete possession of the whole after-part of the ship before any strenuous efforts were made to extinguish it. The wretched captain was never seen again. It was impossible to get near his cabin. The first mate rushed out of his berth with horror depicted on his countenance, and, not knowing where he was going, fell headlong into the flames. Some few of the men exerted themselves to extinguish the fire, under the doctor's orders, but the greater number did nothing effectual, for want of being properly directed. At length he saw that there was no possible chance of saving the ship, and called all those he could get to obey him to lower a boat, that they might endeavour to preserve their lives. What was his dismay to find just then a heavy squall strike the ship; but her after-rigging being already burned, while her head sails were all set, she paid off before the wind. Away she flew. In what direction they were going no one could tell. To lower a boat with any chance of saving her from being swamped seemed now impossible, when suddenly the squall ceased. The opportunity was taken advantage of, the boat was lowered, and he with about a dozen more leaped into her. Before any others could follow some one in the bows cut her adrift, and she floated away from the ship. Dreadful were the despairing shrieks and cries of those who remained, and whom the flames were rapidly surrounding. No help could be rendered them. The boat lay rocking about on the troubled sea for some time, during which a mast and sail belonging to the dingy, and one oar,

LEAVING THE BURNING SHIP.

were found in her. The mast was stepped and the sail hoisted, and the gale once more commencing with far greater fury than before, away flew the boat over the foaming waves. Few if any could have remained alive on board the *Orion* after they had left her. Some thought that a boat or a raft had been launched, by which means the rest might have prolonged their lives.

The doctor concluded his account by saying that when morning came and he saw the distant line of breakers ahead, he had given up all hopes of their lives being saved; and when he had first opened his eyes on the sand, while Tom and I were by his side, he had not expected to find himself still an inhabitant of this world.

Solon ran alongside us and licked the doctor's hand, and seemed highly delighted at having been the means of saving him; and I believe that the doctor was very grateful to him for what he had done.

We soon had a fire lighted. I had a box of lucifers, and also a burning-glass. The latter no one should be without in those regions where the sun is always shining in the day, as a light can thus be instantly produced. Some turtle was quickly cooked, and the strength of all the party was much restored. After this they lay down, as did Tom and I, and we all went to sleep. It was evening before I awoke, when, accompanied by Solon, I went up to the rock to look out for Mr. Henley's boat. After sweeping my glass round in every direction, I returned, sick at heart, to our hut. Indeed, as I gazed over that stormy sea, I felt that there was but little chance of a frail boat such as she was escaping its fury. The doctor slept all the night, but I was sorry to find the next morning that he appeared weak and ill. He said that he felt he had received some severe injury from being dashed against the rocks. He could still walk about a little, though evidently with much pain.

For several days I observed no change either for the better or the worse on our kind doctor. He probably knew what was the matter with himself, and I suspect that his sufferings were aggravated by being aware of the medicines which might have benefited him, and having none to take. I sat and walked with the doctor for the greater part of each day. He could do little more, however, than stroll out on the beach and gaze with anxious eyes over the sea, in the hope of catching sight of some ship which might carry us away from our island. Tom and I at other times used to wander about and collect all the fruits, and roots, and leaves of every description which we thought were likely to prove wholesome for food, and when we brought them to him he was able to tell us which were the most nutritive, and to point out to us those which were poisonous. I thus discovered the very great advantage of possessing a thorough knowledge of botany, and wished that I had paid more attention to the subject before I left home. Strange as it may seem, the days passed away very rapidly. Tom and I had always an abundance of work with which to employ ourselves. The poor doctor could, indeed, do little for himself, and Sills and Brown would do nothing. I had tried at first to make a companion of Sills, but after the effect produced by his narrow escape had worn off, he became very much what he had been before, and as now there was nobody over him, he gave himself up to perfect idleness. He and Brown, whom he made his companion, found a leaf which, when dried, served the purpose of tobacco, and from that time they spent the greater part of every day in smoking and eating. I induced them now and then at night to get up and turn a turtle, which gave us fresh meat when we grew tired of our salted and dried provisions. They seemed to have no wish to leave the island.

"We have nothing to do and plenty to eat—what more do we want?" said Sills, throwing himself back on the grass, when one day I asked him to take his turn in looking out for any ships which might be passing. "For my part, I am ready to remain here till I want a new rig out; it will then be time enough to think of getting away."

I could make no reply to such a senseless answer.

In a short time, however, he and Brown got tired of their daily fare of turtle, and the latter proposed to try and get some fish. Though idle, Brown was not destitute of ingenuity. He first set to work, and out of some nails which he drew from a plank washed on shore, he manufactured several very good hooks, his chief tool being a file which he had in his knife. He soon, also, found several fibrous plants from which he made some strong, and yet fine lines. Among the things left by Mr. Henley was an axe: with this two trees were cut down, and a sort of double canoe, or rather raft, was constructed. The fan-like leaves of the palm served for paddles. Brown and Sills insisted on going off together, though Tom and I would have much liked to have accompanied them. They only proposed, however, to fish inside the reef. The doctor charged them, as they were shoving off, not to get carried outside, and to beware of being capsized, for fear of sharks. They laughed and said that they knew very well how to take care of themselves. We watched them paddling about, and at times, it seemed, catching a good many fish. At length they returned on shore.

"Well, you see, doctor, we were not capsized or eaten by sharks, notwithstanding all your prognostications!" exclaimed Sills as he jumped on shore.

"I am truly glad to find it," answered the doctor, examining the fish just caught; "but let me assure you, if you eat those fish, in a few hours hence it will make but little difference to you; they are without scales, and of a highly poisonous character."

"I don't believe that, doctor," answered Sills, with a foolish laugh. "Brown says he has eaten them a hundred times and not been the worse for them, so I'm not afraid."

"Brown may have eaten the same fish in other latitudes, or at different times of the year; but from my knowledge of them

I should advise you not to touch them, or at all events eat but a very small portion at a time, and see what effects it produces."

After this warning I could not have supposed it possible that Sills would have neglected to follow the doctor's advice; but in a short time I saw him and Brown light a fire, and proceed to cook the fish over it. We had manufactured some flour from one of the palms we had cut down, and with this and some salt they made a hearty meal. Having cooked a further supply they brought it to us.

"Come—nonsense, take some of this, old fellows," exclaimed Sills, holding out a toasted fish at the end of a stick. "We are not a bit the worse for it, you see;—it's very rich and luscious, let me tell you."

"I trust you are right, but wait a few hours; the effects are not likely to be immediate," answered the doctor gravely. He told me at the same time to boil some salt water, and to heat several large flat stones—the only remedies he could think of in his power to apply, should the fish prove poisonous.

Finding that none of us would eat any of the fish, Sills returned to Brown and sat smoking and talking for an hour or more. Some hours had passed after they had eaten the fish, when we saw Sills approaching the hut looking dreadfully ill, and scarcely able to crawl along.

"O doctor, doctor, I am dying—I know I am. I wish that I had done as you told me," he exclaimed in a feeble voice. "There is Brown, he is still worse; he ate more than I did, and was unable to come here."

On hearing this we dosed the poor fellow with hot salt water, and put the hot bricks to his stomach and feet, and then Tom and I ran on with our remedies and applied them to Brown, whom we found in dreadful pain, and looking as if he was dying. I believe both of them would have died had not the

salt water made them very sick, while the hot stones restored their suspended circulation. Still, I would advise no one to depend on such remedies under similar circumstances. They got better; but still for many days were subject to racking pains, and remained weak and ill. While they were in this state, one morning, as Tom and I were at the top of the peak taking our usual survey of the horizon, in the hopes of a vessel appearing in sight, we saw a white speck to the westward, the rays of the sun glancing brightly on it as it rose above the blue sea. At first I thought that it was a sea-fowl flying between us and the horizon; but, after a more steady look, I shouted—
"A sail! a sail!" There could be no doubt about it, but still I remembered that it might not come near us. However, I watched and watched anxiously, and it rose higher and higher above the horizon, and was evidently gliding on towards the island. When I had ascertained this to a certainty, I ran down with the good news to the doctor, for I thought that it would raise his spirits. He had been much depressed and rather worse, I feared, lately.

"She may touch here and relieve us, but we must not be too sanguine," he replied, with a faint smile. "I have ceased to hope for any improvement in my health or strength, and doubt if I should even survive a voyage."

By this remark I guessed how ill the doctor thought himself. I hoped, however, that from being out of spirits he might fancy himself even worse than he was. Again Tom and I went up to the peak. I was surprised to find how fast the stranger had come on. I made out that she was a large square top-sail schooner. On she stood, making directly, and evidently purposely, for the island.

"Could it be possible that Mr. Henley or any of the crew of the *Orion* have escaped and given information of our being left on the island?" I thought to myself.

With this feeling we could not help regarding the stranger as a friend. We waited, watching her till she got quite close, then heaving to, to leeward of the island, a boat was lowered from her side. On seeing this we ran down to the beach to welcome those coming on shore. They clearly knew the place, for they made directly for the opening in the reef. As I looked through my glass at them, they appeared to be a very rough set, exhibiting various coloured specimens of the race of man. I did in no way like their looks. As soon as the boat touched the beach they jumped out, and seemed very much surprised at seeing Tom and me. Much greater was mine, on regarding attentively the officer of the boat, to discover that he was no other than the pretended cobbler who had been a passenger on board the *Orion*. Any doubt I might have had was put to flight by seeing Solon run up to him and bark, as much as to say, "I have seen you before;" then he turned round and growled at two other men of the crew. This drew my attention towards them, and I soon recognized Cobb and Clink, two of the chief mutineers on board the ill-fated ship. They, of course, at once recognized us, and Mr. Barwell, or, as I found his people call him, Captain Hausleig, began to make inquiries about her. When I told him of the fate which had overtaken her, his reply was,—

"I thought so. A drunken captain and mate are pretty certain to lose their ship before long; my only surprise is that she got as far as this."

As we walked along to the huts, he told me what a fine craft he had got, and how successful he had been, but he did not say how she was employed. In the meantime the men who followed us had been talking to Tommy in the same strain. Sills and Brown were evidently well pleased at seeing them, and at once asked Captain Hansleig if he would take them off the island. This he said at once that he would do, if they chose to enter on board his craft, but that he could not undertake to carry passengers. They without hesitation accepted his offer, saying that they liked the look of his craft, and the roving commission which he had told them he held. The doctor received them very coldly, and seemed in no way pleased at their appearance. He seized the first moment that they were out of hearing to warn me against them.

"Depend on it, that if they are not pirates they are little better — slave carriers and men kidnappers," he said with an earnest tone. "Have nothing whatever to do with them."

Before he had time to say more they returned. I managed to whisper to Tom to reply that he would do just what the doctor and I did. As we expected, Captain Hansleig soon after turned to us and said,—

"I suppose, doctor, you and the lads will join us. I have a berth open for you, and for Marsden there, also; he shall be fourth mate soon if he is as attentive as he used to be on board the *Orion*."

"Thank you for your offer," answered Dr. Cuff; "I am too ill to do any duty, and prefer remaining where I am. Marsden and the boy must speak for themselves."

"Thank you for your offer," I answered bluntly, "but I have made up my mind to remain with Dr. Cuff, and I hope Tom Bigg will stay by me."

Captain Hansleig seemed somewhat annoyed at this reply. "Why, what do you think of me and my craft that you refuse to join us?" he asked.

"Provided a person does nothing to offend, really he cannot be called on to express his thoughts," observed the doctor. "It is enough to tell you that Marsden is anxious to reach Ceylon, and unless you are going there it is a sufficient reason surely for his declining to join your vessel."

Dr. Cuff spoke in so calm and yet so resolute a tone that the reply seemed fully to satisfy Captain Hansleig.

"Well, every man to his taste," he answered. "If you prefer living on in this desolate spot, I'll not force you away. Only I warn you that it is very little known, and very many months may pass before any other vessel may touch here. I happened to be in want of a supply of turtle, and cocoa-nuts, and fresh water, or I should not have come near the place."

I told him that I should abide by my first decision, and he did not press the matter further. The slaver traffickers, as the doctor called them, or pirates, as I suspect they also deserved to be called, spent a whole day and two nights on the island. The nights they employed in catching turtles—the days in carrying them on board, and in procuring cocoa-nuts. I observed that they made Sills and Brown work as hard as themselves, ill as they still were from the effects of the fish they had eaten. I doubted, indeed, whether either of them could recover, they looked so wretchedly ill when they went on board. We could, however, have done them no good had they remained; and though it was satisfactory to see them and their new associates take their departure, yet I could not help feeling a pang of regret as I saw the vessel once more spread her sails and stand away to the southward.

The doctor, Tom, and I, were thus left alone on that solitary isle. It soon also became evident to me that the former would soon be taken from us. He had long thought so himself. One day he called me to him, and begged me to write, on a blank page of the journal I had brought from the ship to use as a sketch-book, according to his dictation. I found that I was drawing up a short will, by which he bequeathed all his little property to some sisters in England, with his devoted love. He signed it, and Tom and I witnessed his signature.

There was no power of making his will more valid. By this I knew that he himself did not expect to live many days. He had been latterly spending his entire time in prayer and in giving good advice to Tom and me, and also in reading the Bible, a small copy of which he constantly carried in his pocket. He was a highly scientific man, and as a surgeon first rate; and he was, as I have found many such, at the same time a sincere Christian. I owe much to his counsels and exhortations; and if, as some may observe, a vein showing a mind turned to serious thoughts run through my journal, I am much indebted to him for it. Scarcely did I think as I was drawing out his simple will how soon that voice would cease to sound.

Tom and I slept in his hut, and one of us always kept awake that we might in a moment render him any assistance he might require. I had just been awoke by Tom, who whispered that he thought the doctor was worse. Just then we heard him in a feeble voice uttering a few words of prayer. He was silent. We thought he was asleep. For some time we waited, then we went to his side and took his hand. It was icy cold, and fell down again on the leafy couch we had formed for him. Then we knew that he was indeed gone from us. We both sat down and cried heartily. Daylight came, and we closed his glassy eyes. We knew that we must bury him soon. We dug his grave in the sand with bits of board, and having taken his watch and other things which he had about him, that we might deliver them to his friends should we ever reach home, we buried him in it, and then once more sat down and cried as before.

We, however, soon recollected nearly the last advice he gave us. It was to read some of the Bible every day we remained on the island, and never to give up the practice elsewhere as long as we lived. Not only did we read a chapter at a time, but we were reading it constantly and talking about it. In time it formed the chief—indeed, nearly the only subject of our conversation, and a most delightful one we found it. I certainly before that time could not have supposed that I could have become so deeply interested in the subject; but I am certain that anybody who firmly believes in it as the result of divine inspiration, who will give up his mind to its study, and who feels the unspeakable comfort it is capable of affording, will agree with me that no other book, ancient or modern, can in the remotest degree be compared to it. Too many people read it merely as a matter of conscience. They skim over a chapter at a time with very little thought or reflection. Even that way may be better than neglecting it altogether, but surely that is not the way a book with consequences so immeasurably important depending on the truths it promulgates deserves to be read.

On the death of our kind friend I had fancied it was one of the greatest misfortunes that could have happened to us to be left alone on the island, but I soon discovered that it was an especial blessing. I should never otherwise, perhaps, have become so well acquainted with God's holy Word as I did at that time. At first we had been inclined to regret at times that we had not all gone away in the schooner, and run the chance of being landed at a portion of some civilized country or other. Now we were every day more and more thankful that we had done what was right, and had not consorted with the wicked. We could not help remarking, also, how everything had occurred to produce results the most favourable to us. By the departure of Mr. Henley and his companions we were left to our own resources, and taught to seek strength and support from above. By the arrival of Dr. Cuff, a Bible was brought us, while he, as a friend, gave us counsel the most important, and set us a beautiful example of the calmness and resignation of a true Christian. From Sills and Brown's going away, those who might have tempted us to do evil, or at all events, to be idle, were removed; and at length, when fitted for solitude, and with our minds attuned aright from our previous training, we were left once more alone to employ ourselves in the way most advantageous to us.

Every Christian man who will carefully trace God's dealings with him will perceive that events which may at first have appeared prejudicial to him, have been directed for his benefit, and that many which he at the time thought misfortunes have ultimately proved, without doubt, to have been the greatest of blessings. Such is the result of my own experience, and I feel that I am bound to bear faithful testimony to what I know to be the truth. Would that all who read these pages could make up their minds once and for ever to do the same.

CHAPTER X.

A strange Sail—We Conceal Ourselves—More Visitors—Old Friends—Embark on board a Man-of-War—Kindness of her Officers—Land at Point de Galle—A new Friend—Scenes in Ceylon—Sketch of the History of the Island—Colombo.

AD I not kept a careful diary, we should very soon have lost all note of time, the events of one day were so very similar to those of another. Every day, however, we took a long walk, so that we thoroughly explored the island from end to end. There was scarcely a tree, or a shrub, or a plant on it which we had not noted. We were constantly reminded of the benefit the kind doctor had been to us by pointing out the noxious and the wholesome plants; and as in most instances there is a marked difference between the tribes, when we found a new plant we were able at once to tell to which it belonged. Strange as to some it may seem, the time was a very happy one. I never felt weary; the day never appeared too long. I ought to have said that one of my many sources of amusement was instructing Tommy. I very much improved his reading and his writing; and he was so anxious to learn, and intelligent, and attentive, that it was a real pleasure to teach him.

Thus not only weeks but months passed by. In that latitude we enjoyed an almost perpetual summer, so that there was no change of seasons to mark the lapse of time. We kept our health for all that period, and neither of us ever had a moment's illness. How different would have been the case, however, had we not benefited by Dr. Cuff's instructions, and had the example of Sills and Brown not been set before our eyes to warn us from eating the fish which so nearly killed them!

At last one day, as I was running down from the top of the peak, I put my foot in a hole, and fell to the ground. When I tried to stand, I found that I could not, and I had every reason to fear that I had broken my ankle. I had only Solon with me. Tom was at the huts far out of hearing. I was suffering agonies. Get there alone I could not. Solon looked up affectionately in my face, as much as to say, "Master, what shall I do?"

"Go and call Tom," I said, giving him my shoe. He took it, and off he went as fast as he could gallop.

I groaned with pain as I lay on the ground. I had not long to wait. I soon heard Tom shouting and Solon barking. My dog quickly led the way to where I lay. Tom had understood what had happened, and had brought two sticks to serve as crutches. Even with these I had great difficulty in reaching the huts. Tenderly as a brother Tom nursed me day after day. By bathing my ankle with cold water inflammation was kept down, and to my great satisfaction I at last discovered that though I had given it a violent wrench no bones were broken. I had nearly recovered, though still unable to walk to any distance, when one day Tom came rushing down from the peak almost breathless with haste, and crying out,—

"Mr. Marsden—Mr. Marsden, a sail in sight! a sail in sight! She is standing this way from the eastward, and will be off the island in an hour or so."

My breath came quickly; my heart leaped in my bosom as I heard these words.

"At length we may be released. I may continue my search for poor Alfred, and again get news from home."

These and similar thoughts crowded into my head. Then,

again, it occurred to me, perhaps, after all, the approaching vessel may be only the slaver, or some craft of a similar character. We may be forced to go in her, and at all events we shall be deprived of some of our cocoa-nuts. I hurried out to meet Tommy, for I was able to walk pretty well, and told him my fears.

" Then, sir, I think the best thing we can do is to hide and see what sort of people they are before we show ourselves," he observed.

I agreed with him, but remarked that, if the strangers came into our huts, they would at once discover marks of our having lately occupied them, and hunt about till they had found us. We set to work, therefore, to remove as far as we could all traces of ourselves. We had pretty well succeeded in doing this when the stranger came round the point of the island where we were. She was a ship, with taunt masts, square yards, and very white canvas.

" I do not know what to make of her; she has a very rakish look, and is not a bit like a merchantman," I observed, as I glanced at her through my glass. " Why, I believe she is a man-of-war," I exclaimed, after a more attentive look. " Yes, that she is, and there up goes the glorious flag of Old England at her peak. Hurrah, they expect to find some one here, or they would not have hoisted their flag. They are lowering a boat. See, she is making direct for the passage between the reefs. They must have been here before. Who can they be?"

Such were the words to which I gave expression, on first seeing what I believed to be a vessel come to our rescue. We set off to hasten to the spot where the boat could best land, but on our way the former feeling of doubt and mistrust came over us, and we agreed that it would be more prudent to hide till we had ascertained to a greater certainty the character of the stranger. Calling Solon to keep close behind, we retreated to a spot a little up the hill, where we could securely conceal ourselves behind a mass of rock and thick underwood, whence, at the same time, we had a good view of the landing-place.

"Silence, Solon; silence, good dog," I whispered, as he crouched down at my side uttering, at the same time, a low stifled bark and growl as he eyed the approach of the boat, and seemed disposed to resent the intrusion of strangers.

In a quarter of an hour, or less, the boat, a large gig, touched the land, and six or eight people stepped out of her. Without stopping to look about them, they made directly for the huts. They were in uniform. Others were dressed as men-of-war men, and one was in plain clothes. Solon had planted his fore-feet on the rock, and was looking down at them. Presently, forgetting all my injunctions, he uttered a loud bark, and bounded off down the hill towards them, whisking his tail and giving other signs of pleasure. The person in plain clothes turned round, and, as he leaped up on his shoulders, welcomed him by patting his head and shaking him by the paws. I put my glass to my eye, and looked attentively at him.

"Why, Tom, it is Mr. Henley," I exclaimed.

The next instant, forgetting my lameness, we were running down the hill as fast as our legs could carry us, and most cordially were we welcomed by Mr. Henley and the officers of the ship in which he had come. Johnie Spratt was also there. He had entered on board the man-of-war as a seaman. He at once took charge of Tommy.

I can but afford a brief notice of the account Mr. Henley gave me of his escape. After leaving the island, long before he could reach the burning ship, the gale caught him and he was driven by it away from the land. The utmost that could be done was to keep the boat directly before the seas, and they soon lost all hope of being able to rescue any one from the burning wreck, while every moment they themselves expected to founder. At length, through the darkness, they saw a huge mass bearing down upon them. They shouted and shrieked. Their voices were mercifully heard through the gale by those on board the ship. Sail was immediately shortened. She was hove to. At that very moment the wind ceased, preparatory to another blow, when it changed its direction, and they were enabled to get safely on board. The ship proved to be a large Indiaman, with a number of passengers on board; and the captain said that he could not venture to heave to, even with the prospect of the gale abating, to enable them to return to the island in the morning. The burning ship was seen a long way astern, and he spoke of the great responsibility he felt of delaying his voyage, even for the time necessary to beat up to her. Still, he could not bear the thought of allowing any of his fellow-creatures to perish without endeavouring to rescue them. The ship was hauled on a wind under close reefed top-sails, and stood towards the burning ship. When, however, little more than half a mile off she was seen to blow up, and instantly the spot where she had been was shrouded in darkness. They sailed over it and across it several times, but not a sign of a boat or raft could be discovered. Once more, therefore, the Indiaman stood on her course; and Mr. Henley still remained uncertain whether or not the *Orion* was the ship which was burned. The Indiaman touched at Point de Galle, in Ceylon, to land passengers, and here Mr. Henley and his three companions went on shore, and, reporting himself to the authorities, endeavoured to obtain a vessel to come to the island to take us off. Some of the passengers of the Indiaman had supplied him with the means of existence, and introduced him to several of the merchants at Point de Galle, or he would not have been able to remain there. Week after week passed, and though ships appeared there was some other employment for them. Happily for us Mr. Henley was a man who, having once promised to do a thing, did his very utmost to fulfil his promise. He did not allow his conscience to be soothed by being able to say, "Really, I tried, but I found that I could not."

At length, after waiting many months, the *Star* corvette, Captain Armstrong, came in. He gladly undertook to visit the island and to bring us off; which he accordingly did, and landed us in Ceylon. Captain Armstrong, who was one of the officers we had seen, was a very kind man, and seemed much interested in the account we gave of all that had happened to us.

I had seen a number of beautiful spots during my voyage, but Galle was by far the most interesting and picturesque which I had yet visited. As we approached the land we caught sight of Adam's Peak, a lofty mountain, with its summit enveloped in clouds, and then by degrees the old forts, built as a defence to the city, on rocks rising out of the sea, blue as sapphire, appeared before us, with the bright yellow sand fringed with palm-trees bending over the water, while the ground behind was covered with flowers of the most brilliant hues; and beyond, again, rose hills of graceful shapes, clothed to their summits with forests of perennial green; and, further still, range beyond range of purple and blue mountains, rising one above the other till lost in the distance. It struck me as being a very strong place, all the fortifications being almost entirely surrounded by water. There are two harbours —an outer and an inner one. The *Star* came to anchor in the outer one, among a number of vessels of all sorts of curious rigs—the petamars of Malabar, the dows of the Arabs, the dhoneys of Coromandel, and curious sea boats from the Maldive and Laccadive islands. Still more unlike anything I had before seen were the double canoes of the Singhalese, loaded with fish, beautiful in colour and grotesque in shape, and extraordinary-looking but tempting fruits, &c., manned by half-clad natives, which darted in and out among the shipping. Their most remarkable peculiarity are their long outriggers with balanced log, which—for they can sail both ways—always being kept to leeward, prevents the possibility of their upsetting. Some consist of two logs lashed together; but others are formed of a single tree, hollowed out, often thirty feet long and two feet deep, with a wash-board sewed to the gunwale by coir yarn, not a nail being used in the whole structure.

GALLE.

The captain, knowing how anxious I was to prosecute my search for Alfred, invited me and Mr. Henley to accompany him at once on shore. I parted from the officers with much regret, all expressing themselves most kindly towards me, especially the midshipmen, who invited me, if I was able, at any time to take a cruise with them, and I assured them that I should be very glad to accept their offer if I could do so. I had fortunately kept my pocket-book about me when I left the *Orion*, in which were my letters of introduction, so that, besides having gained the friendship of the officers of the *Star*, I did not land as a stranger in Ceylon, but had the means of forming numerous acquaintances, whom I hoped would render me the assistance I so much required. I had also, according to kind Mr. Ward's advice, kept the gold he had given me about my person, so that when I landed I did not feel that I was altogether dependent on the charity of strangers; but I did not forget that it was necessary, at the same time, to husband my resources to the utmost. Of course, my clothes were almost in rags when I was taken off the island, but my friends, the midshipmen of the *Star*, had rigged me out completely while I was on board, and supplied me with the luxury of clean linen, which I had not enjoyed for a long time. I had so many matters of interest to mention during my stay on the island, that I did not describe how Tom and I had to wash our shirts, and to sit without them while they were drying, and to mend our clothes and shoes with bits of sail-cloth, and how we made hats of leaves; indeed, we looked very much like two young Robinson Crusoes by the time we went on board the *Star*. I was now comfortably dressed, but as I had no right to wear a naval uniform, I was anxious to get a suit of plain clothes as soon as possible. I should have said that we had given Captain Armstrong a full description of the slaver which had visited our island, and of Captain Hansleig, and he said that he should keep a sharp look-out for him, and try to ascertain his haunts that he might catch him if he could.

Passing under the frowning batteries of the old fortifications, we landed at a handsome wharf among a crowd of people of various tints, from the white skin of the European to the ebon hue of the sons of Africa, and habited in every variety of Eastern costume—Englishmen in white dresses wisely shading their heads under japanned umbrellas; Parsees, Chinese, Caffres, and Chetties from the coast of Coromandel, wearing prodigious ear-rings, and with most peculiar head-dresses; then there were Malays, Malabars, and Moors, Buddhist priests in yellow robes; Moodhars, Mohandirams, and other native chiefs, habited in richly embroidered dresses with jewelled swords and pistols.

At first I thought that there were a number of women standing about, for the people, I saw, had their hair drawn back off their foreheads and fastened up in a bunch behind, with a large comb stuck in it, while they wore what looked very like petticoats. Captain Armstrong laughed at a remark made to him on the subject, and assured me that they were men, and they were dressed in the usual style of the country, which had probably existed for many hundred years. Their features are generally delicate, and as many of them have no beards they have often a very effeminate appearance. The women dress much in the same way, and wear a loose white muslin jacket which covers the body, and they seem to delight in loading themselves with jewels. The children, though dark coloured, are especially handsome. Even the principal houses, I observed, consisted only of a ground floor, but of considerable height, with latticed windows and tiled floors—a style which greatly conduced to their coolness. Not only is Galle surrounded by palm-trees, but far as the eye can reach they are to be seen on every side; indeed, the whole of the southern portion of the island is covered with them, and their produce, in a variety of forms, are the chief articles of export from the place.

Captain Armstrong said that he had to go and call on the governor, and so Mr. Henley undertook to accompany me while I left my letters of introduction.

"But you must have some head-quarters where your friends may find you," observed Captain Armstrong; and he kindly took us to a hotel where he introduced us, and laughing, said he would be answerable for our good conduct.

"Remember," he said at parting, "I shall be glad to see you on board my ship whenever you can come; and if you find your brother, tell him from me that I have no doubt that he will be re-instated in the navy. Certain circumstances have come to my knowledge about that ship which make me think this, while also no one now survives to bring any charges against him."

I thanked the captain over and over again for his kindness, and more especially for the encouraging remarks he had made about poor Alfred. Indeed, this made me still more eager to try and discover him without delay. I was received fully as kindly as I expected by all the merchants and other gentlemen to whom I had letters, and after I had told them my adventures they offered me every assistance in their power. My grandfather was known to most of them. His estate was, I found, to the north-east of Colombo, towards the interior of the country. It seemed very uncertain whether he was there or not. None of them had heard of my brother, but they told me that he had in all probability landed at Colombo, and that I should be more likely to hear of him at that place than at Galle.

I have not particularized the various people to whom I was made known at Galle, but one of them, Mr. Fordyce, a kind old gentleman, I must on no account omit. Indeed, he took even more interest in my object than did my many other friends. I have always found myself more attracted towards old men than young ones. When they are inclined to be kind they are so very kind, and considerate, and thoughtful. Mr. Fordyce was especially so. He had been a clerk, without money or interest, but he had steadiness, perseverance, and intelligence, and thus he rose to become junior partner, and was now the head of the firm. He had realized a handsome independence with which he intended to return home; but he was doing so much good in the place with it that he could not be spared, and this he himself could not help seeing also, so he had stayed and stayed on, fortunately for me, till I went there. He had travelled all over the island, and knew as much about it as anybody in it. He was thus able to give me a great deal of interesting information, of which I did not fail to profit. After he had heard the account I gave of myself, he invited me to take up my residence at his house.

"You must bring your dog too," he observed in a kind tone. "We must keep him in a cool place, and not let him run about in the hot sun, or he will be killing himself. And so you wish to set off to your grandfather's property. I think that I can help you there also. A young military friend of mine, Mr. Nowell, is about to travel through the country by way of Colombo to Trincomalé. You may travel together, much, I hope, to your mutual satisfaction. He is a great sportsman, and, very probably, during your journey, without being much delayed, you will be able to see some elephant and buffalo hunting, and get, perhaps, a shot at a deer and a wild boar or two."

I answered that I believed I should very much like to see the sport he described, but that my experience was small in such matters. I had to return to the tailor's to let him fit on my clothes, and to tell him where to send them to.

"I shall now leave you with perfect satisfaction, my dear Marsden," said Mr. Henley in a tone which showed his regard for me. "I must now look out for employment for myself, and have no doubt of finding it. I do not intend to leave these seas for some time, so that I hope we may fall in with each before long. One thing I promise you, that I will make every inquiry I can for your brother; and should I gain any clue to him, I will instantly write to Mr. Fordyce, who will let you know what to do. I had thought of proposing to leave Tommy Bigg with you, but I suspect that in travelling through the country the little fellow would only be an encumbrance to you, so I propose to take him with me, if he does not break his heart at being separated from you.

We had left Tommy, who had come on shore with us, to look after Solon at the inn. He had thought that he was to accompany me; and when he heard that I was unable to take him with me (which certainly I could not have done), he burst into tears, and said that he should never see me again, and begged and entreated that I would change my decision. When, however, Mr. Henley told him that he would take charge of him, and that he hoped to be of service to me by looking out for my brother, the little fellow was at last comforted.

"It will be a pleasure indeed, Mr. Marsden, if we can find out for you where Mr. Alfred has been carried to," he exclaimed, his countenance lighting up with animation. "I don't believe that he could go and hide away from his best friends of his own accord, from all you have told me of him—that I do not—no."

I thanked the honest-minded fellow from my heart for the good opinion he had formed of my brother. Right feeling himself, he at once intuitively perceived how an honest, right-feeling person would act, and he divined, therefore, that Alfred had not the power of communicating with his family.

On parting from Mr. Henley and Tom at the door of Mr. Fordyce's house, I found myself for the first time separated from all those with whom I had left the shores of England. I felt more alone than I had ever done before, till I looked at Solon, and he wagged his tail and rubbed his nose against my hand, as much as to say, "Never mind, dear master, I will stick to you to the last."

Mr. Fordyce's residence was in the suburbs of Galle, on some high ground surrounded by gardens overlooking the ocean. I cannot describe the number of plants and shrubs bearing the most georgeously coloured flowers which adorned it. Everything was done to keep the house cool and airy, with latticed windows, tiled floors, and high roof, such as I have before described. My kind host very soon made me thoroughly at home, and I quickly forgot that I was separated from all my older friends. At dinner I met the young military officer, Mr. Nowell, of whom Mr. Fordyce had spoken. I was altogether very well pleased with him, though he did not show out much at first. He had a firm, independent manner, and a mouth and eye which gave me a favourable opinion of his courage and decision—qualities very important in a travelling companion in a country full of wild beasts like Ceylon. He was not, however, greatly to my disappointment, to start for some days; but I found that in that part of the world things are not to be done in a hurry, and if I attempted it I should exemplify the proverb, "The greater haste the worse speed." I had no reason, indeed, to regret my stay with Mr. Fordyce, as I learned much more about the country than I should otherwise probably have done. He also lent me a horse, and made me ride out every morning for two or three hours after sun-rise, and again in the evening, to get into condition, as he said, for my journey. He also advised me to practise with my rifle.

"I do not wish you to become a mere lion or elephant killer, or to think sporting superior to any other employment in life," he observed; "but in this country a correct eye and a steady hand may often be of great service to you, and they can only be obtained by practice."

Nowell coming in one day, and finding how I was employed, was highly delighted.

"You are just the sort of fellow I like to have with me," he exclaimed. "You take to the work *con amore*. It will not be my fault if we do not have some good sport. I like the look of that dog of yours too; for though he has not, I suppose, been trained to this sort of sport, yet he has evidently got so much sense in his head that I have no doubt he will behave as you tell him."

I was as highly flattered with those encomiums passed on Solon as I was with the compliments paid to myself. As may be supposed, with renewed zeal I continued the preparations for my journey. For the greater part of the day Mr. Fordyce was at his counting-house; but I had the pleasure of spending the mornings and evenings with him, when he gave me very full descriptions of the country through which I was about to travel.

Ceylon is in shape like a ham, with the small end to the north. At the south-west end is Galle, further up on the west coast is Colombo, and on the north-east coast is Trincomalé, all which are now the principal British settlements, while Kandy, the late native capital, is situated on elevated ground surrounded by mountains in the very centre of the island. A well-made road from Galle passes through Colombo and on to Kandy, the native capital, thence it proceeds on to the sanatarium of Neura-Ellia. The country on either side of the high road is for the most part highly cultivated, and would give a stranger an over-favourable idea of it, for but a short distance off on either side of it, especially as it advances north, dense jungles and forests are to be found in a primeval state, full of wild beasts of every description. The island is about 270 miles long and 145 wide. It is divided into five provinces—Central, Southern, Eastern, Western, and Northern.

A large portion of the southern province is covered with palm-trees; the centre is a mountainous region, with magnificent scenery, crowned by the lofty summit of Adam's Peak; while the low lands, where cultivation does not extend, are overgrown with dense masses of forest and impenetrable jungle. This is the condition of the northern and a large portion of the eastern province. Kandy, the capital, is situated in the central province, and in the high lands. In the northern part of it are to be found the newly-established coffee-plantations, which promise to be a source of great wealth to the country.

The country is indebted to Sir Edward Barnes and to Major Skinner for the fine roads which have been constructed in every direction, and have so much tended to civilize the people, to open up its resources, and thus to add to its material wealth, while they have enabled the British with much less difficulty to maintain their authority over it. From the lofty mountains in the centre numerous rivers and streams flow down, and thoroughly irrigate the greater part of this lovely island: indeed, it may well be looked on as the Paradise of the East; for though, in the low country, the climate is relaxing and enervating to European constitutions, in the higher regions the air is bracing and exhilarating in the extreme.

Next to the cocoa-nut and palm-trees, the chief vegetable production of Ceylon is cinnamon, which grows both wild and cultivated wherever there is sufficient moisture for its nourishment. Bread-fruit and jack-fruit trees grow in large quantities, so does cotton, the coffee-tree, the sugar-cane, and tobacco. Rice, cardamom, and the areca-nut are also produced, while the Palmyra palm, teak, and numerous other woods valuable for cabinet-making, grow in profusion.

With regard to wild beasts, in no part of the world are elephants finer or more numerous; tigers are very formidable and destructive. There are savage wild boars, buffaloes, and elks of great size, besides other sorts of deer; snakes are numerous, and some of them of great size, and wild peacocks and other game are to be found in abundance in the higher country.

The aborigines of Ceylon are supposed to have been of the same race as the people of Dekkan. They were demon and snake worshippers, and very barbarous. In the sixth century B.C. they were conquered by Wijayo, a native of India, who first introduced Buddhism among them, which religion was afterwards established by his successors. From the vast ruins and other gigantic works which are found scattered over the country, there can be no doubt that Ceylon was for long inhabited by a civilized and highly intelligent people.

Marco Polo visited it in the thirteenth century, and described it as the finest country in the world. In A.D. 1505 the Portuguese, having doubled the Cape of Good Hope, arrived there, and found the country in a declining state, owing to intestine wars and the invasion of foreign enemies. The Singhalese king besought their assistance, which having afforded, they began in 1518 to fortify themselves in Colombo and Galle, and finally possessed themselves of the greater part of the sea-coast, shutting up the King of Kandy in the interior. In 1632 the Dutch, uniting with the King of Kandy, in their turn drove them out and held the country, though engaged in constant hostilities with the natives till 1796, when the British (Holland having fallen into the power of France) took possession of Colombo, Galle, Trincomalé, and other towns on the coast. We, however, became involved, as had our predecessors, in hostilities with the King of Kandy, and this led to the capture of his capital in 1803. We, however, allowed the king to retain nominal possession of his capital till 1815, when, in consequence of his repeated acts of cruelty, the chiefs invited us to depose him, and the whole island has ever since been under British sway, except during a serious insurrection which lasted from 1817 to 1819, and various other less important attempts at insurrection which have happily without difficulty been quelled.

Such was a rapid sketch Mr. Fordyce one day gave me of the country at large. He remarked, however, that in his mind an especial interest is attached to Galle. He considered it the most ancient emporium of trade existing in the world, for it was resorted to by merchant-ships at the earliest dawn of commerce. It was the "Kalah" at which the Arabians, in the reign of the great Haroun Alraschid, met the trading junks of the people of the Celestial Empire, and returned with their spices, gems, and silks to Bassora. It was visited by the Greeks and Romans, and by the mariners of Egypt under the Ptolemies. But still more interesting is it from its being in all probability the Tarshish visited by the ships of Solomon. They were built, we are told, at Ezion-geber, on the shores of the Red Sea. The rowers coasted along the shores of Arabia and the Persian Gulf, headed by an east wind. Tarshish, the port to which they were bound, was in an island governed by kings, and carrying on an extensive foreign trade. The voyage occupied three years in going and returning, and the cargoes brought home consisted of gold and silver, ivory, apes, and peacocks. Ophir is supposed to have been Malacca, whence ships brought gold to Tarshish. The sacred books of the Singhalese are even now inscribed on silver plates, particularized by Jeremiah as an export of Tarshish. Apes and pea-fowls are still found in great numbers, while ivory must at that time have been even more abundant than at present.

"Hurrah! old fellow," shouted Nowell one day, rushing into my room, where he found me just as I had returned from my morning ride, and was preparing for breakfast, "I have got my leave, and we are to be off to-morrow morning. Are you ready?"

"Of course I am, and could start this moment," I answered. "All right," said he. "We are to go as far as Kandy in a carriage, I find. It will not be so romantic, but far more comfortable in the hot weather. After that we shall get horses and tents, and then our fun will begin, I hope."

Great was my pleasure to find that Mr. Fordyce was going with us through Kandy to Neura-Ellia, a station established as a sanatarium, 6000 feet above the sea. The next morning we found ourselves seated in a primitive-looking vehicle, denominated a mail coach, which ran daily between Galle and Colombo. Nothing could be more beautiful than the road. We were literally travelling under an avenue, seventy miles long, of majestic palm-trees, with an undergrowth of tropical shrubs bearing flowers of the most gorgeous hues, and orchids and climbers hanging in graceful wreaths to all the branches. Birds of the gayest plumage, gaudy butterflies, and insects with wings of metallic lustre, were seen glancing in and out among the trees, while lizards of various hues ran along the road, all adding to the brilliancy of the scene. Whenever there was an opening, on the right side could be seen the white cottages of the natives amid their gardens of cocoa-nuts and plantains, with the purple mountains beyond, and that mysterious Peak of Adam in the distance; while on the left glittered the blue sea, studded with islets, round which were dancing masses of white foam; the yellow beach, approached almost to the water's edge by the green fields and tall palms, while here and there bold headlands rise up and form sheltering bays to the fishermen, whose primitive craft we could see moving along the shore.

There are several resting-places on the road. We remained longest at Caltura—considered, from its position on a height facing the sea breeze, one of the most healthy places in Ceylon. The scenery in the neighbourhood is also magnificent. From the extent of the cocoa-nut groves, arrack is here largely distilled. The toddy or juice is drawn from the trees into bowls suspended to catch it, and numbers of the great bat *Pteropus*, called by Europeans the flying-fox, come and drink from them. They begin quietly enough, but by degrees the toddy takes effect, and, like human beings, they break into quarrels, and continue increasing their noise till it becomes most uproarious.

Having been ferried across several rivers, we reached Colombo in about twelve hours after leaving Galle.

Colombo is not an interesting place. It is on a level, strongly fortified, and has a lake in the rear, from which the inhabitants are nightly serenaded by huge frogs and mosquitoes, and tormented in the day by numberless flies. The European merchants, therefore, have their houses chiefly in the neighbourhood shaded by palm-trees among the cinnamon plantations. We spent but a day here, while, with Mr. Fordyce's assistance, I made inquiries for my grandfather and Alfred, but could gain no information on which I could in any way rely. We again, therefore, continued our journey in the same way to Kandy.

CHAPTER XI.

My New Friends—Journey to the Capital—Kandy—Fine Roads—Magnificent Scenery—Coffee Plantation—Mountain Travelling—Neura-Ellia—Its refreshing Coolness—My First Buffalo Hunt—Unpleasant Consequences—Solon to the Rescue.

WERE I to describe all the wonderful and curious things I saw and heard of in Ceylon, I should very soon fill my pages. After leaving the sea the palm-trees soon disappeared, and we were surrounded by the graceful arecas, mixed with the kitool or jaggery palm, and numberless flowering trees and shrubs, the murutu with its profusion of lilac blossoms, and the gorgeous imbul or cotton-tree covered with crimson flowers. We passed thousands of bullock carts bringing down coffee from the estates in the interior, and carrying up rice and other provisions and articles required on them. They are small, dark-coloured, graceful little animals, with humps on their backs, and legs as slender as those of a deer. The carts they draw are called bandys. They are rough two-wheeled vehicles, with a covering of plaited cocoa-nut leaves.

We were now gradually ascending, the cottages of the natives being surrounded by coffee bushes, with their polished green leaves and wreaths of jessamine-like flowers, instead of palm-trees as in the low country. The latter part of the road was most magnificent, combining the grandeur of the Alps with the splendour of tropical vegetation.

"Some Kandyan prophet had foretold," Mr. Fordyce informed me, "that the kingdom of Kandy would come to an end when a bullock should be driven through a certain hill, and a man on horseback should pass through a rock."

This prophecy has been fulfilled, for we passed along a tunnel under the hill, through which thousands of bullocks have been driven, and under an archway in the rock.

Kandy is a comparatively modern city, having only become the capital of the kingdom about A.D. 1592, since which time it has been frequently burned. It stands closely surrounded by mountains, on the banks of a lake constructed by the last King of Kandy, in 1807. The habitations of the people were most wretched, as the king alone, and members of the royal family, enjoyed the privilege of having glazed windows, whitened walls, and tiles; the palace, and some of the Buddhist temples, are the only ancient edifices which remain, and even these are crumbling to decay. The chief temple was one built to contain the tooth of Buddha. Not that the original tooth really exists, because that was burned by the Portuguese. The present relic worshipped by all the Buddhists is more like the tooth of a crocodile than that of a man. It is preserved in an inner chamber, without windows, on a table, and is concealed by a bell-shaped covering, overspread with jewels.

The view from the side of the mountains above Kandy, looking down on the city with its temples, and palaces, and monuments, and its brightly glancing lake surrounded by hills, is very beautiful. In the lake is a small island, with a picturesque building on it, now used as a powder magazine. A road winding round one of the hills leads to a spot whence we looked down over a wild valley, with the river Mahawelliganga in the centre of it, rushing over a bed of rocks, the whole scene being one of the most majestic grandeur. Altogether, no city within the tropics is more picturesquely situated, or has a finer climate. Still, it is not equal to that of Neura-Ellia, very properly called the sanatorium of the island, to which we were bound.

Mr. Fordyce, before lionizing the place with Nowell, assisted me in making all possible inquiries for Mr. Coventry and Alfred. Several people knew my grandfather. When they last had seen him he was on his way to his coffee estate, which was situated in the extreme east of the district suitable for the growth of the plant, and beyond Neura-Ellia. He had had a young man with him, but who he was and where he was going they could not tell. I was in great hopes, from the account I had heard, that Alfred might have joined him. I was now more than ever impatient to set off, and so was Nowell, for he was anxious to begin his attacks on the elephants, the buffaloes, and elks he was in search of.

"Come along, Marsden, we will set off at once to look for my Will-of-the-wisp old friend, though I suspect we shall have to travel fast to catch him," said Mr. Fordyce to me. "His activity would put to shame many young men, I suspect, and your brother must not let the grass grow under his feet if he wishes to please him."

Mr. Fordyce kindly engaged a vehicle of a somewhat antique structure to convey us as far as Neura-Ellia, a distance of fifty miles. After that we should at length have to engage horses and bullocks to carry our tents and baggage. Although I found the journey exceedingly interesting, as we met with no exciting adventure I will pass over it rapidly. The road for some miles led along the banks of the rapid and turbulent Mahawelliganga. We crossed it by a bridge of a single arch, 90 feet high, with a span of 200 feet. We were told that during the rains of the monsoons the water has been known to rise 60 feet in its bed, carrying carcasses of elephants and huge trees in its current. By the side of the road were numerous shops or bazaars, kept by low country Singhalese, for the sale of all sorts of commodities to the country people. The Kandyans have a strong prejudice against engaging in trade, and indeed dislike to mix at all with strangers. They therefore, when able, perch their residences in the most out-of-the-way and inaccessible positions. The latter are the Highlanders, while the Singhalese are the Lowlanders of Ceylon. The Kandyans have a strong attachment and veneration for their chiefs, by whom, however, they were cruelly oppressed, and both races possess the vices inherent to a long-continued slavery—a want of truthfulness and honesty; at the same time they possess the virtue of strong family affection and respect for their parents and elders.

At Gampola, once the capital of the kingdom, there is a rest-house where we stopped. We had now reached the region where the first successful attempt at the systematic cultivation of coffee was made in the island. It had been tried in several places in the low country, but always had failed. Sir Edward Barnes, the great benefactor of Ceylon, first produced it on an upland estate of his own, in 1825, since which time the export from the island has increased to 67,453,680 lbs. annually. A great stimulus was given to the cultivation of coffee in Ceylon in consequence of the blacks in the West Indies, when emancipated from slavery, refusing to work; but in after-years, from the wildest speculation and the injudicious employment of capital, many of the English who had endeavoured to form estates had no means left to continue their cultivation, and wide-spread ruin was the result. Now, however, those who are able to reside on their property, by judicious management, find the cultivation a most profitable employment for their capital, in spite of the expense of bringing up rice for their labourers, and the destruction caused by winds, insects, caterpillars, wild cats, monkeys, squirrels, and rats. As the natives cannot be depended on as labourers, except in the first process of clearing the forest, the estates are cultivated by coolies, who come over from Malabar and the Coromandel Coast, as the Irish do in the reaping season to England, to find employment.

We continued our journey through a complete alpine region, except that the trees were very different to any seen in Europe. Among them was a tree the stem and branches of which were yellow, with the gamboge exuding from them, called the goraka; there was the datura, with its white flower bells; and the imbul, with its crimson blossoms; while tree ferns by the side of the streams rose to the height of 20 feet.

We stopped at the bungalow of some friends of Mr. Fordyce, now surrounded by a plantation of upwards of a thousand acres of coffee-trees in full bearing, fenced in by hedges of roses. Nothing could be more beautiful than the view from the estate, embracing, as it did, mountains, forests, rivers, cataracts, and plains, seen from a height of nearly 4000 feet above the level of the sea. But a few years ago, about 1845, this very spot was covered with dark forests, wild as left by the hand of Nature. Nowell and I agreed that we should be perfectly ready to turn coffee planters, and settle down here for the remainder of our lives. Mr. Fordyce laughed at our notion.

"Till you got tired of your own society, and then you would be heartily sick of coffee-trees and the magnificent scenery which surrounds us," he observed.

He was right; at the same time, I believe a man with a family round him, who understands the nature of the cultivation and the language of the people, and combines with it the earnest desire to improve their moral condition, and to spread the truths of Christianity among them, would be able to pass his life in a very satisfactory and profitable way. The great secret of happiness in all such positions is the consciousness that we are benefiting our fellow-creatures who surround us. A coffee plantation put me something in mind of a grove of laurels. The leaves are as polished and bright as those of a laurel, but of a darker green. They bloom in the most rapid way, and the flowers are succeeded as quickly by the bunches of berries which soon turn crimson, and are not unlike a cherry in size and colour. The flowers are of snowy whiteness, and grow in tufts along the upper part of the branches. On looking out in the morning I have seen all the trees covered with bloom, looking as if a snow storm had fallen in the night, while the perfume they emitted of a strong jessamine odour was almost oppressive. Within the crimson pulp lies a sheath, which encloses the double seed. This is by various processes freed from its coverings, and the berry we use in England is the result.

Neura-Ellia was reached at last. It is a grassy plain 6222 feet above the level of the sea, and yet surrounded by mountains, some on the north side being 2000 feet higher still. The village, with its pleasant bungalows, stands in the midst of it, with bright streams flowing by grassy fields, and hills covered with the most luxuriant vegetation. Here the air is cool and bracing—a breeze ever blowing, hoar-frost on the grass, and ice on the water in the winter—what a blessed change does it present from the blazing sun and hot sultry air of the sea-coast. It can be reached, too, from Colombo by a capital road of less than a hundred miles in length. I wonder people do not resort to it for their health from all parts of India. I should think that it would be an excellent place for the establishment of schools at which parents in India might place their children, instead of having to send them all the way to England, and to be parted from them, as is often the case, for so many years at a time. Here they might frequently visit them, and greatly benefit their own health. The troops here never change their woollen for lighter clothing, and even great-coats are in request, and blankets on beds and fires in the evening are found pleasant. All our spirits rose in this delightful atmosphere, especially did those of Mr. Fordyce, after we had spent a day there.

"I have made up my mind, young gentlemen, not to let you proceed on your journey alone," he said to us when we met at breakfast. "I shall like to renew my early acquaintance with the wild elephants and buffaloes, and elks and bears, and I think that I may somewhat facilitate your proceedings, and make your journey less expensive to you."

He had, I have no doubt, all along intended to make this proposal, but lest we might have fancied such an old gentleman as he was might prove a considerable bar to our amusement, he had not said anything about the matter. Now that we found how very active and full of spirits he was, in spite of his age, we were both delighted to have his company, besides which we should see a great deal more of the country than we possibly could by ourselves.

"We shall be delighted, indeed we shall," we exclaimed simultaneously.

"But if I do not find my brother Alfred with my grandfather, I must continue my search for him; and if I find him, I shall not like to part from him again immediately," said I.

"Time enough to settle what you will do when you find Mr. Coventry. I cannot insure your catching him even yet," was the answer.

Mr. Fordyce had made all the arrangements for a journey of some length. Should I find Mr. Coventry and remain with him, he intended to proceed with Nowell alone. I was not a little surprised the next morning to see the large cortége assembled in front of our bungalow. There were two elephants to carry our tents, and twenty or more coolies who transported our beds, canteens, and provisions, besides servants, and grass-cutters, and horse-keepers, the mahouts who rode the elephants, and two professional sportsmen, Moors they are called, whose especial business it is to track and capture the elephants. They reside in villages in the northern part of the island, and are a fine hardy race, and show wonderful sagacity in the pursuit of game. Besides the horses we rode, we had several spare ones in case ours should knock up. One man had especial charge of Solon, who, from his ignorance of the nature of the wild beasts we were likely to meet with, it was supposed might otherwise get into trouble. I need not specify exactly the locality of my grandfather's estate; indeed, few of my readers would remember the odd-sounding names of the various places through which we passed. I know that I could scarcely remember them even at the time I was there. Since then roads have been formed in all directions, and already great improvements have taken place besides those I have described. We, however, were now to travel where there were no carriage roads or bridges, and often no ferries, so that we had to construct rafts on which to carry across the streams our saddles, and baggage, and provisions, while our animals swam after us.

"Another warm day, Sandy," observed the Highland soldier to his comrade after many a broiling month had been passed on the plains of Hindostan.

Such was the salutation with which Nowell and I greeted each other after we had descended from the cool heights of Neura-Ellia, and were proceeding towards Mr. Coventry's estate. Most lovely were these days. We always started at the earliest dawn, when all nature was but just awaking from the grateful rest of night. First came forth the gaudy butterflies fluttering from flower to flower, till every shrub had a rainbow-coloured mass hovering over it. Bees full of industry flew abroad, and glittering beetles crawled along the moist grass, then crows, chattering paroquets, and long-legged cranes took to the wing, while the jungle-cock, the dial-bird, the yellow oriole, the grass warbler, and bronze-winged pigeons sent their varied and ringing notes through the forest. Then as the sun arose, the bulbul and the sun-birds were seen quivering in thousands over the nectar-giving flowers of the field. As the heat increased towards noon again all were silent, and fled away panting to seek for coolness beneath the shade of the forest. At this time we also sought shelter in some ruined temple or rest-house, or we had our tents pitched under the shadow of some lofty tree. Once more towards evening the birds took to the wing, the wild animals hurried out to the tanks, and streams, and water-courses, and then moths and numberless night-feeding animals came out to seek for their prey.

At length we reached a plantation which we were told belonged to Mr. Coventry. A small, but comfortable-looking bungalow stood in the midst of it. I cannot describe the anxiety with which I approached the door. A native servant appeared. I had to wait till Mr. Fordyce came up to interpret for me. Mr. Coventry was not there. He had been for some time, but he was lately joined by a young gentleman with whom he had set out for another estate he had purchased to the north of Kandy, and, from his having taken his rifles and other sporting guns, it was supposed that he had gone on some hunting expedition. The information was not altogether unsatisfactory. I hoped at length to come up with him, and my heart bounded with joy at the certainty it seemed to me that the young gentleman spoken of was my brother.

Mr. Fordyce did not appear to sympathize with me as much as I should have expected in my anxiety to find my brother.

" You will fall in with him all in good time, and a few days or weeks cannot make much difference to either of you," he remarked.

Soon after this we heard that there was to be held, at the distance of two or three days' journey off from where we then were, a corral or grand elephant hunt.

" We will without fail attend it," exclaimed Mr. Fordyce. " It is one of the things most worth seeing in Ceylon, and I have not been at one for many years."

Of course Nowell and I were delighted to go. Ceylon has for time immemorial been celebrated for the number and size of its elephants, and for their great sagacity and docility when trained. They have, therefore, annually been caught and tamed, and sent off to different parts of Asia, where they have been highly prized.

We had pitched our tents one evening at the distance of about half a mile from one of those wonderful lakes formed artificially in days long past for the purpose of irrigating the rice fields of the low country. They were usually created by the erection of a dam across the mouth of a valley, oftentimes not less than two miles in length, and from fifty to eighty feet in height, and of a proportionable thickness. Often these artificial pieces of water are ten or a dozen miles in circumference, and of great depth. They are usually full of crocodiles, and are frequented by wild-fowl of all sorts. Our evening meal was preparing, when one of our Moors came in with the announcement that a herd of buffaloes were in the neighbourhood feeding close to the lake, and that we might have a fair chance of trying our powers on them. Delighted at the prospect, Nowell and I seized our rifles, and mounting our horses, rode off towards the spot indicated.

" I will let you go by yourselves, young gentlemen. After a long day's journey, I do not feel that my love of sport would induce me to go through more fatigue," observed Mr. Fordyce.

Solon, of course, was very anxious to accompany me, but the Moor said he would interrupt the sport, so very unwillingly I left him in our camp. Nowell had already had some practice in buffalo as well as in elephant shooting and other wild sports in Ceylon. He explained to me that it is necessary to be very cautious in approaching a herd; sometimes they will

BUFFALOES.

pretend to fly, and all of a sudden turn round and charge their pursuers with the most desperate fury. We were both armed with double-barrelled rifles and hunting-knives, with, as I believed, a good supply of powder and bullets, and so we thought ourselves a match for any wild beasts in the world. The scenery was very beautiful. There was a wide extent of plain covered with richly green grass, and here and there sprinkled with clumps of trees, under which herds of deer crouched in the shade, while others browsed around. Promontories of various shapes, some wooded, and some with only a single palm-tree on them, ran out into the bright lake, at the further end of which rose lofty hills covered thickly with shrubs to their very summits, the bluest of blue mountains appearing one beyond the other in the far distance. As we rode along we put up a number of wild-fowl, teal, and ducks; and the deer, as soon as they saw us, scampered off to a distance, so that we could not have a shot at them had we wished it. The ground now became too uneven for our horses, so Nowell proposed that we should leave the Moor in charge of them, while we walked on towards the spot where we expected to find the buffaloes.

"I am quite up to the work to be done, and it will be much more creditable to attack them by ourselves," he observed.

I agreed. The Moor said nothing, but took the horses and sat down under the shade of a tree. Perhaps he wanted to show us that we could not do without him. Walking on over the uneven ground for about an eighth of a mile, we reached a high ledge of rocks over which we scrambled, and from its summit looked down on a wide plain, bordered on one side by the lake, on the other by an open forest. A large herd of buffaloes—Nowell said there were seventy or more—were lying down at about a quarter of a mile from us in a wide marshy spot such as they delight to frequent. Further off were other herds, scarcely discernible among the grass in the distance. A few bulls were posted as guardians of the rest at a little distance round the herd nearest to us. Not a breath of wind rippled the calm surface of the lake. Scarcely had we shown our heads above the ridge of the rock than the vigilant old scouts perceived us. Instantly the whole herd started up, and gazed at us with astonishment, wondering what were the intruders venturing into these solitudes. There was no cover whatever between us and them, so that our only chance of getting a shot was to advance boldly towards them. As we drew near, the whole herd formed into close order, presenting a regular line like a regiment of soldiers—most formidable-looking fellows they were—and had not Nowell, who had often encountered them before, set me the example, I certainly should not have ventured to face them in the way we did. The buffalo of Ceylon and India is very different to the animal which is called a buffalo in North America, but which is properly a bison. The latter has an enormous head, with a long shaggy mane, and an oblong hump on his back. The real buffalo has short legs for his great size, a rough hard hide, and huge horns which he presses over his back when in motion, so as to bring his eyes on a level with it, sticking out his snout as far as possible in advance of his body. As we drew near, five or six large bulls marched out from the main body, looking most viciously at us as if intending to charge.

"Steady now, Marsden," sung out Nowell, "if we wish to get killed, we shall try to run away; our safety depends on our advancing quietly. Do not fire till I give the word. Single out the second from the right, and aim at the middle of his head. I will take the centre one. Advance at a trot. It will astonish them most."

On we went. The herd stood still. I felt, if not nervous, very curious. The excitement, however, carried me on.

"Shout," cried Nowell. We raised a loud cry, which made the welkin ring. We had got within thirty yards, when the main body, including some of the sentry bulls, turned tail and went off along the plain. Two, however, as if acting in concert, advanced towards us—these we had singled out as our victims.

"Fire!" cried Nowell, when they were about twenty paces from us.

Glad enough I was to do so. To my surprise and delight mine fell over at the instant, and I thought was dead. The one at which Nowell had shot sunk to his knees, but instantly recovering himself, he went off wounded as he was towards the water. Curiously enough, as soon as he was perceived by the herd, the largest of the bulls rushing after him, knocked him over, and tramping fiercely on him, trotted off along the margin of the lake.

"Try and stop the bully!" cried Nowell.

Without a moment's hesitation, off I dashed as fast as my legs would carry me. Nowell would have followed, but both our buffaloes gave signs not only of life, but of renewed activity, and it was necessary to settle with them before it was safe to advance. I was too far off to hear him calling me back. On went the bully buffalo, and I followed after him. Sometimes he would stop and look at me, as if daring me to advance, and then he would run on again for a hundred yards or more, when he would stop as before. I at one time got a little nearer, so bringing my rifle to my shoulder, I fired. I hit him, but in no vital or painful part, for he continued his course as before. I loaded rapidly, and on I went. The lake some way on before me ran up into a deep gulf. The bull, as I fancied, not observing this, steered for the intervening point of land. I thought, therefore, that I had him safe in a corner. I forgot that no animal swims better, or is more fearless of the water. I fully expected that I should be able to bring him to bay. All I wanted was to get a fair shot at his forehead. I had got within thirty yards of him, when into the lake he plunged and began swimming across the mouth of the gulf. The distance round was not great. I thought that I might get to the opposite shore and meet him as he landed. I ran as fast as I could, and got to the point I intended, when he was some twenty or thirty feet from it. I felt something drop as I ran, but I had not time to stop and pick it up. I rushed into the shallow water, thinking that it would be better to attack him there than on dry land. Had I known that his feet were especially formed to tread on marshy places, spreading out as they are placed on the ground, and contracting as they are lifted up, I should have kept on the shore. At about twenty paces off I fired. The smoke cleared away. There he stood, unhurt it seemed, but eyeing me viciously, then slowly and steadily he advanced like a cat about to spring on its prey. Yes, there was a wound, and a stream of blood flowed from it. Had I retreated he would have made a rush. I knew that— I should have been crushed in an instant. I had still a barrel loaded. Again I fired, and eagerly I watched for the result. The fierce animal stood still without moving a muscle, his eye flashing with fury. I was in no better position than before, and he was within a dozen paces of me. My only chance of safety consisted in my being able to load and fire a more successful shot before he was upon me. I brought my rifle down ready to load—I put in the powder—I felt for my shot bag— I could not find it. Again and again, with a sinking heart, I felt about for it—in vain; I had lost it. What hope had I of escape? I kept plunging my hands convulsively into my pockets. My fingers came upon some stones. I remembered to have picked them up some days before at Neura-Ellia. They had been washed down from the mountains above, and were really jewels of some little value—precious, indeed, I thought them. They had been wrapped up in paper. Grasping them all, I rolled them up with a pen-knife and pencil-case, and some small coin, and rammed them all down into the two barrels together—a regular charge of langrage. I knew that none of this was likely to go through his skull, and I feared that my gun might burst, but it was my only chance. If it failed—the full horror of my situation flashed across me. How I blamed myself for having engaged in the useless, I might say senseless and cruel sport. I knew that Nowell must be a long way off, but I hoped that he might hear my voice, so I shouted as shrilly as I could at the very top of it.

Scarcely had I done so, than the buffalo, feeling the pain of his wounds, with a loud grunt rushed on towards me. I fired both barrels in quick succession right into his head. Without stopping to see the effect produced, or till the smoke had cleared away, I turned round, and getting out of the water, ran as hard as my legs would carry me. At length I stopped to look for the buffalo. The monster was only stunned—I thought so. The penknife must have astonished him, but the gems had probably only shattered against his hard skull. He had fallen, but got up while I was watching him, and was now looking about for me. He soon espied me, for there was not an approach to shelter of any sort behind which I could hide myself. With a fierce grunt, which sounded very terrific, on he came. I now more than ever gave myself up for lost. Should I run, or face him, and attempt to leap aside as he came near me? I knew that the spot where I had dropped my bag of bullets was too far off for me to hope to reach it before he could overtake me. I felt exactly as I have often done in a dream, as if what was taking place was almost too dreadful for reality. I turned my head over my shoulder as I ran. The buffalo had begun to move. I could hear his panting breath—his snort of rage. I stopped short, and in desperation faced him. I mechanically poured powder down the muzzles of my rifle barrels. My eye was all the time on the huge and infuriated brute which was, I believed, about to destroy me. He was not to be awed by powder, or I might have hoped to have frightened him by firing my blank charges in his face. I felt as if all the colour had left my cheeks, and I own that I could have cried out most lustily for help, had I fancied anybody would hear me.

Just then a loud bark reached my ear from a long distance through the pure air, and I saw a small animal scampering along through the grass towards me. Directly afterwards I heard a shout of a human voice. I shouted in return. It gave me confidence. On came what in the distance had appeared to be a small animal. It was my faithful Solon. The furious buffalo had got within ten paces of me, and in another instant I should have been crushed by his forehead, when Solon, instinctively observing what was best to be done, flew at his neck, and compelled him to turn round to ascertain who was his new opponent. I took the opportunity to leap aside, when Solon, letting go his hold, kept barking away furiously and flying at the buffalo's neck, to draw away his attention from me. The success of his sagacious proceedings restored my nerve and courage, and I kept dodging the buffalo, each time getting further and further from him, till the faint shouts I had heard were repeated nearer, and I saw Nowell running at full speed towards me. I was now more alarmed for Solon than for myself, lest he should meet with some injury in his courageous attacks on the buffalo. The fierce animal was, however, evidently getting weaker and weaker from loss of blood, still his determination to punish me was unabated. Notwithstanding all the escapes I had had, I feared that he would succeed, when Nowell came up directly in front of him, and though nearly out of breath from his long run, without a moment's hesitation lifted his rifle to his shoulder and fired. In an instant our huge enemy rolled over, and never again moved a muscle. I had had enough of buffalo-shooting for that day. Even then I felt what a senseless sport I had been engaged in. Still I cannot deny the excitement and interest it afforded us. All we got were the tongues of the three buffaloes we had killed, and a steak out of the last for Solon. He, noble fellow, had evidently broken away from his keeper, and came up just in time to save my life. We got back at length to our tents.

CHAPTER XII.

Visit to great Elephant Corral—Mode of Capturing Elephants in Ceylon—Wonderful Sagacity of Tame Elephants—Mode of Taming Elephants—Their Habits when Tame—Habits when Wild.

TWO days after I had enjoyed my first experience in buffalo-hunting we arrived in the neighbourhood of the great elephant corral, or great elephant trap, as it might very properly be called. We had been travelling through dense forests scarcely penetrated by the sun's beams, where but seldom we had heard the song of birds, the hum of insects, or even the roar of wild beasts. I was astonished at this till Mr. Fordyce pointed out to me that under the dense shade of the tall trees there could be no pasture for the graminivorous animals, and consequently no prey to tempt the carnivorous ones to invade those silent solitudes.

But a few hours' ride after leaving the gloomy solitudes I have described brought us into the midst of a scene such as the gorgeous East can alone produce. Thousands of people appeared to be collected with gaily caparisoned elephants and horses in vast numbers in the midst of a village of boughs and branches, the houses being thatched with palm-leaves and the sweet smelling lemon grass. The people of all the neighbouring villages appeared to have made the hunt an excuse for a complete holiday. There were, besides those engaged in the work, some thousands or more natives—men, women, and children—crowding round the corral—the men armed with their long spears in picturesque costume, the women with children of the colour of bronze, and destitute of a rag of covering, clinging to them, while many of the young girls were habited in the graceful robes of that part of the country, with a scarf which, after being wound round the waist, was thrown over the left shoulder, leaving the right arm and side free. There were conjurors, and tumblers, and story-tellers to help to pass the time, but the great interest was concentrated on the business for which all had collected.

Mr. Fordyce had sent forward to have preparations made for our arrival, and we found a delightfully cool arbour ready for our reception. We had not only an airy dining-room, but a bed-room a-piece, fitted up with our tent furniture, while habitations had been run up for our attendants outside.

"There is nothing like travelling with 'a mighty, magnificent, three-tailed bashaw,'" observed Nowell to me, laughing. "Now, if you and I had been alone, we should have to rough it by ourselves, with no one to care for us or look after us."

After we had taken possession of our mansion we strolled out to see what was going forward. We could not help stopping to watch the feats of a juggler. First, he jumped upon a pole six feet from the ground, on which he placed a cross bar, and balancing himself on it made prodigious leaps from side to side. He had a companion, who assisted him in his feats, but how they were done it seemed impossible to discover. After leaping along to some distance, he returned to the centre of the admiring circle of spectators. Steadying himself on his pole, he caught a handful of pebbles thrown up to him by his companion. He held his hand up, and away flew a number of small birds. Next, an egg was thrown up to him. Holding it in his two hands, he broke it, when out fell a serpent and glided away among the crowd. After watching the serpent till it had disappeared, we found that he was keeping a number of brass balls in constant motion by striking them with his elbows and then with his hands. He next performed a still more difficult feat. He balanced on his nose a small stick, which had at the top of it an inverted ball or cup. From the rim of the cup were suspended by silken threads twelve balls with holes in them. He next placed in his mouth twelve rods of ivory, and while the balls were made to fly round, by managing the rods with his lips and tongue, he contrived to fit a rod into every ball, when, letting the centre stick fall, they remained suspended by the twelve rods. A ball of granite being thrown him, fully seven inches in diameter, and not less than fourteen pounds' weight, he took it in one hand, when, extending his arms in a line, he rolled it backwards and forwards from wrist to wrist, across his shoulders, by some scarcely perceptible exercise of muscular power. This done, grasping it in both hands, he threw it up to the height of twenty feet or more, and watching as it came down till it was close to his head, he bent forward and caught it between his shoulders. Then, as if this last performance had afforded him intense pleasure, he jumped forward for fifty yards or more, returning as before. All this time, it must be remembered, he was balancing himself on the horizontal bar placed across his single pole. Those I have mentioned are only some of the extraordinary feats the juggler performed. What suppleness of limb he must have possessed, and what an immense amount of practice he must have gone through before he could have accomplished any one of the feats he performed.

Strolling on with one of our Moors as a guide, we reached the corral. By ourselves we should not have found it, for the front part of it especially was left purposely concealed by trees and jungle. This is done that the elephants might not be frightened when they are driven in towards it. The space occupied by the corral was about 500 feet long and 250 feet wide. From one end, in the centre of which was the entrance, on either side a palisade extended, growing wider and wider, and reaching some way into the forest, somewhat in the same manner as a decoy for wild-fowl is formed. The trees were allowed to stand untouched in the interior of the corral. The

WATCHING ELEPHANTS IN CORRAL FROM STAGE.

palisades which enclose the corral were formed of trunks of trees about twelve inches in diameter. They were sunk three or four feet into the ground, and rose about fifteen feet above it. They were connected by transverse pieces of timber lashed

HOW THE CORRAL IS BUILT.

to them with jungle ropes. These jungle ropes are formed of the flexible climbing plants with which the forests abound. On the outside were fixed forked supports placed against the tie beams, so that very great force would be required to drive the palisade outward. Between each upright there was sufficient space left to allow a man to pass through. Strong as the work was, I could have fancied that a number of infuriated elephants would very speedily demolish it, but we were told that they rarely or never even make the attempt, for the whole corral is completely surrounded by men and boys, who hoot, and shout, and cry so vociferously, that the poor animals can never face them, but quickly rush back into the centre, to be as far off as possible from the noisy crowd. Amid a group of trees which looked down into the corral, stages had been erected for the use of the spectators who had assembled to witness the scene which was to be performed, and here Mr. Fordyce soon secured seats for himself and us. For six weeks or more beaters had been employed in driving up to the neighbourhood of the corral several herds of elephants.

The elephant is one of the most peaceably disposed of animals, and all he wishes is to be allowed to feed undisturbed. The beaters knowing this, having extended themselves in a circuit of many miles, and ascertained that a sufficient number of elephants are within it, commence making just sufficient noise as to disturb them, and to induce them to move slowly in towards the centre of their circle. They are supplied with flutes, drums, guns, a quantity of gunpowder, and other means of making a noise. In this way three or four, or even more, herds are collected together, and kept within such an area as will allow of their being watched day and night by the huntsmen. Six weeks or more are sometimes thus consumed. By slow degrees they are driven in towards the corral. Two or even three thousand huntsmen—or beaters they may more properly be called—are employed in the operation; and as the elephants begin to show symptoms of alarm, fires are kept up by day as well as by night at a dozen paces or less apart throughout the entire circle, with paths of communication, while the head men keep going constantly round to see if their followers are vigilant. Should any attempt be made by the elephants to break through the magic circle, instantly a strong force can be assembled at the point to drive them back. By the slightest carelessness or mismanagement the result of the whole previous labour might be lost. It must be remembered that the object is to take the noble animals alive, and to tame them that they may be employed for the use of man.

I was reminded, as I saw one of those vast creatures humble and obedient to the commands of its keeper, of the stories in the "Arabian Nights," of some huge geni which rises out of a bottle and swells to the size of a mountain being brought under subjection by a magic ring, and made obedient to the commands of a fair princess, or some delicate young lady or other.

At length the herds of elephants are driven within a circumference of a couple of miles or less, in which is included the wide-spreading jaws of the corral. It was at this juncture that we happily arrived at the spot. Not a word was spoken above a whisper among the immense multitude, as it was important to preserve the greatest possible silence so as to tranquillize the elephants till it was necessary to move them, and then that the effects of the shouting and other noises might be greater when they were commenced.

We had all taken our places to watch the proceedings. It was curious to look down from our perch into the forest, and to know that fully five thousand people were assembled close to us, and fifty or sixty huge elephants, without a sound being heard.

The signal was given. Suddenly a terrific noise was heard

from the furthest end of the magic band which enclosed the elephants—the beating of drums, playing of fifes and other wind instruments, firing off of guns, and shouts and shrieks of men and boys. Gradually they closed in on the astonished herd, no one making any sound till they were in the rear of the elephants. The poor animals naturally rushed away from the noise, and thus drew nearer and nearer to the opening in the corral. This was furnished with stout bars, and men were stationed there to let them drop the moment the elephants were in.

Suddenly we saw the boughs of the smaller trees and brushwood violently agitated, and the leaders of the herds appeared rushing towards the gateway. We fancied that in a moment more they would be secured, when a wild boar, which had remained concealed in the brushwood, equally astonished with them at the terrific sounds, scampered out of his hiding-place, close in front of the headmost elephant. Whether the boar or the sight of the corral frightened him most, I cannot say, but he turned round, followed by the rest, and the hunters had again to extend their line, while the elephants took up the position they had before occupied in the middle of the jungle. There they stood astonished, not knowing which way to turn, and waiting the course of events. It was therefore determined by the director of the hunt to wait till night to attempt the capture of the animals, the torches and fires at that time producing a much greater effect.

We descended, therefore, from our trees to enjoy a very luxurious repast in our sylvan abode, and as darkness came on again ascended to our lofty perch. As before, not a sound was heard, but the watch-fires blazing up shed their ruddy glow over the dark forest, and lighted up the picturesque figures of the men employed around them. Suddenly the roll of a drum was heard, then a discharge of musketry, and then shrill wind instruments, and shrieks and cries resounded wildly through the forest. The fires burned up brighter than ever, and an entire line of flame extended round the whole opposite to where we sat away from the corral. Near the corral all was profound silence and darkness. On came the mass of hunters with flambeaus, closing in, shrieking and shouting, driving the whole body of elephants before them. Again the huge leader of the beasts crushed through the brushwood, pressing the smaller trees before him. Nearer he and his followers approached the gateway. Wilder blazed the torches, and louder rose the shouts. In he dashed, followed by the rest, the bars were let drop behind them, and sixty wild beasts of the forest were made captives. The corral, it must be remembered, was full of trees, and left in as perfect a state of nature as possible. The moment they were in, all the sides of the corral blazed up with brilliant flame, the hunters having rushed to the nearest watchfire to light their torches as they came up.

The first impulse of the elephants was to rush across the corral, hoping to make their escape; but they were brought up by the strong palisades, and driven back by the flaming torches, the muskets fired in their faces, and the loud cries of the hunters. Then they turned, and dashed back to the entrance-gate. It was closed, and in vain they attempted to force an exit; the torches, and music, and cries, drove them back; and at length they all formed in one group together in the centre of the corral, the very picture of hapless captives. Then they would start round and round the corral, looking out for some weaker place through which they might escape; but, finding none, they again returned to the centre of the enclosure, not in silence, however, for, as if to mock the shouts of their tormentors, they set up the most terrific trumpeting and screaming I have ever heard.

Sometimes one of the larger male elephants would leave the crowd, and go round trumpeting with fury, trying to get through here and there at some spot not before examined, but with the same result. Then he would return, sullen and bewildered, to his companions, who stood in the centre of the area, formed in a circle round their young ones.

Thus they passed the night—the hunters sleeping near the line of blazing fires kept up outside the corral, and hundreds of men and boys with spears, and white wands ten feet long, being on the watch to turn the elephants should they attempt to charge the stockade. This, however, they were too astonished and subdued to attempt to do.

The next morning preparations were made to conduct the tame elephants, who were to play a very important part in the capture, into the corral. There were a dozen or more of these intelligent creatures, belonging to the different chiefs as well as to the government. Some had only, we were told, been captured a year, and yet they seemed fully to comprehend the work they had to perform, and to take the keenest pleasure in making prisoners of their former companions. Some also belonged to the Buddhist temples, the priests employing them in their religious ceremonies. One or two, we were assured, were upwards of a hundred years old. One of the most intelligent was a female elephant about fifty years old, which we called Bulbul. She showed herself to be a keen sportswoman.

A large quantity of rope is required for noosing the elephants. This is made from the fresh hides of the buffalo and deer. As no Singhalese will touch a dead body, the only people who will manufacture these ropes are the outcast Rodiyas, a party of whom stood at a distance from the crowd. These unfortunate people are the most degraded race in the country. Their very name means filth. They were compelled to go almost naked; to live under sheds, not being allowed to build a house with two walls. They could not enter a court of justice, or even a temple, though nominally Buddhists. They are compelled to stand aside on the road when any traveller passes them; and they fall on their knees when they address any man of recognized caste. Their habits are dirty in the extreme; and they eat any food, even carrion, which comes in their way. They are, indeed, like the Cagots of France; and as little is known of the cause which reduced their ancestors to their present degraded state as in the instance of the last-named race. One thing alone could, and assuredly would, restore them to communion with their fellow-creatures, and that is the introduction of pure Christianity among them and the population at large. Curiously enough, both people have, from time immemorial, been employed in skinning cattle and making ropes.

All things being prepared for the capture of the elephants, two tame ones were ridden in by their mahouts, each with an attendant, and followed by two head men of the noosers—"*cooroowes*," they were called—eager to capture the first animal on that hunt. Each elephant had on a collar made of coils of rope of cocoa-nut fibre, from which hung cords of elks' hides, with a slip knot, or rather noose, at the end. Operations were now commenced, and most interesting they were. The chief actors were certainly the tame elephants. Bulbul began by slowly strolling along, picking a leaf here and there, as if she had nothing very particular to do. Thus she advanced, till she came close up to the herd, all of whom came out to meet her in the most friendly way, seemingly to inquire if she could explain what all the commotion had been about. Their leader entwined his trunk round hers, and passed it gently over his head, as if to invite her to join his party.

" Watch the treacherous creature," exclaimed Nowell,

laughing. "She fully intends to betray him, and yet she appears to be captivated by all the soft things he has been saying to her."

Such, in truth, was the case. She placed herself close to the leader, but it was to allow the nooser to stoop down under her, and to slip his noose round the hind foot of the wild one. The rope was very nearly made fast when the elephant, discovering what had been done, shook it off, and turned his rage upon the hunter. Had not Bulbul interposed, the latter would have paid dear for his temerity; and, as it was, he got an ugly touch of the elephant's foot, which compelled him to creep limping away out of the wood. Now the cleverest thing was done which we had yet seen. Bulbul and another elephant were made to advance, and to place themselves one on each side of the leader of the wild ones. He did not attempt to run away, but was evidently not very well satisfied with his company, as he kept moving the weight of his body from foot to foot, as elephants invariably do when standing still in any doubt or perplexity.

The second nooser, who was a young active man, now crept in and took the noose, which hung suspended from Bulbul's collar, and holding it open in both his hands, slipped it adroitly under the huge hinder leg of the monster. I was reminded, on seeing the act, of workmen touching the piston-rod of a steam-engine, or some other part of some powerful machinery, one blow of which would almost annihilate them. This time the noose was secured; and as soon as the cunning Bulbul saw that it was so, she began to back towards the nearest large tree, dragging the elephant after her, till she was able to give it a turn round the trunk. The wild elephant did his best to break away, but she kept him tight; at the same time she could not manage to draw him nearer to the trunk. The other tame elephant now stepped up to her assistance, and, by pressing his shoulder and head against the shoulder and head of the wild one, forced him back step by step, Bulbul all the time hauling in sagaciously on the slack of the rope, till he was brought close up to the trunk of the tree. The cooroowe people then rushed in and secured him to it. The nooser now passed another noose under the other hind leg, which was secured like the first. Bulbul and her comrade now ranged up one on each side of the poor animal, and while, as it seemed, holding him in conversation, and consoling him for his misfortune, the active nooser slipped under them and secured the two fore-feet as he had done the first. The other ends of the ropes were then carried to a tree, and secured round it immediately in front of the other. All four legs were also hobbled together, and then the huge monster stood, in spite of all his strength, in the most complete bondage. The ropes used for the latter purpose were made of the kittool or jaggery palm, as they are of a more flexible nature than those of the cocoa-nut fibre, and less likely to cause ulcers on the poor elephants' legs.

While the treacherous tame elephants remained alongside the captive to console him for his misfortune, he was perfectly quiet; but no sooner were they withdrawn than he made the most violent efforts to set himself free. His first endeavour was to untie the knots of the ropes which bound him; but when he found that this was beyond his art, he tried to burst them asunder. Now he leaned backwards to free the fore-feet —now forwards to clear the hind ones, till, literally lifting them off the ground, he balanced himself on his trunk and fore-feet, lifting his hind ones up in the air. Wonderful were the exertions he made to free himself; and as he crushed the branches within his reach, it seemed as if he would bring the stout tree itself to the ground. He uttered the most terrific screams in his agony, now bending his huge proboscis under him into the ground, now lifting it high in air; now pressing one cheek, now the other, on the earth.

I have since heard of a tame elephant exhibited in England having been taught to stand on his head, and, I fancy, dance the polka; and from the extraordinary positions into which I saw the animals throw themselves on this occasion, I fully believe in their power to do anything of the sort.

The mighty captive was close to us. At length, after continually exerting himself in this strange way, he lay quiet; but every now and then he would burst out again into a fit of fury, soon however to discover how vain were his efforts to free himself; and then, overcome and exhausted, he remained perfectly motionless, giving up for ever, it seemed, all hope of freedom.

Meantime the other wild elephants were in a state of terror and nervous excitement. Now they would all stand huddled together, not knowing what to do; then one, braver than the rest, would advance, and by degrees the others would follow, and the whole herd made a desperate rush towards the end of the corral.

It was a nervous moment. It seemed scarcely possible that they would not dash against the barrier, and, strong as it might be, hurl it in fragments to the ground, and trampling over their persecutors, escape into the forest. I held my breath, believing that this would be the result of their charge; but at the same moment crowds of young men and boys hurried up to the point threatened, holding long white wands and spears in their hands. As the elephants approached, with their trunks raised high in the air, their ears spread out, and their tails erected, trumpeting and uttering the loudest screams indicative of their rage, the young men, with the most perfect nerve and coolness, struck their thin lances through the openings in the palisades, at the same time shouting and whooping at the top of their voices.

Just as I expected to see the fatal crash come, the huge

brutes turned round, and off they went once more to take shelter under the trees in the centre of the corral. One after the other, the wild elephants were bound in much the same way as was the first. What appeared to me very wonderful, was that the wild ones never molested the mahouts or cooroowes who rode on the backs of the tame elephants. They could at any moment have pulled off the riders, but not the slightest attempt of the sort was made. One of the chiefs or managers of the corral rode in among the herd on so small an animal that his head was not higher than the shoulder of many of them, but no notice whatever was taken of him. The operation of noosing each elephant occupied altogether from half an hour to three quarters.

Not only did the cunning Bulbul seem to take pleasure in capturing a male elephant, but she evidently had equal delight in assisting to make a slave of one of her own sex. A large female elephant was fixed on. She and her assistant, placing themselves one on each side of her, cut her off from her companions, and the nooser slipping a rope under her foot, Bulbul carried it to the nearest tree. The wild lady, however, grasped the rope with her trunk, and, carrying it to her mouth, would quickly have bit it through, had not the other tame one, perceiving what she was about, with wonderful sagacity torn it away from her, and placing her foot on it, prevented her again from lifting it.

At last most of the leaders were captured, and it was curious to watch the proceedings of the rest. At first they were too timid to move, but after a time they came up, and entwining their trunks together, seemed to express their sympathy and sorrow. The captives expressed every variety of emotion. Some trumpeted, and bellowed, and screamed in their fury, tearing down the branches of all the trees they could reach, and struggling violently, ultimately sinking exhausted, and only now and then uttering the most pitiable groans and sobs. Some remained perfectly silent. Most of them twisted themselves about, however, in the most extraordinary way. I could not have supposed that an animal of such apparently unwieldy bulk as an elephant could possibly have distorted himself as many did. Some curled their trunks about till they looked like huge writhing snakes. One kept curling up his proboscis and letting it fly open again with the greatest rapidity. It was almost harrowing to our feelings to see the whole ground below us covered with such huge, struggling, writhing masses. I made a remark to that effect to Nowell.

"Look through a telescope shut up, which will diminish objects some hundred times, and you will think nothing of it," he answered. " Or, the next time you wish to harrow up your feelings, just walk over an ant's nest, and apply a large magnifying-glass to the spots where your feet have been placed. You will see worse sights even than this, I suspect."

From what I saw I should say that elephants have as great a variety of character as human beings. In one point only all acted much alike. After their most violent struggles were over, and the ground in front of them had been beaten into dust, they took it up with their trunks and scattered it over their bodies, and then, withdrawing a quantity of water from their mouths, they in the same way sprinkled it over themselves, till the dust was converted into a cake of mud. From the quantity of water thus employed it seemed clear that they must have a large internal receptacle to contain it, as for a whole day or more they had had no opportunity of drinking, and had been exposed to unusual alarm and exertion.

The most curious and interesting part of the whole exhibition was the sagacity displayed by the tame elephants, and especially by Bulbul. They went coolly and calmly about their work, never creating the slightest confusion, and seeing in a moment exactly what was best to be done. They stepped carefully over the ropes which were being twisted round and round the trees, and never by any chance trampled on any of the captured ones lying on the ground. One of the wildest had managed to twist the first rope secured to him several times round the tree, when Bulbul, walking up, pressed against him, and made him untwist himself. She even, on another occasion, put her own foot under that of one of the wild ones, and kept it up till the nooser was able to slip the rope over it. Not only do the tame elephants assist materially with their great strength in dragging the wild ones up to the trees, and in securing them, but without their aid, and the cover they afford, even the most active and daring of noosers would not venture to approach a herd.

The most amusing incident in the strange drama was the appearance and behaviour of two young elephants, about ten months old. They seemed to be general pets of the herd, following them wherever they went, running in and out among their legs, and being nursed not only by their own mothers, but by all the females whenever they appeared. When the mother of one of them was captured, the little creature followed her up to the tree round which the rope was fastened. It then did its utmost to liberate her, and actually attacked the men, striking them with its trunk, and endeavouring to prevent them from fastening the other nooses round its mother's legs. At last it so interfered with their proceedings that they were obliged to drive it back to the herd. It went away at a slow and disconsolate pace, looking back every now and then in the most affectionate way towards its captive mother. On reaching the herd it attached itself to one of the other females, when she hung her trunk over it and caressed it in the kindest way. As soon as the noosers had finished securing its mother, it returned to her side, and appeared to be attempting to console her, but it very soon grew angry at finding that she could not move, and began to attack everybody who passed. As this inconvenienced the men, they had to tie it up, when, as it was dragged along, it caught at all the branches in the way, and trumpeted and cried with grief. Both the small ones were tied up together, and screamed louder and more incessantly than all the rest. They put one much in mind of two young babies, for when food was given them they ate it up greedily, but before their mouths were empty began to cry and roar away again as loudly as ever.

Among the elephants driven into the corral was a rogue, or outcast elephant. They are supposed to be driven out of the herd on account of their vicious disposition, and none of their kind will ever associate with them. They live, consequently, morose and solitary lives, and are always the most dangerous to attack. He was captured like the rest, and as a proof of his bad temper, as he was dragged by one of those lying on the ground, he attacked him furiously with his tusks, and would have injured him severely had he not been torn away from him. No one trumpeted and screamed louder at first, but in a short time he lay down quietly, as if he saw that it was folly to fret himself about what could not be helped.

"That fellow will soon become tame and humble as the rest," I observed.

"The hunters say that sudden quietness is a sign that he will not live long," said Mr. Fordyce. "We shall see if they are right."

We watched the poor brute. He was covering himself with dust and water like his companions in misfortune, and continued to do so incessantly.

There were still a great number of elephants to be noosed when night closed in on us. A large herd, we understood, were also kept in check outside, ready to be driven in as soon as the first batch had been disposed of.

The next day we spent much in the same way as the former ones. Most interested we were, for certainly we could never expect to have so good an opportunity of studying the character of elephants in their wild state. Everything we saw tended to raise them higher in our estimation as the most sagacious of brute beasts, while there was the marked difference between the manners of the wild and the tame ones which civilization is calculated to create. The behaviour of the tame ones was most wonderful. They seemed to enter so thoroughly into the spirit of the affair, and to observe so immediately what was necessary to be done. There was especially no cruelty or malice displayed. They were apparently happy and contented themselves in captivity, and they did not seem to consider that there was any hardship for others to be reduced to the same state. The wild ones also, when they found that escape was impossible, bore their captivity with wonderful dignity and composure. Some even seemed to listen with pleasure to the notes of the Kandyan flute which the natives played near them; and though at first they would not eat, at length when some juicy stems of the plantain were offered them, they could not resist the temptation of the luscious morsels. The young ones, however, though they ate everything given them, screamed and bellowed louder than any of the rest, attacking every one who came near them, and never ceasing their struggles to get free. Indeed, their conduct throughout reminded me very much of petted and rather violent-tempered children.

When we took our seats the rogue lay on the ground, moving his head about slowly and heavily. Suddenly he was quiet, and almost at the same moment his body was pounced on by innumerable crowds of black flies.

"The rogue is dead," observed Mr. Fordyce.

Instantly two elephants entered with some of the outcast Rodiyas, who undid the cords from the tree, when the elephants dragged the dead body to a distance from the corral. I need not further particularize each capture as it occurred, though each was in itself especially interesting. Most remarkable was the sagacity they displayed in trying to loose themselves from their bonds, as also in avoiding having the noose thrown over their feet. One fine fellow tried to uproot the tree in front of him to which his fore-legs were secured, and then sat down on his haunches like a dog, trying to undo the knots with his trunk. When he found that all his efforts were unavailing, he threw himself on the ground, while the tears coursed each other down his rugged cheeks. Many, indeed, of the elephants wept and sobbed when they found themselves hopelessly captives.

Corrals are always erected near some river or lake, where the newly-captured elephants may be indulged in the luxury in which they so much delight. To convey the wild elephant to the water, a tame one is placed on each side of him. A collar is then formed round his neck of cocoa-nut rope, to which ropes are attached, secured also by similar collars round the necks of the tame ones. This done, the ropes round his legs are removed, and he is marched away by his companions to the water. The curious part of this operation, we remarked, was the way in which the tame elephant defended his rider from the blows of the wild one's trunk. No attempt, I observed, was made to noose the trunks. Probably from their being very sensitive organs, too much injury would be inflicted on the elephants by so doing.

After the poor animals had enjoyed their baths, they were secured to trees in the forest, with three or more grass or leaf cutters a-piece to supply them with food. Their education was now to begin, and Mr. Fordyce told us that in three or four months they would be sufficiently tamed to go to work. Both he and Nowell, who had seen a bull-fight in Spain, said that it did not at all come up in interest to the scene we had been witnessing, while there was far more cruelty employed, and a larger amount of danger, in consequence of the assistance afforded by the tame elephants. At the same time, the courage and activity displayed by a Spanish piccador or matador is infinitely superior to that which a Singhalese nooser is compelled to exert. Of one thing I am certain, that in a state of freedom the elephant as a rule is certainly neither savage nor revengeful, and considering his power to inflict injury, he is rather a timid animal than otherwise. In captivity, if he gets out of health, he is liable to fits of obstinacy and irritability, when he has been known to inflict injury for which, on his recovery, he has afterwards exhibited the most undoubted sorrow and repentance. How often is the same disposition exhibited by children from the same cause, and how speedily, on recovering their health, is their amiability restored! So we must not be over-harsh in judging of the poor elephants, who have not the reasoning powers even of a young child.

The mode of training an elephant, as described to me, and as we saw it going forward, is interesting. For the first three days, during which he will seldom take food, he is allowed to stand quiet, with a tame one by his side to give him confidence. When he takes to his food, he is placed between two tame ones, and the head groom stands in front of him with a long stick having a sharp iron point. Two men are also stationed on either side, protected by the tame ones, with sticks with sharp crooks, while others rub his back and talk to him in a consoling and encouraging tone. At first he is excessively indignant, and strikes in every direction with his proboscis; but his blows are received by the men on the sharp points of their sticks and crooks, till the end is thoroughly sore. Finding that he has the worst of it, and seemingly acknowledging that his captors have established their supremacy, he coils it tightly up, and seldom again attempts to use it as a weapon of offence. The next process is to take him to bathe between two tame elephants, and to compel him to lie down. This is done by tightening the ropes which unite his feet, and by the driver pressing the sharp point of the crook on his back-bone. Often for several days he resists and roars most lustily, and the assistance of the tame ones is required to keep him in order. In about three weeks, perhaps, he may be left alone, and then when he is taken to bathe with his feet only hobbled, a man walks backwards in front of him with the point of his pike presented at his head, and two others, one at each ear, holding their pointed crooks. On reaching the water, the dread of having the crook pressed against his backbone makes him immediately lie down. After this the process is easy. They vary much in disposition. Some will within even a day or two feed out of a man's hand. The great secret is, while proving to them the power of man, to treat them with kindness and to win their confidence. From the treatment their feet receive when being captured, they will not allow them to be touched for months and years afterwards without exhibiting signs of anger. Though in other respects tamed, they cannot be put to work for three or four months—indeed, till they take their food eagerly, and flourish on it. Otherwise they quickly die, as the natives say, of a broken heart. They are taught to draw a waggon, or to tread clay for forming bricks; but by far the most important service they render is in piling timber and removing large blocks of stone. It is most curious to observe the way in which one will take up a huge log of timber in his trunk and carry it through a narrow road, turning it longways when there is not width to allow it to pass, and avoiding all impediments, and finally placing log after log on the pile with the greatest regularity. This he will do without any driver to guide his movements, and directed entirely by his own sagacity.

From what I could learn, the average age of elephants is about seventy years, though some have been known to have lived twice as long; and one elephant, who only lately died, and whose skeleton, I have heard, is in the Museum of Natural History at Belfast, was successively in the service of the Dutch and English Governments—certainly for upwards of a century. Probably he was a hundred and twenty years old at least. The natives believe that elephants bury their own dead. Certain it is that they remove them from any spot which they are accustomed to frequent, shoving their bodies on with their heads or tusks, or dragging them with their trunks. Others believe that elephants select some remote and sequestered spot by the side of a lake surrounded by mountains, and thither they resort when they feel their death approaching, that they may lie down and die tranquilly. The popular belief, however, is that they live to an almost illimitable age when in a state of freedom; and that is the reason why their dead bodies are seldom or never found, unless they have met their death from the sportsman's rifle.

An elephant requires three men to attend to him. One is his mahout or attendant, and two, as leaf-cutters, to supply him with food; so that the cost of his keep is upwards of three shillings a-day. The elephants of Ceylon have sometimes, but not often, tusks, while those of Africa are generally supplied with them. So peaceable and amiable are their dispositions, that they are provided with no other weapon of offence; for the trunk, though powerful, is too delicate an organ to be used willingly for the attack of other animals, except in cases of necessity. Indeed, he has no enemies who venture to attack him except man; and of late years, in consequence of the wide distribution of firearms among the natives, and the great number of English sportsmen who have invaded the country, their numbers have greatly diminished.

I heard of one Englishman having killed upwards of a thousand of those noble brutes, and of others, five hundred or more I cannot say how I might think of the matter if I was to indulge in the sport, but my present feeling is that of unmitigated horror that any man should willingly be guilty of such wholesale slaughter, unless in case of necessity. If it was important to rid the country of them, they might engage in the work for the sake of becoming public benefactors. Lions, tigers, and wild boars should be killed, because they are dangerous to human beings; and the time may come when, the wilds of Ceylon being brought under cultivation, it may be necessary to exterminate the sagacious elephant, or, at all events, to reduce him to subjection, and to keep him within limited bounds.

Elephants delight in the shade, and shun the heat of the sun. Thus they are found often in large herds on the mountain heights in Ceylon, at an elevation of some thousand feet above the sea. With regard to their sight, that is supposed to be somewhat circumscribed, and they depend for their safety on their acute sense of smell and hearing. The sounds they utter are very remarkable, and by them they seem to be able to communicate with each other. That of warning to the herd is a deep hollow ringing sound, like that of an empty cask being struck; a common caution to their friends is a simple quiver of the lips, which makes a noise like *prur-r-r*; that of pain is a deep groan from the throat; that of rage is a shrill trumpeting through his proboscis. But they also make many other scarcely describable noises. The height of the elephant is generally over-estimated, the ordinary height being from eight to nine feet, though in some instances they may be found exceeding it. His agility, the gentleness of his tread, considering his size, and the silent way in which he escapes through the forest, is worthy of remark. The elephant, when he lies down, stretches his legs out behind him, not under him, as does the horse—a beautiful arrangement for an animal of his vast bulk, as thus, without any violent strain, he is able to lift himself up. The thigh-bone is very much longer in proportion to that of the *metatarsus*—the one below it—than is the case with other animals, and thus the knee is very much lower down. He has also no hock, and can thus bend his knee as completely as a human being. By this arrangement he is able to descend declivities without difficulty. In traversing a mountain region he invariably selects the ridge of a chain, and takes the shortest path to the nearest safe ford. They are generally found in herds of about twenty each, which are evidently distinct families; and though they may mingle with other herds at times when they meet to drink at the same tanks or water-courses, they invariably unite together again at the slightest alarm. Elephants become rogues from various causes; chiefly when they have been separated from the herd, and, from living a life of bachelor solitude, become morose and vicious. They at length generally resort to the neighbourhood of human habitations, where they commit serious depredations on the rice grounds and among the cocoa-nut plantations. Sometimes they will approach a dwelling, and travellers are frequently attacked and even killed by them. The natives, therefore, give every encouragement to European sportsmen who will undertake to destroy them; and in this case they really can be of very great service. Nowell and I, on hearing this account of the rogues, agreed that the first we heard of we would undertake to attack, and we quite longed for an opportunity of exerting our powers in so useful an undertaking.

No one seemed able to account for the reason why elephants are so much afraid of wands or spears. They will not even, unless driven by terror, attempt to pass through the slightest reed fence but a few feet in height. Thus a single watcher is able to keep them off the rice and coracan lands; and in some places, where these intervene between their haunts and the tanks where they are accustomed to drink, passages are made, lined by bamboo fences, and they pass up and down them without attempting to break into the fields, though full of their favourite food. Their instinct tells them exactly when the products of the ground in which they most delight are ripe, and they regularly make their appearance in that part of the country where they are to be found. Now, curiously enough, as soon as the rice and coracan are removed and the fences are broken, the elephants walk into the fields and regularly glean them. When this is done they move on to some other district. In the same way they visit those parts of the country where the palmyra palm flourishes, at the time the fruit from its ripeness is about to fall to the ground. Some are said to be very inquisitive, and will not only examine any structure which has been put up in the locality they frequent, but rogues especially will often even pull down huts or cottages, and do all sorts of mischief, apparently from mere wantonness. Elephants live on the leaves of all sorts of trees, as well as grass, and grain, and fruits. They especially like the cocoa-nut. Stripping off the fibre, they crush the shell with their tusks, and let the juice trickle down their throats. The position of the trunk is very graceful when they feed themselves; as it is also when they hold a branch and fan off the flies from their backs. I forgot to say that, though they often lie down, they are frequently found asleep leaning against a tree or a rock, and often in captivity stand on their feet for months together without ever lying down. However, I might go on, I find, recounting the curious circumstances about elephants till I had filled my journal; and I must therefore continue without further interruption an account of our journey.

CHAPTER XIII.

Singhalese Torches—Chewing Areca-Nut—The Veddahs—Devil-Dancers—Chena Cultivations—A Rogue Elephant—Rat Snake—My First Elephant Hunt—Horrible Situation—Nearly Killed by an Elephant—Providential Escape.

ON leaving the scene of the great elephant hunt I described in my last chapter, we turned our faces once more towards the region of the northern coffee estates.

Mr. Fordyce then told me that he had dispatched a messenger to inquire whether Mr. Coventry was residing on his property, and if not, where he was to be found. Before we had proceeded far we met the messenger, who brought word that Mr. Coventry, and a young gentleman who was staying with him, had set off a short time before for Trincomalé, where they probably now were.

"Then to Trincomalé we will go," exclaimed Mr. Fordyce. "We will run our fox to earth, at all events, provided he does not take to the water and swim away."

"Then I, however, must follow wherever he goes," I observed. "I feel sure Alfred is with him; and yet I cannot account for his not having written home. Oh, how I long to find him, poor fellow!"

I could not help fancying that Mr. Fordyce, kind and liberal as he was to me, did not quite enter into my feelings about finding Alfred. Perhaps, through my impatience, I did him injustice. I thanked him most cordially for his kindness; for I felt that, at all events, if left to my own resources I should have been utterly unable to follow my grandfather from place to place as I was now doing.

Again we plunged into the gloomy shade of a Ceylon forest. I have already described the large retinue with which we had to move ; and though we carried a great deal of food, so much was required for so large a number that we had to depend mainly on our guns for the meat to put into our pots. Of this, however, neither Nowell nor I complained, as it gave us the very sort of employment we most enjoyed.

One ordinary day's journey was very much like another. The first morning we were aroused before sunrise, and on going out of our tents we found our attendants with torches in their hands ready to accompany us. These were not only to light us on our way, but to frighten off any bears, wild boars, or elephants, who might be crossing our path, and would be ugly customers to meet in a narrow road. These torches are called *chules*. They are made out of the straight and dry branches of the "welang tree," which is bruised into loose strips, still, however, holding together. They last burning for a couple of hours. No scene could be more picturesque, as our numerous cavalcade wound down a mountain path, with rocks and woods on either side ; some thrown into shade, and others standing out prominently in the ruddy glare thrown around by the torches. We rode on till the heat of the sun warned us that it was time to stop ; and while our tents were pitched by the side of a stream of pure water, which had its source in the neighbouring mountains, the servants lighted the fires, and commenced active preparations for breakfast. Rice was boiled, coffee was made, curries concocted, and game— which had just before been shot—spitted and set to turn and roast. We meantime enjoyed the luxury of a cool bath within the shade of our tents. There were no crocodiles in the stream ; but in most places it is dangerous to bathe in the tanks and rivers, which abound with them, as many are large enough to carry off a man between their jaws without the slightest difficulty.

By the side of the stream grew numerous tall trees, in many places completely overarching it. The most remarkable was the kombook, from the branches of which hung the pods of the large puswel bean. The pods are the most gigantic I have seen, measuring six feet in length, by five or six inches in width. From the calcined bark of this tree the natives extract a sort of lime, with which they mix the betel they are constantly chewing. The inhabitants of Ceylon have the same enjoyment in it as Europeans have in chewing tobacco. It is used with the areca-nut, the product of the graceful areca palm. They thus take, unconsciously, as a corrective to their somewhat acid food, a combination of carminative, antacid, and tonic. Every Singhalese carries in his waist-cloth a box containing some nuts of the areca and a few fresh leaves of the betel pepper, as also a smaller box to hold the chunam or lime. The mode of taking it is to scrape down the nut, and to roll it up with some lime in a betel leaf. On chewing it, much saliva is produced of a bright red colour, with which the lips and teeth are completely stained, giving the mouth a most unpleasant appearance.

While we were seated at breakfast we observed a dark small figure moving out in the skirts of the forest nearest to us. At first I thought it was a monkey; and so did Nowell, who was going to fire at it, but Mr. Fordyce happily restrained him.

"Let us see what the creature will do," said he. "I am not at all certain that it is not a human being."

After looking about cautiously, the figure came out of the shade of the wood, and then we saw that it was really a human being—a large-headed, mis-shapen man, with long black hair hanging half-way down his body, the only clothing he wore being a piece of dirty cloth round his waist. He looked starved and wretched, so we held out some food to him. He eyed it wistfully, but seemed to have the same fear of approaching us that a strange dog would. We observed that our followers looked at him with expressions both of mistrust and disgust, so I volunteered to go and take him some food. I put it on a plate, and carried it towards him. He looked at it without saying a word, and then seized it with both hands, and ate it up with the greatest avidity. He had evidently been nearly starving, when the smell of our cooking operations brought him to our encampment. I signed to him that I would get him some more food, when he sat himself down on the grass at a short distance only from our circle, and near enough for Mr. Fordyce to speak to him. Our friend addressed him in a variety of dialects, and at last he answered with some scarcely articulate sounds. After a short conversation had taken place, Mr Fordyce said :—

"The man is a remnant of one of the tribes of Veddahs. They are the most degraded, or rather least civilized of all the people of Ceylon. They are divided into Rock Veddahs, Village Veddahs, and Coast Veddahs. This man belongs to the first, who are the most barbarous of all. They are omnivorous, eating carrion or anything that comes in their way—roots, or fish, or wild honey, or any animals they can catch; but their favourite food is monkeys and lizards. They live either in caves and nooks in rocks, or on platforms among the boughs of trees. They hunt the deer with bows and arrows, and dry the flesh, which they sometimes barter for articles for which they have a fancy, such as cocoa-nuts, arrow-heads, hatchets, cooking bowls, and coloured cloths. Each family has a head man, who manages domestic affairs, but exercises very little sway over them; their language is of the most limited description; they have no religious rites, no knowledge of a superior being or idea of a future state, and they do not even bury their dead, but cover them up with leaves in the recesses of the forest. They have no names for years, days, or hours; they can scarcely count beyond five on their fingers, and they have no music, games, or amusements of any sort. The Village Veddahs are a degree superior to them, as they live in huts, and roughly cultivate the ground. The Coast Veddahs are somewhat less savage than the first, and employ themselves in fishing and in cutting timber. They have much gentleness of disposition, and though, as might be expected, their morals are in the lowest state, grave crimes are seldom committed. Our government have made most laudable attempts to reclaim them, and in many instances, seconded by the devoted efforts of the missionaries, have met with great success. When I said they have no religious ceremony, I ought to have mentioned that when they are sick, they fancy that they are affected by an evil spirit, and so they send for a devil-dancer to drive it away. Something eatable is made as an offering to the evil spirit, and placed on a tripod of sticks. Before this the devil-dancer, who has his head and girdle decorated with green leaves, begins to shuffle his feet by degrees, working himself into the greatest fury, screaming and moaning, during which time he pretends to receive instructions how to cure the malady. The Wesleyan missionaries especially have laboured indefatigably among these wretched beings, and notwithstanding the low state of barbarism into which they had sunk, have succeeded in converting many hundreds to a knowledge of the glorious truths of Christianity, and in bringing them within the pale of civilization. They are settled in villages, cultivate the ground, and have schools among them. One or two stations, in consequence of the missionaries having been carried off by fever, have been abandoned; but even there those Veddahs who had come under their influence continued to build cottages and practise the various arts they had learned. Still, throughout the length and breadth of Ceylon, there is a wide, and, I firmly believe, a fruitful field among all castes and tribes for the labours of the Christian missionary."

Having won the confidence of our Veddah, Mr. Fordyce desired him to light a fire by means of two dried sticks—a difficult operation, in which they are said to be great adepts. He replied that he would do as we wished; and breaking one of his arrows in two, he sharpened the end of one into a point, and making a hole in the other, he held it between his feet and twirled the first rapidly round between the palms of his hands. But a few moments had passed before smoke ascended and charcoal appeared; that quickly ignited; and some leaves and sticks being applied, a blazing fire was soon made.

Mr. Fordyce, after questioning the savage, inquired if more of his companions were in the neighbourhood. He said yes, and that he could soon bring them. He disappeared, and we got some food ready. In a short time he returned, with nearly twenty wretched-looking beings, their hair and beards hanging in masses down to their waists. Each carried an iron-headed axe in a girdle, a bow about six feet in length strung with twisted bark, and a few ill-made arrows with peacocks' feathers at one end and an iron unbarbed head tapering to a point at the other. After we had given them the deer's flesh we had prepared, we set up a mark and told them to shoot at it. They were miserable marksmen, not one arrow in half-a-dozen hitting the target. They said that all they required was to wound their game, and then that they ran it down till it died; that they could kill an elephant by wounding him in the foot. The shaft breaks short off, when, the wound festering, the poor brute becomes so lame that they can easily overtake him, and eventually worry him to death.

Travelling on through the forest, we came suddenly on an open space of three hundred acres or more, with a number

A CHENA PLOT.

of huts in the centre, and people actively employed in cultivating the ground. The space was divided into patches, containing paddy or dry rice, grain, Indian corn, coracan, with sweet potatoes, cassava, onions, yams, chillies, as also cotton-plants. I was surprised to find that the cultivators had only a temporary occupation of the ground. It is called chena cultivation. Pumpkins, sugar-cane, hemp, yams, millet, and other grains and vegetables are grown.' A number of families obtain a license from the government agent of the district to cultivate a plot of ground in this way for two years, and no more. Most of the products I have mentioned are cleared off in a shorter time, but the cotton plant and a few others require a longer period. A part of the community remain to gather them, while the rest move on to another chena plot, which they treat in the same way.

A day or two after this, emerging once more from the forest, we found ourselves approaching a village of mud-huts, of different sizes—one of them, built round an open court-yard, had been prepared for our reception, the rooms having been hung with white cloths by the head washerman of the place, whose official duty it is to attend to visitors. He had borrowed them for the occasion from the villagers, and would have to return them well washed and whitened. They served to hide the dirt on the walls. The rooms had each but one small window, or hole rather. They all opened into the court. They kept out the air, but certainly no sun could get in. Such a building is the usual habitation even of chiefs. Some, however, have handsome carved furniture, both tables and chairs, and cabinets, while their wives and daughters are decked in flowing robes and ornaments of gold and precious stones.

Scarcely had we taken up our quarters in our new abode, when the head man of the place and some of the chief villagers came in due form to pay their respects to Mr. Fordyce. They said that they understood that he was accompanied by some renowned sportsmen, to whom they could offer a magnificent opportunity of displaying their prowess. We pricked up our ears as Mr. Fordyce translated this. The neighbourhood was infested by a huge rogue elephant, whom none of these people could succeed in killing. He was not the only one, as many other rogues frequented the tank where he was usually seen, but he was by far the most mischievous. He would walk into fields at night and eat up the corn, and even into gardens and consume the vegetables; several times he had pulled down huts to get at corn stored within them, and once he had upset a cottage and very nearly destroyed the inhabitants. He had besides killed several people—some of whom he had met by chance, and others who had gone out to kill him.

Nowell was not at all daunted by these accounts, and told Mr. Fordyce that he had made up his mind to try and kill the rogue. I begged to accompany him, and Mr. Fordyce said that he would go and keep us out of mischief. We had our two Moor-men—the chief of whom we called Dango; and several of the villagers volunteered to accompany us and show us the haunts of the rogue. All arrangements were soon made—we were to start by dawn the next morning.

Delighted with the prospect before us, I was about to lie down on a sofa prepared as my bed, when I saw a snake fully four feet long glide in at the door of the room, and coil itself away under my pillow. I had no fancy for such a companion, and not knowing whether or not it was venomous, I shouted to Dango, whom I saw in the court, to come and help me to kill it. Nowell, who had left the room, heard me call, and came at the same time. Dango fearlessly put in his hand, and turning out the snake, said that it was only a rat-snake kept tame about the house for the purpose of killing rats, and that it was perfectly harmless. Still I could not bring myself to lie down on the couch with the expectation of such a visitor. Nowell very good-naturedly said that I might take his sofa, and that he would sleep on mine. I placed myself, therefore, on three cane chairs at the table, on which a lamp was burning. I fell asleep, but was awoke before long by hearing a rattling and scampering noise about the room, when, opening my eyes, I saw a dozen or more rats making free with our boots and eatables, and a number of other articles. Just then from under Nowell's pillow out glided the rat-snake; quick as thought he seized one rat, then another, and then another, by which time the rats had scampered off. He glided away in pursuit, and I conclude returned and carried away the rest, if he did not eat them on the spot, for they were gone when I awoke.

After hurriedly discussing some coffee and biscuit, we started on our expedition. Mr. Fordyce and Nowell had each two rifles. I had only one. Dango was told to keep near me. Poor Solon was very unhappy at again being left behind, but he was so very likely to get killed if he flew at an elephant that it was but prudent not to take him with us. Torches were lighted to show us the way and scare off wild beasts, as we sallied forth from our tapestried chambers. There was a slight crescent moon, and the stars were shining with the most wonderful brilliancy in the dark blue sky on the calm waters of a lake or ruined reservoir, along which our course for some little distance lay. There we had to border round a piece of country which had some years before been subject to the process of chena cultivation, but which, having been again deserted, was covered with a dense thorny jungle such as no man could force his way through without being almost torn in pieces, but which affords a secure retreat to elephants and all other wild animals. Close to the edge of this the cultivated land of the village extended, and people were stationed in watch-houses erected up among the branches of the trees, shrieking and yelling, and beating drums, and making every conceivable noise to drive back into the jungle the elephants who were accustomed to take their morning repast off their fields of coracan, and maize or millet. It was well known that the rogue elephant was near, and so audacious had he become, that though driven off from one part, he was very likely to appear directly afterwards in another. After waiting for some time in the hopes of getting a shot at him from the trees, we came to the conclusion that he suspected danger, and would not again appear. Nowell, who took the lead, therefore resolved to follow him. Dango was too keen about the matter to object, though, as he observed, " Many mans get killed so."

I ought to have said that Dango had been so much with the English, and so often out with English sportsmen, that he could express himself very tolerably in English. Mr. Fordyce, laughing, said that he should prefer watching outside with the horses; so, accompanied by four of the most active villagers, Nowell, Dango, and I prepared to penetrate through the jungle. Our only mode of escaping the thorns was to crawl on our hands and knees, trailing our rifles after us; and to do this without the certainty of their going off, we had to secure the locks in cases. Then we had the possibility of meeting unexpectedly with a cobra di capello, or boa constrictor, or a wild boar, or more dangerous still, a bear, besides running a risk of having our eyes scratched out, and other little inconveniences of that sort. Our chief object was to avoid making any noise.

After proceeding some way, we could hear the rustling sound of the leaves, as the rogue, as we supposed, moved his head or perhaps only his ears among them. I held my breath. There were no tall trees near behind which we could run should he espy us. Our only chance of safety was in bringing him down by a shot. We were well to windward of him, and he had not yet discovered us. We all stopped, holding our breath, with our rifles cocked, ready to fire. We were not a dozen yards from him, but so thick was the jungle that nothing of him could be seen. Suddenly the peculiar "prur-r-r" sound I have described was heard. I saw Nowell and Dango exchange glances. Suddenly the almost perfect silence was broken by a loud shrill trumpeting, followed immediately by a terrific crash such as an elephant only can make, as with his huge body he rushes through the jungle.

"Here they come," cried Nowell; "it is not a single rogue —there may be a dozen; we must turn them, or we shall be done for. Fire at the biggest, and perhaps the rest will take to flight."

I had no time to ask him how he knew this. In truth, I am not ashamed to say that I felt as I had never felt before. Just as I expected to see the herd of monsters appearing through the jungle, and either to see one of them roll over from the effect of my rifle, or to have one of his huge feet placed upon me, or to feel myself wriggling, like a worm in the beak of a bird, in his trunk, Nowell shouted out, "They have winded us —they have turned—they are running. On, on—follow, follow."

This was more easily said than done. The herd had, as we soon found, formed a lane; but thousands of thorny creepers, from the size of cables to the thinnest wires, still hung across it from bush to bush, and cactus plants, from twenty feet and upwards in height, many overthrown and partly crushed, presented their sword-like points as a *chevaux-de-frise* to impede our advance. Still, in the excitement of the chase we scarcely felt the pricks and punctures our bodies were receiving, or saw the tatters to which our clothes were being reduced. On we pushed, creeping under or jumping over obstacles, or hacking at them with our knives—Dango and the natives using their axes with great effect. It seemed wonderful how their nearly naked skins did not get torn off their bodies; but by long practice they knew how to avoid obstacles far better than we did.

The elephants were going along before us at a great rate, for at least twenty minutes had passed since we had last seen them; still, we could not tell at what moment we might again be upon them. Dango once more cautioned us to be ready. Not a sound was heard. The boughs were still quivering which they must have set in motion. We knew that we must be again close upon them. Stealthily as North American Indians on a war trail we crept on. I began to feel much more confidence than I had before done. Still, I only hoped that the elephants would not charge us. We got our rifles ready for a shot. Every instant we expected to be upon them, when suddenly the warning "prur-r-r-r-r-t" was heard, followed by a loud crashing of boughs and brushwood. Were they about to charge us? No; off they were again. The sun was getting up. There was but little air that we could feel. Still, there was enough to carry our scent down to the elephant. It was intensely hot. We had had very little breakfast, and I began to think that elephant-shooting was rather a serious sort of sport after all. Nowell was too practised and keen a sportsman to think anything of the sort, so hallooing me on again, we went ahead in the chase. We had much the same sort of ground as before. I longed to be out of the jungle, but the cunning elephants well knew that it was the safest sort of country for them. They could always keep out of sight in it, and might if they wished charge us at any moment. Had they been the ferocious creatures some people describe them, this they would have done long before. By degrees, the little wind there had been died away, and Dango intimated that the elephants were circling round, probably making for the lake we had before passed. This gave us fresh hope of overtaking them. On we pushed, therefore. At length we came to a point where the thick trail separated in two parts—one keeping to the left, the other straight on. Nowell determined to follow the latter, though it was the narrowest, made by only two or three elephants, or perhaps only one. We knew now that we were less likely to be discovered by the elephants, as they know of the approach of their enemies more by their scent than their sight, which is supposed to be rather short. Working our way on, we entered a low jungle which had been a short time before a chena plantation. It was about five feet high, and it was of so dense a character that no human being could have penetrated it unless in the track of elephants. We had not entered it more than five minutes, when just before us appeared the retreating form of a huge elephant. Nowell started with delight and rushed on. I followed close at his heels, and Dango and the natives followed me.

It seemed extraordinary foolhardiness that a few men should have ventured to follow close on the heels of a huge monster armed with powers so prodigious as the elephant. So it would have been had it not been for those deadly little rifle balls we carried in our guns.

Nowell had almost got up to the monster, who, however, still went on. What was my surprise to see Nowell suddenly stop, and lifting his rifle, give him a bow chaser. He must have expected to cripple him, and thus to be better able to give him a shot in a vital part. The elephant in a moment halted, Nowell being almost close upon him. Round the monster turned with a terrific shriek of pain and fury. Nowell sprang back only just in time to get out of the way of his trunk. The elephant for a moment stood facing us, and blocking up the path in front. We had the narrow pathway he had formed through the jungle alone to retreat by. Nowell had only one barrel loaded, and was not ten paces from the huge brute. Still, he stood calm as a statue. I could not help expecting to see him crushed the next instant beneath the elephant's feet, and believed that I and those behind me would share his fate directly after. In a clear grass country, with some trees to get behind, they might have hoped to escape, as a man can run as fast as an elephant, and keep it up longer; but in the tangled brake through which we had passed they would not have the remotest chance of it. If Nowell fell, I believed that I should fall also. The suspense lasted but a short time. Raising his trunk, and trumpeting with rage, on came the elephant. Nowell still stood steady as a rock, showing the firmest nerve; the elephant was within six paces of him. I stepped forward with my rifle levelled and my eye on the elephant's forehead. Nowell fired. Through the smoke which hung thickly around I saw the monster's head appearing with terrible distinctness I heard Nowell's voice. Whether or not the elephant was crushing him I could not tell. I fired my first barrel. I was about to fire the other, when the huge head sank down to the ground, and from the cloud of smoke Nowell appeared standing within two feet of the monster's trunk.

"Bravo! capitally done, Marsden!" he exclaimed in a clear voice. "Your shot is not far off mine, that I'll be bound."

The elephant lay dead before us. He was right; his bullet had taken effect in the elephant's forehead, and mine was two inches below it. Which had killed him I do not know. Probably either would have proved mortal. Certainly he dropped the moment he got mine. We had done some good; we had commenced the destruction of the marauding herd, but still we had not killed the rogue. Excited to the utmost by our success, and ready for anything, we resolved if possible to accomplish that undertaking before we returned to the village.

One of the natives cutting off the tail of the elephant we had killed, we worked our way as well as we could out of the jungle, and found ourselves in a more open country, with the lake on one side and some hills on the other—the intervening space, sloping up the side of the mountain, being covered with dense lemon grass, which we found on approaching was twelve feet high. Dango, on looking about and examining the ground, assured us that the herd had gone in that direction, and that the rogue himself was not far from him. The spot was altogether a very secluded one, and very likely to be the resort of large herds of elephants. Before us a promontory stretched out into the lake. We proceeded to the end to look out for elephants, as there was no doubt that they frequented the lake to drink; but none were seen, so we judged that they had retired into the cooler jungle after their morning repast. We turned, therefore, back to the foot of the mountains on our left, when the loud trumpeting or roaring of elephants brought us to a halt. The roaring grew louder and louder, and as it reverberated among the cliffs and rocks, it seemed more like distant thunder than any sound which living animals could make, and more dread-inspiring than anything I could have conceived. Dango said at once that the sound must be made by a large herd, and that they were a quarter of a mile off at least. On drawing nearer, Dango discovered the tracks, though the ground was hard and sandy, and covered with rocks. He pointed out here and there a stone displaced, and pieces of twigs, and crunched grass, and leaves which the elephants had dropped while browsing as they sauntered on. Here and there also we came to a soft place, where they had left the marks of their huge feet.

It was now necessary to proceed with the greatest caution, for we knew that we could not be many paces from the herd. Having clambered over and among a number of rocks with no little difficulty, we found ourselves on the margin of a level space, so completely covered with the lemon grass of which I have spoken that it was with difficulty we could force our way through it. Still, Nowell did not hesitate to enter it, and of course I went with him, followed closely by Dango and the natives. Presently Nowell put his hand on my shoulder, and pointing forward, I perceived the dark lump just rising above the tall grass, less than forty yards off, with something moving about, which I soon guessed was an elephant's ear, which it was flapping up and down.

Directly afterwards we made out another elephant close to it; and from the peculiar movement of the grass in different places there could be no doubt that we were close upon a large and just now scattered herd; but as the grass was above their heads, we could not make out exactly how many were in each spot. Again we all stopped, and Nowell signed to the men to be excessively careful; the slightest noise would have alarmed them. They might either have charged at us from different quarters, or they might have turned tail and trotted off before we could get a shot at them. The two elephants we had at first seen, there could be little doubt, from their superior height, were the leaders of the herd, and probably the rogue was, as usual, at no great distance. It was very important, if we could, to ascertain his position, as he, we knew, was most likely to be on the look-out, and to come suddenly upon us. We retreated slowly to a rock, from whence we thought we should get a better view over the sea of grass, when I stumbled and hit the butt of my rifle against a stone. Slight as the noise was, it was enough to awake the vigilance of the watchers. At the same moment, high up above the grass went their trunks, and they blew the loud shrill note of alarm. Immediately from different directions other trunks were thrown up, each sounding an answering blast; and here and there the vast heads of elephants appeared, with eyes glancing around, trying to ascertain the nature of the danger of which their leaders had forewarned them.

All this time the two leaders were keeping up the most

terrific, rumbling roar, like peal upon peal of thunder, thus summoning the herd to unite. However, they did not show any disposition to retreat, but kept gazing at us with ears cocked, as if they fully intended us mischief. We still kept as quiet as possible, hoping to see all the herd unite before they attempted to decamp. In a short time a very considerable number had assembled round the two leaders, and there they stood gazing at our faces just appearing above the grass, and seemingly meditating whether they should make a rush at us or not. Nowell seemed to think that this was a favourable opportunity to advance towards them. On we went through the high grass. Had I not been with a good sportsman like Nowell and a practised hunter like Dango, I should have thought that what we were doing was the height of madness. No sooner, however, did we thus boldly advance than the greater portion of the herd turned round and retreated before us. At the same time the two leaders, and a third who had joined them, as was the duty of the warriors probably of the party, formed in line, and beating the grass right and left with their trunks, with ears cocked, tails up, and uttering loud screams, rushed forward directly at us. My legs felt a strong inclination to turn about and run away; but as Nowell in the coolest manner advanced to meet them, so of necessity did I.

"Marsden, mark the right fellow, and aim carefully at the forehead," said he. "I'll take the two left. Dango, have the rifle ready to hand me if I want it."

He spoke as calmly as if there was not a particle of danger. I began to fancy that there was none, and that in a wonderful way gave me coolness. I kept my rifle on the cock, ready to fire when he gave the word. On they came in a perfect line, till they were within ten paces of us.

"Fire!" he exclaimed.

The smoke obscured all before us. There was still a tramping sound. I saw a huge head projecting out of it, while a terrific roar sounded close to me. I had still one barrel. I fired, and the monster dropped dead. When the smoke cleared off we found that the right and left beasts had been killed by our first shots, but that he had only wounded the second elephant, my shot having killed him outright. I was exceedingly proud of my achievements, and it excited me to further exertions. I forgot all about my previous dislike to the idea of killing the sagacious animals. Indeed, after the tales the villagers had told us of the devastations they had committed, I felt that we were really conferring a great benefit on the poor people.

"On, on after them!" cried Nowell, as soon as we had reloaded and inspected the elephants we had killed.

A wide lane was formed by the retreating elephants as they had crushed through the tall grass, and we could see them in full retreat before us. We rushed after them at a rapid rate, forgetting all the necessary caution. We soon gained upon them, and one of them turning his head, Nowell fired, and over he went. All the savage part of our nature was, I believe, excited. For my own part I only thought of how many elephants I could kill. Another animal turned—I believe that he was going to stand at bay or to charge—I fired, the bullet hit him, and down he went. I was rushing up to him when Nowell shouted to me to stop. Fortunately he did so, for up got the monster with a cry of fury, and charged us. Nowell fired, and before the smoke had cleared away he had ceased to struggle. Still there were many more elephants, but they began to scatter. Nowell followed some to the right, while I, not seeing that he had gone in that direction, went after some to the left. They made up the mountain. I found that Dango was coming after me, having handed Nowell's second rifle to one of the other men. Before us appeared a large elephant and a little one not more than three and a half feet in height. We very quickly caught them up, when the mother —if mother she was—instead of protecting the young one, retreated up the mountain towards a thick jungle near at hand, leaving it in our power. Dango, with a spring, caught it by the tail, but so strong was it, that it was dragging him towards the jungle, when it turned round its trunk, and he then caught that also, and there he held it, shouting lustily for me to come and help him, while the little elephant kept bellowing and roaring louder than even the big ones. I hurried up and assisted in dragging the poor little poonchy up to a tree, to which Dango, with some of the flexible creepers which grew about, very quickly made it fast, at the same time hobbling its feet so, that had it broken loose it could not run away. Just as we had done, while roaring away as loudly as a full-grown elephant, it gave me a blow with its trunk which very nearly flattened my nose in a very disagreeable way. However, I felt that I richly deserved the infliction, so did not retaliate.

All this time we fully expected to see the mother return to the assistance of her charge, but still she kept away. We therefore retired to a little distance behind some rocks to wait for her; but we were not wholly concealed, and although little poonchy kept roaring on, she still kept carefully within the cover. It was Dango's opinion, as it was mine, that she was not the real mother of the little animal, but that its own mother having been killed, it had gone to her for protection, and that her own was somewhere else with the herd. Indeed, we had seen another young elephant running off with the main body.

On looking down over the now well-trampled sea of lemon grass, we saw in the distance several more elephants. Wishing to rejoin Nowell, and to have another chance of a shot, I descended the hill, followed by Dango. We worked our way up to the spot where our three elephants lay, when my companion shrieked out at the top of his voice,—

" Sahib, sahib, look dere, look dere—elephant come! "

CHARGED BY A WILD ELEPHANT.

I did look towards the point indicated, and there, sure enough, came a huge beast—who was evidently, from his peculiar characteristics, every inch a rogue—bursting at full charge through the tall grass. He carried his trunk high up in the air, while—with ears cocked, and his tail standing out above his back like the ensign staff at the stern of a man-of-war's boat—screaming terrifically, he rushed at me with scarcely credible velocity. To escape from him through that tall, thick grass was utterly impossible. What to him were mere gossamer threads served effectually to stop my progress. I had all along at first had some slight doubts as to the wisdom of the expedition in which I was engaged. I then remembered that I foolishly had not loaded after I had fired my last shot. I had, consequently, only one barrel ready. I felt that my last moment had come. Awful and dreadful was the sensation which came over me. I need not say that I tried to pray for mercy, for protection; but I could not help feeling that I had brought my fate upon myself.

"Home!—in vain will they wait my return. Alfred too! who will now search for him?"

Such thoughts passed like lightning through my brain. With his trunk raised I could not hope to hit the elephant on the forehead even if I fired, so I resolved to wait till the last moment, when he was close upon me, thinking that he might then lower it to strike me, and expose a vital spot. On he came with a speed greater than I had supposed an elephant could use. Right and left flew the long grass, louder and louder grew his horrid screams as he saw that I was within his power. Still his trunk was raised, and I could not fire. In another moment, with a scream of triumph and gratified rage, he was within three feet of me. I fired, and immediately exerting all my muscular powers to the utmost, I sprang on one side. In vain it seemed. Down like a flash of lightning he lashed his powerful trunk at me, and I felt myself hurled through the air as a ball is sent off from a golf-stick, to the distance of a dozen yards from him, or even more, I thought. Happily it was among the still standing grass. I had been struck on the thigh, and was not stunned, though the limb felt numbed, and I thought must be smashed to pieces. That little mattered, though, as I fully expected to have my head in another moment in as bad a condition. I looked up; I could see where he was by the movement of the top of the grass. He stopped and kept beating the grass about on every side with his trunk, evidently searching for me, that he might squeeze the breath out of my body with his huge knees. I lay as still as death, not daring to breathe, for I knew that my only hope of safety lay in his not discovering me till some one came up to my rescue. What had become of Dango I could not tell. Nearer and nearer he drew. It is impossible to describe my sensations. When I was standing upright with my weapon in my hand, and hoped to bring him down by a shot, they had been very terrible—now they were ten times worse. I could hear the grass rustling as he drew close to where I lay. I should have liked to have shut my eyes and resigned myself to my fate, but I could not. Closer and closer he drew. His long black trunk waved several times about the grass over the very spot where I was. He bent it to the right and left, as a heavy fall of rain with a strong wind does a field of corn. Tighter I held my breath, and mercifully, in consequence of my having reserved my fire till the muzzle of my rifle almost touched him, had so nearly blinded him, and so dulled his power of scent, that he was less able to discover me. Had his trunk but grazed me as he struck it about above my head, I should instantly have been discovered, and my fate would have been sealed. Round and round me he walked, roaring away in his fury and disappointment at not finding me. The circle grew larger, and the noise of the rustling of the grass grew fainter. Once more I began to breathe, and to consider what was the matter with my leg. Still I dared not move. Perhaps the rogue was only standing still watching for me. No;

the rustling continued, but every moment was growing fainter. It ceased altogether. Then I heard some shouting and loud trumpeting, followed quickly by three shots in succession. I earnestly hoped that Nowell had not been caught by the rogue. I felt thankful that I had thus far been saved, but still I was not certain that I was safe. At length I ventured to move my limbs to ascertain if my thigh was broken. I first found, to my great joy, that I was able to crawl, and then that I could stand upright. My cap was gone, and so was my rifle, I could not tell where. I felt the pain too great to proceed, and so I shouted at the top of my voice for help. An answer was made to my cry, and soon Dango came working his way through the grass up to me. The tears streamed down his cheeks when he saw me, for he thought I was killed. Unarmed it was useless for him to come to my rescue, and from behind one of the dead elephants he had watched the proceedings of the rogue. He was now almost as anxious as I was to ascertain what had become of Nowell and the natives. He feared, as I did, that the rogue might have caught them.

The conduct of the brute was a fair example of the mode in which rogues generally proceed. He had waited concealed, probably close at hand, while we were attacking the rest of the herd, and then the instant he saw that we were unprepared, had dashed out on us. Had I attempted to run when he got near me, he would have killed me in a moment by striking me on the back; or, had I not jumped aside, he would equally have finished me by a blow on the stomach; had he struck me on the shoulder, he would only have knocked me down, so that the mode in which I was struck was the only one by which my life could have been preserved. Dango hunting about at length found my rifle, on the stock of which the elephant had actually stepped, leaving his impress on it, and I having picked up my cap, after loading the rifle, we followed the track of the retreating rogue towards the spot where we had heard the last shots fired.

On we went till we came on the huge body of the rogue, with Nowell and the natives standing near. He was measuring it, and found it nearly fourteen feet in height, a huge monster even for Ceylon. He had heard my shot, and even when he saw the rogue with a wounded head, believing that I had turned him, he had had no notion of the danger to which I had been exposed. I was helped to a stream of cold water which flowed down from the mountain, and in this my thigh was bathed till the pain was somewhat assuaged. A litter was then formed of bamboos and creepers, on which the natives bore me back towards the spot where we had left the horses, while Dango led away the poor little poonchy. At first the baby elephant cried and roared most lustily; but, on food being given it, after a short time it seemed reconciled to its fate. A young elephant is very soon tamed.

Mr. Fordyce was delighted to see us back after our long absence, for he had become really anxious about us. He could scarcely credit the account we had to give of the number of elephants we had killed, and I suspect regretted that he had not been of our party. Of course he was very much concerned at finding how serious was the injury I received, though, when we arrived in safety at the village, he could not help saying in his usual facetious manner,—

"Well, Marsden, I hope that you are satisfied with the specimen you have had of the delights of elephant-shooting, and I only trust that you may never meet a greater rogue than you did to-day."

CHAPTER XIV.

A Wounded Veddah—How a Christian can Die—Attacked by Black Ants—Abundance of Game—Catch a Crocodile Asleep—Fight with a Bear—Chase a Deer—Lose my Way—Climb up a Tree—What I saw when there.

LAY on a sofa for the remainder of the day and during all the night, suffering great pain. There was no surgeon within some hundred miles of us, and the surgical knowledge of the natives was of a very limited description. Mr. Fordyce and Nowell did their best for me, and kept continually fomenting the limb with cold applications of vinegar and water, by which the swelling was somewhat abated. The skin, however, was much broken, and soon became of a bright purple hue. I felt somewhat alarmed, but Dango begged that I would allow him to apply a balsam composed of what I was told was margosse oil. The odour was as disagreeable as that of asafœtida, but not only did it keep all flies away, but it had a most healing and cooling effect, so that after the rest of another day I was able to mount my horse and proceed on our journey. Nowell passed the time by going out and shooting pea-fowl, partridges, and small deer, which added considerably to our bill of fare at dinner time.

During three days after this, we travelled through the dense forest country I have before described. Though nothing could be more sombre or gloomy compared to the bright and open plain we had sometimes traversed, I was thankful for the shade and coolness we obtained, as the heat might again have inflamed my injured leg. I felt at first as if I had had a lump of lead hanging on one side of my horse, but by walking a little every day, that sensation gradually wore off, and in less than a week I was as well as ever.

"You did well in destroying the elephants who were committing depredations on our friends' fields, but I cannot allow you to undertake, as knight-errants, to attack the rogues infesting all the villages we pass through," observed Mr. Fordyce. "You will certainly get expended yourselves, if you make the attempt."

Nowell was rather annoyed at this, as he, not having had the severe lesson I had got, was still eager for more elephant-shooting. While Mr. Fordyce was speaking, we were approaching the spot where we proposed pitching our tent, near one of the many tanks I have mentioned, now, in most instances, in a sadly ruined condition. Suddenly our ears were assailed by a wild and mournful cry.

"What can that be?" I asked.

"Some human being in pain," answered Mr. Fordyce, pressing on his horse in the direction from whence the sound came.

We followed him till we came to a tree round which stood a number of Veddahs, far less repulsive than those we had before seen. In the centre of the circle, sitting on the ground with his back against the trunk, was a young man with a horrible wound in his stomach, through which his intestines protruded. There he sat, the picture of fortitude and resignation; and though his companions exhibited their grief by their wild howls, he did not show, by the contraction of a muscle, or by any sign of impatience, that he felt the agony his wound was causing, or that he feared the death which must be its result; at the same time the perspiration streaming from his forehead, cheeks, and neck, showed the terrible pain he was suffering. Dango, who came up, inquired how the accident had occurred, when he was told that the young Veddah had just passed a wild buffalo in the cover, scarcely noticing it, when the animal rushed out at him from behind, knocked him down, and gored him from the groin upwards, as he fell. It was pitiable to see him when we felt how little aid we could afford him. He looked up calmly in our faces as if to seek for assurance and consolation there, but he could have found but little of either.

"Such might be your fate, or indeed that of any one of us, as we are traversing these wilds," observed Mr. Fordyce.

The Veddah looked up at him that moment and spoke. Mr. Fordyce produced a small copy of the New Testament from his pocket, and read some verses. Instantly the young man's countenance brightened. He knew and believed the truths contained in that sacred book. He had been educated at one of the missionary establishments, afterwards abandoned; but the seed had not fallen on stony ground. Now our kind friend could afford both comfort and consolation. He continued reading to the poor man till a litter could be formed, and some of the balsam I have mentioned could be procured; his wound was washed and dressed, and bound up, and he was carried to one of our tents. Some of his companions followed and sat outside, but did not attempt to enter. Not a sound all the time did he utter of complaint. Now and then he pointed upward to show us that it was from thence he received strength; that it was there he hoped soon to go. He had come, he said, to speak the truth to some of his tribe who were yet unconverted, and totally ignorant of all knowledge of the gospel; that he would be prevented from bringing those glad tidings to them was the only cause he had to regret being so speedily summoned from the world; but "God's ways are not man's ways," he observed, and he had no doubt that He in his infinite wisdom had good reason for allowing what had happened to occur.

Mr. Fordyce asked him the names of those he would wish to speak to, and he having given them, we went out with Dango to try and find them at a spot a short distance from the camp, where we were told that the tribe were assembled. Some hundred people almost black, and destitute of clothing, were assembled under the boughs and among the stems of a huge banyan tree, which formed, as Nowell remarked, a sort of natural temple. In front of it was a small stone altar, with fire burning on it, the flames from which shed a lurid glare on the rapidly darkening shadows of the huge tree. Before the altar were two figures; the most unearthly, horrible—indeed, I may say demoniacal—I have ever set eyes on. I could scarcely believe that they were human. They were black, and with the exception of a piece of cloth round the loins, totally destitute of clothing; they had huge mouths, with grinning teeth and large rolling eyes, while their hair hung from their heads in long snake-like locks, like horses' tails, reaching almost to the ground. They were shrieking and howling, and making all sorts of horrible noises, while they jumped, and leaped, and whirled round and round with the most extraordinary grimaces, distorting their bodies in every conceivable form, while their hair was tossed up and down in all directions, and whisked about like the reef points of a sail in a gale of wind.

Dango looked at them with supreme contempt. "They are devil-dancers," he observed. "They have been sent for by this ignorant people to dance for the recovery of the poor fellow we found wounded."

He was a Mohammedan himself, and had many superstitions which we could not help thinking as sad.

After some difficulty he found the men we were in search

of, and got them to accompany us to the tent where the poor
Veddah lay. He sat up while some came in, and others stood
in front of it, and asked them some questions, to which they
replied briefly. I had little doubt that it was about the devil-
dancers, and that they told him they had been doing their
best for his recovery. Then he spoke to them long and
earnestly, though it seemed to me that his voice was growing
weaker and weaker. Still so eager, so absorbed was he in
his subject, that he felt neither pain nor weakness. Now and
then he asked questions, and his auditors replied. Then he
went on again speaking rapidly, and oh, how earnestly! He
was evidently full of his subject; he was well aware how short
might be the time allowed him to impart to his friends those
sacred, precious, all-important truths he had himself learned.
As he went on speaking, his countenance seemed to assume an
almost beatific expression; the tones of his voice were full of
melody. His friends listened with rapt attention, tears streaming down from their eyes, their breasts heaved; but not one
moved his position, not a gesture was made. Truly it
seemed as if some holy blessed spirit animated the dark form
of one whom, under other circumstances, we should have supposed to be a mere ignorant debased savage. I thought he
must have sunk exhausted from the effort he made to speak,
but the spirit which animated him gave him strength which
seemed not his own. The sun went down, darkness came on
rapidly, still he continued speaking. How solemnly impressive
was that night scene!

Our tents had been pitched under a tope of tamarind trees,
near a small but beautiful lake, which seemed to reflect every
star which shone so brilliantly in the cloudless and clear sky,
while the constellation of the Southern Cross assisted to re-
mind me that we were in a far-off land, and in another hemi-
sphere to that in which I was born. At the same time, it

seemed a sign and assurance that the glorious truths of the Christian's faith, so long but dimly known in those regions, should from henceforth be widely scattered throughout the whole of those broad lands where that magnificent group of stars can be seen.

As I looked around I could see the elephants standing a little way off under the trees, fanning themselves lazily with branches of trees to drive off the mosquitoes, which tormented them. Nearer were our attendants sitting round their watch-fires, and close to them were picketed the horses, to take advantage of the protection afforded by the fires against any prowling bear or active leopard. Perfect silence never reigns in these grand solitudes. Near us I could hear the incessant metallic chirp of the hyla, the shrill call and reply of the tree cricket, and the hum of myriads of insects of every description, while from a distance resounded the hoarse voices of thousands of tank frogs, which kept up a spirited concert till daylight.

Within our tents, where I went to lie down for a short time, overcome with fatigue, numberless night-moths were fluttering about, and suddenly I could see brilliant flashes circling around, now disappearing, now returning, caused by a covey of fire-flies which had entered, and could not for some time find the means of escape. At length the tent was left once more in darkness. I slumbered uneasily for a few hours, and again arose. I was anxious to know how the poor Veddah was getting on. I scarcely expected to find him still alive; but as I got outside the tent, I could hear his voice still addressing his people. Mr. Fordyce had preceded me to the spot, and was listening attentively. It was already dawn. As I looked at the party, it seemed to me that they listened with as much attention as when he began. They looked in the dim uncertain light like a group of bronze statues. As it grew lighter, I perceived that the voice of the young man grew weaker.

The tent faced the east, looking across the lake. The glow of the rising sun increased. A wide expanse of the most brilliant golden hues was spread over the whole of that part of the sky. Then upward rose the sun himself in all the glorious brilliancy of that lovely clime. I saw the young Veddah make a sign with his hand. His friends stood aside. He gazed at the glorious orb of day, then he spoke once more, pointing to it. His friends turned and looked towards it. Its rays fell full on his countenance, and, dark as that was, from the expression which animated it, it was perfectly beautiful. His voice rose. He was telling his people of the glories of heaven; of Him who placed that warmth-giving luminary there for their benefit, and who so loved the world that He sent his only Son, that all who trust in him might be saved from destruction. This I was told afterwards.

I began to hope, from the strength the Veddah exhibited, that he was less injured than we had supposed. On a sudden, with his hand erected, still pointing to the sky, with the words of the gospel still on his lips, he fell back, and as his friends stooped down around him, their cries and tears told us that he was gone.

"Oh," I thought, "who would not wish to die as that man we call a savage has died! What minister of Christ's holy truth could desire a more glorious, a nobler end to his labours on earth; standing like a brave soldier to the last moment at his post? I am sure that young Veddah has not died in vain. Those he has been addressing have deeply imbibed the truths of which he has told them. Perhaps in no other way would they have listened to them."

I was right. The Veddahs soon recovered from their grief, or rather ceased from exhibiting it, and placing the body on the litter on which he had been brought to the tent, they carried it to the banyan tree, where the rest of their tribe, with the horrible devil-dancers, were still assembled. Mr. Fordyce, Nowell, and I followed. They halted with the bier, and one of them stepping forward, addressed the tribe, pointing occasionally with great significance at the body. The countenances of many of them exhibited great astonishment; still more so, when six of those who had been listening to the dying Veddah's exhortations stepped forward, and taking the devil-dancers by the shoulders, marched them away to a distance, first addressing them vehemently in the hearing of the rest. What they said I do not exactly know, but I believe it was to point out to them the utter inefficacy, besides the wickedness and folly, of their incantations.

The custom of the wild Veddahs is to cover up their dead with leaves, then to desert the spot where they are laid; but we assisted in forming a deep grave, into which the body of the young Christian Veddah was lowered, while Mr. Fordyce offered up prayers, that those who attended might all in time come to a perfect knowledge of that truth which had during the past night been so forcibly explained to them. With much regret we left those simple-minded savages, to continue our journey. I trust and believe that the seed sown that night ultimately brought forth fruits, and that many of the tribe embraced the truths of Christianity.

For the greater part of the year the ground in Ceylon is so hardened by the sun, that one is able to pass across the country without difficulty in every direction. The elephants and coolies, with our tents and baggage, could rarely in a straight course make good more than fifteen miles a-day, whereas Nowell and I found that we could even walk further than that, and ride more than twice the distance. We therefore frequently used to push on, either before or after our noon-day rest, so as to get some shooting, and, at all events, to kill some game for provisioning our party.

One day a strongish breeze, which had somewhat cooled the air, tempted us to start away rather earlier than usual after our rest at noon, we having heard that we were approaching a country where a number of deer and a quantity of other game was to be found. By-the-bye, I had run a great chance that night of being devoured by—not a leopard, or a bear, or a crocodile, however. I was asleep, when I suddenly began to dream that I was Gulliver, or some such person, and that a thousand Liliputians were attempting to bind me, running their swords and spears into me in the most unmerciful manner. I awoke, and, putting out my hands, began to pull off from my neck, face, and arms, handfuls of insects. I jumped out of bed, and instantly my legs were covered in the same manner. I shouted lustily for a light, awaking all the camp, when Dango came running in with a torch, and I found myself covered with a battalion at least of an army of black ants, each half an inch long, which were marching across the country. Their line was fully five feet in breadth, and, as their custom is, they went straight up and down, and over everything, never deviating to the right hand or the left. Finding our tent in the way, they had passed under the canvas, but, as my ill luck would have it, exactly over my bed, and away they streamed out again on the opposite side of the tent. When I got out of the way, and swept those on me off, they joined the main body and continued their march. Although provided with formidable mandibles, they are destitute of venom, so that I only felt the punctures they made, without any inflammation following. When my sheets had once more assumed a snowy appearance I turned in, and quiet was restored.

As we were setting off, Mr. Fordyce told us that he would join us perhaps in the cool of the evening, and charged us to take care of ourselves, and not to follow any elephants or bears likely to teach us that we had caught a Tartar. Of course we said that we could and would take very good care of ourselves. Away we rode. Dango with another man led on foot, with Solon under their charge, Nowell and I following on horseback. Little did I think when I was a poor, knocked-about midshipman on board the *Orion*, that I should be able to travel about in Ceylon or anywhere else in such luxury.

I think that I have scarcely done justice to the beauty of the scenery of the island and the infinite variety it presents. The forests are not without their peculiar attractions; the changes and number of tints are very remarkable. The old leaves are constantly turning red, and yellow, and brown. Falling to the ground, they are immediately replaced, without being missed, by the young buds, some of the brightest yellow, others of deep crimson, and others of green of every shade.

We suffered at first, this day, much from the heat, while travelling along a narrow path cut through the dense jungle; and doubly delighted were we when we once more emerged into a partially open country, interspersed with clumps of trees and jungle, with hills, and a water-course, and a tank or small lake in the distance. We rode on till we came to a part of the water-course, at which our horses and Solon eagerly slaked their thirst. We did not disdain to drink also. While seated near the water, under the shade of a lofty wide-spreading kumbuk-tree, called by the Tamils maratha-maram, which extended its long branches far over the water, we saw from a jungle a hundred yards directly in front of us a noble buck step out, and, after throwing up his head and gazing with surprise at us, begin leisurely to graze where he stood. Nowell was for trying the range of his rifle on him, but I entreated him not to fire.

"No, no," I exclaimed; "let him have a chance for his life. We might as well hit a poor fellow who was down in a boxing-match. Wait till we invade his territory. We shall find plenty of others to shoot."

Directly afterwards, three or four peacocks, one of whom had a train of remarkable splendour, marched out on the green sward, and strutted up and down, certainly offering tempting marks. They were followed by a number of jungle fowl, whose plumage gleamed with metallic lustre, and who were so little fearful of man that they came within pistol-shot of where we sat, on the opposite bank of the stream. I had often seen pictures of our first parents in Paradise, surrounded by the animals of the field and the birds of the air, and here we had an exemplification of how true such pictures may be to nature as it was before sin entered into the world, and the brutes learned to dread man's cruelty and tyranny. We had directly after a further example of this. Happening to turn my head, I saw, not twenty yards behind the kumbuk-tree, what at first I thought was a log of wood under some bushes of a buffalo-thorn. I scarcely know what impulse made me approach it, as did the rest. Solon set up a loud bark, and instantly the seeming log shoved out four feet, and exhibited to our astonished eyes a hideous crocodile fully twelve feet long, and evidently of prodigious strength. Still more terrific did he look when he began to turn round in a circle, hissing and clanking his bony jaws, with his ugly green eye intently fixed on us. I felt a strong inclination to run away, for it seemed to me that he might make a rush and snap one of us up in a moment; but as Nowell and the natives stood their ground without fear, so did I, while Solon continued his barking, but at the same time kept wisely at a very respectful distance. The truth was, that the crocodile, suddenly aroused from his balmy slumbers, was far more frightened at us than we had cause to be at him, and was completely paralyzed. Dango, knowing this, struck him with his long pole, when he lay perfectly still, looking to all

CROCODILE OF CEYLON.

appearance dead. In a minute, however, while we were watching, he looked cunningly round and made a rush towards the water, which his instinct told him was the safest place for him to be in. On receiving, however, a second blow, he lay motionless and feigned death as before. Nowell then did what I certainly should not have thought of attempting; he caught him by the tail, and pulled away with all his might, but he could as easily have moved an elephant. Dango poked him on the back with his long pole. Solon kept barking away, but did not get within range of his jaws, knowing full well that he could use them to good effect if he chose, and gobble him up in a moment; while I, at Nowell's desire, belaboured his hard scales with a stout stick. Meantime the other native was cutting a thin, long twig from a creeper, and, while we were all hallooing and shrieking, and trying to arouse the monster, he quietly inserted it under his arm, tickling him gently. In an instant he showed that he was alive, by drawing in the limb closely to his side. Again the native touched the huge monster gently under the other arm, and he drew that in, twisting and wriggling about in the most ridiculous way, just as a child does to avoid being tickled. We could not help bursting into shouts of laughter at the exhibition, and all my respect for the

RIDING ON A CROCODILE.

mighty brute's powers vanishing, I gave way to an impulse which seized me, and leaped on his back, while he began to crawl off at a rapid rate to the tank. The long twig again brought him to a stand-still, not feeling, probably, my weight upon him, and I was thus enabled to leap off free of his jaws, which I had no desire even then to encounter. My return to *terra firma* was hailed with delight by Solon, who was in a great fright on seeing me borne away on the back of a creature for which he had evidently an instinctive dread. This was shown when we attempted to cross the stream a little higher up by a ford. He kept falling back, and making every sign of an unwillingness to enter the water, and it was only when I rode in that he consented to push across close to my heels, barking furiously all the time. Scarcely was I out of the water when a huge head was protruded from a hole close to the ford, and the jaws of a crocodile snapped with a loud clank just behind my faithful dog's tail. It made him spring forward like a bolt shot from a bow, while my horse lashed out with his hind-legs, giving the brute a blow under his jaw which must have knocked in some of his teeth, and, as Nowell observed, somewhat spoiled his beauty.

Coming to another kumbuk-tree, close to which Dango said the cavalcade would pass, we determined to leave our horses there under charge of the native, and with Dango go after the game, which we were every instant putting up in prodigious quantities. Off we went with a good supply of ammunition in our pouches, our rifles in our hands, and some biscuits and small flasks of brandy and water in our pockets, which Mr. Fordyce made us take, though it was wisely somewhat weak.

The country was tolerably open. There was jungle here and there, and patches of wood, and then open grassy spaces, along which we were easily able to make our way. There were hills in the distance, spurs of the centre chains, and water-courses and lakes. I find that I have frequently spoken of artificial and natural lakes. It must be understood that we often travelled for days together without meeting them, through dense forest country; but such regions were almost entirely destitute of game, because there was neither food nor water for them, and there we had hitherto met with no adventure.

We very soon bagged three or four brace a-piece of jungle fowl and pea fowl, as well as some black and red partridges, a hare, some pigeons, and two little mouse deer; when in a grassy hollow before us, surrounded by jungle, and interspersed with bushes of the long cockspur thorn, we saw a herd of fifty or more deer feeding quietly and not aware of our approach. It was important to get near them without being seen or winded, and to do this we kept close in under the taller trees, many of them giants of the forest. Dango led the way, Nowell followed, and I brought up the rear, holding Solon back with a leash, for he was so eager to pursue them that even I could not have restrained his impatience.

Suddenly, as we thought that we were getting close to the deer, we heard Dango exclaim, "Wallaha! wallaha!" (a bear, a bear), and a huge grizzly monster, descending from a tree in which he had been ensconced, appeared directly in front of him, so much so, that we should have run the risk of killing him had we ventured to fire. His cry startled the deer, and off they went fleet as the wind, we being left with the task of bagging Master Bruin. Dango had a spear in his hand and a hatchet in his belt. He instinctively threw forward his left arm to receive the attack of the brute, who was upon him before he could present his spear's point. He dropped it therefore, and felt for his hatchet. With a fierce growl the shaggy monster seized his arm. At the moment I let Solon escape from his leash, and off he flew, courageously leaping up at the bear's back, which he seized with a grip which made the blood gush out. This made us still more afraid of firing, but we rushed up as fast as we could to the encounter. I thought that the bear would completely have torn off the Moor man's arm; but, lifting up his axe, he struck the brute so heavy a

DANGO AND THE BEAR.

blow that he almost cut his head in two; but yet, though the blow was mortal, he did not fall, but, turning round, made off through the jungle followed by Dango and Nowell, with Solon still hanging pertinaciously on his flanks. Anxious for Solon's safety, I was rushing on at the same time, when from behind another tree another bear appeared confronting me. I presented my rifle and was about to fire, when off he went through the thick underwood. I saw that it would be bad generalship to leave so formidable an enemy in our rear, so I felt that it would be my duty to follow him. This I did as fast as I could, but he waddled along at a quickish pace, breaking the stout boughs with wonderful ease as he forced his way through them. I managed, however, to keep his shaggy back in sight, and again got pretty close up to him, following at his tail with the intention of shooting him between the shoulders, as soon as an open space in the brushwood would allow me to do so. It was a hazardous experiment, but the seeming cowardice of the crocodile had made me feel somewhat of contempt for the bear. I was on the point of lifting my rifle, when with a fierce roar he rapidly turned round and literally leaped on the muzzle. I remembered my narrow escape from the rogue elephant, and scarcely expected to be so fortunate again. I fired first one barrel, then the other in rapid succession, directly in his breast, as he threw his whole weight against my rifle, and completely forced me back. All I remember was a crackling of bushes, a terrific roar, a confused cloud of smoke, and a dark mass above me. I lay stunned, I believe, for some time, and then I heard a bark, and some one exclaim,—

"Poor fellow; O dear, O dear, he is killed."

"No, I'm not quite," cried I from under the bear.

Then there was a pulling and hauling, in which Solon lent his jaws, and paws, if not his hands, and the huge bear was partly pulled off me stone dead, and I was partly pulled out from beneath the bear, both my friend and I fully expecting to find all my bones broken, and my rifle doubled up. My astonishment was as great as my satisfaction and thankfulness, when I discovered that when I tried to get up I could do so, and that when I shook myself none of my bones rattled; indeed, except a bruise or two, there was very little the matter with me, while my

ATTACKED BY A BEAR.

rifle was in the same perfect condition. I had, too, single-handed killed the bear, a thing, Nowell said, to be somewhat proud of in the sporting way. I did not allude to the horrid fright I had been in, and certainly hoped that I might never have such another encounter.

The Ceylon bear, indeed, is a very savage amimal, and will, I heard, frequently attack people without the slightest provocation. Dango cut out the bears' tongues and put them in his game-bag; while I, having swallowed a few drops of brandy and water, felt perfectly recovered.

We now once more turned our attention to the deer. The report of our rifles had frightened the herds nearest to us, but after walking on for a mile or so we came upon some tracks of deer, by following up which, with great caution, hiding behind every rock and bush, we espied at length another large herd. They were at some distance on the opposite side of a grassy level, and near what may best be described as open forest country. To approach them near enough to get a good shot, without being discovered, was the difficulty. Following Dango's example, who crept on through the high grass on hands and knees, now finding some bushes behind which we could run on at a more rapid pace, now once more crawling on as before, keeping our bodies concealed merely by a high tuft of grass, we at length got within a distance at which Nowell thought that we might hope to bring down our game.

Suddenly we saw one of the deer, acting sentinel to the rest, raise his antlered head, and look anxiously around. We were all kneeling behind a low bush. Whether or not they heard any noise we might have made in bringing up our rifles to raise them to our shoulders, or that Solon gave a low bark of impatience, I do not know, but like a flash of lightning, almost before we had singled out which of them we would fire at, away they dashed towards the forest. We each of us fired both our barrels. We felt convinced that two deer at least were struck, and now concealment being no longer necessary, across the wide glade we ran at full speed, and soon came up to the spot where the herd had been feeding. Drops of blood on the grass showed us that our shots had taken effect, and following them closely, we hoped soon to come up with the wounded deer, as we could still see some of the herd among the trunks of the trees in the distance. On we went, not stopping to reload our rifles, Solon, highly delighted at having his talents brought into requisition, leading the way at full speed, but without barking, which he seemed to know would only frighten the game. After running on rapidly for some way the forest became much denser, and it was more difficult to see any distance ahead.

Probably in consequence of the cuff I got from the rogue elephant, and my late encounter with the bear, I was not so strong and active as usual, and was bringing up the rear at some little distance from my companions, when a creeper caught my foot and over I went. I struck my head, I fancy, against the thick root of a tree rising out of the ground, and was so much hurt that a minute or more passed before I could rise. By the time I was on my feet, and had looked about me, Solon and my companions had disappeared. I had little doubt about overtaking them speedily, as I had still before me the bloody track of the wounded deer. Keeping my eyes on it, I went on as fast as I could run. Again the forest opened a little. I thought that the traces had grown less distinct, or rather lighter than before. Whereas hitherto every foot nearly of ground had been marked with a drop of blood, now I could only discover one at the distance of one or two yards from each other. I did not shout even to ask my companions to stop for me, so fully persuaded was I that I should soon come up with them. I was conscious, however, that I was not making such good way as at first, and I knew that till they brought the stag to bay, or till it dropped, they would probably outstrip me. On I went. Every moment I thought that I must overtake Nowell and Dango. Sometimes I even fancied that I heard their voices before me, and Solon's well-known bark. This encouraged me to proceed, and I ran even faster than before. Of course I was in a terrific heat, having to carry my heavy rifle, and to go along at such speed for so long a time. At length I came to an open glade. Still the deer tracks marked the grass, so I hurried across and found myself in another open clump of trees. I thought by the direction in which the trees cast their long shadows over the ground that I was making a straight course, and so I believe I was. On, on I ran; an unnatural excitement, it seems to me, had seized me; I did not like the idea that Nowell was hunting a deer with my dog, and would catch it when I was not present, so I said to myself, " I am determined to be in at the death at all events." I could not possibly calculate how far I had gone, nor how time had passed. At length my legs began to feel an excessive weariness, and my usual senses returning, I observed that the sun was rapidly sinking towards the horizon. On stopping and reflecting for a moment, the thought struck me with painful vividness, that I must by some means or other have followed a different track from my companions and missed them altogether. The thought that such was too probably the case almost took away my breath, and made my heart sink within me. I was aware that bears and leopards were likely to abound in the neighbourhood, with probably serpents of various sorts, and I knew not what other wild beasts or reptiles I might have to encounter during the dark hours of night. The first thing I did was wisely to stop and load my rifle, which I ought to have done long before. This is a safe rule in shooting in a wild country, never to be tempted to move without first having reloaded one gun. I next looked out for some elevated spot whence I could make a survey of the surrounding country, that I might take the best line to regain the camp. I searched in vain, and at last I determined to climb a tree from which I might obtain an extensive look-out. It was some time before I found one which I could manage to get up, and from the topmost boughs of which I at the same time might obtain such an extensive view as would be of any use to me. I at last found a tree answering my wishes. Of course I could not carry my rifle up with me, so I had to leave it leaning against the trunk. I did not know the name of the tree I was climbing, but it was a tall and very handsome one, having dark purple flowers at the end of its branches, of peculiar richness and beauty. Up I went to the very top, and when I got there I wished myself down again, for I could not see any points to assist me in finding my way, while, having bruised some of the fine-looking flowers, so horrible an odour proceeded from them that I could scarcely bear to remain where I was. I soon, therefore, descended; but just as I reached the lower branches, I saw below me an object which made me thankful that I was safe up the tree. I have since ascertained that the tree is called the *Sterculia fœtida*. It is one of the greatest and tallest of the Ceylon forest trees, but the flowers as well as the fruit emit a stench so detestable as properly to entitle it to its characteristic botanical name. The fruit also is curious. It consists of several crimson cases of the consistency of leather, which enclose a number of black seeds, bean-like in form. On the bursting of their envelope these, when ripe, are dispersed.

CHAPTER XV.

Encounter with a Boa-Constrictor—Meet a Giant—Find myself among the Ruins of an Ancient City—Surrounded by Snakes—Take Shelter in a Ruin—Horrible Adventures in it—Attacked by Bears—How I passed the Night—Solon's Return—See a Leopard about to spring on me—Solon watches me while I sleep.

THE object I saw, when perched up on the bough, was sufficiently terrible in appearance to make my hair stand on end. It was a huge boa-constrictor, which came gliding along the grass noiselessly towards the foot of the tree. I was entirely unarmed, for my rifle was on the ground below me, and I had no time to descend to obtain it. I felt, too, that my position was very insecure, for I had heard of boas raising their heads ten feet or more from the ground by the strength of their tails, and of climbing to the very topmost crests of the loftiest palm-trees. I thought that by some means or other the vast snake had scented me out, or seen me, and that he would climb the tree to get at me. I had heard of birds being fascinated by serpents, and falling helplessly into their jaws, and I really felt a sensation something akin to what I suppose they must. I did not exactly feel inclined to jump down into his mouth, but I thought that very likely I should let go my hold and fall down. I am not ashamed to confess having had that feeling, but I tried to conquer it, and it soon wore off, and then I began to consider how I might best escape the dreadful Python. At first I thought that I would climb up to the very highest branch, in the hopes that the boa would not venture to follow me there, for fear of breaking it with his weight; and then it occurred to me that I might possibly escape by working my way along to the very end of one of the lower branches, and, while he was climbing the stem, drop to the ground and run off. The height was great, though, and the ground so hard that I had sufficient reason to fear that I might injure myself in my fall. Besides this, I felt certain that the huge serpent could drop the moment he saw what I was about, and make chase after me. Terrible indeed were my sensations. What was passing seemed like a horrid dream. I could scarcely believe that it was all true. The serpent seemed fully twenty feet long, with a large head, and a yellow body covered with black marks—a more hideous-looking creature it was scarcely possible to conceive. How I longed for my rifle, which stood up uselessly against the stem of the tree; I only hoped that the serpent would catch hold of it, and perhaps shoot himself! Perhaps he might think fit to swallow it, and then there was a great chance of its sending its two bullets through him. The idea tickled my fancy so much, that, terrible as was my position, I could not help bursting into a fit of laughter. The operation seemed to do me good. I laughed away till I could not refrain from descending to where I could watch the rifle, with the full expectation of seeing the boa swallow it. I saw my rifle, but I also saw, what was curious enough, a deer, probably the one I had wounded and followed, and who had come out of the jungle to take shelter under this very tree. At once I fancied that I had discovered the cause of the boa's appearance. He, in his wanderings in search of prey, had undoubtedly come upon the blood-stained tracks of the wounded deer, and had followed them up, till it had by chance espied the poor animal where it then was. I was only too thankful that it had not overtaken me, for it would have undoubtedly seized me, under such circumstances, with as little ceremony as it would the deer.

and have as quickly disposed of me. In the excitement of the chase I should probably not have heard its stealthy approach, and I shuddered as I thought of the narrow escape I had had. Still, I was not quite certain that I was safe. I watched anxiously for what was going to occur. The poor deer did not attempt to escape, but, trembling in every limb, looked at the boa as he glided on stealthily towards it.

A BOA-CONSTRICTOR ATTACKING A DEER.

When the snake had got close to it, it butted at him with its antlers, as if it had hopes of driving him off. With a sudden spring, however, which made me start by its rapidity and force, the boa threw itself on its prey. He first thrust out his long black tongue and felt it, then he seized it by the leg, and throwing it down in an instant, had wound the huge folds of his body round it, crushing every bone in its body. The deer bleated out its complaints, but its cries grew fainter and fainter, and soon ceased. The boa then, having unwound himself, taking it by the nose, began to lubricate its body all over with saliva, and gradually sucked it into his capacious mouth. I expected to see the horns act like a spritsail-yard, and prevent its going down, but they went in also, and glided down his elastic and muscular inside without causing him any inconvenience! I waited till he had thus effectually put a gag in his mouth, and then, though his head was scarcely a yard from my rifle, I descended the tree and eagerly grasped it. So busy was he in gorging the deer, that he did not attempt to move off, though it seemed to me that his wicked eye was fixed on me with a meaning, which signified:—" Wait a little, my boy, and then, when I have got down the deer, I will have a bite at you as a *bonne bouche* for my supper."

" We'll see about that, Master Boa," said I, stepping back a little, and levelling my rifle. " I suspect that I shall spoil your supper, as you have spoiled mine by eating up my deer."

Firing, I sent a ball right through his head, blowing it almost into fragments. The creature was not killed, but lashed out furiously with its tail, twisting and turning in the most dreadful manner. I had always felt a dislike to put any creature into unnecessary pain, besides being fully aware of its decided wrongfulness. Loading, therefore, as rapidly as I could, I got as near as was safe, and fired at the upper part of its tail. The shot was successful, and that instant it ceased to move. Seizing the boa, which had given me such a fright, by the tail, I hauled it out to its full length, when, pacing along it, I found it to be nearly, if not quite the length I had supposed, with a body thicker than my thigh, and a head as big as a cocoa-nut—the throat and mouth now distended in a wonderful way by the sausage-like body of the deer.

A considerable time had been thus spent, and when, having shouldered my rifle, I began to consider which direction I should take, I felt that I had very little chance of finding my companions before dark. While up the tree, I had observed at some short distance what I took to be rocks or ruins, and I bethought me that I might find among them some cave or stronghold where I might rest for the night; or, better still, meet with the habitation of a hermit or priest, some of whom still, I had heard, occasionally take up their abode near the shattered temples of their ancient faith. With this hope I walked on in the direction I supposed the rocks to be. I kept my eye warily about me. I felt that I was surrounded by enemies. I had already that day had experience enough of the nature of the creatures which might attack me.

"A battle with a bear and a boa-constrictor in one day is pretty well enough to satisfy a knight-errant," said I to myself. "I have now only to meet a rogue elephant, a wild boar, a buffalo, and a leopard, to fill up the list of my possible opponents. However, there is no use having a faint heart; I'll push on boldly, and trust that I may be preserved from all the dangers which may surround me."

I had remarked a distant hill top, and that, of which I occasionally got a glance, together with the glow in the sky where the sun was sinking, enabled me to steer a tolerably direct course in the direction I wished to go. After I had killed the serpent I loaded one of my barrels with small shot, that I might kill a bird for my supper, the pangs of hunger warning me that I should not get on at all without eating. I very soon knocked over a pea-fowl and a parrot. Of the latter

I had frequently eaten pies during our journey. I was thus in no fear of starving, and I thought that if I could have had Solon with me I should have had no cause to fear. As it was, I felt very solitary, and not a little uncomfortable.

The gloom increased. I pushed on through a dense wood. I thought that I must be near the spot I was seeking. It appeared to be a lighter a-head, and I fancied that I saw the gray of the rocks against the sky above them. Eager to get out of the forest, where a bear or a boar might, without giving me warning, pounce down on me, I pushed on, when suddenly I saw what appeared to be a monstrous giant standing in the portal of a cavern. Instinctively I drew back. Naturally my nerves were in a very excited state after all that had occurred. I expected to see him, like the giants in fairy stories, rush forward and try to seize me by the nape of the neck, to clap me into his pockets, or his caldron or cavern, or any other receptacle for his victims.

"I'll have a shot at him, at all events, if he makes the attempt, and show him the effects of a good English rifle," said I to myself.

I was standing under the shade of the wood, close by the trunk of a huge tree. As I peeped out, more clearly to observe the monster, it seemed as if a bright light was playing round his head, while his eyes, I fancied, kept moving round and round in search of something. I thought that perhaps he had heard my approach and was looking for me. I could almost have shrieked out with horror, but the so doing, it occurred to me, would betray me. So wonderfully real appeared the monster to my excited imagination, that I was about to raise my rifle to my shoulder to be ready to fire should he approach me, when the light on his head faded away, and I saw that it had been caused by the glow of the setting sun in the sky— the eyes sunk into their sockets, the features no longer appeared in the bold relief in which they had before been presented, and I discerned what I should probably, under other circumstances, have at first discovered, that what I saw before me was but a colossal statue. I now boldly advanced, half ashamed, though laughing at my previous fears. Its size made it appear nearer than it really was, and my surprise was great indeed, when I

A COLOSSAL STATUE.

at length got close up to it, to find that it was at least fifty feet in height, and carved apparently out of the solid rock. I had no difficulty in determining that it must be a statue of Buddha, and that I was standing amidst the ruins of one of his temples. Hungry as I was, I could not help examining it before I cooked my supper, or looked out for a secure spot in which I might pass the night.

The statue had with infinite labour been carved out of the living rock, but so much detached from it that only two slender ties remained to connect it with the vast mass of which it had once formed a part. It stood on a high platform, with a large bowl before it, in which the offerings of worshippers, I conclude, were once wont to be deposited. On either side huge pillars rose to support the roof which once covered it. Altogether, the mighty figure and the surrounding edifices were more like what I should have expected to have seen in Egypt or among the ruins of Nebuchadnezzar's once proud capital, than in that far off and hitherto but little known region.

On every side, as I wandered on, I found ruins of what I have no doubt were once temples, and palaces, and public edifices, some still in a wonderful state of preservation, and others little more than shapeless masses of debris and fallen brickwork. As I clambered over them I saw before me some arches in the side of the rock, which I thought probably were at the entrance of chambers, one of which might serve as my abode for the night. I hurried on, for it was already getting so dark that I had good reason to fear I should be unable to find the sort of place of which I was in search before I was altogether benighted. I had cut a stick to help me along, or I should not have been able to get over the rough ground so well. I had gone on some way when a loud hiss close to me made me start, and I could just discern a big snake wriggling out from a crevice near which I had passed. I turned aside, when I was saluted in the same way. I was about to go back, when I saw two snakes wriggling along across the only place I could have passed. I felt that I was in for it, as the saying is. I cannot describe my sensations. They may be far more easily supposed. To go forward seemed the best course I could pursue. So on I went. I tried not to jump, or shrink, or cry aloud when every now and then a serpent darted out his long forked tongue at me and hissed; but it was difficult to command my nerves. I knew that a large number of the snakes in Ceylon are not venomous, and all I could do was to try and persuade myself that these were among the harmless ones. Those that came near me I struck at with my stick, and quickly sent them to the right-about, for, happily, most serpents are cowardly creatures, and only seize their prey when they can do so unawares or at a great advantage. Even the deadly cobra di capello, one of the most venomous of all, is speedily put to flight, and only bites when trod on or carelessly handled. The knowledge of this gave me a courage I should not otherwise have possessed, and so I continued my course undaunted across the ruins.

On reaching the perpendicular face of the cliff, I found, as I had supposed, that the arches I had seen formed the entrance to chambers of some size, and on inspecting one of them, as far as the waning light would let me, I resolved to take up my abode in it for the night. As, however, I could not eat the game I had killed raw, I had first to collect materials for a fire. They were not wanting in the forest, where I had observed an abundance of fallen branches and leaves. I had remarked also a welang-tree, from which the Veddahs form their arrows, and also torches are made from it. I now discovered a much shorter path across the fallen ruins than the one I had come. I hurried on, for I had only a few more minutes of daylight to expect. Picking up two or three fallen branches of the welang-tree, and as large a bundle of other wood as I could carry, I retraced my steps to the excavation in the rock, where I threw it down, and went back for more. I was not long in this way in collecting a supply to last me for some hours, I hoped, for so hot was the atmosphere that I could only have borne to sit by a small fire. I had picked up some rotten wood to serve as tinder, and, as I had a match-box in my pocket, I had no difficulty in creating a flame. Some steps led up to the archway I had selected for my quarters. I carried my sticks up them, and made up my pile of wood in the mouth of it. I had an idea that it extended a considerable way into the interior; but it was now so perfectly dark only a few feet from the mouth, that I could not by possibility explore it till I had made some of the torches I intended. I collected a few large stones to sit on, and made a platform on which to light my fire, that I might the better roast my birds. I put the tinder with some dry leaves close to it under the pile, and then having lighted my match, I knelt down and began to blow away to get it up into a blaze. This, to my great satisfaction, I had just accomplished, when suddenly I felt a pretty hard slap on the side of my face, then another, and next my cap was knocked off, and such a whisking, and whirling, and screeching took place around the fire, and about my head especially, that I could not help fancying for some time that a whole legion of imps, or fairies, or hobgoblins of some sort had taken it into their heads to hold their revels in the cavern, totally regardless of my presence. My sober senses, however, in a short time returned, and as the flames blazed up more brightly I saw that my tormentors were a vast number of bats, on whose long quiet retreat I had intruded. There seemed to be a great variety of them, and of many different bright colours—yellow and orange, and red and green. Some were small, but many were of great size, formidable-looking fellows, with wings three or four feet from tip to tip. While I kept up a bright flame, however, they were enabled to see me and to steer clear of my head. I soon discovered the reason why they kept so long flying round and round the fire. It was that a number of moths and winged insects were attracted by the flames, which they followed to gobble up. Their presence was anything but pleasant, but I soon saw that it was utterly impossible to avoid them. The odour they caused was very disagreeable, while the suffocating heat of the rock on which the sun had been shining with full force for many hours was scarcely sufferable, and I wondered how the former inhabitants of the city could have existed there.

Just then, I must observe, my own hunger absorbed my mind, and I had to exert my wits to convert the food I had with me into an eatable state. I very rapidly plucked the birds, and having cut out four forked sticks, I stuck them among the stones, and with two others as spits I soon had my birds roasting. I had some biscuit, and some pepper and salt in my bag, so that I had now no fear about making a satisfactory meal. In a country abounding in game like Ceylon, a person with a rifle in his hand, and a supply of powder and shot or bullets, need never be in want of an ample supply of food. While my supper was cooking I cut the sticks of the welang-tree into convenient lengths, and, taking a large stone, beat them away, turning them round and round till all the fibres were thoroughly separated, and they became fit to serve as torches. I had plenty to do, for I was at the same time turning my spits to prevent the birds from being burned. In a short time I had the pea-fowl and partridge ready to eat, though, I daresay, that they might not quite have satisfied the fastidious taste of an aldermanic epicure. I was so hungry that I believe I could have eaten a couple more of birds if I had had them. I kept a portion, however, to serve me for breakfast the next morning in case I was unable to kill any more. I might, to be sure, have added as many bats as I wished to my repast, but I saw none of the flying squirrel species, the flesh of which is said to be very delicate and nice.

When I had finished my supper I felt very drowsy, but was afraid of going to sleep till I had ascertained what other beings might have occupied the cavern. Lighting one of my torches, I was delighted to find that it burned brightly and steadily. Holding it in one hand, while I felt my way with my stick with the other, I advanced cautiously further into the recess. As I could not carry my rifle also, I had left that leaning against the arch near the fire. The ground was tolerably smooth, and covered over with sand, and earth, and dirt. To my surprise, after going a little distance I discovered that the cavern not only extended straight forward into the rock, but that long galleries had been excavated right and left within its face, like those in the rock of Gibraltar, while others branched off again into the interior. Altogether I was in a very different sort of place to what I wished for, or to what I expected to find. Still, it was now too late to look out for an abode of smaller dimensions, and I determined to make the best of this one. I did not like to be long absent from my fire lest it should go out, when I might not be able to find the place and my store of fire-wood. I therefore turned to go back to it. I thought that I should have no difficulty in finding my way, but I had not gone many paces before I had to stop and consider whether I was mistaken or not. The bats, too, considerably annoyed me. Wherever I went they flew about, knocking against my torch, and almost putting it out. Still, I did not think it possible that I could have missed my way. I stopped to reflect. How often I had turned round I could not tell. The horrid bats had been so constantly attacking me, or rather my torch, and I had so frequently whisked about in vain attempts to drive them off with my stick, that I could not help arriving at the very unpleasant conclusion, that I was unable in the remotest degree to tell in what direction lay my fire, and what was of very much greater importance, my rifle. The torches manufactured by the natives will last two hours, but mine I saw would burn out in a much shorter time, and then I asked myself, In what condition should I be? It was impossible not to anticipate something very dreadful. I had heard of people being eaten up by rats in similar places, and I could not tell what liberties the bats might take with me in the dark. I remembered having been told all sorts of terrible things which they were capable of doing. I did not reflect whether they were likely to be true or not. Then there were serpents in abundance in the neighbourhood. Of their existence I had had ocular demonstration. But, besides them, I could not tell what wild beasts might not have their habitations in the secret recesses of these long deserted mansions. These thoughts passed very rapidly through my mind. I had no time to spare in thinking uselessly about the matter. I must decide at once what course to take. The glare of my own torch would, I found, prevent me seeing so easily that caused by the fire, so leaning it against the wall in a recess, I hurried along what I conceived to be the chief passage as far as a slight glimmer from the torch would allow me to go in a direct line. I could see no sign of my fire in that direction. I hurried back to my torch. It was burning dreadfully low. I repented my folly in coming away without an additional one, and in leaving my rifle behind me. I now seized it in my hand and hurried on with it. I came to a place where two passages branched off at right angles to each other. One must therefore, I concluded, run right away into the interior of the rock; the other on my left might possibly lead towards the arch by which I had entered the labyrinth. I took, therefore, the one to the left, and once more placing my torch in a niche I walked on, waving my stick in front of me. I had gone twenty paces or so, though it seemed five times that distance, when to my great delight I observed a slight glare reflected on the wall on the right, which, as I supposed, was opposite the arch I was in search of. So eager was I to ascertain this that I did not go back for my torch, but pushed on, believing that I should have light enough when I got near the fire. On I went; in my eagerness I should have broken my nose by tumbling over bits of stone, had I not brought myself up with my stick. As it was, I got an ugly tumble, and hurt my knee not a little. I picked myself up and on I went. My fall taught me the prudence of caution, and once more I went forward not quite so rapidly as before.

To my great joy I at last saw my fire still blazing up, and rather more than I had expected too; but a moment afterwards my joy was turned into dismay, for there, seated before the fire, and munching the remainder of the birds I had kept for my breakfast, I saw a huge bear. His back was towards me, and I had approached so silently over the soft ground that he had not heard me. His olfactory nerves also were too well occupied with the fragrant smell of the roast pea-fowl and pigeon to scent me out, which he might otherwise probably have done. He was evidently enjoying his unexpected repast, and daintily picking the bones. Had I left my spirit flask, I suspect that he would have taken a pull at that to wash down his meal. If I had but had my rifle in my hand I should have had no cause to fear him, but as it was, I need not say that I did not feel at all happy about the matter. My weapon was leaning against the wall not two yards from him, and I could not hope to get at it without being discovered. I had already had sufficient experience of the savage nature of Ceylon bears to know the necessity of approaching him with the greatest caution. I bethought me that my safest plan would be to go back for the end of my torch, and by keeping that before me

AN UNWELCOME GUEST.

dazzle his eyes, so that I might get hold of my rifle. I instantly hurried back to put the plan in execution. The torch was still burning, that I could see by the glare it sent forth across the gallery. In my eagerness I stumbled twice and hurt my shins very much. I picked myself up and went on. I was afraid of my torch burning out. I had already got well within its light when I thought I heard something moving over the ground behind me. I turned my head. Horror of horrors! The light from the torch fell on the shaggy breast and fierce muzzle of a huge bear—the brute I had no doubt who had made free with my breakfast. He was waddling along with his paws extended, as if he fully purposed to give me a hug, which would certainly have squeezed the breath out of my body. I could have shrieked out, but I did not. Instead of that, I sprang on with frantic energy towards my torch, which was already almost burned to the very end. I seized it eagerly, and facing about as the bear with a loud growl made a spring at me, I dashed it full in his face, and under the cover of a shower of sparks which were scattered from it I ran as fast as my legs could carry me towards my fire. The bear was so much astonished by the unexpected reception of his amiable overtures that he did not attempt to seize me, and, as may be supposed, I did not stop to look whether he was about to follow me. My first aim was to get hold of my rifle. With that in my hand I did not fear him. On I ran. I happily did not stumble this time. I daresay I was as pale as death—I am sure I felt so. Gasping for breath, I at length reached the fire. I hurriedly threw some branches on it to make it blaze up, that I might see if my enemy was approaching, and how to aim at him, and then I seized my rifle and stood with it ready to fire. Master Bruin, however, had been taught to feel a certain amount of respect for me. He did not make his appearance as I expected, and I began to hope that I should not be drawn into another battle with him. I had had fighting enough for that day. After waiting a little time I sat down, for I was sadly tired; still I thought that for worlds I would not go to sleep. Had I done so I should have expected to have found myself in the jaws of some monster or other.

The most important thing was to keep up a good light till sunrise, and so my first care was to manufacture as many more torches as I had wood for. I had already found a torch so efficacious a defence, that I was unwilling to be without one in my hand.

While thus employed, I thought I heard a low growl, and looking up, I saw moving along the gallery within the aisle to which the glare of my fire extended, not one bear, but two, looking at me evidently with no very amiable intentions! I should have had little fear of one, because, had I missed with one of my barrels, I might have killed with the other; but two such cunning and fierce fellows as bears were a fearful odds against me, which I would gladly have avoided. Still, I of course determined to fight it out as best I could. I threw still more wood on my fire. I lighted another torch, and stuck it between some stones by my side, so that I might have a steadier light than the fire afforded, the flickering flames from which very much confused the objects in the further recesses of the galleries, and would have prevented me getting a steady shot at my enemies. Then I knelt down with my rifle presented, ready to take a steady shot at the bears, should they show signs of intending to attack me. They looked at me, and I looked at them. They were licking their paws; whether they did so expecting to find some more roast partridge and pea-fowl, or with the anticipation of a feast off me, I could not tell. I had no doubt that one of my visitors was the bear I had seen, and the other his better half. I was only very glad that they had not a whole tribe of young bears and bearesses with them.

Under circumstances of such fearful suspense, it is difficult to say how long a time may have passed—seconds appear minutes, and minutes hours. The bears growled, and their angry voices sounded through the vaulted passages like the echoes of distant thunder. I felt inclined to roar too. Sometimes I thought that a loud shout might frighten them away. I was considering how loud I could shout. Then I considered that my wisest course would be to keep the most perfect silence, for roar loud as I might, I could not roar as loud as they could. Once more they uttered a horrible growl. They were evidently holding a consultation as to what they should do to me. On they came nearer and nearer, uttering the most menacing growls. I had, I thought, but one chance—to knock over one of them with one barrel, and the other with the second. I pulled the trigger. The first barrel missed fire; the next did the same. In my agitation when last loading *I had forgotten to put on the caps.* I had no time even to remedy my neglect. I was completely at the mercy of the angry monsters. I had but one chance, it seemed, of my life left. Igniting another torch, I grasped one in each hand, and whirling it around my head, I rushed boldly towards the bears, shrieking at the top of my voice, and as I got up to them, dashing the blazing brands at their muzzles. The sudden and unexpected onslaught, and the noise I made, had their due effect. The bears halted, and then to my great joy turned round and waddled off as fast as they could go.

Thankful for my preservation when I had given up all hopes of life, I ran back again to my fire, put on caps to my rifle, and sat down pretty nearly exhausted with my exertions. Though I had driven the bears away for the moment, I could not help fancying that they would very soon again return. In spite of this consciousness I felt most terribly sleepy. I would have given anything to be able to take half-an-hour's sleep in safety. Now, I knew if I fell asleep that I should fall into the claws of the bears. I was nodding. I heard another low growl. I could endure it no longer, but, seizing my rifle in one hand, tucking a bundle of torches under the same arm, and holding a lighted torch in the other, I rushed from the ruins into the wood opposite. I did not reflect that I might have fallen from Scylla into Charybdis, or as some less elegantly express the idea, have jumped from the frying-pan into the fire; but, at all events, I had got further off from those terrible bears.

Having thought of making so many torches was—no pun being intended—a very bright idea. I was now able to collect ample materials for another fire. I did not fail to do so, and soon it blazed up brightly, sending its glare far and wide into the recesses of the wood. I knew from experience that it would be effectual in keeping elephants and buffaloes at a distance, and I hoped that other wild animals might be scared off. What crocodiles might have to say to me, I did not like to reflect, but I thought that they could scarcely come out of their tanks at night to pick me up by the side of a blazing fire, unless they might mistake me for a roasting monkey, and as they prefer underdone meat, might carry me off before I was completely cooked.

I had lighted my fire near the trunk of a large tree, against which I leaned my back, part of the root rising above ground serving me as a seat—indeed, it formed not a bad arm-chair. I thought that I could manage to sit up in this and keep awake till daylight, employing myself in throwing sticks on the fire, and by using other devices to prevent myself from going to sleep. I went on doing this for some time, and thought that I was doing bravely, then I found that one stick would not leave my fingers. By great exertions, however, I at last threw it in, then I got another ready, but that tumbled down at my feet, and a third slipped from my fingers, and then my arm fell down powerless by my side.

How long I slept I do not know. I dreamed over all the scenes I had witnessed since I came to the island, confusing and exaggerating them in the most extraordinary manner. I was galloping away on the backs of wild elephants, charging huge boars, and tweaking ferocious bears by the nose, while I had seized a huge boa-constrictor by the tail, and was going away after him at the rate of some twenty miles an hour. This sort of work continued with various kaleidoscopic changes during the remainder of that trying night. Nowell, and Alfred, and Solon came into the scene. Nowell was riding on a wild buffalo; Alfred had mounted on the shoulders of a bear; and Solon, with the greatest gravity, was astraddle on the back of a monster crocodile, to which St. George's green dragon was a mere pigmy, when the crocodile took it into his head to plunge into the sea, at which Solon remonstrated and barked vehemently.

I awoke with a start, and looking up, I saw a big leopard which had with a bound alighted not six feet from me, while my faithful Solon was standing over me tugging at my clothes and barking furiously at the leopard. The brute was preparing for another spring. He had providentially missed me with the first he made. I felt for my rifle, which I had placed by my side, but I dared not take my eyes off the creature for a moment, lest he should be upon me. My heart gave a jump when I found my rifle, and knowing that it was now all ready, brought it to my shoulder ready to fire. I all the time kept my eyes intently fixed on the leopard, for I was certain that in so doing lay my best chance of escape. The creature was in the very act of springing forward. Not a moment was to be lost. Aiming directly at his head, I fired. Onward he came with a snarl and a bound, which brought him to the spot where I had been sitting; but as I fired, I leaped aside behind the tree, and he fell over among the ashes of the fire, which had long completely gone out.

It was broad daylight; the sun was shining brightly among the branches of the trees, and the parrots were chattering, and other birds were singing their loudest, if not very musical notes. All nature was awake, and I felt how deeply grateful I ought to be that I was still alive, and able to enjoy the numberless blessings and objects to delight, and interest, and gratify the senses, with which the world abounds. I considered how mercifully I had been preserved during the long hours I had slept in that utterly helpless state of deep sleep into which I had fallen, till my faithful dog had been sent to warn me of the danger threatening my life. The moment Solon saw the leopard fall dead he leaped upon me, licked my face and hands, and exhibited every sign of the most exuberant joy and satisfaction, arising both at having found me and at having been the means of preserving my life. He then flew at the body of the leopard, and pulled and tugged at it to assure himself that the beast was really dead. When he had done this, he took not the slightest further notice of it.

On examining him, I found that his coat was much torn, and so were his feet, with thorns and briers, and I had little doubt that he had been travelling all night to find me. He looked also very tired and famished, and as I also felt very hungry, I bethought me of trying to kill some birds, to supply the place of those my friend Mr. Bruin had deprived me of in the night. I therefore reloaded the barrel I had just fired with small shot, and before many minutes a fine jungle-cock got up, which I brought to the ground. I loaded again, and killed a couple of parrots. So, as they would be ample for Solon and me, I instantly plucked them, and kindling a fire, in ten minutes I had them on spits roasting away merrily— merrily, at least, as far as Solon and I were concerned, though, perhaps, the poor birds would have had a different opinion on the matter. I had, as may be seen, thus become a capital woodman. I kept, depend on it, a very bright look-out all the time for my former visitors, the bears, lest a whiff of the roasting birds might induce them to come back to get a share of the banquet. I had now, however, a vigilant watcher in Solon, who sat by my side wagging his tail and observing the process of roasting with the greatest interest. I wish, poor fellow, that he could have spoken, to tell me what had become of Nowell and Dango. I examined him to ascertain whether he had brought me any note from my friend, but if he had had one tied round his neck, it had been torn off by the bushes; but I thought it much more probable that he had left them as soon as he had missed me, and set off without letting them know, to try and find me out.

After he and I had breakfasted, I felt very weary and sleepy; and so, feeling certain that he would keep a more vigilant watch over me than I could myself when awake, I lay down with perfect confidence on the ground, in the shade of a bo-tree, and slept as soundly as I ever did in my life. No dream disturbed me—not a thought passed through my mind. The last thing I saw, before I closed my eyes, was Solon sitting up with his head stretched over me, his ears outspread, his eyes looking sharply round, and his nose pointed out, ready to catch the slightest scent of a dangerous creature. What a perfect picture, I have since thought, did he present of true fidelity!

CHAPTER XVI.

Wonderful Statues—Dagobas—Temples and other Ruins—Consider how to find my way back to the Camp—Meet a Hermit—Attacked by a Buffalo—Kill it with one Shot—The Unexpected Meeting with an old English Gentleman—Accompany him to his Camp—Who he proves to be—Meet Lumsden, my Schoolfellow—Inquiries about Alfred—Anxiety as to Nowell's Fate—We set out in Search of him and Dango—Colony of Paroquets—The Anthelia—Find Dango—The Fate of an Elephant-hunter.

SLEPT for an hour or more under the bo-tree, held sacred by the worshippers of Buddah, in front of those strange, fantastic, and gigantic remains of a bygone age and people. When I awoke, there was Solon sitting exactly in the attitude in which I had seen him when I went to sleep. The moment I opened my eyes, he began to lick my face and hands, and to show every sign of satisfaction.

"It is your turn to sleep now, old Solon," said I, patting him on the head, and pressing him down on the ground.

He seemed to understand me, and giving a couple of turns round, he coiled himself up, and in a moment was fast asleep. I do not think that he had been asleep ten minutes before he jumped up, wagged his tail, and ran forward, as much as to say,—

"I am all ready now, master, to begin our journey; and it is high time, I am sure, to be off."

I thought so likewise, but in what direction to go I could not tell, nor did Solon seem to know much more about it.

Anxious, however, as I was to rejoin Nowell, I scarcely liked to leave the extraordinary place in which I found myself without exploring the vast ruins by which I was surrounded. Daylight showed me that they extended to an immense distance; the whole surface of the ground, as far as my eye could reach, was covered with fragments of an ancient city; the ground in many spots was literally coloured red by the masses of brick crumbled into dust, while around I saw scattered in vast quantities large and massive columns, which once must have formed a support to innumerable temples, palaces, and public buildings of various sorts. Many parts of the ruins were completely overgrown with jungle. I was forcing my way through it, when I saw at a little distance, partly concealed by the foliage, a large elephant. I thought that he appeared to be standing listening to ascertain in what direction I was coming.

"An undoubted rogue," I said to myself, examining my rifle to ascertain that the caps were on, and to be ready to fire should he attack me. I signed to Solon to keep close at my heels, and approached the monster cautiously. It was just the place where I might expect to meet with a perfect rogue. I crept on slowly. I was surprised to find that Solon took no notice of the elephant, though he kept, as I ordered him, close behind me. The elephant did not move. I got nearer and nearer. There he stood, ready, it seemed, to make a rush at me. I expected to see him lift up his trunk and commence the assault; but he did not make the slightest movement that I could perceive. To be sure he was considerably hidden by the foliage. Perhaps he might be asleep. Elephants do sleep standing. That I knew. He might have been stamping with his feet, or cocking up his ears, for very frequently, as I advanced, he was almost entirely concealed by the thick bushes. I had got within twenty paces of the monster, when, obtaining a clearer view than before, I was struck by the unusual colour of the hide. Still nearer I got. Surely an ear was wanting, and the trunk was of a very odd shape. In another minute I was indulging in a hearty fit of laughter, as I found myself standing close under the elephant. No wonder it did not move, nor had it for many hundred years, for it was carved, though roughly, out of a mass of stone; there it stood—a beast of great size and excellent workmanship; and further on were fragments of other elephants and bulls, as also of pedestals and stone sarcophagi, covered with the most grotesque human figures, and many other curious designs.

Wandering on for some distance, and passing all sorts of ruins, and figures, and pillars, I came to what I took to be a lofty circular hill covered with shrubs. On getting nearer, I found a terrace, or platform, surrounding it, out of which protruded the heads of gigantic elephants, as if their bodies were supporting the seeming hill, but which I soon discovered to be no hill, but a vast edifice, shaped like half an egg-shell, composed of bricks, like the pyramids of Egypt. I went up the steps leading to the terrace, and entered beneath this wonderful structure through a low archway. Passages appeared to run through it in different directions, but the horrible odour of the bats, which had taken up their abode in those dark recesses for ages, and the fear I naturally felt of meeting serpents or bears, induced me to refrain from going further. The wonderful building I have been describing, was, I discovered, a dagoba—of which there are numbers in Ceylon—built much with the same object as the pyramids of Egypt, and unsurpassed, except by them, by any edifices in the world in point of size, and I may add, in utter want of utility or beauty. They were constructed, likewise, in all probability, with pain and suffering, amid the groans, and tears, and sighs of some conquered or enslaved people like the Israelites of old. Many of them were built from two to three hundred years before the birth of our Lord.

Hurrying on, and feeling like one of the heroes in an Eastern tale who suddenly finds himself in an enchanted city, as I gazed from side to side at the wonderful ruins and remains I met, I reached another dagoba of far vaster size than the one I had left. It was covered with trees, and huge masses of brick had been driven out of it by their roots; but still its stupendous outlines were, it seemed, but little altered from what they had been originally. I afterwards heard particulars about it. It had been originally 405 feet from the ground to the summit of the spire. It was built before the Christian era, and it is even now—most of the spire having been destroyed—250 feet in height. The radius of its base is 180 feet, which is, I believe, the same measurement as the height of the dome from the ground. I was struck by the way in which these huge structures, commemorative of man's pride and folly, have been triumphed over by nature. Tall trees grow on their very summits, and their roots have wrenched and torn asunder the most gigantic and massive masonry, and hurled it crumbling to the plains below. Sir Emmerson Tennent, in his delightful work on Ceylon, describes one of these dagobas, that of Jayta-wana-rama, erected by Mahasen, A.D. 330 :—

"It still rises to the height of 249 feet, and is clothed to the summit with trees of the largest size. The solid mass of masonry in this vast mound is prodigious. Its diameter is 360 feet, and its present height (including the pedestal and spire) 249 feet, so that the contents of the semicircular dome of brickwork and the platform of stone, 720 feet square, and 14 feet high, exceed 20,000,000 of cubical feet. Even with the facilities which modern invention supplies for economizing labour, the building of such a mass would at present occupy five hundred bricklayers from six to seven years, and would involve an expenditure of at least a million sterling. The materials are sufficient to raise eight thousand houses, each with 20 feet frontage, and these would form thirty streets half a mile in length. They would construct a town the size of Ipswich or Coventry; they would line an ordinary railway tunnel 20 miles long, or form a wall one foot in thickness and 10 feet in height, reaching from London to Edinburgh. In the infancy of art, the origin of these 'high places' may possibly have been the ambition to expand the earthen mound which covered the ashes of the dead into the dimensions of the eternal hills—the earliest altars for adoration and sacrifice. And in their present condition, alike defiant of decay and triumphant over time, they are invested with singular interest as monuments of an age before the people of the East had learned to hollow caves in rocks, or elevate temples on the solid earth."

Having somewhat satisfied my curiosity, I felt that I should not delay a moment longer in trying to find my way back to my friends. How this was to be accomplished I could not tell. I tried to get Solon to lead the way; but though he wagged his tail and looked very wise when I spoke to him, running on ahead a short distance, he always came back again to my heels, and evidently did not know more about the matter than I did. The affair was now growing somewhat serious. Nowell would, I had no doubt, be wandering about searching for me, and Mr. Fordyce could not fail to be excessively anxious at our not returning. To start off again through the forest in the expectation of falling in with them seemed worse than useless. We might be wandering about day after day, searching for each other in vain, till all our ammunition was expended, and might easily then fall victims to rogue elephants, or bears, or other wild beasts. The contemplation of such a catastrophe was not pleasant; but still, what was to be done? I asked the question of myself over and over again. I examined my ammunition, and found that I had eight bullets and a dozen or more charges of small shot, with an ample supply of powder; so that, if I did not throw my shots away, I might hope to supply myself with food for several days. To stand still would never do. I believed my friends were to the south of me, so I was pushing on in that direction, when suddenly I came upon an open space free from jungle, with a beautiful expanse of water, blue and glittering in the sunshine, spread out before me. Tall trees fringed the greater part of its banks; but here and there columns, and domes, and carved arches, and huge statues appeared among them, their strange and fantastic images reflected in the mirror-like surface. Beyond them, towering up into the clear sky, rose at different distances several of those prodigious structures, the dagobas, which I have described. The whole scene, as I beheld it in the light of that clear atmosphere, under the blaze of the noon-day sun, was most enchanting, while I sat down to shelter myself from the heat beneath the shade of a mass of ruins, with wide-spreading branches extending from their walls, which formed a complete roof over my head. The site of the ruined city into which I had wandered must thus, I discovered, be of many miles in extent, and gave me an idea of the power and magnificence of the monarchs who once possessed the territory. While England was scantily inhabited by tribes of painted barbarians, here existed a people who had attained a high state of civilization, living in richly adorned palaces, having magnificent temples, carving statues of gigantic proportions, erecting tombs and monuments equal in height to mountains, and forming reservoirs of lake-like extent. And now, how great the contrast! Those people were then, and have ever since remained, sunk in the grossest superstition; while the British, blessed with the light of gospel truth, have risen to that height of civilization which has given us the complete mastership over the now fallen race which inhabit the country.

I do not know that I said this in exactly these terms, but such was the tenor of the thoughts which passed through my mind.

While I was resting and trying to determine some definite plan to pursue in order to find either Nowell or Mr. Fordyce, I saw a figure emerge from some ruins on my right, and approach the lake. It was that of an old man. His skin was of a dark brown, and he wore a long white beard, with a loose robe cast over his shoulder and round his loins. His whole appearance was in thorough keeping with the scene. He filled a gourd he carried with water, and was returning to the place he came from, when his eye fell on me. He started on seeing me, and then, putting down his water-pitcher, advanced towards where I was sitting. I rose to receive him, as I should have done had he been the poorest peasant; but from the dignity of his air and the gravity of his counntenance, he seemed to be much above that rank. He salaamed, and so did I, imitating his action; but it appeared that here our power of intercourse must cease, for I soon discovered that he did not understand a word of my language more than I did of his.

"Though I cannot speak to him, I will try, however, what effect signs may have," I said to myself.

I set to work at once. I took my stick and drew an outline of the shape of the island on the sand. Then I made a mark in the position of Kandy, and another on the east side to show the position of Trincomalee, clearly pronouncing the names of those two places. Then I mounted my stick, to show that I was riding along from one to the other, and I put my arm out in the shape of a trunk, to show him that there were elephants, and I changed my stick from hand to hand, by which I wished him to understand that there were a number of people with us. Having marked a line somewhere between Kandy and Trincomalee, I drew some tents on the sand, and seizing my gun, and putting it next to the stick twice, to show that two people accompanied me, I ran on as if in chase of animals. Then I left my stick and ran up to the ruins, and putting my head down to the ground, showed that I had slept there. Then I got up and ran about in different directions, to show that I could not decide which way to go. The old man seemed fully to comprehend me, and I understood by the signs he made that if I would accompany him to his abode, he would show me the way I was to take. I accordingly followed him, when, taking up his gourd of water, he led me to a small hut in front of a large and aged pippul-tree, a species of banyan or Indian fig. The tree was surrounded by a wall covered with a variety of carved work. There were steps leading up to it, and a number of statues and monuments within the enclosure. I remarked the leaves, which were constantly moving, like our own aspen. Its leaves were heart-shaped, with long attenuated points, and were attached to the stems by the most slender stalks. I had no difficulty in recognizing it as one of the sacred bo-trees of the Buddhists. The great bo-tree of Ceylon was planted B.C. 288 years. It is, consequently, at the present time, upwards of 2150 years old. I also at once guessed that the old man was a Buddhist priest, the guardian of the tree, and of a little temple close at hand, built apparently out of the ruins which lay scattered around.

To show that he was hospitably inclined, he placed before me a dish of rice mixed with sugar and honey, which I thought very nice; as also some mangoes, and several other fruits, of which I was not sorry to partake, as the not over-well cooked repasts of tough birds and buffalo flesh, on which I had subsisted for the last two days, had made me wish for vegetable diet.

Having partaken of all that the old man set before me, I signified that I was anxious to commence my journey, the hottest time of the day having now passed away. He understood me, and, taking a long staff in his hand, he led the way, Solon and I following close behind him. He had gone on some distance, when he stopped before a vast number of granite columns fully twelve feet high, standing thickly together like the trees of a forest. I do not exaggerate when I say that there were hundreds of them, covering an immense extent of ground. The old man pointed at them, then, sighing deeply, on he went. I afterwards learned that these pillars are the remains of a vast monastery for Buddhist priests, built by King Dutugaimunu one hundred and sixty years before Christ. It obtained the name of the Brazen Palace, on account of it having been roofed with plates of brass. It was raised on sixteen hundred columns of granite twelve feet high, which were arranged in lines of forty in each, so that it covered an area of upwards of two hundred and twenty square feet. The structure which rested on these columns was nine stories in height. It contained a thousand dormitories for priests, as well as halls and other apartments for their exercise and accommodation.

"All these apartments were ornamented with beads which glittered like gems. The roof of the chief hall was supported by pillars of gold, resting on lions and other animals. The walls were adorned with pearls and flowers formed of jewels. In the centre was a superb throne of ivory, with a golden sun on one side and a silver moon on the other, while a canopy studded with diamonds glittered above all. The rooms were provided with rich carpets and couches, while even the ladle of the rice-boiler was of gold."

This account gives us a tolerable notion of the luxury of the priestly order of Buddhists in those days. Indeed, they seem to have taught their followers that the most virtuous acts they could perform would be to bestow their wealth upon them.

I certainly had no idea that such vast and magnificent

edifices had existed in that part of the world in those days. Leaving this region of pillars, and passing several broken statues of different animals, we were pursuing our way along the shores of another of those wonderful tanks of which I have spoken, when suddenly I heard a shot in the forest, then there was loud shouting and barking of dogs, and a huge buffalo, mad with rage and fear, burst through the jungle, and catching sight of the priest and me, with his head on the ground dashed towards us. There was a tree at a little distance, but it was too far off for the old man to reach before the buffalo would be up to us. I signed to him to fly to it, intimating that I would defend him with my rifle. He took my advice, and hastened towards it. Solon meantime ran off, barking loudly, towards the buffalo. This distracted somewhat the animal's attention, and he stopped to consider, apparently, which he should attack first. I might have hit him where he stood, but I preferred waiting till he came nearer, that I might have less chance of missing him. He first made a charge at Solon, but the brave dog was too quick for him, and nimbly leaped out of the way of his terrific horns. Several times he stopped to butt at Solon, but without being able to touch him. Then he turned towards me. When my faithful dog saw that, he attacked him still more pertinaciously. I was afraid, however, when I fired, that I might hit the dog should I miss the buffalo, and I therefore kept shouting, "Solon, Solon," to call him off. I never felt more cool and composed. I really believe that I could have taken a pinch of snuff if I had had one. It was very necessary that I should be cool. The buffalo had got within ten paces of me, and in another instant he would have been over me, when, aiming at his forehead, I fired, and down he dropped in midway career, stone dead.

"Bravo, my lad, bravo!" I heard a voice exclaim from among the trees, it seemed. "Capitally done, capital!"

I looked round and saw riding out of the wood on my left a somewhat thin, but active, wiry-looking old man, but evidently from the tone of his voice and his appearance a gentleman. Meantime the old priest came back, and threw his arms round my neck to express to me the gratitude he felt for the service I had done him. I thought that I even saw tears trickling down his eyes. While this ceremony was going on, the old gentleman rode up to the dead buffalo, and leaping from his horse examined its head.

" A first-rate shot steadily planted. You are a young sportsman. How came you here?" exclaimed the old gentleman.

I told him briefly how I was travelling through the country, and following a deer had lost my companions.

" Not an uncommon occurrence. However, I can help you out of your difficulties, I hope, and enable you to find your friends," he answered, in a brisk, kind tone. " Come to my camp. We shall find it pitched not more than two or three miles from this, towards the other end of this wilderness of ruins."

While we were speaking, a couple of Moors, hunters by profession they seemed, and other attendants, brown and scantily clothed, came up with a number of dogs. They expressed great satisfaction at seeing the buffalo dead, and cut out its tongue to carry away. The stranger directed them, as I understood, to return to the camp, saying that he would follow leisurely in a short time. He then turned to me.

" Thank the old Santon, and tell him you will not trouble him to come further," said he.

'I explained that I could not speak a word of his language.

" Oh, you have only lately come to the country," said the old gentleman. " I will then act interpreter for you."

He spoke a few words to the hermit, and gave him a silver

coin, which the latter placed reverently in his bosom, bowing low at the same time.

"That is for himself, not for Buddha, though, I must tell him," observed the old gentleman. "We have no business to support their false gods and impious worship, under any pretext whatever. It only encourages them in their errors, and brings down retribution on the heads of those who ought to know better. Now, come along, my lad. I cannot take you up on my horse, nor can I walk, but you appear to possess a pair of good legs, which will carry you over the ground at a rate sufficient to keep up with me. Is that your dog? He is a fine beast. I must make his acquaintance. Now, wish the old hermit good-bye. Salaam to him. That will do. Come along.

"A fine old man that," he continued. "It is a pity he should be a priest of so absurd a faith. Do you know anything about Buddhism? The Buddhists believe in the transmigration of souls (the doctrine of the *metempsychosis*, as it is called). . In that respect they are like the followers of Brahma. It is doubtful, indeed, which is the older faith of the two—whether Brahmanism is a corruption of Buddhism, or whether Buddhism is an attempt to restore Brahminism to its original purity. Buddhism has existed for upwards of two thousand years; it is the chief religion of the Chinese, and that indeed of upwards of one-third of the human race at the present day. Buddhists are practically atheists. Buddha Gotama, to whom all Buddhists look up, was, they believe, the incarnation of excellence. They fancy that everything was made by chance, and that Buddha was only infinitely superior to all other beings, and therefore that he is a fit object of admiration and contemplation, and that the height of happiness is to be absorbed in some way, after having been purified by many changes, into his being. They believe in the perfectibility of man, and therefore their great aim is to become moral and virtuous, while the employment of their priests is chiefly to contemplate virtue, and to inculcate its precepts and practice. Indeed, it may be said to be less a form of religion than a school of philosophy. Its worship appeals rather to the reason than to the imagination, through the instrumentality of rites and parades; and, though ceremonies and festivals are introduced, the more enlightened are anxious to explain that these are either innovations of the priesthood, or in honour of some of the monarchs who have proved patrons and defenders of the faith. No people, perhaps, are so destitute of all warmth and fervour in their religion as the followers of Buddha. They believe because their ancestors believed, and they look with the most perfect complacency on the doctrines of the various sects who surround them. As Sir Emmerson Tennent says—'The fervid earnestness of Christianity, even in its most degenerate form, the fanatical enthusiasm of Islam, the proud exclusiveness of Brahma, and even the zealous warmth of other northern faiths, are all emotions utterly unknown and foreign to the followers of Buddhism in Ceylon. Yet, strange to tell, under all the icy coldness of this barren system there burns below the unextinguished fires of another and a darker superstition, whose flames overtop the icy summits of the Buddhist philosophy, and excite a deeper and more reverential awe in the imagination of the Singhalese. As the Hindus in process of time superadded to their exalted conceptions of Brahma, and the benevolent attributes of Vishnu, their dismal dreams and apprehensions, which embody themselves in the horrid worship of Siva, and in invocations to propitiate the destroyer; so the followers of Buddha, unsatisfied with the vain pretensions of unattainable perfection, struck down by this internal consciousness of sin and insufficiency, and seeing around them, instead of the reign of universal happiness and the apotheosis of intellect and wisdom, nothing but the ravages of crime and the sufferings produced by ignorance, have turned with instinctive terror to propitiate the powers of evil, by whom alone such miseries are supposed to be inflicted, and *to worship the demons and tormentors*, to whom this superstition is contented to attribute a circumscribed portion of power over the earth.' They call their demons Yakkas, and, like the Ghouls of the Mohammedans, they are supposed to infest grave-yards. They believe also in a demon for each form of disease—delighting in the miseries of mankind. Thus in every domestic affliction the services of the *Kattadias*, or devil-priests, are sought to exorcise the demon. Although the more intelligent Singhalese acknowledge the impropriety of this superstition, they themselves resort to it in all their fears and afflictions. It has been found to be the greatest impediment to the establishment of Christianity; for, though the people without much difficulty become nominal Christians, they cling to the terrible rites of their secret demon-worship with such pertinacity, that while outwardly conforming to the doctrines of the truth, they still trust to the incantations and ceremonies of the devil priests. Notwithstanding this we must not despair. The struggle with Satan, the author of devil-worship, may be long and fierce, but if we go on perseveringly endeavouring to spread a knowledge of the gospel, we shall most assuredly gain the victory over him in the end."

Such were the remarks of the old gentleman as Solon and I walked alongside him on our way to where he expected to find his camp pitched. We found the tents pitched under a wide-spreading tamarind tree, in the immediate neighbourhood of a number of cocoa-nut palms. Close at hand were piles of curious ruins, near a beautiful lake bordered by trees; while carved slabs, fallen columns, and broken statues lay scattered around. The stranger's cortege was much of the same character as was Mr. Fordyce's. Camp-fires were already lighted, near which the horses were sheltered, while four or five elephants stood, as usual, busy fanning off the flies in the background.

"I have a young companion with me, also a stranger in this country. He met with a slight accident, and could not come out hunting to-day. I have no doubt he will be glad to make your acquaintance."

The moment the old gentleman said these words my heart beat quick. He saw my agitation. I thought of Alfred.

"Who is he—pray tell me?" I asked.

His hand was on the curtain of the tent. He made no answer, but threw it back. I entered. A young man was there. He looked up. No, it was not Alfred, but my old schoolfellow whom I had met at Teneriffe, Lumsden.

"Marsden, my dear fellow, I am delighted to see you," he exclaimed, jumping up. "How did you find your way here?"

"Marsden!" ejaculated the old gentleman, looking earnestly at me. "Marsden!—who are you?"

"Ralph Marsden, sir," I answered hurriedly. "My father has lately died; my mother was Miss Coventry."

"Then you are my grandson, young gentleman, and right glad I am to welcome one who has proved himself so true a chip of the old block!" exclaimed Mr. Coventry.

I had had no doubt who he was from the moment I had seen Lumsden with him. He seized me by the shoulders, and, gazing in my face for a minute, gave me as kind and warm a hug as I could expect to receive.

"Your old friend here told me to expect you, as you were come out in search of poor Alfred. What has become of him I cannot tell. You heard nothing of him at the Mauritius, I fear?"

"No, sir," I answered, much agitated and grieved. "Cannot you tell me where he is?"

"No, indeed, I cannot, my boy," replied Mr. Coventry; "I would give much to discover. I have kept him actively employed ever since he found me out. He has been twice at the Mauritius, once I sent him off to Singapore, and the last time I despatched him on a mission of importance to Mozambique, after which, before returning here, he was again to go to the Mauritius. This was many months ago. Not a line have I had from him, nor can I obtain the slightest information as to what has become of him. He is not a good correspondent, as I daresay you have discovered. After he left his ship, he took it into his head that his family would consider that he had disgraced them, and begged that I would allow him to call himself by a different name, hoping if he did not write home that he might be considered dead, and be soon forgotten. I did not oppose his fancy, because I hoped that he would soon reason himself out of it. This will account for your not having heard of him, as also for your father's not receiving any information when he wrote about him. Had he written to me, poor man, I would have replied, and might have perhaps induced the lad to return home. However, let bygones be bygones. I am pleased with you, Ralph. I like your notion of coming out to look for poor Alfred, and your way of proceeding, and I will help you by all the means in my power."

"Thank you, sir; thank you for all you say of me and promise to do," I replied, taking my grandfather's hand. "Now that I find you do not know where Alfred is, the necessity of my searching for him is greater than ever. I feel that I hitherto have not been as diligent in carrying out my object as I ought to have been. I was always buoyed up with the idea that you knew where Alfred was to be found, and was much less anxious than I should have been had I known the true state of the case."

"It is happy for you that you did not know the true state of the case; it is better for all of us that we do not know what the future may bring forth," observed my grandfather. "When you were at the Mauritius, it appears Alfred had not reached the island, and I shall hear on our arrival at Trincomalee whether he has since got there. I expect also to receive replies to various inquiries I have instituted in different places, from Aden down the whole of the eastern coast of Africa. I have traced him as far as Aden, but I do not know the name of the vessel in which he left that place. I feel confident that he did not go up the Red Sea, nor is he likely to have come eastward again. You have thus, then, a definite direction in which to search for him. Rather a wide region, certainly, and difficult of access, but by perseverance you may in time succeed in your object."

My grandfather's remarks again raised my hopes of finding my brother. At first when I discovered that he was not with him, I felt my heart sink within me.

"I will continue my search for him in spite of pestiferous climates, or savages, or any other difficulties which I may have to encounter," I exclaimed, half speaking to myself.

"That is the spirit which will enable you to succeed, my lad," said my grandfather, putting his hand on my back. "And now I want to know all about your family at home. You have not yet told me."

I briefly told him all that had occurred, of my father's death, and of the poverty in which my mother was left. He looked very grave and sad as I spoke.

"This should not have been," he muttered to himself. "I have been an unfeeling, unnatural father; wild, reckless, thinking only of myself, and of gratifying my own roving propensities."

He was silent for some time. "Ralph," he said suddenly, "I have made up my mind to go home to see your mother. I shall leave my property here and in the Mauritius under the charge of careful agents, and set off as soon as I can make the necessary arrangements. I will leave ample means with you to prosecute your inquiries, and you can return when you have found your brother, or should you be led to believe that further search is hopeless."

I need not enter into the particulars of our conversation during the evening. We had, however, a great deal. My grandfather had numberless questions to ask, which I had to answer; while I also had much information to gain from him on a variety of subjects, on which he was in no way unwilling to satisfy me. I found him, as I had expected, somewhat eccentric, but at the same time far more kind-hearted, generous, and liberal, than I had been led to believe he was.

My great anxiety was now to get to Trincomalee as soon as possible, and I believe that Mr. Coventry equally wished to be there. We could not, however, proceed without letting Mr. Fordyce know that I was in safety. We were on the point of sending off messengers to try and discover his camp, when a couple of armed natives were seen coming from among the trees, followed by two laden elephants and a number of bearers, whom, as they approached, I discovered to belong to Mr. Fordyce's party. On finding who we were, they pitched their tents close to ours, and he himself very soon afterwards made his appearance. I could not but be gratified at the pleasure he expressed on discovering that I was safe, but I was much concerned to find that Nowell and Dango had not been heard of. He had sent scouts out in every direction; but not a trace of them had hitherto been discovered.

As soon as I heard of this, I wanted to set out to search for my friend, but both the old gentlemen protested against my doing so; indeed, I myself was scarcely aware how tired and worn I was. Mr. Coventry was also able to send out scouts to search for Nowell, so that I became now reconciled to not going out myself for that purpose. Lumsden, however, volunteered to go out early the next morning to look for him should he not have been found in the meantime. We had an hour or more to spare after we had dined before darkness would set in; and both my grandfather and Mr. Fordyce, having heard of a curious temple in the neighbourhood, hewn in the bare rock, were anxious to employ the time in visiting it. We set off on horseback, the distance being considerable, hoping to find Nowell safe at the camp on our return. We passed on our way heaps of ruins, very similar to those I have before described, till at length we found ourselves before the precipitous side of a hill of granite. On approaching nearer, we saw directly in front of us a temple about twenty feet in height, the roof supported by pillars, with a sitting figure of Buddha in the centre, the whole hewn out of the solid rock. On the right was a standing figure upwards of twenty feet in height, and beyond it a recumbent one between forty and fifty feet long. On our left was another sitting statue placed on a pedestal, elaborately carved, with a great deal of carved-work on the wall behind it. All these statues were of Buddha, the different attitudes being intended to represent his calm and contemplative character.

"What is Monasticism but Buddhism under a slightly different form? What are hermits but Buddhists? How different is true Christianity, with its active spirit of benevolence ever going about to do good, and thus to repress and overcome evil," I heard Mr. Fordyce remark to my grandfather

He responded to the sentiment warmly. "Unhappily, Buddhism is to be found, not only in Asia, but in civilized

Europe and America," he remarked. "What was the 'Age of Reason' in France but Buddhism fully developed?· What were its results? Tyranny, murder, cruelty unexampled. Sinful and corrupt man—had we not the Bible to tell us, history does so in every page, and the present state of the world speaks loudly the same lesson—never has, and never can, guide himself by reason alone. Here we have throughout Asia one-third of the inhabitants of the globe attempting openly to do so, and see in what a state of moral degradation they are, and have been, as far back as their records can carry us. How lifeless, how soul-debasing is the system! Though in theory the religion of Buddha is infinitely superior to that of Brahma, how exactly similar are its effects on its votaries! While the Sepoy worshippers of the one in India were ruthlessly murdering men, women, and children, the Chinese were attempting precisely the same acts at Singapore and Sarawak, and wherever their numbers afforded them any prospect of success; while nothing can exceed the cruelties they inflict without compunction on each other. This people, too, profess to believe in a faith which inculcates mildness and gentleness; which forbids taking the life of any living creature; which copies, indeed, all the precepts of Christianity, but which, unlike Christianity, trusts implicitly to the guidance of human reason, and ignores any other influence. Now, the true Christian does not ignore the guidance of reason, but he does not trust to it. To one thing only he trusts—the guidance of the Holy Spirit of God, to be obtained through his grace by faith, prayer, and obedience."

"I am glad to hear you speak thus, my old friend," said Mr. Fordyce. "No man can begin to think too early on the subject of religion; but it is better late than never, when, through God's mercy, our lives have been spared to do so at all. How dreadful it is to contemplate a man gradually sinking into the grave, who year after year has had the gospel freely, liberally offered to him, nay, pressed upon him, and yet who has refused, and continues to refuse, to accept it!"

"Yes, Fordyce, I feel deeply what you say," answered my grandfather. "I have lived too much to myself. Henceforth I hope to live to serve One to whom all honour and allegiance are due."

I need not say how thankful I felt at hearing my grandfather speak in this way. I had been taught to believe, and not incorrectly, that he had led a thoughtless life, utterly indifferent to religion, and that it was owing to this that he had lived abroad and shown no regard for my mother. Lately it seemed that a new heart had been given him, and that he had become a changed man.

The conversation I have described took place in front of the rock-hewn temple. We were struck by the immense amount of labour bestowed on it. First, a perpendicular face must have been given to the solid rock. On this the outline of the temple and the figures must have been drawn, and then with chisel and hammer inch by inch cut out. These temples, it must be remembered, were formed at a time when art in Europe was at its lowest ebb, and unable to produce anything at all equal to them.

Much interested in our trip, we rode back to the camp, where we hoped to find Nowell; but though some of the scouts had come in, not a trace of him had they discovered.

We passed the night in a state of the greatest anxiety for his safety. I shall not forget the provoking din caused by a colony of paroquets settled in a group of cocoa-nuts near at hand. They had been away searching for their evening repast when we arrived; but just at sunset they came back in prodigious crowds, screaming, chattering, and frisking about in the most amusing manner, as if delighted to meet each other after the termination of their day's labour. For some time, till darkness warned them that it was time to go to rest, the din they made literally prevented us from hearing each other speak. At length they were silent. I was awoke, however, at the earliest dawn, by the voices of one or two who called up their fellows.

"Good morning," said one, bowing and coquetting to another; "I hope that you have passed a pleasant night."

"Fresh and moist, I thank you," was the answer, as Miss Polly shook the dew from her feathers. And thus one after the other woke up, and such a chattering and clamouring commenced, as they walked up and down along the thick leafstalks of the palms in the highest state of excitement, preening their wings and making remarks on us, probably, and talking over the plans of the day. I jumped up and dressed, for I was anxious to set off without delay to look for Nowell. While a cup of coffee was boiling, I walked out a little way from the camp to enjoy the freshness of the morning air. I had been admiring the glorious refulgence with which the sun rose over the small lake, on the west shore of which we were encamped, when, as I turned to retrace my steps to the tents across the dewy grass, I was almost startled to see my shadow cast along it with peculiar distinctness, while the shoulders and head were surrounded by a brilliant halo. I rubbed my eyes; I looked again and again; I turned round and changed my position several times; but as often as my back was turned to the sun and my eyes on the grass, there was exhibited that most curious and beautiful appearance. I walked on for some way, endeavouring to account for the phenomenon, till I came to a spot covered with blocks of stone and powdered bricks, and there it entirely disappeared. On reaching another grassy spot once more I saw it before me, but much fainter than before;

and by the time I reached the camp scarcely any of the halo was to be seen.

My grandfather and all the party were on foot, and as soon as we had partaken of some coffee and biscuit we mounted our horses, intending to make a systematic search for Nowell. With so experienced a hunter as Dango in his company he was not likely to have lost his way or to be far off, and therefore it was generally feared that some serious accident must have happened to him. Mr. Fordyce, with some of the natives, went in one direction; Lumsden, with some others, went in another; and Mr. Coventry said that, as he could not part with me, I must accompany him. I took Solon with me, of course. His sagacity had taught him the importance of keeping directly behind me, and he showed no inclination to stray. Our journey must have appeared to him like travelling through some enchanted country, full of strange monsters, with whom it would be almost hopeless to contend. We sent on the tents and canteens, and agreed to rendezvous at a spot about three miles in advance should we not find Nowell.

As we rode along I told my grandfather of the phenomenon I had seen at sunrise. He said that it is called the *Anthelia*. It arises from the rays of the sun thrown on the concave and convex surfaces of the dew-drops, each particle furnishing a double reflection. The halo is caused chiefly, I fancy, by the contrast of the excessively dark shadow with the surrounding brightness. The further off the dew-drops are from the eye the more brilliant do they appear, and thus cause the brightest halo round the head.

We rode on for some way, sending our scouts out in every direction, while we examined every spot in a more direct line where we thought it possible our missing countryman might be found. We had proceeded some miles, and were about to turn off towards the spot we had agreed on as a rendezvous for breakfast, when one of our hunters said that he perceived recent signs of an elephant in the neighbourhood, and told us to be careful, as he had little doubt from their being only one that it was a rogue, and probably a fierce and cunning one. This information, of course, put us on the alert. We looked to our rifles, and directed our horse-keepers to walk at our horses' heads, that we might dismount in a moment and be ready for action, while we kept our eyes about us in every direction. The hunter made a sign, pointing towards a thick jungle. We dismounted, leaving our horses with their keepers. We had been passing through a somewhat open country, with trees scattered about here and there. We advanced cautiously. I saw the jungle in the distance move. Solon barked as a signal that danger was near. Presently there was a loud trumpeting and roar, I may call it, not of fear, but of rage, though it was sufficient to inspire fear. There was a crashing of boughs and underwood, and a huge elephant, with trunk uplifted, broke through the jungle and rushed furiously at us.

"Now, my lad, I hear that you have already hit more than one elephant, let me see what you can do," exclaimed my grandfather, the spirit of the old sportsman rising within him.

He had with him a Moor, a first-rate hunter and shot, armed with a rifle. There was not much chance, therefore, of our missing the elephant between us. We all advanced towards him as soon as he appeared. As he kept his trunk up in the air, the difficulty of shooting him on the forehead was much increased. Our bold air somewhat disconcerted him. He stopped, apparently to single out one as his victim. At that same moment he lowered his trunk.

"Now, Ralph," cried my grandfather; "fire!"

I did so, aiming at the monster's forehead, though I was upwards of thirty yards off. Up went his trunk. He rushed on, fury in his eye, and the excess of rage indicated by his trumpeting. It seemed scarcely possible that some one of us should not suffer. Yet I felt wonderfully cool. I waited a second; and then taking full aim, fired my second barrel. In an instant the huge monster stopped, and before the smoke cleared away lay an inanimate mass on the ground, within twenty yards of us.

My grandfather, when he saw what had occurred, seized me in his arms and gave me a hug which well-nigh squeezed the breath out of my body.

"Well done! capitally done, my boy!" he exclaimed. "I thought your shot at the buffalo might have been chance, but I can now see what you are made of. Don't suppose, though, that I care so much about your being able to kill a buffalo or an elephant, but it is the calmness of nerve and the steadiness of eye I admire."

Just then we heard a cry, and looking round to ascertain whence it proceeded, we saw a person perched up in a tree beckoning to us. Leaving Solon, who was snuffing round and round the dead elephant, we hurried on, when, as we got near the tree, I recognized Dango. He cried out that he was too much hurt to descend, and entreated that some of our people would come up and help him to do so. We waited with great anxiety till he was got down, which was done by means of the ropes with which the horses were tethered. Poor fellow! he seemed to be in a state of great suffering, and looked almost starved. He was placed on the grass, and as soon as a few drops of spirits and water had been poured down his throat he was able to speak. He then told us, that after I had been separated from Nowell and him, and Solon had run after me, they had set off to try and find me. It was, however, close upon sunset when they reached this spot. They very soon discovered the traces of an elephant, and were looking about to ascertain whether he was in front of them, when a loud crashing of the boughs was heard, and he emerged from the jungle close to them. He first made at Dango, who knew that the most dangerous thing he could do was to fly, unless he had a tree near at hand behind which he could conceal himself; so facing the elephant he boldly stood his ground, hoping that Nowell would kill the monster, or that he should be able to leap out of his way. Now on came the elephant, trumpeting loudly. Nowell lifted his rifle and fired. Dreadful was the momentary suspense. With a cry of rage the elephant threw himself at Dango. The Moor leaped aside, but not far enough to prevent the elephant from knocking him over with his trunk, and putting one of his huge feet on his leg. He would have been killed had not Nowell shouted and shrieked, to draw off the elephant's attention, while he was reloading his rifle. He succeeded almost too soon, and the brute rushed at him. He fired, but his eye had lost its accustomed exactness, or his nerves were shaken, for again he missed hitting a vital part. The moment Dango found himself free, he crawled away towards a tree at some little distance, which the elephant had already passed. Nowell retreated, then halted, and once more pulled his trigger; his piece missed fire. Again and again he tried. He had no time to put on a cap. He endeavoured to escape his impending fate by flight. He ran fast. He saw a tree some yards off. He hoped to reach it. At first he outstripped his savage pursuer; then his strength, it appeared, failed him; he dropped his rifle and ran on. Once more he gained ground on the elephant. He reached the tree, but he did not look to see on which side the elephant was coming. He ran round it and met his ruthless foe face to face! Not a cry escaped him. Who can picture his sensations? on another instant, the huge monster's whole weight was upon him.

"Dere—dere is de tree," said Dango, pointing to a large ebony tree at a little distance.

We approached the spot with awe and dread. There lay, recognized only by parts of the dress, all that now remained on earth of the once gay, gallant, and handsome Arthur Nowell, slain in an inglorious and useless strife with a wild beast. I shuddered as I thought how narrowly I had escaped such a fate, and felt thankful for the mercy which had been shown me. Then as I looked once more at the spot, and remembered that he who lay there had lately been my companion and friend, and that but a few hours before I had seen him full of life and animation, with cheerful voice eagerly pursuing the chase, I gave way to my feelings and burst into tears.

Such has been the fate of many an elephant-hunter. It was almost impossible to carry the mangled remains to the camp, so with our hunting-knives and spades, manufactured by our followers, in the course of a few minutes we dug a grave in which we placed them. Rudely carving his name on the stem of the tree, while our followers carried poor Dango, with sad hearts we returned to the camp.

CHAPTER XVII.

Grief of Mr. Fordyce—Mahintala—Catch a Crocodile—Singing Fish—Arrive at Trincomalee—Embark on board the *Star*—Visit the Maldives—Aden—News of Alfred—Island of Perim—Magadona—Further News of Alfred—Find a Shipwrecked Seaman on a rock—Who he proved to be.

"AND where is Nowell? Have you not found him?" asked Mr. Fordyce, as we rode up to the rendezvous, where breakfast was being prepared under the shade of a banyan-tree. I thought my kind old friend's heart would have broken when he heard what had occurred.

"I had begun to love him as a son, for the son he was of the friend and companion of my youth. His poor, poor mother, how this news will wring her heart! What grief and anguish is in store for her!"

I need not further dwell on Mr. Fordyce's grief; but I cannot leave the subject without reminding those of my readers who may some day be inclined carelessly to risk their lives as Nowell and I had been doing ours, first, that they have no right to do so—that they are committing a great sin by the act; and then, also, that though they may be careless of the consequences, that they have mothers and sisters, fathers and brothers at home, to whose loving hearts their untimely fate will bring many a bitter pang of grief. It is a soldier's duty to be ready to die fighting for his country; and though those at home mourn, and mourn deeply, their grief is not bitter or full of anguish as it would be if those they have lost had died in consequence of their own folly or wickedness.

Nowell's death threw a gloom over our little party which it was difficult to shake off. I was struck by the way, the instant poor Dango was brought into camp, my grandfather set to work to examine and dress his hurts.

"My great fear is that mortification will set in before we can reach Trincomalee," he remarked. "His limb is so much crushed that I fear amputation will be necessary to save the man's life."

He attended on the poor fellow with as much care and skill as any medical man could have done, but his fear proved too well founded, and before two days were over the daring and expert hunter had breathed his last.

Anxious as we were to get to the termination of our journey, we could not travel much faster than we had been doing. As our progress was in no way retarded by it, my grandfather took Lumsden and me to see any object of interest which was within our reach. The most extraordinary was the mountain of Mahintala. It rises suddenly out of the plain to the height of upwards of 1000 feet; its sides are covered with wood, huge masses of granite towering up on the summit. The southern face is almost precipitous, but on the north there is a sufficient slope to have allowed of the formation of a thousand stone steps, leading from the base to the highest point of the mountain. Some of them are cut out of the mountain itself, but others are formed of slabs of granite, fifteen feet in width. Each step averages a foot in height. It was on the summit of this mountain that the great prophet of Buddha, Mahindo, first stopped when he came to Ceylon to establish his religion, and it was here that he met the monarch of the country, whom he converted to his faith. On a platform near the top stands a dagoba, with a sort of convent, intended for the habitation of the monks; and from thence the steps continue upwards to the summit, which is crowned by a dagoba 100 feet in height.

which is said to enshrine one solitary hair from the forehead of Buddha.

This wonderful building has stood for upwards of eighteen centuries, having been constructed about the first year of the Christian era. It is said that when it was completed the king had it covered by a rich canopy, ornamented with pearls and other precious stones, while he spread a carpet, eight miles in length, from Mahintala to Anarajapoora, that pilgrims might proceed over it without washing their feet. On the level of the convent a tank has been formed for the use of the priests. The whole level space near the summit must at one time have been covered with buildings, from the vast quantity of ruins and fragments of statues, and carved work of every description strewn about. In spite of the height we climbed up to the top. The view is superb, extending almost across the island from sea to sea. Below us was a wide expanse of forest, spreading around till lost in the far distance, while out of it were seen rising the dagobas of Anarajapoora, with the artificial lakes I have described glittering among them, and several curious rocks and mountain heights dim and indistinct in the far distance.

We met with nothing which I can properly call an adventure during the rest of our journey, and yet there were numberless objects we saw well worthy of description. I have spoken of our encampments, but often, instead of erecting our tents, the natives rapidly built for us huts of boughs, which they covered neatly with palm leaves, and in these abodes, from their being much cooler than tents, we frequently passed the night. We had a number of rivers to cross. Sometimes we passed over in canoes, but very frequently we placed ourselves and our saddles on rafts formed of two or more hollow trunks of trees, with branches laid across them, while our elephants and horses swam over after us.

WOMAN CARRIED OFF BY A CROCODILE.

As we drew near the sea we stopped one night in the neighbourhood of a lagoon, in which the crocodiles were said to be very numerous, and of prodigious size. As we walked out by the side of the sheet of water just before sunset, we found a number of natives collected there, who seemed to be in a state of great agitation. On inquiring, we were told that

WOMEN ATTACKED BY A CROCODILE.

a number of women were engaged in cutting rushes for making nets. They were almost up to their waists, when great was their horror to see the scaly back and tail of a huge crocodile appear among them. They turned to fly towards the shore, but at that instant a piercing shriek gave notice that one of their number was seized. The rest, as they reached the shore, saw their helpless companion dragged away into deep water. In vain she shrieked—in vain she lifted up her hands imploringly for assistance. The horror-stricken group looked on without attempting, probably without being able, to rescue her; and dreadful it was to hear her cries and to see her struggles till, dragged into deep water, she was concealed beneath its surface. Some men having assembled, they resolved to try and catch the crocodile, to punish him for his atrocity. For this purpose they baited a large hook. It was made fast, not to a single thick rope, but to a bunch of small ones, which the monster cannot bite through as he does a large one, as they sink into the spaces between his teeth, and thus secure it more firmly in his mouth. This collection of lines was carried out into deep water by a buoy, and the end secured to some strong stakes driven in where it was sufficiently shallow for the purpose. The hook was baited with the entrails of a goat. Thus prepared, it was left during the night.

On leaving our tents the next morning, we found a strong strain on the rope, and the natives soon collecting, a canoe was launched, and some men getting into her, the line was made fast to her bow. No sooner did the crocodile feel himself hauled towards the shore, than he resisted strongly, and away spun the canoe off towards the middle of the lagoon. The crew tugged one way and the monster the other, and now and then he raised his fierce-looking head above the surface, clashing his jaws together with the most horrid sound, which showed that if he once got the canoe between them he could easily crush it and its crew.

The crocodile has no fleshy lips. All his mouth is composed of hard bone, so that when he snaps with his teeth and jaws, it sounds exactly as if two large pieces of hard wood had been struck together, and warns any one of the fate they may expect if caught by them.

The natives, however, did not appear to fear him. They let him haul away and exhaust his strength, and then once more they paddled towards the land. Having at last carried the end of the line on shore, all hands hauled away on it, and though he struggled vehemently, the monster's huge snout was seen emerging from the water and gradually approaching the dry land. No sooner, however, was he fairly on shore than he appeared stupified, or else he was pretending to be so, that he might have an opportunity of catching some one unawares. I was about to go up to him to examine him more closely, when, with a terrific wag of his huge tail, up he started and made a desperate effort to regain the water. He was soon hauled back again, however, and Lumsden and I had to put an end to him by sending a couple of rifle balls into his side. We thought that we had killed him, for he lay perfectly still with his eyes closed. We were again running up to him, when one of the natives called us back, and another pricking him with a spear, up he started as full of life as ever once more, making a push for the water, with the hook and line still in his mouth. He was, however, soon brought back again, when one of the natives pushed a long sharp spear into his neck, and drove it home till it reached his heart. Whether or not he was the monster who had killed the woman we could not tell. Certainly he had not swallowed her, for on being cut open, his maw was found to contain only some tortoises, and a quantity of gravel, and stones, and broken bricks. Those hard substances he had swallowed to assist his digestion. The opinion of the natives was that he certainly was not the monster who had carried off the woman, because had he been, he would not have returned for more food.

Crocodiles are said never to attack people except when

pressed by hunger. On such occasions they watch for deer and other animals which come down to the tanks or lakes to drink, and, seizing them by their heads, quickly draw them in. I should think that a crocodile would find an elephant a very tough morsel, though he might give him a very awkward nip at the end of his snout. At the same time, if any living creature could crush a crocodile, an elephant's knees would do it.

It was a day's journey from this neighbourhood that we heard of the existence of musical fish. It was asserted that they sang so loudly that their notes could be heard by those floating over the calm surface of the lake where they were said to live. My grandfather was a man who never was content to believe anything from mere hearsay, when he had the power of investigating the truth of an account. Accordingly he engaged a canoe, and the evening of our arrival, when the moon arose, we pulled off to the locality spoken of. The surface of the lake was like glass, and as we listened there could be no doubt of it. Sweet, gentle sounds came up faintly, but clearly, from the depths below. They reminded us of those produced by a finger-glass when the edge is gently rubbed round and round. There was not one continuous note, but a number of gentle sounds, each, however, in itself perfectly clear from a bass to the sweetest treble. On putting our ears against the side of the canoe the sounds were much increased in volume. They varied, too, in different parts, and at some places we lost them altogether. If the sounds proceeded from fish this might have been caused by the shoals swimming about, but then, on returning to the spot the notes were again heard as before. The natives asserted that they were produced by the inhabitants of shells, and they showed us some which they called the crying shells, from which they asserted the sounds proceeded. From what we observed and heard we were very much inclined to be of their opinion. *Cerithium Palustre* is the scientific name of the shell in question; but I cannot pretend to decide the point.

Shortly after this we reached Trincomalee. Few harbours in the world possess more beauty or are more perfect in their way than that of Trincomalee. It is so completely landlocked that its surface is as calm as that of a lake. Over its wide expanse are many lovely islands of various sizes, while here and there bold headlands run into its waters, and in other places the shores rise to a considerable height, covered with trees, and lofty mountains are seen towering up in the far distance. We at once agreed how infinitely superior it was to Point de Galle, in whose unsafe roadsteads so many noble ships have been cast away. On the other hand, not only is the harbour of Trincomalee renowned for its extent and security, but for its accessibility for every description of craft at all seasons and in all weathers. Of course my own opinion is worth but little, but I heard it stated by those who knew the country well, and are at the same time thoroughly disinterested, that it possesses every requisite to make it both the capital and the great commercial port of the island. Except in the immediate vicinity of the sea, the soil is far superior to that near Point de Galle and Colombo, while the reasons which induced the former possessors of the island to make those places the chief ports have now ceased to be of importance; the chief of these reasons was the existence of the cinnamon plantations near them, the greater number of which are now abandoned.

Trincomalee is but a poor town, the only buildings of importance being those belonging to Government. There are also a number of Hindu temples kept up, but they are in the most barbarous style. They contributed to make the crime of which England is guilty appear more glaring, that so miserable a religion should still be in existence, after the country has been so long governed by a Christian people. I do not say that any religion should be put down by force, but I do say that the example of Christian men and the preaching of Christian ministers ought, and would, by this time, have influenced the votaries of Brahma and Siva, had they been brought to bear on them in a place where, as in Trincomalee, the religion of the country differs from both of them. The town has extensive fortifications in the neighbourhood, but, under the modern system of warfare, they would prove, I was told, of little or no value as a defence to the place. I thought it best to give this short account of Trincomalee before resuming the narrative of my own adventures.

We had been in the place two days when a brig-of-war entered the harbour, which, on her making her number, I found with great satisfaction to be the *Star*. Captain Armstrong was known to my grandfather, so he accompanied me at once on board. I was anxious to go, as Captain Armstrong had promised to make all the inquiries in his power about Alfred, and I could not help hoping that he might have heard something about him. Captain Armstrong received us most cordially. When I inquired about my brother, he said that he had, after almost abandoning all hope of hearing of him, discovered that he sailed in a merchant brig, bound down the African coast, to trade chiefly in ivory, gold, and other precious articles; but that there were rumours that the vessel had been wrecked or cut off by the natives. He did not altogether credit this rumour, and he assured us that had he been at liberty he would at once have followed her supposed course, and endeavoured to ascertain its correctness. He had, however, to return to Ceylon and Madras. Some repairs being required for his brig he had put in to Trincomalee, in consequence of which I had thus happily fallen in with him.

" And Marsden," he continued, " you remember the invitation I gave you to take a cruise in the *Star*. I now repeat it, and I am glad to tell you that, after visiting Aden, I have been directed to proceed down the east coast of Africa, as far as Natal. The object is that I may inquire into matters connected with the abominable slave-trade, which has for some time past, in spite of treaties and protestations, been carried on from numerous places along that coast, especially at and near the settlements belonging to the Portuguese. I shall make it my especial business to inquire after the missing vessel, and probably, indeed, my ostensible object, so that we may hope to gain some tidings of your brother."

My grandfather thanked Captain Armstrong very much for his kindness, and so, of course, did I; and it was arranged that I was to go on board as soon as the ship was ready for sea. This, however, would not be for nearly another week. On leaving the cabin, what was my surprise to see William Henley walking the deck with a gold lace to his cap, and the crown and anchor on the buttons of his jacket. I went up to him and warmly shook his hand.

"What! have you entered the navy?" I exclaimed.

"Not exactly," he answered; "I have joined this ship as pilot, as I am pretty well acquainted with the parts of the coast she is about to visit, and, perhaps, the hope that I may assist in discovering your missing brother may have influenced me in accepting Captain Armstrong's offer of the berth."

I was very certain that this was the case, for I had, I knew, gained his regards, and that he would be ready to do a great deal to serve me.

"By-the-by, you will find two other old shipmates aboard, who will be glad to hear that you are going to join us," he continued, when I told him of Captain Armstrong's kindness. "There they are."

I stepped forward, and there I found Johnie Spratt and

Tommy Bigg, both metamorphosed into regular men-of-war's men, though the latter was certainly a very little one. Johnie, I found, had entered before the brig left Point de Galle. He met an old shipmate belonging to the *Star*, who persuaded him to enter, and he told me that he never regretted having done so, as he was far better off in every respect than he had been in the merchant-service. Tommy had followed Mr. Henley, and only joined when he did. He also seemed very happy, and looked twice as brisk and active as he had ever been on board the *Orion*. I was afraid that Solon would not be allowed to accompany me, but when I spoke to the captain, he answered good-naturedly,—

"Oh, bring him by all means. You will soon find that he makes plenty of friends on board, for sailors delight in all sorts of pets, and more especially in a little child, a monkey, or a dog. I suspect that they will soon get him out of his gravity, however."

So it was arranged that Solon should accompany me. I should have been very sorry to have parted from him, and yet I would not have declined Captain Armstrong's offer on that account. I was so impatient to be off that the week I was detained at Trincomalee appeared to pass very slowly by. I spent a good deal of my time with Mr. Fordyce. I wished to show him, as much as possible, how sensible I was of all his kindness to me, and I felt as if I had somewhat neglected him after I had met my grandfather. He had begun to get over poor Nowell's death, but he had very far from recovered his usual buoyancy of spirits. My grandfather was very much engaged, partly in the business which had brought him to Trincomalee, but chiefly in placing his affairs in a condition which would enable him to return to England. I was very glad to find that he intended to intrust the charge of many important matters to my friend Lumsden. I had always found him at school a highly honourable and conscientious boy; and I had every reason to believe that he was still guided by the same high principles which then influenced his conduct.

The last words of my grandfather to me were, " Good-bye, Ralph, my dear boy; I trust that we may meet again before many months are over, in Old England, and that you will bring home Alfred safe with you."

Scarcely had Solon and I set our feet on the deck of the *Star*, than the anchor was hove up, and sail being made, we ran out of the harbour and stood away to the southward. The first land we sighted was that of the Maldive Islands, of which there are said to be upwards of forty thousand. They are all of a coral formation, and rise to an elevation not exceeding fourteen feet above the ocean. Generally they are much lower. The sea might easily be sent rolling over them, were they not protected by long coral reefs and sandbanks of a circular form. Through these reefs there are passages of great depth, called atolls. The water inside is perfectly smooth. We entered by one of them, brought up off Mali, the chief island, which is about seven miles in circumference. It is the residence of the chief of all the group, who is called the Sultan, and is now dependent on the British Government of Ceylon. The people are Mohammedans, and their numbers are said to amount to upwards of one hundred and fifty thousand souls. They produce Indian corn, and millet, and sugar, and cotton; and there are numerous fine trees on the islands—the uncultivated portions being covered with an impenetrable jungle. There are few animals on the islands. Fish, however, is very abundant, so that all the inhabitants might exist on them.

The captain's business with the sultan was soon concluded. It was interesting and curious to sail among the tree-covered islands, some of the woods appearing to rise directly out of the water, while we threaded our way out again from the group to the westward. Our passage across the Arabian Sea was as smooth as the most timid of navigators could desire. We made the mountainous, rocky, and somewhat barren, though considerable island of Socotra, belonging to the Imaun of Muscat. Soon after this we sighted the mountain mass of Jebel Shamshan, or Cape Aden as it is called, rising 1776 feet above the sea, with the town of Aden built on the eastern base of it.

The capture of Aden, in 1839, was one of the first naval exploits which took place during the reign of Queen Victoria, and most gallantly was it accomplished by an expedition sent from India, under the command of Captain H. Smith of the *Volage*. As we approached the lofty headland of Cape Aden it looked like an island. Its position is very similar to that of Gibraltar, as it is connected with the mainland by a piece of low swampy ground. I was struck by its grand picturesque appearance, though it is barren and wild, and utterly destitute of vegetation. We ran in and anchored not far off the fortified island of Sirah, four or five miles from the town.

Aden, when captured, consisted of little more than an assemblage of mud huts with matting coverings, and contained scarcely six hundred inhabitants. It is now a flourishing place containing twenty-two thousand inhabitants, and is surrounded by orchards and gardens. This change is owing to its occupation by British troops, and the constant visits of steamers with numerous passengers to and from India.

I went on shore with Captain Armstrong to make more inquiries about Alfred, or rather the vessel in which he sailed. She was, I found, called the *Dragon*. The master, Captain Redman, was a very plausible person, and my brother had undoubtedly thought him a very respectable one; but things had come out after he had left Aden considerably to his discredit, and I had reason to fear that he was utterly unprincipled and reckless, and intimately connected with slavers—indeed, it was very probable that he would without scruple have taken a cargo of slaves on board if he had had the opportunity. Should he have attempted to obtain slaves on some parts of the coast, it was very likely that he would have been cut off, as the natives in many places are strongly opposed to the slave-trade, having discovered how greatly it is to their disadvantage. For the sake of it wars are fostered, and a horrible system of kidnapping is practised; while commerce, the cultivation of the land, and the general resources of the country are neglected, the only people who benefit being the chiefs and the foreigners who assist in carrying away the unhappy slaves. Every piece of information I gained raised my hopes, although often it might have appeared to be of a very discouraging nature. I felt that it added another link to the chain by which I hoped to find my way to where Alfred was concealed.

What may properly be called the British settlement of Aden is embraced in a peninsula of about fifteen miles in circumference. It is in reality a huge crater joined to the mainland by a narrow neck of sand. The town and cantonments are within the crater, and thus entirely surrounded by hills, except on the east, where it has a gap opening on East Bay. The town is neat and well built, and the fortifications entirely new. It is very strong by nature, and as large sums and the best engineering skill have been employed in refortifying it, it may now be considered impregnable, and is deservedly looked on as the Gibraltar of the Indian Ocean. It used to be supplied with water from tanks formed on the sides of the mountains, and these the governor has much improved. Wells also have been sunk, and the sea-water has been distilled to supply that most necessary fluid.

Instead of at once going north, we stood up the Straits of

Bab-el-Mandeb, to the island of Perim, when we came to anchor in a remarkably fine harbour, capable of accommodating a numerous fleet. It had lately been occupied by the British, who were then building a lighthouse on it. The only safe passage by it is that on the north, or Arabian shore, barely half a mile in width. That on the southern side, between it and Africa—though eleven miles wide—is exceedingly difficult, so that it might easily be rendered impassable. Thus strong fortifications on the north side might prevent any fleet from forcing the passage of the Red Sea. As about a quarter of the island consists of a low plain of sand and coral, covered with salt-loving plants, and the remainder is overspread with loose boulders and masses of black lava, without a drop of fresh water, it cannot be considered a desirable residence. The garrison, however, is supplied by means of tanks constructed to catch the rain, and the fort is also furnished with an apparatus for distilling salt water. The highest point is only about 245 feet above the sea.

My heart bounded with satisfaction when once more we made sail to the southward. We were at length, I felt, fairly on our voyage to discover my brother. Keeping an easterly course, we steered along the coast of Berbera till we doubled Cape Guardafui. We then once more stood to the southward along the coast of Ajan. We saw no towns or even villages, though we constantly kept close in with the land. This part of Africa is inhabited by tribes of people called the Somauli, who are in general Mohammedans. Some live in towns, but they are mostly a pastoral people. Those who live on this part of the coast occupy themselves almost entirely as fishermen. We landed at several places to communicate with them, and got glimpses of fertile-looking valleys, and here and there of fine open grassy plains. We could hear of no vessel answering to the description of the *Dragon* having been seen off the coast; indeed, from the business in which she was said to have been engaged, it was not likely that she would have called off there. We entered also the harbour of Magadoxa, formed by a coral reef. It is a curious place. There are scarcely a hundred and fifty houses in the place—all of them with thick walls, and built round court-yards, but one-half of the town consists almost entirely of tombs.

We should not have been the wiser for our visit had we not fallen in with the master of an Arab dow, who had been some way to the southward of the Portuguese settlements. Captain Armstrong had on some occasion rendered him some service, and when he saw the *Star*, he came on board with some small presents to show his gratitude. On being questioned, he told us that some voyages before he had fallen in with a brig answering exactly the description of the *Dragon*, and that he had heard that an attempt had been made by her master and his crew to carry off some of the negroes from a village on the coast against their will. He had succeeded in securing a few on board, but when returning on shore for a further supply, the natives had set on him, and murdered him and most of his people. They had then gone on board, rescued their countrymen, and carried off the survivors of the brig's crew as captives into the interior.

Though I trembled while the account was being translated to me, yet on considering over the subject, I felt sure that Alfred would not have joined the party who had attempted to kidnap the natives, and I therefore had great hopes that he was among those who had been made prisoners, and that I should ultimately be able to discover the place of his captivity. The Arab did not know the exact position of the spot where the occurrence had taken place, as it was some way further to the south than he had gone. Yet from the information he gave, Captain Armstrong had little doubt about finding it.

Leaving Magadoxa, we continued our course to the southward. A few days after this we were standing on with a fair breeze and a light wind, when the look-out from the masthead hailed the deck, to say that there was an object on the port bow, but whether a rock, or a ship with her masts gone or capsized, or a whale, he could not tell. Several of the officers went aloft with their glasses, as I also did, to try and ascertain what it was which had hove in sight. We looked and looked, however, for some time, without being able to settle the point. The object was a long way off, and we drew only very slowly up to it. As we approached it seemed to grow larger and larger. It was pretty clearly not a ship's bottom, nor a whale, and finally it resolved itself into a high rock surrounded by a coral reef—so we judged from the line of surf which every now and then we saw rising up out of the blue sea. It was a very dangerous-looking place, on which, during the fierce gales of those latitudes, in thick weather or on a dark night many a fine ship has probably been cast away.

"There appears to me to be something moving on the rock," observed Mr. D'Arcy, the second lieutenant. "Perhaps there are only birds there."

"No, sir; there is a man, and he is waving a shirt or a flag, or something of that size," I exclaimed, after looking attentively for some moments.

I was right. In a quarter of an hour or less we got near enough to make out clearly a man, who was standing on the highest point of a conical mass of black rocks, which looked like the peak of a volcano rising out of the sea. He had stripped off his shirt as a signal, and was continually waving it above his head. Of course, he could not see us as clearly as we, with our glasses, could see him—a fact which he had probably forgotten. Not only was he waving, but by his gestures he was evidently shouting and leaping up as high as he could from the rock, in his eagerness to call our attention to him.

A SHIPWRECKED MARINER.

Poor fellow! it was not surprising, for it was a dreary spot to be left out in mid-ocean all by himself. Having got as near as we could venture, we hove to, to leeward of the rock, when a boat was lowered, of which Mr. D'Arcy took command, and very kindly allowed me to accompany him. As we pulled up to the rock, we found how much we had been deceived by the distance as to its size, for instead of being anything like the size of a ship, the rock, or rather the islet, proved to be nearly a mile in circumference, though when first discovered only the conical rock in the centre had been seen, the lower portion being very little above the level of the water. As soon as the man discovered us approaching, he ran down from his lofty post towards us. Why, I could not tell; I almost expected to see Alfred. We had to pull round some way before, guided by the signs he made, we could find a passage through the reefs. At length, however, one was found, and dashing through it, we were soon close to the shore. But even before we touched it, the man plunged into the water in his eagerness to meet us. I looked eagerly, but I soon saw that it was not Alfred. He was an oldish, roughish-looking man, and had all the appearance of a seaman.

"Thank Heaven, friends, that have been sent to save me," he exclaimed, as he was helped into the boat; "I don't think I could have held out many days longer. I have been living on dried whale's flesh and shell-fish for I don't know how many months past, and I was beginning to feel the scurvy breaking out in me; but all's right now; I've no fear."

Mr. D'Arcy wished to have a look at the rock before leaving it, so he and I, and one of the midshipmen, landed. Our idea of its being the extinct crater of a marine volcano was undoubtedly correct. At the foot of the cone was a pool, deep and clear, of pure fresh water, forced up it must have been from beneath the ocean. On one side of the islet were the remains of a large sperm whale, the flesh of which had supplied the poor man with food. He had also constructed a hut very neatly out of the bones, near the top of the crater. Already young palm-trees and a variety of vegetable productions were springing up round the base of the cone, so that this spot in a few years hence may afford ample support to any one cast away on it. After a very cursory inspection of the place we hurried back to the boat, and returned on board.

The rescued man expressed himself most grateful for the assistance afforded him. He did not, however, at first say much about himself, merely observing that he had gone through a great number of adventures, and had at last, after having been a prisoner among the blacks, and effected his escape, been wrecked three months before on this rock, when he was the only person whose life had been saved.

"And what is your name, my man?" asked Captain Armstrong.

"Bigg, sir—Thomas Bigg," answered the seaman.

"He seems to be an active, intelligent man. As we are short of hands, we may as well allow him to enter if he wishes it," observed the captain to the first lieutenant.

The stranger was asked if he would enter, and expressed no objections to do so, but said he would think about it.

When I heard the name of Thomas Bigg, I looked at the man very hard, to see if I could discover any likeness between him and Tommy, for I could not help thinking that he might possibly be Tommy's father, who was supposed to have been lost at sea. I waited till the seaman was sent forward, and then I followed him.

"I say, my man, your name is not strange to me," said I. "Will you tell me, have you ever had a son called after yourself?"

"Why do you ask, sir?" said he, looking surprised, and yet very eager.

"Because I once had a shipmate of that name, a little fellow, who told me that his father had been so long at sea without coming home, that he was supposed to be lost," I replied.

"Did he remember me? Did he talk about me, the poor dear little chap?" inquired the seaman, eagerly.

"Indeed he did," I answered. "He told me how fond you were of him. He was sure that you would have come back if you could; and he, I am sure, loved you dearly, as a son should a kind father."

"Bless him! bless him!" exclaimed the seaman, brushing away a tear from his eye. "But where is he now? Can you tell me nothing more about him?"

Just then Tommy came on deck. "What do you think of that little fellow out there?" I asked.

The seaman looked at him eagerly. In another moment he had sprung from one side of the ship to the other, and, to Tommy's great surprise, had seized him in his arms, and gazing anxiously in his face, began to hug him as if he was about to squeeze all the breath out of his body. Tommy looked up at length in return.

"Father!" he exclaimed, hesitatingly, drawing deeply his breath; "is it you, is it you indeed?"

"Tommy, Tommy, it is," cried the seaman. "I've found you, and you've found me; and if they were to tell me that you were not my own boy, I wouldn't believe them, that I wouldn't. I know you as well as if I'd never lost sight of you, that I do!"

I cannot describe how happy I felt at this meeting of the father and his boy. The tears came to my eyes as I watched them. I soon, however, went away and left them to themselves. "I trust I may be as fortunate in finding poor Alfred, after my long search for him, as Tommy has been in finding his father without looking for him at all," was the tenor of my silent prayer.

CHAPTER XVIII.

Old Bigg's Narrative—My Plan to rescue Alfred—Fall in with an Arab Dow in a Sinking State—Catch Sight of the Pirate—She tries to Escape—The Chase—She blows up—The Fate of Sills.

THERE is an old saying, that "it's an ill wind that blows no one any good." I found it a very true saying, for I have scarcely ever known a misfortune, or what might be called an ill, happening in the world without, before long, having actually seen some good derived from it, by which somebody or other has benefited. I do not mean for one moment that evil may be done that good may come of it. Very, very far from that. There is no more hateful morality in the sight of God. But what I mean is, that God often causes events to happen, which we in our blindness may think ills or misfortunes, but which, in reality, tend to our ultimate happiness. If we could only bring ourselves firmly to believe this, it would enable us to bear with far greater patience than we do the sickness and losses, the sufferings and annoyances which meet us constantly in our course through life.

The day after we had rescued Tommy Bigg's father from the rock, as I was walking the deck, he came up to me.

"Sir," said he, touching his hat, "my boy tells me that you have been his best friend from the time you first set eyes on him, and I am grateful, sir, indeed I am. I'd do anything to serve you, and from what Tommy tells me I think I might serve you. I hear from him that you came away from home to look for a brother, and that you believe he was aboard the *Dragon*. Now, sir, I belonged to that unfortunate craft, and it was a bad day for me that I ever set foot on her deck, so I have had reason to think. I didn't know what her calling was, or I would never have stepped up her side, that I know.

"Well, sir, when we last sailed from Aden, a young gentleman came on board for a passage down to Natal. I soon found out that he was a seaman, though he took no part in the navigation of the brig, but when he discovered, as I had done, her character, kept himself aloof from the captain and officers, and, indeed, everybody on board. He did well; for, to my mind, it would be hard to find a greater villain in existence than Captain Redman. I would have liked to have spoken to him, to tell him that he might trust me if the worst came to the worst and he required my services; but it wouldn't have done for me to have been seen addressing him.

"We called in at Mozambique, and then some of the government officers, and merchants, and great people of the place, came on board, and were hand and glove with Captain Redman. Thinks I to myself, I wonder now if you knew what sort of a rogue he is whether you would be so friendly? But I soon found out that it would have made no difference with them, for they were one and all interested in the slave trade, and were friendly with him because he paid them hard cash for the slaves they got for him. I believe that they had arranged for a cargo for him, when a new governor of the place came unexpectedly out from home, and gave notice that he would not allow anything of the sort. Whether he was in earnest about preventing the traffic, or whether he only wished to show that a new broom sweeps clean, I don't know. Certain it was that we had to get out of the place as fast as we could, and made sail to the southward.

"I ought to have told you, sir, that I didn't know the name of the young gentleman who was aboard us, but from what Tommy tells me I have little doubt that he was your brother. I believe that he would have left the brig at Mozambique, but Captain Redman persuaded him that he was going on direct to Natal, so he remained on board.

"Now the captain had, I found, engaged to supply a cargo of slaves, and he was determined to get them by fair means or foul. Before many days had passed, I found that the vessel was headed in towards the coast. In a short time we dropped anchor in a snug harbour with a narrow entrance, where we lay completely concealed from any vessel in the offing. In a short time a chief came off in a canoe, and the captain had some palavar with him, and he returned on shore. The captain then said that a number of blacks had agreed to come on board to take their passage to some place or other, to work as labourers, but that after having signed their papers they had refused to come, 'so you see, my young men, we shall have to use force to make them do their duty,' he observed.

"We had a strong crew for the size of the brig—some thirty hands or more—and twenty or more, without a word, agreed to the captain's proposal. All the boats were lowered, and away they went, as soon as it was dark, to the shore. I did not know at the time why they took so much precaution, but I afterwards learned that there were two parties in the place—one headed by the chief who had come aboard, and who lived on the coast, in favour of the slave-trade; the other, who owned the country further inland, who had determined to put a stop to it, from having discovered that it was doing them every possible harm. They had also won over a good many of the coast natives to see things in the light they did.

"I and about eight other men remained on board, so did

our young gentleman passenger. We waited for some two hours or more, wondering why the captain and the rest were so long in returning, when at last the boats appeared loaded to the gunnel with thirty blacks or more in them. The poor wretches were chained two and two. They were quickly passed below, and secured between decks, which had been fitted up for them. Everything was done in a great hurry. I guessed that something was wrong. 'Now, my lads, we must be off again; no time to be lost,' sang out the captain.

"Away they went, and three more of our people, so that there were still fewer left on board. We waited and waited for their return, but still they did not come. At last we heard some shots fired on shore, and we began to think that something had happened. Still longer we waited, and we grew very anxious, and one proposed one thing and one another. There was only the second mate left on board of all the officers, and he did not know what to do. We had given up all hopes of seeing them when the splash of oars was heard, and we saw, as we thought, three or four boats approaching. It was just before break of day, and it was very dark. It was all right, we thought, and we were expecting to see our shipmates come up the side, when, all of a sudden, I don't know how it was, there were some fifty black fellows screeching and howling away on the deck. Some of them attacked us; and while we were struggling with them, others rushed below and liberated the slaves, and in less than a minute up they all came pouring on deck, shouting and shrieking, and threatening vengeance on us. Two or three of our fellows were killed. Still we fought on, for we knew that we had no mercy to expect from them.

"When daylight broke, the young passenger and I, and two others, were the only ones on their legs, and the two last were wounded and bleeding. Seeing this, the blacks made a rush at us. I thought all was over, and expected to be knocked on the head and thrown overboard. I fought as long as I could, but my foot slipped, and some of the blacks throwing themselves on me, I lost my senses, and when I recovered I found myself bound hand and foot. The young passenger was in the same condition; so was another man. The rest, I feared, had lost their lives. The blacks now swarmed round the brig in their canoes and rafts, and commenced taking everything out of her, and stripping her of her rigging and sails. They were all as busy as ants, and this, I believe, prevented them from paying much attention to us. Perhaps our lives might otherwise have been sacrificed, but the occupation gave time for their anger to cool, and the wealth of various sorts they found on board put them in the highest good humour.

"In the course of the day we three prisoners were carried on shore. We could hear nothing of our shipmates, and had too much reason to fear that they all had been murdered. I do not mean to say that they did not deserve their fate. They were concerned in a plot to reduce those very people who had killed them to a condition, in many instances, worse than death, and thus they brought their fate upon themselves. When we were landed a little farinha was given us, and we were ordered to march forward, followed by a dozen guards or more. We travelled on all day, and at night slept in a native hut, with three or four negroes guarding us.

"The country was generally very fine, with grassy plains, and forests, and hills, and valleys, and numerous streams. We had only a little more farinha given us, and dirty water; indeed, it was very evident that the blacks were treating us as we should have treated them if they had been made slaves of.

"I will not further describe our journey except to say that it was most miserable. If we did not go fast enough the blacks pricked us on with their spears or beat us with sticks, and all the time gave us only just enough food to support life. At last we arrived at a village where we were handed over to three of the principal people of the place; and signs were made to us that we were now slaves, and must work to support ourselves, as well as to obey our masters. I set to work to learn the language of the people, and soon was able to talk to them. I resolved to make myself as happy as I could, and never grumbled or looked angry. My master, however, was a great tyrant, and used often to beat me and to threaten my life, so I resolved to try and run away.

"I have not told you more about the young gentleman, our passenger. I have no doubt he was your brother, and I will call him so. He seemed pretty content with his lot, for though he had to work hard his master was pretty kind. I told him what I thought of doing; and he agreed to accompany me if he could, but advised me to run away without him if I had the chance, and that he would try and follow by himself. The other poor fellow about this time caught the fever and died. The blacks were not a bad or a cruel set of people after all; and when they saw that we appeared contented and happy, they were much kinder to us. We learned their language and all their ways; and then we showed them how to do all sorts of things which they did not know anything about. When my clothes were worn out I took to dressing like the blacks. There wasn't much difficulty in doing that. Then I began to hunt about to try and see if I couldn't make my skin like theirs. At last I found some berries which I thought would do it. After trying a number of things, to my great pleasure I found that I could make my skin as black as that of any of the negroes in the country. To make a long story short, I collected plenty of the dye, and one evening I covered myself all over with it. When it was done I crept out of the hut where I lived to try and see your brother, to get him to run off with me, intending to colour his skin as I had done mine. I found, however, that he had been sent off up the country by his master. If I waited I might be discovered; so, doing up my old seaman's clothes in a bundle, with as much food as I could scrape together, I set off towards the coast. I knew that I must meet with unnumbered difficulties. I travelled by night chiefly, when the natives were not likely to be about; and as I had to go round about to avoid villages and huts, it took me a week to reach the coast. When I got there, however, I was no longer afraid of showing myself. I felt pretty sure that I should be taken for a native of the interior. I therefore walked into the first hut I came to on the shore, belonging to a fisherman, and told him that I had been sent by one of the chiefs to learn what was going forward along the coast, and what the slave-dealers were about. I did not let him know whether I was for or against them.

"He, I found, was in favour of slave-dealing; and from him I learned that a few miles to the north there was an Arab dow taking in a cargo, supplied by one of the Portuguese dealers. Off I set as fast as my legs could carry me. I had a little oil in a calabash, with which I knew I could soon make myself white, so I had no fear of being shipped on board as a slave. It was the evening before I came in sight of the dow. She lay in a little bay about a quarter of a mile from the shore. There were no boats to be seen, and no means of communicating with her. I judged that she had got her cargo on board, and was about to sail; but it was perfectly calm, and she was waiting for a wind to get under way. I was eager to be on board her: I wanted, at all events, to be away from the blacks. I sat down and rubbed my skin over with the oil till I was almost white. I did not think of sharks, or of the distance I had to swim; but, hunting about, I found some pieces of light wood. These I fastened on each side of me, and secured another piece under my breast; and then in I plunged and struck out for the dow. It was a long way to swim, and I couldn't help fearing that before I reached her a breeze would spring up. Now and then I saw the water ripple before me, and my courage almost failed me. I can but die once, I thought to myself; but still it seemed very hard to have to die just then.

"I had got almost up to the vessel when I saw another thing which might well have made my heart sink: it was the black three-cornered fin of a shark appearing just above the surface. I knew that it was now high time to kick about, and sing out, and call to the people on board the dow to help me. They came, on hearing my cries, to the side of the vessel, and they saw me and also my most unwelcome companion. They at once did what was best: while some shouted and got sweeps out to stir up the water, others lowered a boat. Anxiously I watched their proceedings, kicking about, and shouting as loud as I could, while I swam on as before. Still, there was the shark's fin not five fathoms from me. I dreaded every instant to see it approach nearer. The Arab boat got close up to me, the men seized me by the arms, and at the very instant that the shark, thinking that he was about to lose his prey, made a grab at my legs, I drew them up, and, as it was, I felt his mouth touch my foot.

"The Arabs were very kind to me when I had put on my clothes, and told them that I was an Englishman. At first they thought that I was a black man, for I had forgotten to rub the black off my face, and afterwards had more difficulty in getting that white than any other part of me. I could very easily talk with them, as I had learned to speak the lingo in very common use along the coast in those parts.

"The dow was, as I expected, a slaver. She had seventy

OLD BIGG AND THE SHARK.

or eighty poor wretches stowed closely together in her hold, and was going to take them to an island in the north of Madagascar, where they were to be shipped on board a French vessel bound for some French island or other. Soon after I got on board a breeze sprung up, and the dow made sail. We had been at sea four or five days when a large schooner hove in sight. The Arabs took her for an English man-of-war, and made all sail to escape. As I looked at her, however, I felt pretty sure that she was no other than a villainous piratical craft which had been cruising about in these waters for some time—shipping a cargo of slaves when she could do so easily, robbing other vessels of them when they came in her way, and committing acts of piracy on every opportunity. In either case the Arabs had every prospect of losing their cargo. If she should prove to be a man-of-war our lives would be safe; but if the pirate, as I suspected, her crew would very likely murder us all, and sink the dow, on the principle that dead men tell no tales.

"As soon as I hinted my suspicions to the Arabs they made all sail, and stood to the northward in the hopes of escaping. The weather had before been threatening. A heavy gale sprung up, which increased every moment in fury. Still the Arabs held on. The schooner came after us at a great rate. Night was coming on: we hoped to escape in the darkness. On we drove. Where we were going no one seemed to know. The little vessel plunged and tore through the fast rising seas, every timber in her creaking and groaning. The wind howled, the waters roared, and the poor wretches below cried out and shrieked in concert.

"After some hours of this terrible work I felt a tremendous shock: I was thrown down flat on my face. Another sea came up and washed every soul off the deck. The dow was on the rocks. Scarcely a minute had passed before she began to break up under my feet. I cannot describe the terrible cries of the poor slaves as the sea rushed down upon them. I had seized a spar, and a sea rolling on lifted me up and carried me forward. I knew no more till I found myself clinging to a rock. I climbed on till I discovered that I was safe on shore. When daylight broke not a human being could I see—not a vestige of the wreck remained. There I remained for a long time—till you came and took me off."

Thus ended old Tom Bigg's yarn. It was much longer, and

not perhaps in the same language exactly in which I have given it. When Captain Armstrong heard the particulars he promised to go to the spot described by the seaman, and to form some plan by which Alfred might be rescued from slavery. Tom was called in to consult.

"I have been thinking about it, gentlemen, ever since I came on board," he answered. "Now, Mr. Marsden has been very kind to my little boy, and I want to show him that I am grateful. The only way I can think of to get your brother, sir, is for me to go back for him. I can easily turn myself into a black man, and it will be very hard if I can't find an opportunity of letting him know that he has friends at hand. If the *Star* can remain off the coast so as to take us on board, I have no doubt I shall be able to bring him away."

I thanked Bigg very much for his offer, and said that I would accept it on condition that I could go with him. I could not allow another person to run the risk of losing his life for my sake without sharing the dangers. I proposed that I should stain my body and dress as a black; and by pretending to be dumb should I fall in with any natives, I thought that I might possibly pass muster as a real negro. There was no great novelty in the design; but the natives were not likely to have had the trick played on them before, and would therefore not be suspicious, while, from the way in which Bigg imitated the negroes, I had great confidence in his being able to deceive them if necessary. Of course, it would be more hazardous going back to the very place from which he had made his escape; but as he had told me that none of the natives knew that he had assumed the appearance of a black, they very probably might not recognize him. Although Captain Armstrong did not altogether approve of our plan, he could not suggest any other: and he therefore promised to assist me in carrying it out, with any improvements which might be suggested.

I have not attempted to describe the gales and calms, and many of the various incidents we encountered on our voyage. We had had one of those tremendous gales to which the Mozambique Channel is peculiarly liable, when at early dawn a vessel was made out right ahead, with her masts gone, and her bulwarks rising but a little way above the water. Had it been dark we should have run directly over her. We soon caught her up, and found her to be an Arab dow, just like the one Bigg had described, and full of slaves. Poor wretches!—those who had still strength to make a noise were howling fearfully, expecting every instant to go to the bottom. Never shall I forget the horrible scene she presented. More than half the blacks had died from fright, or starvation and fever, or had been drowned; but the Arab crew had been so occupied in pumping, and in trying in other ways to keep their vessel afloat, that they had been unable to spare time even to throw the dead overboard, and there lay their festering remains—decomposition having already commenced—still chained to the living. The *Star* was hove to; and Mr. Henley, who could speak a little Arabic, went in the boats to assist in rescuing the crew and their wretched cargo. He had to tell the Arabs that we would not receive one of them on board if they did not work away to the last to keep the dow afloat, or they would have deserted their posts, and allowed the poor blacks to sink. We meantime set to work with hammers and chisels, and liberated the negroes as rapidly as we could; but it was with the greatest difficulty that any one of us could stay below, so terrible was the odour from the dead bodies. To such a state had they been reduced that many died while we were attempting to liberate them, and others as they were being carried on board the *Star*, while several breathed their last as food was being put into their mouths. Scarcely had we got the slaves out of the vessel than down she went, carrying most of the Arab crew with her, and several were drowned before we could rescue them. The reis or Arab captain of the dow told Mr. Henley that he had engaged to land the negroes on a small island to the north of Madagascar, whence they would be taken off by a French vessel, and carried to the French island of Reunion. The plan of proceeding was this:—On board the French vessel was a government agent, and also an interpreter who could speak to the blacks. These wretches went on shore with a strong guard. Then the poor blacks were collected without a particle of food or shelter, and with every prospect of dying of starvation. They were asked if they would like to go off to an island where they would have plenty of food and be well treated, if they would engage to serve a master for a certain number of years. Of course, very few refused these terms, and they were carried off as free labourers to Reunion or to other places. Those who refused were allowed to perish, as a warning to the rest. The Arab master declared that all the blacks we found on board had come voluntarily; and though they themselves told a different tale, Captain Armstrong had no means of punishing him or his people. They were, therefore, to be landed at Mozambique; while Captain Armstrong resolved to carry the poor blacks, if they wished it, back to the part of the coast from whence they had been taken.

Scarcely had we stowed our unexpected passengers away, and very much crowded up we were with them, than a sail was reported to the southward. We stood towards her. For some time she did not alter her course. Probably we were not perceived. We made her out to be a large top-sail schooner. Suddenly she kept away, and went off before the wind under all the canvas she could carry. This at once made her character suspected, and we accordingly made sail after her. The *Star* sailed remarkably well. The midship-

CHASING A SLAVER.

men always declared that she ought to have been called the *Shooting Star*. The schooner evidently also had a fast pair of heels, but we came up with her. I saw Johnie Spratt looking at her very attentively, when after three or four hours' chase we had got near enough to see her hold from the deck.

"Well, Spratt, what do you think of her?" I asked.

"Why, sir, I may be wrong or I may be right, but to my mind that schooner out there is no other than the craft which that Captain Hansleig, who was aboard us in the *Orion*, is said to command. I have fallen in with her two or three times since I have been out in these seas. He has been bold enough when he has no slaves on board, because he thinks that then no one can touch him; and so I have no doubt he has got some now, or he wouldn't be in such a hurry to run away."

On hearing Spratt's remark, I looked at the schooner more attentively than before through my glass, and had little doubt that she was the very vessel which had carried off Sills and the seaman Brown from the island. When Biggs saw her he pronounced her at once to be the piratical craft from which he had urged the Arabs to try and escape when he was wrecked, and declared that from his certain knowledge her captain was a most atrocious villain, and that as the schooner was well armed, and he had a very strong crew, he was not likely to give in without fighting hard to get away.

The drum now beat to quarters; the guns were cast loose; shot and powder were handed up; the men buckled on their cutlasses, and stuck their pistols in their belts. It was an interesting sight to observe the ship's company as they stood grouped round their guns, ready to commence the battle at a signal from their commander. At length we got the schooner within range of our guns. We fired a shot past her, but she showed no colours, nor did she heave to. We therefore fired two more at her; one of the shots glanced against her side, and one of the midshipmen declared that he could see the white splinters flying off it. We waited a few minutes that we might get still nearer, so that our shot might tell with more effect. The schooner did not fire in return.

"Now," cried Captain Armstrong, who was fully convinced of the character of the stranger, "give it them, but aim high at the rigging. Fire!"

We yawed, so that our guns could be brought to bear on

the stranger. Every shot seemed to tell, and several of her spars were seen to come tumbling down on deck. Then once more we were after her, and again, when a little nearer, another broadside was fired. This produced almost as great an effect as the former one, but I suspect that some of the guns were trained low, for I saw distinctly masses of white splinters flying off from her quarters. Notwithstanding this, she would not give in. Perhaps those on board her dared not. They fought with halters round their necks. Captain Armstrong seemed to hesitate about continuing to fire on a vessel which did not return it. He was a humane man, and he probably felt that he might be destroying unnecessarily the lives of the unfortunate beings on board. Still he could not tell what trick they might be intending. The guns were again loaded and run out. We had now got within musket range. We could, however, only see a couple of men at the helm, and another walking the deck, yet there was no sign that the pirate ever thought of giving in.

"Shall we give him another broadside, sir? Nothing else will make him heave to," said the first lieutenant.

"No, no; stay. He will probably lower his sails when we range up alongside, and ask why we fired at a quiet, harmless trader like him?" answered the captain.

The words were scarcely out of his mouth, as the *Star* got almost abreast of the schooner, when up on her deck rushed a crowd of men with muskets and pistols, and began peppering away at us, while her ports at the same time were hauled up, and her guns opened a hot fire on us. She at the same time put up her helm, and attempted to run us aboard.

"Now, fire away, my lads. Boarders, prepare to repel boarders!" shouted Captain Armstrong.

Those of the crew not required to work the guns, drawing their cutlasses, divided into two parties. Some came aft to range themselves under the captain, while others, led by the second lieutenant, sprang on to the top-gallant forecastle. The schooner was within a dozen fathoms of us. Her crew seemed considerably to outnumber ours; and I certainly never saw a more desperate set of villains crowded together. I had no fear, however, that our honest British crew, though somewhat diminished in numbers by sickness, would be an ample match for them. Our men worked away at their guns in silence. The pirates shouted and shrieked, and kept up a terrific fire at us. Several of our men were hit, and one poor fellow standing near me fell suddenly on the deck. I tried to lift him up, but not a groan did he utter. There was a round mark on his forehead. He had been shot through the brain. In another moment I thought the pirates would be aboard us. I heard a terrific explosion, a hundred times louder than the loudest thunder, I thought, and looking up I saw to my horror the masts, and spars, and sails of the schooner rising in the air, the hull seemed to rock to and fro, and directly afterwards down there came on our heads fragments of spars, and burning sails, and blocks, and planks, and ropes, and the mangled bodies of men, all mingled together in horrible confusion, while the sea around us was a mass of wreck. Many of our crew were hit by the spars and blocks, and several were struck down and killed. Every one, however, who was uninjured began instantly to heave overboard the burning fragments, but it was not without difficulty that the brig was saved from catching fire. The instant her safety was secured, the captain ordered the boats to be lowered to try and save some of the unfortunate wretches who might have escaped destruction by the explosion. I jumped into one of them, followed by Solon, and off we shoved. Before, however, we could reach the hull of the blazing schooner, she gave one roll, and down she went stern first, dragging with her into the vortex she made the few struggling people clinging to the spars or bits of wreck near her. Still, at a short distance off, I observed a man holding on to a spar. We pulled towards him. As we approached he lifted up his head and looked at us. His countenance bore an expression of rage and hatred. It was that, I felt sure, of Captain Hansleig. Before, however, we could reach him, shaking his fist at us, and uttering a fearful imprecation, he let go of the spar, and throwing himself back, sank beneath the waves. Horrified as I was, there was no time to lose in thinking of the circumstance, as I had to look round to see if there was anybody else to whom we could render assistance. I caught sight of another person struggling in the water. He was trying to get hold of a plank, but was evidently no swimmer, and I thought he would sink before we could get up to him. I urged the boat's crew to pull as fast as they could, as did the officer in command. Just before we got up to the struggling man he sank, but I thought I saw his head far down below the surface. So did Solon, who was watching the direction of my eyes, and leaping in, he dived down, and in an instant brought up to the surface the person, of whom he had a gripe by the collar of his jacket. When Solon saw that the seamen had got hold of the person, he scrambled on board again by the help of the oars.

"Poor fellow! he seems a mere lad," observed the officer in command of the boat.

The man did not breathe, but he had been so short a time under the surface that we had hoped he might be recovered. We saw, however, that his side was injured, apparently by the explosion. Finding that there was no one else to assist, we pulled back to the ship. For the first time, as I was helping to haul the rescued man up the side, I looked at his countenance, and changed as it was, I felt sure that it was that of Sills. He was at once put under the surgeon's care. He was stripped, dried, put between warm blankets, and gently rubbed, and in a short time animation returned; but he was suffering very much from the injury he had received. I told the surgeon who he was, and asked him if he thought he would recover. He replied that he had not the slightest chance of doing so, and that if I wished it, I had better see him without delay. I went accordingly to his cot in the sick-bay, and told him who I was. He was very much surprised to see me, and thankful that I came to speak to him.

"I have had a dreadful life of it since I parted from you, Marsden," he observed. "I was not allowed to act even as an officer, but was made to serve before the mast, and was kicked and knocked about by all the men who chose to vent their spleen on me. I had no idea that the vessel was what she was, a slaver and a pirate, and every man on board would have been hung if they could have been proved guilty of the things I often saw done by them, without sorrow or compunction. I have never known a moment's happiness since I left the island, and I wish that I had followed your advice, that I do."

I spoke of the thief on the cross, and tried to point out where true happiness can alone be found. While he was speaking to me his voice grew weaker and weaker, and now a rapid change came over him. I sent for the surgeon, but before he could arrive the poor misguided fellow was dead.

CHAPTER XIX.

Mozambique—Description of the Neighbouring Country—Slave-Trade—How carried on—Prepare for my Expedition into the Interior of Africa—Bigg and I land—Transformed into Blackamores—Fortunate Shot at an Elephant—Meet Natives—Feast off the Elephant—Search for Water—An unwelcome Visitor—A Night in an African Desert.

I WAS glad to get away from the spot where the catastrophe I have described occurred, but it was very, very long before I could get the scenes I had witnessed out of my head. How different would have been the fate of Sills had he been guided wisely, instead of foolishly, and endeavoured by every means in his power to perform his duty. We first made sail for Mozambique, where Captain Armstrong had to communicate with the governor to arrange a plan for the suppression of the slave-trade.

Mozambique belongs to the Portuguese. It is the chief of their settlements on the east coast of Africa. They claim the whole coast from Cape Delgado in the north, situated in about eleven degrees south latitude, to Delagoa Bay, which will be found at about the twenty-sixth degree south latitude; an extent of nine hundred miles in length, but reaching, I fancy, a very little way inland. Their authority does not in reality exist except at their fortified ports and towns. We brought up in an extensive harbour before the city of Mozambique, which stands on an island of the same name. This island with two others, St. Jago and St. George, and the mainland, form the confines of the harbour, and shelter the vessels riding between them from every wind.

I and several of the officers landed with Captain Armstrong, who wished to communicate with the governor-general. It was said that he was very anxious to suppress the slave-trade, but that he was actually intimidated by the slave-dealing community.

The island is defended by two forts, and we heard that the guns had been dismounted and sent to Portugal, in order that should the place be captured by the natives, it might be the more easily retaken by the slave-dealers. We were not prepared to find so handsome a city as Mozambique is in many respects. We landed at a fine wharf built of the most massive masonry. The palace of the governor-general is a handsome building, erected round a court-yard, with lofty rooms and floors of timber. The roof is flat, and covered entirely with lead. The floors of most of the other houses are of chunam, or lime. All the houses are very substantially built, for the sake of coolness; and many of them look as if at one time they may have been comfortable abodes when the slave-trade flourished, and they were inhabited by the principal slave-dealers in the place. The town is irregularly built; the streets are narrow; there are two large churches and several chapels, and two or three squares, with fair-sized houses round them. As we were passing through the principal one, we observed a pillar of wood fixed in a mass of masonry. We inquired its object, and were told that it is used for securing the negroes when they are ordered to be publicly whipped. I have little more to say about the city of Mozambique, except to remark that it is difficult to conceive how civilized beings can allow the place they live in to be kept in so very dirty a condition. The truth is, that the blighting influence of slave-dealing affects every one, from the highest to the lowest Portuguese; and their whole thoughts are taken up in the consideration of how they can in the greatest degree benefit directly or remotely by it. While the Portuguese government persists in sending out ruined men to govern the country, or under-paid officers, they cannot wash away the stigma which now rests on them of wishing to support the slave-trade in spite of treaties, and their promises to put a stop to it. There are about two hundred white soldiers in the place, all of them convicts, and some doubly convicted of the worst of crimes. There are certain government officials and some foreign merchants, Germans, banyan traders, Arabs, and others; and all the rest of the inhabitants are negroes and slaves, or, as the Portuguese call them, Gentiles. Altogether there was nothing attractive in the place, and we were very glad that we had not to remain there.

As we stood down the coast we touched at another Portuguese settlement, that of Inhambane. The town, though it has been established nearly three hundred years, is a miserable place. It consists of about a hundred and fifty ill-built houses, thatched chiefly with the broad leaves of the cocoa-nut tree, posted generally along the margin of the harbour, but some of them can be seen peeping out here and there between the mangrove bushes or cocoa-nut trees along the beach. There is a fort, the garrison of which consists of some sixty convicts, sent from Goa to Mozambique, and then, after further misbehaving themselves, sent on to this place, so their character may well be supposed. There is a church, but it is in a very ruinous condition. Altogether the place is a very miserable one, and is evidently withering under the blighting curse of the slave-trade. The huts of the natives are built in a square form, instead of round, like those to be seen further south. We heard that the natural productions of the country in the interior are very abundant. Among them are indigo, coffee, cotton, trees producing India-rubber, bananas, plantains, oranges, lemons; the natives collect gold and ivory; amber and turtle are found on the shore, while all sorts of fish and the sperm whale exist off the coast. But the slave-trade, by encouraging international wars, effectually prevents the development of all these numerous resources, and will prevent them as long as it is allowed to exist.

We were now approaching the spot whence Bigg told me that he had made his escape. My heart beat more anxiously than ever as I thought of the possibility of soon rescuing poor Alfred. I thought of all he had suffered, of his long banishment from civilized society, and of the hopeless condition to which he must have been reduced when deserted by his companion in slavery. I, of course, could think of nothing else, and my only satisfaction was in being employed in making preparations for our expedition on shore. Johnnie Spratt was very anxious to accompany us, and so was little Tommy Bigg.

"He might be of use dressed up as a little nigger," I heard his father remark. "But I don't know; the risk may be very great, and though I wouldn't grudge it for the sake of serving young Mr. Marsden, I think we may do very well without him."

On hearing this I begged that Tommy might on no account accompany us, but I determined to take Solon. We weighed the advantages against the disadvantages in so doing. He might certainly make the natives suppose that we were not negroes by his foreign appearance, he being so unlike any dogs they have; but then, it might appear probable that he might have been obtained from some slaver or vessel wrecked on the coast. He might possibly also remember Alfred, or Alfred might see that he was an English dog, and call him and talk to him. To have a further chance of communicating with Alfred, I wrote a note telling him that I was looking for him, that the *Star* was off the coast ready to receive him on

THE INDIA-RUBBER TREE.

board, and urging him to endeavour to make his escape without delay. I wrote also to the same effect on an immense number of bits of paper, which I proposed to fasten to all the trinkets, and knives, and handkerchiefs, and other articles which the natives value, which I could obtain on board, in the hopes that one of them might fall into Alfred's hands, and that he might thus know that efforts were making for his liberation.

The appearance of the coast as we stood along it was not attractive. Beyond a white sandy beach, which looked glittering and scorching hot in the sun, the ground rose slightly, fringed on the upper ridge by low, stunted trees bending towards the south-west, exhibiting proofs of the force of the hurricanes, which blow down the Mozambique Channel from the north-east. Talking of the hurricanes which prevail hereabouts, I ought to have mentioned that it was during one of them in this channel that the poet Falconer, whose deeply interesting poem of "The Shipwreck" had been a great favourite with Alfred and me, lost his life. The ship in which he sailed as purser foundered, and he, and I believe everybody on board perished. No work, either in prose or poetry, so admirably, so graphically, and so truly describes a shipwreck as does his. It is curious that after its publication he should have lost his life amid the scene which he has so perfectly described. In the same way no writer has more vividly painted the horrors of a fire at sea than Mr. Eliot Warburton, in the last work he wrote, just before embarking for the West Indies. But a few days afterwards he perished by the burning of the steamer on board which he sailed.

We were looking out anxiously for the bay, which Bigg believed he could recognize again. Mr. Henley knew the coast generally, but he had been unable, from Bigg's description, to fix on the exact spot. We looked into two or three places which somewhat answered the description, but had to stand out again. At last we ran into a little

THE COCOA TREE.

bay, which Bigg said he was positive was the one in which the Arab dow lay when he got on board her. Accordingly we stood in and brought up. No people could have been kinder to me than Captain Armstrong and all his officers were while I was preparing for my expedition.

"I might employ force, and endeavour to compel the natives to give up your brother, but they might declare that they knew nothing about him, and of course, with my whole ship's company, I could effect but little against the hosts they could bring against us," he remarked, as he was speaking on the subject. "Your pacific plan is far more likely to succeed. At the same time, should you find yourself discovered and placed in difficulties, you may threaten the natives with all the vengeance which the *Star* and her ship's company can inflict on them."

The boat was lowered to carry old Tom Bigg and me to the shore. I was fully aware of all the risk I was running, and though I was full of hope, I could not help feeling sad as I wished Mr. Henley and all my kind friends on board good-bye. Our various articles were done compactly up in cases, that we might carry them on our backs. I had my trusty rifle, which I covered up carefully, so that what it was might not be seen. My ammunition belt I fastened round my waist, under my shirt, and in it I stuck a brace of small pistols, lent me by one of the officers. Bigg was armed with pistols and a stout stick. I had on a flannel waistcoat, and drawers tucked lightly up, and a loose shirt over all. The ship's barber had tightly curled my hair, and Bigg said he knew exactly where to find the berries with which he proposed dyeing our skins. I had been going about without shoes or socks since I resolved on the expedition, that I might harden my feet; indeed, since I had come to sea I had very frequently gone without them; at the same time I expected to suffer more inconvenience at having to travel through the bush with bare feet than from any other cause. Still, of course, I should at once have been discovered had I worn shoes, or even sandals. All the officers wished me success as I stepped into the boat, and seemed to take a great interest in my proceedings. We looked anxiously out to discover if we were watched as we pulled towards the shore, but we saw no natives, and we had great hopes that we had not been observed.

Old Bigg took an affectionate farewell of Tommy as he sprang out of the boat, and Mr. Henley, who had accompanied us, cordially grasped my hand as I stood up to leap on shore.

"May Heaven guide and prosper you. This is an enterprise for the success of which I can heartily pray, and I never wish a friend of mine to undertake any for which heartfelt prayers cannot be offered up."

I thanked him heartily, and sprang on the beach, followed by Solon.

"Come along, Mr. Marsden, the sooner we can get out of sight the better," exclaimed Bigg, as he led the way towards a thick wood which appeared a quarter of a mile or so in front of us.

The boat pulled back to the ship, while we ran as hard as we could towards the wood. It was at all events satisfactory to find that there could not be many natives in that neighbourhood. In less than five minutes we were safe inside the wood, and Bigg lost no time in hunting about to find the berries with which he proposed to dye our skins. He soon discovered them, as also the leaves of some other plants, which assisted to heighten the colour. We had the means of lighting a fire, and a pot for cooking our food. A stream was near at hand, and in a short time we had a strong ink-like decoction formed, which, when I applied it to my hand, very quickly gave it a fine glossy black hue. I could not help hesitating for a moment, when I saw the effect produced, about covering my whole skin with it, lest I should never get white again.

"Never fear, sir, a little oil and hot water will soon take it all off again," said Bigg, who had observed my proceedings.

I felt ashamed of myself when I remembered the object I had in view; and setting to work at once, with Bigg's assistance, very soon got myself turned into a very respectable looking young blackamoor. I helped Bigg, and touched him up here and there where he had left spots uncovered. Solon all the time sat watching our proceedings with the greatest astonishment. He looked up in my face and gazed earnestly at it, and when he found that it was entirely black, he whined piteously, as if some great misfortune had happened to me. He, however, knew me by my voice, so that I had no fear of his running away from me, and in a very little time he got perfectly accustomed to my appearance.

Having done up our bundles again, and got ourselves ready for our march, we started off towards the interior. We had a journey of three or four days at the least before us. Bigg had been fully that time finding his way to the sea. We had numberless dangers to encounter—not only from natives, but from wild beasts and venomous reptiles. I had known of them before, but they now presented themselves more vividly before me, and I felt how grateful I ought to be to Bigg for his readiness to encounter them for my sake. We soon left the region of mangrove-trees. We got on easily enough across downs and grassy plains, but we had often great difficulty in forcing our way through the bush and the dense forests which lay in our course. We had gone some miles, and had not hitherto seen any natives. Just as we were emerging from a wood, Bigg touched my shoulder and pointed to several black figures with calabashes on their heads, some three or four hundred yards off, across an open glade which lay before us. In another moment we should have been discovered. I signed to Solon to keep behind me, and we turned on one side, skirting the border of the forest to avoid them. We were not quite certain whether we had altogether escaped detection, for we observed them looking about as if their quick eyes had detected something unusual in the wood. As soon as we had got round, still sheltered by trees, we were able to continue our proper course. We had arranged what Bigg was to say should we meet any natives, and we were to give them some small present to show our friendly disposition; at the same time hinting that we had friends who would wreak their vengeance on the heads of any one ill-treating us. We had not gone far before we came to the outside of the forest, and now for a great distance an open, undulating country, with here and there trees scattered over it, appeared before us.

Suddenly Solon stopped, pricked up his ears, and looked intently back towards the point whence we had come. We followed with our eyes the direction at which the dog was pointing, and directly afterwards the brushwood and the branches of the trees were bent outward, and the head and trunk of a huge elephant appeared, as he dashed furiously out of the forest. No sooner did he catch sight of us than he set up a loud trumpeting, indicative of rage, and rushed towards us. He was, fortunately, still at some distance, so I had time to take off the covering of my rifle, and to cock it ready for his reception. The experience I had gained of elephant-shooting in Ceylon now stood me in good stead. My sailor companion, who was not aware of what I was able to do, was naturally much alarmed on my account.

"Much better climb up this tree out of the way of the brute. I'll help you up, sir," he sung out, beginning to make his own way up the gnarled and crooked trunk.

"No, no; I'll stand below and kill the elephant. You get

up out of his way. In case I should miss him, I'll dodge round the tree," I answered; "I am safe enough; don't fear for me."

While we were speaking, I observed directly behind the elephant a considerable number of blacks—some dozen or more—armed with spears and darts. They were evidently in chase of him, and had not perceived us. When Solon saw the elephant, he began to bark furiously, rushing towards him, and then retreating again to me. His barking attracted the attention of the natives, who now first perceived us. The elephant had halted, trumpeting and shrieking louder than ever, when some of the natives again darted their spears at him, while Solon assailed him with his barking in front. The monster probably thought that the dog had inflicted the pain he felt, for he now rushed at him with such fury that I became not a little anxious for his safety. Solon, however, seemed perfectly well aware what was best to be done, and contrived nimbly to keep just beyond the distance that his huge antagonist's trunk could reach. Once the elephant had tried to strike him with his trunk, but he was then a long way off from me. He had now come within twenty yards of the tree behind which I stood. Again he lowered his trunk to strike the dog. The opportunity was not to be lost. I took a steady aim and fired. Never have I made a better shot. The bullet struck the monster directly on the forehead; and without advancing another foot, down he sank an inanimate mass. Solon sprung on the body, barking with delight. Bigg slid down from the tree; and forgetting his character of a negro, was about to give a true British cheer, when I stopped him; and the negroes who had been in chase of the animal came rushing up, staring with astonishment at his sudden death. The moment I found that I had killed the elephant, I had again covered up my rifle, so they could not even see by what means the deed had been done. As they assembled round the animal, I pointed to it to let them understand that they were welcome to make what use of it they might wish. My companion also addressed them, and told them a long story, at which they seemed highly pleased, for they clapped their hands and gave other signs of satisfaction. What they thought of us I could not tell; but I could not help fancying that they had strong suspicions that we were not real blacks. This, however, did not appear to be of much consequence, as they were evidently impressed with the idea that we were very important personages, and were prepared to pay us all possible respect.

Bigg discovered that the elephant had only been slightly wounded by their arrows; and that, had it not been for my shot, he would very probably have escaped from them. I was, therefore, in high favour with them, and they were all very curious to know how I had done the deed. This I thought it prudent not to tell them, and Bigg tried to mystify them as much as possible. They were also equally puzzled to know who I was. In this case also Bigg did his utmost to mystify them; and I believe that they were under the impression that I was a regular black prince, the son of some mighty potentate or other to the north of their country. I had no difficulty in keeping up my character of being dumb, but I found it necessary to pretend to be deaf also, as they were constantly addressing me, and of course I could not understand a word they said. In the meantime, Bigg talked away for both of us; and although I very much doubt if his language was particularly grammatical, he seemed to get on famously with the savages; and acting on an idea which came into his head, he confirmed the notion they had adopted that I was a person of no little importance.

By degrees more natives came up from different parts of the forest, and seemed highly delighted at finding the elephant dead. I had to go through the ceremony of being introduced to them, and in a short time I found myself on the most friendly and sociable terms with them all. They now began to cut down boughs and erect huts under the surrounding trees. Bigg followed their example; but when I offered to assist him, he begged that I would not, saying that such work would be derogatory to a person of my exalted rank. He took the opportunity of telling me, while no one was listening, that the natives were going to cut up the elephant for the purpose of obtaining the fat, which they prize exceedingly.

"You'll see, Mr. Marsden, they will eat the whole of him up in a very short time, though they value most the trunk and the fat."

It was now getting late in the day; and all hands having built their huts, set to work to collect sticks and to dig holes in the ground. Each hole was about two feet deep and three wide. Having lit huge fires in them with rotten branches of trees, they proceeded to cut off the trunk and feet of the elephant. They then scraped out the ashes, and put a foot or a piece of the trunk in each hole, covering it first with sand, and then with the hot ashes. A fresh fire was then made above the hole; and when that had burned out, the feet were exhumed, and scraped clean of the ashes. While these operations were going forward, I sat in the hut Bigg had formed watching the proceedings. He had made a fire also in front of the hut, at which he boiled some tea, which, with some ham and biscuit, formed our evening meal. He had secured a piece of the elephant's feet for Solon, who ate it with considerable satisfaction.

It was late in the night before the natives had finished their culinary operations. They then came and invited us to join their feast; and though I would gladly have excused myself, I did not think it prudent to do so. I had a slice from the trunk and another from a foot presented to me; and though I took it with reluctance, I was agreeably surprised to find how very palatable it was. Bigg seemed also to relish it exceedingly. Having made a good supper, we retired once more to our hut; when Bigg having made up our fire to scare away any wild beasts who might be disposed to pay us a visit, I fell asleep, with my faithful Solon by my side. I knew full well that he would arouse us at the approach of danger. Probably the noise made by the natives kept the wild beasts away, otherwise the smell of the baked elephant would have attracted them to the spot. When we awoke in the morning, we found the natives preparing to cut up the elephant. Having removed the rough outer skin, they cut off an inner one, with which they make bags for the conveyance of water. The flesh is cut into strips and dried, while the fat is carefully removed and preserved. We left them engaged in this operation, several men having completely disappeared inside the huge carcass. They were all too busy and eager in the work to notice our departure, and so we got off without the ceremony of leave-taking. We went on in good spirits, for we had made a fair beginning, and secured friends in our rear, which was of great importance. We walked on for about two hours in the cool of the morning, when, beginning to get very hungry, we looked about for water to cook our breakfast. None, however, could we discover. At length, pushing on ahead, we saw before us a small antelope called a sassayby. Bigg said that he was now certain that water was not far off. As the antelope did not take to flight, and we wanted food, I unslung my rifle, and aiming steadily, shot it through the body. It ran on for some way, and I thought we should have lost it; but Solon gave chase, and in a few minutes brought it to the ground. We hurried up, and having killed the animal, and cut off as much of the flesh as we could consume, proceeded on in the direction where we thought water was to be procured. Still we did not reach it, and our thirst and hunger became excessive.

While considering how we could best direct our steps, a flight of birds passed over our heads to the east. They, however,

MARSDEN AND BIGG IN THE WILDS OF AFRICA.

circled round after some time, and flew back westward. Soon after another flight passed over our heads, and appeared to descend a quarter of a mile or so a-head. This encouraged our hopes. The country was undulating, and there were hollows which at no distant period had contained water. Then we came to one which was still muddy; and ascending a hill near it, we saw before us a bright mass glittering in the sunbeams. Solon gave a bark of delight, and trotted on, and we followed as fast as we could, till we came to a pool of pure, clear water. We soon had a fire lighted, and some water boiling for our tea; while our venison, stuck on little sticks round it, was toasting, and hissing, and bubbling away right merrily. After this we lay down in the shade of a tree to rest. We might have travelled through a part of the country where more water was to be found, but then we should have been certain to meet with more natives, who might have impeded our progress.

Scarcely had we proceeded half a mile after our forenoon rest, than, emerging from a wood, we saw before us a very beautiful and to me most extraordinary sight. Before us stood, with their heads lifted high up, a troop of eighteen or twenty giraffes, or camelopards. Few of them were under eighteen feet in height, of a delicate colour, and very graceful. They turned their small heads at the noise we made, and perceiving us, switching their long tails with a loud sound, cantered away before us. I could easily have brought one of them down, I fancied, but I had no wish to merit the appellation of the destroyer, and we continued our course as before. It was some time, however, before we lost sight of them.

I cannot describe the variety of animals we met with in our progress. Many of them I had not seen before, but had no difficulty in recognizing them from the descriptions I had read of African wild beasts. We were beginning to look out for a spot on which to camp for the night, when before us appeared a grove of wide topped mimosa-trees. If water was to be found near at hand we agreed that this would just suit us. We were approaching the place when up started a huge white

A HERD OF GIRAFFES.

she-rhinoceros with her calf. I got my rifle ready, expecting that she would attack us; but after looking at us a minute, she and the calf turned aside, and away they went, greatly to our satisfaction. I had never seen a more hideous monster. She was inferior only to an elephant in size, and had two horns, one before the other, on the top of her long head; the hinder horn was not more than half a foot long, while the front horn, which inclined forward, was nearly four feet in length. She carried her strange, wrinkled head low down to the ground.

In spite of her ugliness she seemed to be a very inoffensive creature.

There are four varieties of the rhinoceros—two white and two black. The black are smaller, and by far the fiercer of the two. They will turn round and charge their pursuers, ploughing up the ground with their horns. They are subject to paroxysms of rage, when they will attack a bush or a tree, and with loud snorts and blowing they will plough up the ground round it, and charge it till they have broken it in pieces. Is not this the animal referred to by Job when he says, " Canst thou bind the unicorn with his band in the furrow? or will he harrow the valleys after thee? Wilt thou trust him, because his strength is great? or wilt thou leave thy labour to him? Wilt thou believe him, that he will bring home thy seed, and gather it into thy barn?" (Job xxxix. 10–12).

Not finding water as we expected, we had to walk on till it was very nearly dark, when we came to a large pool fed by a stream which appeared never to be dry. On going round it, however, to find a convenient place to dip in our water-bottles, we discovered so many traces of lions, elephants, rhinoceroses, and other savage animals, that we agreed it would be wiser to pitch our camp at some distance from the spot. We accordingly pushed on an eighth of a mile or so out of sight of the water, and built our hut and lighted our fire.

We were cooking some of our antelope flesh, and I had put on our saucepan to boil the water for our tea, when by some carelessness I upset it. To go without our tea would have been most disagreeable, so I at once jumped up and said that I would go off and replenish it. Bigg wanted to go and let me stay.

"No, no," I answered; "it was through my fault that the water was lost; it is my duty to get some more. You keep up the fire and take care of the camp." Just as I was going off I took up my rifle. "I'll have my old friend with me," I observed.

Solon of course followed me. I had got to the pool and refilled both the bottles, while Solon was lapping at the water, when on looking up I saw standing on the top of the bank above me a huge lion. He was regarding me attentively, as if considering what sort of strange animal I was who had come to his drinking-place. Solon discovered him at the same time, and turned round ready to fly at him had I given the word. I signed him to lie down, knowing that one pat of the lion's paw would have killed him in an instant. I unslung my rifle, ready to fire should it be necessary, but I did not wish to throw a shot away. Keeping my weapon presented, and covering the kingly animal, I walked steadily up the bank towards him, crying out, "Boo, boo, boo!" gradually raising my voice. The lion stared at me without moving, but as I got nearer he gradually drew back till he fairly turned round and trotted off into the bush. As I got to a distance I looked round, and saw two or three other lions, followed by some elephants and a couple of rhinoceroses, all of which animals live on amicable terms; as the two latter have no wish to eat the lion, and the lion finds them rather tough morsels to swallow. I hurried back, with Solon close upon my heels, to the camp, when Bigg and I congratulated ourselves that we had pitched it away from such unpleasant neighbours.

It was quite dark before we had finished our meal. We were sitting before the fire still discussing our venison with no little appetite. Solon was sitting by my side, and I was every now and then throwing him a piece, which he seemed to relish as much as we did, when suddenly he pricked his ears, and jumping up, threw himself into an attitude of the most earnest watchfulness. I was certain that some animal or other was prowling round, so seizing my rifle I stepped out a little way beyond the fire to try and discover what it was. Scarcely had I done so when I heard a roar, and there stood, the bright glare of the fire lighting up his tawny mane, either the huge lion I had seen at the pond, or one equally large and powerful. He had, I suspected, regretted letting me off so easily, and had followed me to our camp. He stood looking fiercely at me for a few seconds, then, uttering a terrific roar, he seemed about to spring on me. I held my rifle ready to fire, but I felt that there were many chances of my missing him. I would much rather have had to encounter even the fiercest of elephants.

I shouted out to Bigg, "A lion! a lion!"

Scarcely were the words out of my mouth, when he was on his feet by my side with a large burning log in his hand. He sprang forward, and before I could stop him had dashed it full in the face of the savage brute. So astonished was the lion that, without an attempt at retaliation, he turned round, and with Solon barking defiance at him, dashed off again into the bush. Though we did not think that the same lion would come again, the lesson was not lost on us, and we resolved to have a large fire blazing, and to keep watch during the night. As I sat up during my part of the watch, constantly keeping my eyes around me, I could hear the lions muttering and calling to each other with sounds very unlike the roar they utter when they are quarrelling over a carcass or about to spring on their prey. There were, too, the cries of jackals, the laughing of hyenas, the occasional trumpeting of an elephant, the croakings of night-birds, or of insects or reptiles of various sorts, which, all mingled together, formed a concert which effectually banished sleep, and was anything but enlivening and inspiriting. Thus passed my second night in the midst of an African desert.

CHAPTER XX.

Fresh Plan Adopted—Hunt for a Suit of Clothes—Kill a Lion—Turned into a Black Prince—Arrive at the Village—Cordial Reception—A Native Feast—How I established my Reputation—Find Alfred—Our Escape—Reach the *Star*—Sail for Cape Town—Conclusion.

WE were not many miles, according to Bigg's computation, from the village where I supposed that Alfred was held a prisoner. My success as a hunter had made me think of a plan of operations which I had great hopes would succeed. It was bold, but I considered that from its very boldness it was more likely to succeed. I proposed it to Bigg.

"You see," said I, " you made me out to be a great person to the first natives we met when I killed the elephant, and I see no reason why I should not succeed equally well with these people, if we take more pains to prepare ourselves for the characters we are to assume. My idea is this: We will kill a giraffe or a stag, or some other wild beasts with handsome skins, and with the trinkets we have got we will dress ourselves out in a very fine way. I can be a prince as before, deaf and dumb. You can be my attendant and prime minister, doctor or medicine-man. You tell me that though they do not like being made slaves themselves, they do not object to hold others in slavery. Well, then, you can say that I am anxious to obtain their opinion on the subject of the slave-trade, and that I have visited them accordingly; and then you can say what a great hunter I am, and that I make nothing of killing an elephant or a lion, or any other wild beast you like to mention."

I need not enter further into the particulars of my plan. Bigg highly approved of it, and so we lost no time in making the necessary preparations. I doubted whether the skin of a zebra, or a giraffe, or a lion would make the handsomest regal cloak, and resolved to be guided by circumstances. We were proceeding along the side of a valley, when just below us there appeared, grazing, a herd of zebras, and not far off from them several giraffes, most of them with young ones by their sides. We were to leeward of them, so I hoped to get near enough to have a shot at one of them without being discovered. Had I been on horseback, I should have had no difficulty in catching them up; as it was, I had to proceed with the greatest caution. Keeping along as much as possible under shelter of the brushwood, we descended the hill towards them. I then took post behind the nearest clump of shrubs, and told Bigg to go on ahead as far as he could, and then, showing himself, turn them towards me. In a short time I heard his shout, and on they came bounding towards me. I selected a young one, handsomely marked; for I thought that the skin would be lighter, and suit better for a cloak than that of an old one. I fired at its breast, and over it fell, scarcely struggling for a moment. The shot put the rest to flight. I, however, had gained my object. We at once skinned the animal, and then set to work to scrape the skin as clean and thin as possible. This done, Bigg hung it on to the end of a stick, which he carried over his shoulder, that it might thus dry in the sun and air as we walked along.

Soon after this I killed a fine deer, which we skinned to serve as a robe for Bigg. I thought that he would be soon tired if he had to carry both skins, and so I proposed at once cutting them into the shape of the robes we required. This we did with our knives, and two very fine-looking garments we produced. I, however, was not satisfied that my appearance would be sufficiently regal, so I proposed, if I could, to obtain a lion-skin with which further to deck myself. We marched on, however, without encountering a lion all day.

Towards the evening we reached a water-hole, where we determined to encamp. Near it stood the huge hollow trunk of a tree. This, with a little addition and cleaning out, would make us, we agreed, a very comfortable hut for the night. We examined it thoroughly, to see that there were no snakes in it, and soon had it fit for our reception. We put a roof to it of leaves, and stuck some stout stakes into the ground in front of it, to keep off any wild beasts which might be disposed to leap on us unawares.

By the time we had got a fire lighted to cook our tea it was almost dark. Just then I saw a huge white rhinoceros come up to drink. We were inside our hut. I let him drink his fill, and as he was about to turn aside I fired and hit him on the side of his vast head. He did not fall, but looked about him as if to see whence the injury had come, and in what direction to charge, and so I was afraid that the bullet had glanced off. I therefore fired again. The rhinoceros trotted off a little way from the pool, looking angrily around, but suddenly stopped, and then, much to our satisfaction, down he came to the ground. The body lay still within point-blank range of my rifle. This was a matter of great importance. It must be understood that I killed the rhinoceros, not in mere wantonness, but that the carcass might serve as a bait to a lion, of which I was so anxious to get possession. I waited for some time, during which an unusual stillness seemed to reign through the night air.

Suddenly a terrific roar sounded in our ears. It was not to be mistaken; it was that of some huge old lion. I looked out eagerly, expecting to see the monarch of the forest emerge from the darkness. Still he did not appear; but a troop of jackals replied to the roar, and their savage, hideous cry was echoed by that of a number of hyenas. Before long I saw them emerging out of the neighbouring thickets, and stealing down towards the body of the rhinoceros. They quickly flung themselves on it, and began tearing away at the flesh, wrangling and fighting over every mouthful. I should have fired to drive them away, had I not feared that by so doing I should have prevented the approach of the lion. I had just lost all patience, and was about to let fly among them, when I caught sight of a magnificent lion, with a fine black mane almost reaching to the ground, which stalked with majestic steps up to the carcass. He was followed by two others. They commenced their banquet without disturbing the former guests; indeed, none of the animals seemed to take any notice of each other. I refrained from firing at once, for I knew that the lions would not take their departure without drinking. I waited also to get rid of the jackals and hyenas, for I was certain that no sooner should the king of beasts be dead than they would set upon his carcass and devour it. I observed that the other beasts did not attempt to dispute a bone with the lions, but at the same time they seemed to pay them very little respect, and would look up and absolutely laugh in their faces without ceremony.

At length scarcely a particle of the big rhinoceros remained, except some pieces over which the three lions kept watchful guard. The other animals stood at a little distance watching them till every particle was consumed, and then finding that their banquet was at an end, ran off to their lairs, or in search of some other prey. The lions meantime approached the water. The leader presented his side to me; I could resist no longer, but fired at his shoulder. He gazed round with a

SHOOTING A LION.

look of rage and defiance, uttering a loud roar. Then, seeing no enemy, he turned to fly, but his roar changed into a mournful, groaning cry, and before he had gone many paces he sank down helpless on the ground. He continued his roar of pain for some minutes. I was about to rush up to despatch him at once, but Bigg entreated me to remain quiet, saying that it is very dangerous to approach a dying lion, as, with a last effort, he may spring up and destroy the incautious intruder As soon as I had fired, the other lions, scared by the noise, trotted off and disappeared in the bush. At last the big lion's groans ceased, and then, carrying as many sticks as we could lift, with torches in our hands, we approached the carcass. Solon ran up to it with evident mistrust, but after he had sniffed round it, the lion making no movement, we felt satisfied that it was dead. We at once lighted a large fire close to the carcass, to scare away his comrades, or the hyenas or jackals, should they be inclined to return; and then forthwith set about skinning him. It was no easy operation, and we had also to collect sticks to keep up our fire, while we were several times alarmed by Solon's barking at the approach of wild beasts. The night was far spent before the skin was in what we fancied a fit state for use, and we then returned with our trophy to our tree. We lighted another fire in front of it, and afterwards, while Bigg kept watch, I took a couple of hours' sleep. He laughed at the notion when I roused up and told him to lie down, and said that, on a pinch, he could do very well without sleep for a night or two.

Daylight showed us that the lion's skin would require a great deal more scraping and drying before it could be fit for use. We employed ourselves on this work while breakfast was cooking, and as soon as we had breakfasted and our garments were ready, we dressed up in them. I could not help laughing at the ridiculous appearance we presented. The lion's head hung down behind my back, while his front claws were brought over my shoulders like a lady's boa, and the others trailed down behind me. I had made a sort of crown or cap of the camelopard's skin, as also some sandals, while another piece served me as an apron. Bigg had on a kilt and a shorter cloak, without cap or sandals, as became his inferior rank.

My heart beat anxiously as we drew near the village. The people stared at us as we approached, pointing, and running, and chattering away most vehemently, evidently not knowing what to make of us. My rifle was still covered up, and Bigg carried both our bundles. We advanced boldly, as if we were confident of meeting with a friendly reception. As we drew nearer, Bigg began to shout out all the titles he could think of, to make it appear that I was some very wonderful person. I looked about, meantime, eagerly for Alfred. I did not see him, and I began to fear that he was not there, or that he might be ill, or perhaps, worse than all, had sunk under the climate and the labour he had to perform. The people crowded round us, and the chief made his appearance, and I saw Bigg pointing to my lion-skin robe, and talking away very vehemently. He was explaining, I found, that I was a great slaughterer of lions and other wild beasts, and that I wore this robe as a mark of my prowess. I need not repeat all the extraordinary things he said. The result was, that the chief and all the people of the tribe looked on me with the most profound respect. To show it, they forthwith prepared a feast, and when Bigg told them that I must have a hut to myself, one of the principal men in the place volunteered to vacate his. The chief, however, expressed his hope that I would give him a specimen of my skill, and that as the neighbourhood was much infested by lions, I should be conferring a great benefit on the community by killing them. Bigg explained this to me when I returned to my hut, and I was very glad to learn of the proposal, as I knew that I should thus the more easily establish my credit among them. My first question on finding myself alone with Bigg was about Alfred. He said, that from what he had heard he felt sure that he was in the place, and that if we walked about the village we should very likely fall in with him. It might have been more prudent to remain in my hut, but after waiting a little time, I could not resist the temptation of taking a stroll to try and discover my brother. A good many of the natives followed me as I walked about, but the chief and others were occupied in preparing for the banquet, and no one seemed inclined to impede my progress.

I had not gone far when I saw a person in a field digging with a wooden spade. As I got near I saw that he was white, though I could not be certain if he was my brother or not. I walked close up to him. I did not think that he would suspect who we were. He was dressed in the remains of a jacket and trousers, but they were almost in tatters, while a palm-leaf hat covered his head. Twice I had to pass close to him. At last he looked up, and stared at me earnestly. Then I was certain it was Alfred, but worn and ill, and sadly changed. I longed to rush forward and embrace him, but I had to restrain my feelings, and to content myself with pointing at him as a sign to Bigg, who, I trusted, would make some arrangement for him to meet me. I then, flourishing the long case in which my rifle was enclosed, walked away, followed by the mob of negroes, leaving Bigg to speak, if possible, to Alfred.

I had no time again to communicate with Bigg, for on returning to the village I found that the feast was ready, and that the chief was waiting to do the honours. I have not space to describe it. I exerted myself to do it justice, and so did Bigg, who succeeded much better than I did. Some of the dishes, composed of baked roots and fruits, were not bad, but the animal food was of a very doubtful character. Some of the smaller creatures might have been hares or rabbits, but they looked remarkably like monkeys, while there were other things which might have been eels, but were, I had a strong suspicion, snakes cut into bits.

When the feast was over, Bigg told me that the chief was anxious that I should go out that evening and kill some lions. I nodded my head in assent.

"I have told him you would do so if his people would show you where they are to be found," he observed.

Accordingly, the chief and a large number of his people set out with us. Some dozen were, I found, said to be experienced hunters. Solon followed at my heels. He had created almost as much interest among the natives as we had. I was looking out for a deer or a zebra, or some other smaller animal to serve as a bait for the lions, when I heard a loud trumpeting in the forest, and presently a huge elephant rushed out directly in front of us. I was delighted to see him, but the natives hurried off right and left to escape from him. I, to their surprise, stood my ground, though his trunk was lifted, and he was evidently about to charge. I had a tree near me. Solon, as before, performed his part faithfully, rushing on and barking close up to him. The elephant lowered his trunk to strike him when within fifteen yards of me; I fired, and in a moment he sunk to the ground.

This feat alone satisfied the natives of my prowess, but I was determined to show that I could kill lions also. I left a large party of them cutting up the elephant, and walking on, shot a zebra. The body, I knew, would attract the lions, so I signed to Bigg to get a hole dug near the spot, that it might serve as a rifle-pit for us. He and I took up our post there, while the natives hid themselves away in the surrounding bush to watch my proceedings. I had not long to wait before some jackals came screeching up to partake of the banquet they had scented far off. Before long two magnificent lions followed. My ambition was to kill both of them. They soon began to attack the carcass of the zebra, but I waited till they both at the same moment had their sides turned towards me. Then I let fly first one barrel, and then the other. I gave a shout of satisfaction as I knocked them both over. They got up, however, roaring, and advanced towards the pit where Bigg and I, with Solon, lay concealed. One fell, but the other bounded on. I had no time to reload, but I had my pistol, and Bigg had his. We held them ready. The terrific monster, with a roar of rage, was close above us, his eyes glancing fire; we could almost feel his breath. We both fired right at his head at the same moment, and then slunk down in our pit. I thought it would prove our grave, but the lion bounded clear over it, and on jumping up again to reload, I saw him a few paces off stretched out in the agonies of death.

We agreed that we had done enough for one afternoon, and Bigg, calling to the natives, they crowded round the bodies of the lions, and gave strong signs of their satisfaction.

While they were not observing us, I whispered to Bigg that I was anxious to get back at once to the village, that I might communicate with Alfred. It seemed an age, however, before the natives retired to their huts, and I was alone with Bigg and Solon. Still longer after that did it seem before, while I was watching eagerly at the door, that I saw a figure creeping towards the hut. I had to hold Solon down, for he seemed inclined to fly out and bark.

"Ralph, Ralph, is it you indeed come to look for me?" said a voice which I recognized as Alfred's, and the next moment we were in each other's arms, and I found myself crying almost as if my heart would burst. Alfred was not much less moved, while Solon sprang up, and leaning against us, licked his hand.

Bigg had gone to sleep, but he soon roused up, and a very happy party we were. We had not much time to talk though. Now was the moment for action. Alfred was of opinion that the natives would soon suspect me and Bigg, and that it would be our wisest course to make our escape without any delay. I completely inclined to the same opinion.

"Why should we wait a moment then?" exclaimed Alfred. "Let us be off at once."

"Stay," said I; "you shall rig up in my princely gear, and

I will appear as a humble little blackamoor. You shall have my pistols, and I will carry my trusty rifle; we shall then all be armed, and I have no doubt but that we shall be able to make our way among either natives or wild beasts. Quick—quick—here, take the things."

I would not allow Alfred to expostulate. In a very few minutes the change was complete, and the black mane of the lion so completely covered his features, that it was scarcely possible to distinguish what was the colour of the skin beneath. Solon sat watching the whole process with great interest. I thus once more appeared in my negro shirt, with bare feet and head. We all then crept out of the hut. No sound was heard. The stars told us the direction we were to take. Alfred knew of a well-beaten native path which led eastward. We crept on cautiously along it till we were out of hearing of the village, and then we all ran on as fast as our legs could carry us. It mattered little how tired we might be at the end of our journey, provided we could get in safety on board the *Star*. We had had a good supper, so that we had not to stop for feeding. Before sunrise, we had made good, I believe, full twenty miles, perhaps still more. We were not likely to be pursued, but still we pushed on. At length, when the sun rose high, we stopped to breakfast and rest. Alfred and I had a great deal to talk about. He had to tell me his adventures, and I had to tell him how I had found him out.

In the afternoon we were again on foot, pushing on as rapidly as before. We saw elephants and rhinoceroses and several lions, but while we were moving on none of them appeared inclined to attack us. At night we rested with large fires in front of us, and a tall tree with some thick stakes at our backs. Once we were startled by a bark from Solon and a fierce growl close to our ears, and there stood a huge black-maned lion. I lifted my rifle to fire and Alfred and Bigg each seized a burning brand and dashed it in his face. The reception was warmer than he expected, and with a roar of surprise he bounded off again into the bush.

We had more difficulty in dealing with the natives the nearer we approached the coast. They evidently suspected us, and wished to stop our progress. Bigg talked to them a great deal, but I suspect that they did not even comprehend his very extraordinary lingo. We, however, pushed on and made our escape from them. It was some hours after noon when, from the summit of a high ridge, we caught sight of the sea. We cast our eyes along the horizon, and thought that we could make out the *Star* in the offing. How thankful we felt, and how our spirits rose! We hurried down the hill; when at the bottom, we were annoyed to find ourselves close to a large negro village. We were going to pass round it when some of the natives saw us, and we agreed that it would be best to put a bold face on the matter, and to march openly into the village. Bigg did his utmost to talk over the people, but I suspect that his language betrayed him. They collected in numbers, and by their gestures it appeared to us that they contemplated detaining us. To this it would not do to submit; so having observed a path which we believed led down to the sea, we hurried along it, Alfred leading. We supposed that there was no person of authority in the village to stop us, and we agreed that it would be wiser to go ahead before one should arrive. We looked round every now and then; when at length we saw that no one was watching us, we pushed on as fast as we could go. It was generally a descent, but now and then we had to climb a hill. At the top of one we saw the sea glittering below before us, and what was our delight to observe three boats pulling in towards the shore from a man-of-war brig, which we had no doubt was the *Star*. On we ran faster than ever, and good cause we had to do so, for some loud shouts made us look behind, when we saw a whole posse of natives brandishing their spears and running after us at the top of their speed. Still the boats appeared to be too far off to reach the shore before the natives would overtake us. On they came with dreadful shrieks and cries. As far as we could see, on looking back, none of them had fire-arms, and had I chosen, of course I could have picked off two, and perhaps even more, before they could have got up to us; but I was most unwilling to shed blood, and besides, I thought that if matters could be explained to the natives they might be disposed to be friends instead of enemies.

Still, unfortunately, this could not under the present juncture be ascertained. What we had to do was to keep out of their way. Lightly clad as they were, they ran very fast; so did we. The people in the boats pulling in towards the shore must have seen them, we fancied, and gave way with a will to get in in time to assist us. I looked at the savages, and then I looked at the boats, and I felt utterly hopeless that this could be done. The blacks were almost close enough to have hurled their spears at us, when, as I had given up all hope of escape, a loud cheer saluted our ears close to us, and Mr. Henley with a dozen blue jackets well armed, appeared from behind a high rock overhung with lichens and creepers on our left. They presented their muskets, and the natives halted. The latter, though they might not possess them, knew perfectly well the effect of fire-arms. Mr. Henley, who knew something of the language of the coast natives, addressed them, and after a little palaver, first one and then another came down towards us. He had no great difficulty in persuading them that we were friends, for they saw that had he wished it he could have allowed his men to fire, and might have killed numbers of them. He assured them that the English were not only friends, but that they wished to put an end to the slave-trade, and to encourage agriculture, and would assist them by every means in their power. The result was that we parted on very good terms.

Our appearance on board caused a great deal of amusement, though nothing could exceed the kindness with which Alfred and I were received and treated by all the officers.

After calling at several places, we went on to Cape Town. Two other ships of war were there, the officers of which came on board the *Star*. No sooner did the captain of one of them see Alfred, than he held out his hand towards him, exclaiming,—

"I am delighted to meet you again, my dear sir. Why, you are the very person who in so gallant a manner swam off to my ship when she was cast away on the coast of Chagos, and were the means of saving the lives of all on board."

Alfred, to my great joy, acknowledged that such was the case, for he had not told me of the circumstance. The result was that Captain Armstrong, who had a vacancy on board, at once gave it him; and as there were a sufficient number of captains at the Cape at the time, he was allowed to pass his examination as a mate, and was rated as such accordingly. Several of my other friends were equally fortunate. A large ship, homeward-bound, had lost her master, and Mr. Henley being known favourably to the agents at Cape Town, he was appointed to take charge of her. Captain Armstrong, knowing that it was important that Alfred should return home, gave him leave to accompany me in Mr. Henley's ship, the *Susan*. We were on the point of sailing, when, to my still greater satisfaction, my grandfather arrived from Ceylon, also on his way home. We accordingly all agreed to go together on board the *Susan*. Just before we sailed, however, the *Star* was ordered home; and as it was much better that Alfred should return in her, he once more donned his newly-made mate's uniform and rejoined her. As the *Susan* was not a very fast sailer, he had thus the satisfaction of reaching England first, and with joy and thankfulness was he received by all the dear ones at home. He had learned a severe lesson from all he had gone through, and no better officer now exists in the service. We were not less welcome when, a few days afterwards, we joined the family-circle. All our troubles seemed to have vanished.

Little did I think when I left home that I should so soon see all the dear ones I had left, with our grandfather, kind Mr. Ward, Mr. Henley, and Henry Raymond, assembled round our dinner-table, while Solon was sitting up attentive to all that was going forward; and Tommy Bigg, and his father, and Johnnie Spratt were enjoying a good supper in the kitchen below. I ought to have said that my grandfather brought a good account of kind Mr. Fordyce, who was soon coming to England, while Lumsden, my old school-fellow, had now the chief charge of his affairs in Ceylon.

I had learned much by my voyages and travels. One truth had been impressed more firmly than ever on my mind, that under every circumstance in which we can be placed, if we will but do our duty to the very utmost of our power, and rely firmly on our Maker's kind providence and mercy, all will ultimately turn out for the best, and we shall not fail to see his finger guiding and directing every event for our ultimate happiness and prosperity.

www.ingramcontent.com/pod-product-compliance
Lightning Source LLC
Chambersburg PA
CBHW022141300426
44115CB00006B/292